POSSIDIUS OF CALAMA

THE OXFORD EARLY CHRISTIAN STUDIES series includes scholarly volumes on the thought and history of the early Christian centuries. Covering a wide range of Greek, Latin, and Oriental sources, the books are of interest to theologians, ancient historians, and specialists in the classical and Jewish worlds.

Titles in the series include:

The Body in St Maximus the Confessor
Holy Flesh, Wholly Deified
Adam G. Cooper (2005)

The Asketikon of St Basil the Great
Anna M. Silvas (2005)

Marius Victorinus' Commentary on Galatians
Stephen Andrew Cooper (2005)

Asceticism and Christological Controversy in Fifth-Century Palestine
The Career of Peter the Iberian
Cornelia B. Horn (2006)

Marcellus of Ancyra and the Lost Years of the Arian Controversy 325–345
Sara Parvis (2006)

The Irrational Augustine
Catherine Conybeare (2006)

Clement of Alexandria and the Beginnings of Christian Apophaticism
Henny Fiskå Hägg (2006)

The Christology of Theodoret of Cyrus
Antiochene Christology from the Council of Ephesus (431) to
the Council of Chalcedon (451)
Paul B. Clayton, Jr. (2006)

Ethnicity and Argument in Eusebius' *Praeparatio Evangelica*
Aaron P. Johnson (2006)

Union and Distinction in the Thought of St Maximus the Confessor
Melchisedec Törönen (2007)

Contextualizing Cassian
Aristocrats, Asceticism, and Reformation in Fifth-Century Gaul
Richard J. Goodrich (2007)

Ambrosiaster's Political Theology
Sophie Lunn-Rockliffe (2007)

Coptic Christology in Practice
Incarnation and Divine Participation in Late Antique and Medieval Egypt
Stephen J. Davis

Possidius of Calama

A Study of the North African Episcopate at the Time of Augustine

ERIKA T. HERMANOWICZ

UNIVERSITY PRESS

2008

OXFORD
UNIVERSITY PRESS

Great Clarendon Street, Oxford OX2 6DP

Oxford University Press is a department of the University of Oxford.
It furthers the University's objective of excellence in research, scholarship,
and education by publishing worldwide in

Oxford   New York

Auckland Cape Town Dar es Salaam Hong Kong Karachi
Kuala Lumpur Madrid Melbourne Mexico City Nairobi
New Delhi Shanghai Taipei Toronto

With offices in

Argentina Austria Brazil Chile Czech Republic France Greece
Guatemala Hungary Italy Japan Poland Portugal Singapore
South Korea Switzerland Thailand Turkey Ukraine Vietnam

Oxford is a registered trade mark of Oxford University Press
in the UK and in certain other countries

Published in the United States
by Oxford University Press Inc., New York

© Erika T. Hermanowicz 2008

The moral rights of the author have been asserted
Database right Oxford University Press (maker)

First published 2008

All rights reserved. No part of this publication may be reproduced,
stored in a retrieval system, or transmitted, in any form or by any means,
without the prior permission in writing of Oxford University Press,
or as expressly permitted by law, or under terms agreed with the appropriate
reprographics rights organization. Enquiries concerning reproduction
outside the scope of the above should be sent to the Rights Department,
Oxford University Press, at the address above

You must not circulate this book in any other binding or cover
and you must impose the same condition on any acquirer

British Library Cataloguing in Publication Data

Data available

Library of Congress Cataloging in Publication Data

Data available

Typeset by SPI Publisher Services, Pondicherry, India
Printed in Great Britain
on acid-free paper by
Biddles Ltd., King's Lynn, Norfolk

ISBN 978–0–19–923635–0

1 3 5 7 9 10 8 6 4 2

To
Nancy Wegerdt Thorgerson
in loving memory

Preface

We do not know much about the friends of Augustine, the bishop of Hippo. The intellectual and historical influence that he exerted has pulled them so tightly into his orbit that their personalities have become distorted, at times to the point of obfuscation. The moments we do see them as distinct personalities are brief and usually mediated through Augustine's writings. We do know that Alypius watched in astonished silence as Augustine wept and pulled his hair in frustration (*conf.* 8.8 [20]). Evodius once caused embarrassment to the African Catholics when he was deliberately rude to an important Donatist bishop in what was supposed to be an amicable debate (*ep.* 33.2–3). Anthony of Fussala, the young man Augustine took in as a boy and elevated, too soon it seems, to the episcopate, dramatically stormed out of a meeting with Augustine and returned moments later, with a great deal of screaming, to reiterate his displeasure (*ep.* 20*.25). These rare glimpses of character are welcome, if only because they help satisfy a prurient wish to know what Augustine's colleagues were like as men. But what did they *believe*? On matters such as theology, law, discipline, and literature, many assume that they thought as Augustine did. The assumption is off the mark, as it turns out, yet this false impression is not entirely of Augustine's, or history's, making. In times of crisis, the bishops themselves presented a unified front.

This book is about Possidius of Calama, an episcopal colleague and friend of Augustine's, who wrote the only contemporary biography about the bishop of Hippo. The *Vita Augustini* depicts Augustine as the single, dominant religious force in North Africa. The other bishops, whom Possidius never even identifies by name, comprise an amorphous crowd of grateful supporters, and this is because his portrait of Augustine engages in a great deal of wishful thinking, informed more by the fear that Augustine's reputation was waning in the years after his death than by a strict adherence to events. The fact is that Augustine's episcopal colleagues, Possidius included, had their disagreements with the great man, and they prevailed more often than Possidius liked to admit.

The *Vita Augustini* was written at a difficult time. Augustine was dead and the Vandals now held the cities and territories the bishops had spent their careers traversing. Possidius, well aware that Augustine's theological views were meeting stiff resistance among Christians in Africa, Italy, and Gaul, was entangled in his own religious difficulties. There is a good chance he wrote the *Vita Augustini* after he was deemed intractable by the Vandal king and consequently exiled from Africa. Under these circumstances, it is easy to see why Possidius would want to depict Augustine's career as one of unmitigated success, but the same circumstances make it harder to explain why Possidius would also choose to contradict so much of what Augustine wrote about himself. Possidius garbles the events surrounding Augustine's conversion, an event we know well from the *Confessions*. Possidius mistakenly attributes the writing of the *Retractationes* to Augustine's realization that he was close to dying, when in fact the bishop had at least eighteen more years to live when he first conceived of the project. Very basic errors such as these do not make sense when read against the *Vita Augustini* which consists of successive allusions to Augustinian text, like baubles on a chain, strung together to create a narrative. Possidius knew Augustine's corpus well, so why he deliberately tried to manipulate it, as well as distort various facts about Augustine's life, constitutes one of this book's principal areas of investigation.

Possidius' ideas on the use and meaning of the written word differ significantly from Augustine's. The bishop of Hippo always placed texts in a subordinate relationship to scripture. Scripture alone contained truth; all other texts, even trustworthy ones like transcripts from Church councils, were human creations and consequently subject to error. Possidius' attitude toward the written word, on the other hand, crystallized in the years he engaged the law. All African bishops, Augustine included, were well versed in the solicitation of directives from the imperial consistory, and this book seeks to articulate the close relationship to Roman law enjoyed by both Donatist and Catholic clergy. While Augustine regarded favorable legislation as useful, his gaze remained focused on the Bible. The *Vita Augustini*, however, where heresy is thwarted and Catholicism made victorious by the circulation of Augustine's books and accompanying legal injunctions from the emperor, suggests that Possidius' trust in the efficacy of text was both deeper and more broadly applied. And why not? The bishop of Calama had seen what the written word could do. The law dispersed the Manichaeans, broke the Donatist hold on Africa, and compromised the status of those who supported Pelagius. Possidius himself traveled to the imperial court twice, personally appealed to the emperor to initiate what would become the conference of 411 and, as far as we know, spent a great deal of time in his city of Calama lobbying the municipal council and other men of influence by use, not of scripture, but of transcribed records from the town council or the latest directive from Ravenna.

Like most urban bishops, Possidius' career largely revolved around evidentiary dossiers. His was the age of the document, and matters such as ownership of church property, appeals on behalf of prisoners, and questions regarding heresy required that the appropriate texts be presented to authorities for scrutiny. Council minutes, episcopal correspondence, the transcripts of debates, and even the theological writings of Augustine were acceptable as evidence, and since such dossiers decided what, exactly, constituted orthodoxy—a matter of imperial law—the influence they exerted on Possidius' imagination was considerable. In the *Vita Augustini*, we can see the beginnings of what we now call patristic literature: the use of nonscriptural works for theological proof. It is a striking departure from what Augustine thought the proper use of text, but thoroughly consonant with Possidius' manipulation of Augustine's literary corpus. Augustine's intellectual vibrancy was in large part a measure of his willingness to reassess his beliefs. He could change his mind, and when he did so, he liked to share that experience with his readers. To the contrary, Possidius was interested in definitive statements and the intractability of imperial pronouncements. Consequently, at a time of retrenchment and assessment of losses, Possidius grabbed hold of Augustine's life and text and tried to make them stop moving. The *Vita Augustini* is very much like an evidentiary dossier, giving us a man who consists of the books he wrote, which, unchanging and unchanged, affirm religious and legal truth. Had Augustine the opportunity to read Possidius' biography, he might have found it perplexing, but I do not think he would have been surprised. Possidius had always exercised a great deal of independence, even in the presence of Augustine.

This book began as a doctoral dissertation submitted at Princeton University in 1999. Peter Brown was my adviser, and I thank him for being such a wonderful man and teacher. His wife, Betsy Brown, is one of the most gracious people I have ever known. Elaine Fantham, Robert A. Kaster, and Mark Vessey, whose generosity continues unabated to this day, comprised my reading committee. Mark's critique of my work at the initial stage of rewriting changed my entire way of thinking about Possidius. I am grateful to him for the challenge. I thank Peter Brown (again), Nancy Felson, Christine McCann, Jane Merdinger, Naomi J. Norman, James J. O'Donnell, Sarah Spence, and Maureen A. Tilley for reading and commenting on parts or the whole book manuscript. Kevin Uhalde helped me restructure the penultimate draft. Gillian Clark and the anonymous reader at Oxford University Press offered sound criticism and good direction. I apologize to them, and to all the other people listed here, for at times ignoring their excellent advice.

My research was supported by an Andrew W. Mellon Research Fellowship for Junior Faculty from the American Council of Learned Societies (ACLS) in 2003–4. I am most grateful to the ACLS. I also thank Betty Jean Craige and the Willson Center for the Humanities and Arts at the University of Georgia for a research fellowship in the spring semester of 2007. The final editing of the manuscript was supported by the President's Venture Fund through the generous gifts of the University of Georgia Partners. I offer my thanks to Ellen Harris for her excellent work. Mr. Tom Perridge at Oxford University Press was very kind in guiding me through the intricacies of submitting successive typescripts as well as metaphorically holding my hand while I waited for official responses. Virginia C. Feher and the entire staff at the University of Georgia's Interlibrary Loan Office are marvelous people. The smiles they had for me when I frequently appeared at their door may have in fact been the gritting of teeth, but without their efficient, professional service, writing this book would have been impossible.

A version of Chapter 5 was previously published under the title 'Catholic Bishops and Appeals to the Imperial Court: A Legal Study of the Calama Riots in 408', *Journal of Early Christian Studies*, 12 (2004), 481–521. It appears here with the kind permission of The Johns Hopkins University Press.

The following people make the world a wonderful place to be, and I count myself fortunate to know them: Joe Hermanowicz, Christine Albright, Elissa Bell Bayraktar, Priscilla Kidder Blevins, Lisa Daliere, Timothy N. Gantz, Ann Pickering Lang, Michelle A. Swagler, W. Glenn Doak, and Eric Thorgerson. I thank all of them for their goodness.

E.T.H.

Athens, GA

Contents

Abbreviations   xiii

Introduction   1

PART I. THE *VITA AUGUSTINI*: AUGUSTINE'S LIFE AND TEXT ACCORDING TO POSSIDIUS

1. The *Vita Augustini*   17
   Possidius Defends Augustine   23
   Legal History   43
   The *Vita Augustini* as Catalogue Raisonné   54

2. The Literary Possidius   64
   Possidius Takes the Stage   66
   'Vox Tua Nempe Mea Est': Autopsy and Allusion   72
   'He Himself Told Me'   75
   A Life as a City as History as a Book   77

PART II. POSSIDIUS AND THE LEGAL ACTIVITIES OF NORTH AFRICAN EPISCOPATE

The Life and Carrer of Possidius   83

3. Donatists, Catholics, and Appeals to the Law: 392–404   97
   Attempting to Rouse the Law   100
   Theodosius' Law of 392   102
   Crispinus and Possidius, the Bishops of Calama   108
   The Law of 381 Against the Manichaeans   120
   The June Council of 404   124
   The Donatists and the Law   126
   Conclusion: Heresy and Schism   129

4. Donatist Strategy and Catholic Response, 403–5   132
   The Violence   134
   The Response   142
   A Display of the Wounded   149
   The Edict of Unity   150
   The Problem with Success   153

5. Possidius Goes to Court, 408–9	156
The Riots at Calama, June 408	157
Local Rule and Imperial Law	164
The Fall of Stilicho and Violence in Africa	168
Sirmondian Constitution 14	174
Possidius and Augustine in Disagreement?	180
6. The Conference of 411	188
The Conference of 411: Preliminaries	192
The Legal Details: Rescripts and Mandates	196
Neither Council nor Court Case	200
The Legal Strategy	203
Donatist Numbers and Catholic Lies	212
Ending to Begin Again	218
Conclusion	221
Bibliography	229
Primary Sources	229
Secondary Sources	230
Index	251

Abbreviations

Journal titles are abbreviated in the text (according to the conventions of L'*Année Philologique*), but spelled out in full in the bibliography.

BA	*Oeuvres de saint Augustin*, Blibliothèque Augustinienne (Paris, 1949–).
CCL	Corpus Christianorum Series Latina (Turnhout, 1953–).
CJ	*Codex Justinianus*, ed. P. Kruger, Corpus Iuris Civilis, ii (Berlin, 1877; reprint 1954).
Coll. Carth.	*Gesta Collationis Carthagine habitae*, published as *Actes de la Conférence de Carthage en 411*, ed. Serge Lancel (Paris, 1972–91).
Concilia Africae	*Codex canonum ecclesiae Africanae*, ed. Charles Munier, CCL 149 (Turnhout, 1974).
CSEL	Corpus Scriptorum Ecclesiasticorum Latinorum (Vienna, 1865–).
CTh.	*Codex Theodosianus:* (1) *Theodosiani libri XVI, cum Constitutionibus Sirmondianis*, ed. Th. Mommsen, with P. Meyer and P. Krüger (Berlin, 1904; reprint Berlin, 1962); (2) *The Theodosian Code and Novels and the Sirmondian Constitutions*, tr. Clyde Pharr (Princeton, 1952; reprint New York, 2001).
PCBE Afrique	*Prosopographie chrétienne du bas-empire*, i: *Prosopographie de l'Afrique chrétienne (303–533)*, ed. André Mandouze (Paris, 1982).
PCBE Italie	*Prosopographie chrétienne du bas-empire*, ii: *Prosopographie de l'Italie chrétienne (313–604)*, ed. Charles Pietri and Luce Pietri (Rome, 1999–2000).
PL	Patrologiae cursus completus, series Latina, ed. J-P. Migne (Paris, 1844–1964).
PLRE	*Prosopography of the Later Roman Empire*, i: *A.D. 260–395*, ed. A. H. M. Jones, J. R. Martindale, and J. Morris (Cambridge, 1971); ii: *A.D. 395–527*, ed. J. R. Martindale (Cambridge, 1980).
Sirm.	*Constitutiones Sirmondianae*; see *Codex Theodosianus*.
v. Aug.	*Vita Augustini*, ed. A. A. R. Bastiaensen (Milan, 1975).

Introduction

Augustine established his monastery at Hippo in 391. Possidius joined Augustine's community soon after and lived there until about 401, when he was made bishop of Calama (Guelma, Algeria).[1] The two men were friends for almost forty years, visiting each other regularly and working closely on council business, legal issues, and theological matters.[2] Augustine's friendships were central to his life, and the dominant image modern readers have of Augustine's relationships comes from the *Confessions*, or even his early dialogues, where he and his associates enjoy a gentlemanly like-mindedness. In other sources, we rarely see tension, personal or professional, among the North African bishops.[3] In Possidius' *Vita Augustini*, the only biography of the bishop of Hippo written by a contemporary, the author's relationship with his subject is likewise portrayed as respectfully harmonious. Possidius' unwavering dedication to Augustine is representative of the entire African episcopate, which looked to the bishop of Hippo as to how to behave and what to believe. That image Possidius cultivated is still prevalent today, and much of Augustinian scholarship credits the bishop of Hippo with directing Africa's intellectual and

---

[1] The traditional date for Possidius' ordination is 397 (*PCBE Afrique*, 'Possidius 1', 890, and Mark Vessey, 'Possidius', in Allan D. Fitzgerald [ed.], *Augustine Through the Ages: An Encyclopedia* [Grand Rapids: William B. Eerdmans Publishers, 1999], 668), but the excerpts from the North African Church Council of 410 indicate that Possidius was a junior colleague of Florentius, the bishop of Hippo Diarrhytus, who we know was appointed in September 401. See *Concilia Africae, Registri Ecclesiae Carthaginensis Excerpta* 107.

[2] Possidius often visited Hippo, which probably explains why there exists only one confirmed (and another probable) letter addressed to Possidius from Augustine. See *epp.* 91, 137, 23*A; *civ. Dei* 22.8; *v. Aug.*, *passim*, which testifies to Possidius' presence at Hippo. We assume that whenever Possidius went to Carthage, he stayed at Hippo on the way there and on the way home.

[3] See, for example, Augustine's *ep.* 148 to his friend Fortunatianus, wherein Augustine explains that he has offended a fellow bishop because he ascribed physical attributes to God. Augustine asks Fortunatianus to seek pardon on his behalf, as the rebuke deeply offended this bishop. Augustine also makes it clear (*ep.* 185.25) that the bishops attending the 404 conference in Carthage disagreed about how best deal with the escalating violence between the Catholics and Donatists.

All Latin citations from Augustine's letters taken from the Goldbacher edition *CSEL* 34.1–2, 44, and 57. Translations of Augustine's letters (including *epp.* 1*–29*) from Roland Teske, S.J., *The Works of Saint Augustine: A Translation for the 21st Century* (Brooklyn: New City Press, 2001–5).

theological pursuits. His Catholic contemporaries, as exhibited by the paucity in substance and style of their books, were silent 'followers'.[4]

In 430, as the Vandals marched east in their conquest of North Africa, Possidius fled Calama and returned to Augustine's monastery. Hippo came under siege, and in the months that followed, the bishops spent their time in conversation, prayer, and mutual exhortations to accept affliction with humility. Possidius then watched Augustine succumb to fever and was among the few present at his burial. An image made famous by Peter Brown in the final lines in *Augustine of Hippo* portrays a now solitary Possidius gazing at the library shelves filled with Augustine's treatises, letters, and sermons. Knowing as we do the history of the second half of the fifth century, and how much Augustine's colleagues relied on him for direction, we think we can see helplessness in Possidius' eyes as he looks at all those books.[5]

The assumption, however, is not quite on the mark. Possidius' devotion to Augustine was no doubt true, expressing itself in the creation of a biography, but more important, in the foresight to stop gazing at the books on the library shelves and *move* them. Possidius catalogued Augustine's library (and attached a copy of the catalogue at the end of the *Vita*) and helped send its contents to a safer location. It is largely through his efforts, we think, that most of Augustine's enormous corpus survives.[6] It is also true that Possidius, far from always requiring Augustine's cue, was a man of energy and his own opinions. He was stubborn, too, and his truculence often landed him in difficulties. He was once ambushed and beaten by armed Donatists in retaliation for having insulted their bishop. On another occasion, angry mobs (his fellow townsmen) set his basilica on fire and killed one of his clerics. He successfully argued in front of proconsuls and members of the imperial consistory, but his methods could be provocatively blunt. Flavius Marcellinus, who by all accounts is rare in the history of late antiquity for being a bureaucrat of gentle demeanor, grew visibly impatient with Possidius' aggressive talk at the 411 conference. In 437, Possidius was exiled from his see by the order of the Vandal king, Geiseric. Prosper of Aquitaine reports that Possidius, by now one of the most senior

---

[4] A call for reassessment comes from Peter Brown, *Augustine of Hippo: A Biography* (Berkeley: University of California Press, 1967; reprint 2000), 499, with assent from Allan D. Fitzgerald, 'Tracing the Passage from a Doctrinal to an Historical Approach to the Study of Augustine', *RÉAug*, 50 (2004), 301–2.

[5] For a discussion of the passage in *Augustine of Hippo*, see Mark Vessey, 'The Demise of the Christian Writer and the Remaking of "Late Antiquity": From H-I. Marrou's Saint Augustine (1938) to Peter Brown's Holt Man (1983)', *JECS*, 6 (1998), 377–8.

[6] Jean-Paul Bouhot, 'La transmission d'Hippone à Rome des oeuvres de saint Augustin', in Donatella Nebbiai-Dalla Guarda and Jean-François Genest (eds.), *Du copiste au collectionneur: mélanges d'histoire des textes et des bibliotheques en l'honneur d'Andre Vernet* (Turnhout: Brepols, 1998), 23–33.

bishops in Africa, had earned the personal enmity of Geiseric for, not surprisingly, refusing to humble himself before the new Arian ruler.[7] Possidius had, Prosper reports, the attribute of *constantia*.

Despite the author's assurances of an easy episcopal concord, Possidius sometimes argued with his colleagues, including Augustine. The bishop of Hippo once reprimanded Possidius for speaking ill of someone at the dinner table, and threatened to retire to his room unless the gossip stopped.[8] In an undated letter, Augustine is patently exasperated with Possidius' request to write a scripture-based explanation regarding a matter he considered self-evident.[9] Augustine once asked Paulinus of Nola to talk sense into Possidius, as a trip he planned to Ravenna to appeal to the emperor against his fellow townsmen was beginning to look like a pursuit of vengeance. Augustine tells Paulinus that the kind of punishments implemented by imperial law were inappropriate for solicitation by clergy, and that a disagreement about this issue with Possidius was damaging their friendship (*ep*. 95).

The dissonance between his literary presentation and the historical evidence is of Possidius' deliberate manufacture. Harmonious collegiality is a crucial aspect of the constructed image, as is Augustine's role as the undisputed arbiter of Catholic doctrine. At the time of the biography's

---

[7] T. Mommsen (*MGH Auctorum Antiquissimorum IX*) *Chronica Minora I* (Berlin: Weidman, 1892), 1327 (p. 475): 'In Africa Gisiricus, rex Wandalorum, intra habitationis suae limites volens catholicam fidem Arriana impietate subvertere, quosdam nostrorum episcopos, quorum Possidius et Novatus ac Severianus clariores erant, eatenus persecutus est, ut eos privatos iure basilicarum suarum etiam civitatibus pelleret, cum ipsorum constantia nullis superbissimi regis terroribus cederet.'

[8] *v. Aug*. 22.7: 'quod ego et alii, qui illi mensae interfuimus, experti sumus.'
The bishops at Augustine's table ignored the injunction inscribed on the dining table: 'Quisquis amat dictis absentum rodere vitam hac mensa indignam noverit esse suam.' Augustine's response was sharp: 'Nam et quosdam suos familiarissimos coepiscopos, illius scripturae oblitos et contra eam loquentes, tam aspere aliquando reprehendit commotus, ut diceret aut delendos esse illos de mensa versus, aut se de media refectione ad suum cubiculum surrecturum.'
This, and all, citations from the *Vita* have been taken from A. A. R. Bastiaensen (Milan: Fondazione Lorenzo Valla, 1975). English translations are adapted from H. T. Weiskotten, *Sancti Augustini Scripta a Possidio Episcopo: Edited with Revised Text, Introduction, Notes and an English Translation* (Princeton: Princeton University Press, 1919).

[9] The letter dates perhaps around 401 (and thus near the time of Possidius' elevation to the episcopate), and is listed as number 245 in the Maurist catalogue. Possidius, always dependent on the authority of textual citation, asked Augustine for specific passages of scripture he could read to his parishioners to make them stop wearing bodily adornment. Augustine's response urges Possidius to apply some interpretive sophistication to the texts in front of him, as surely specific injunctions for each and every rule he wants to impose will not be found in scripture. Makeup is no more than a form of lying, and women must therefore not apply it. It is natural and to be expected that women wear jewelry in order to appear comely to their husbands as well as for husbands to comport themselves to make their wives happy, but amulets, for obvious reasons, are not to be tolerated.
For dating of *ep*. 245, see Le Nain de Tillemont, *Mémoires pour servir à l'histoire ecclésiastique* (Brussels: E. H. Fricx, 1706–28), 14.256–7. Cf. *PCBE Afrique*, 'Possidius', 890, n. 5.

composition, that is, within a few years of Augustine's death, his legacy was in a precarious state. Possidius' aims in writing the biography were to protect the bishop's career and help preserve his books, with the first in large part designed to ensure the second. Immediate survival of Augustine's lifework was paramount. The Vandal army, largely Arian with little interest in the well-being of Augustine's corpus, was waiting to enter Hippo in 430, and the large collection at Hippo's monastery library might suffer destruction.[10] The biography describes the ailing Augustine as not caring for any possession save his books, and he repeatedly urged the bishops, especially Possidius, to protect them. The library was a personal concern, an inheritance explicitly bequeathed by a dying man in the final hours of conversation. As such, Possidius' biography, in its role as catalogue raisonée accompanying a list of Augustine's books, letters, and sermons, organized the corpus to facilitate understanding and circulation.

There were other matters for Possidius to address, too, such as Augustine's uncertain reputation among some religious circles—African, Italian, and Gallic—in the 430s.[11] We learn much about the conversations regarding Augustine's worth as a theologian in the years immediately following his death by noticing the topics that arise in the biography. Manichaeism is one. It is well known that Augustine's ties to Manichaeism in his youth continued to pursue him into middle and old age. His detractors, and there were many, exploited the former affiliation with some success. Other items of interest (and revision) were the legitimacy of Augustine's ordination, the way he ran his monastery at Hippo, his obedience to the decisions made at Church councils, and his attitude toward the secular courts. That Possidius is at pains to delineate the unswerving allegiance pledged to Augustine by the Catholic clergy as well as his preeminence as a theologian are two more examples of this kind of clarification, based more on the perceived need to defend his hero than the desire to describe him. Possidius would be delighted to discover that a modern reading audience accepted these assertions as fact.

Possidius' objectives in writing the *Vita* call for a broad view of geography because some of Augustine's most effective detractors came from Italy and

---

[10] Yves Modéran, 'Une Guerre de religion: Les Deux Églises d'Afrique à l'époque Vandale', *An Tard*, 11 (2003), 21–44 emphasizes the tenacity with which the Vandal kings tried to convert Africa to Arianism. Even if Augustine's works survived invasion, there was very little sympathy among the conquerors to protect Augustine's textual legacy.

[11] Ralph W. Mathisen, *Ecclesiastical Factionalism and Religious Controversy in Fifth-Century Gaul* (Washington: Catholic University of American Press, 1989), 122–40, esp. 123, reminds us that Augustine was highly respected among Gallic theologians, and was regularly cited as an authority. It was his writing on predestination that caused alarm. See, for example, Vincent of Lérins, *Commonitorium* 17.7: without naming Augustine, he calls his views on predestination, 'the lowest abyss of heresy'.

Gaul. Possidius looked beyond Africa for his reading audience, but at the same time he adopted a very narrow chronological outlook. The biography addressed a very specific group of people who all were living in the empire of the 430s. There are therefore few, if any, theological abstractions in the *Vita*, but matter-of-fact statements of whom Augustine met and what he did: Augustine heard Ambrose, converted to Catholicism, and then returned to Africa, where for the rest of his life he dedicated himself to communication and persuasion. He dictated and preached. He engaged in numerous debates where his honest arguments bested the rhetorical tricks employed by heretics. The descriptions of his encounters with opponents are sketchy because their importance lies in the fact that Augustine handily defeated anyone who faced him, but as Possidius repeatedly states in the *Vita*, those who required detail and extended proofs could verify his statements by comparing the corresponding documents in Augustine's corpus. Augustine behaved in the monastery according to the precepts he publicly exhorted others to follow and continued to preach with a keenness of mind until the onset of his final illness. With Hippo under siege, his death, at least the way it is described by Possidius, went largely unremarked save by his closest friends. The point was that his books were still available, waiting to be copied and circulated.

When placed beside the *Confessions* or the *Retractationes*, Possidius' *Vita* displays little of the imaginative vigor Augustine brings to his autobiographies. Augustine writes about who he is, and who he has come to be. Possidius writes about what Augustine did. The impulse to lead Augustine away from internal introspection and instead offer the readers a portrait that insists on accomplishments and victories comes, again, from the external pressure on Augustine's reputation in the 430s. Some readers preferred Augustine's earlier works on grace while asserting that his later treatises promoted idiosyncratic notions. These kinds of preferential distinctions, Possidius believed, had to stop. Whereas Augustine allowed his readers to follow his thoughts as they evolved, his biographer made him a man of unmoving parts. Upon conversion, and perhaps more important, upon elevation to the episcopate, Augustine always remained the same, his consistency continually reaffirmed by public acts of orthodoxy.

Many readers assume Possidius' literary approach is naive and banal. We know very little about Possidius' education, but it has been previously assumed to be limited to a few books. Augustine once told Bishop Memorius that Possidius was not versed in the liberal arts; instead, all that Possidius knew was from his, Augustine's, teaching (*ep.* 101). Certainly this means he was given, within a decidedly Christian context, the best education the late antique West had to offer. It is good to keep this in mind when reading the modern scholarship, because while some studies note a lack of disagreement among Augustine's episcopal colleagues, others assume that those who do, in fact, depart from Augustine's views are either misinformed or dull-witted. Efforts to understand the intellectual relationships Augustine enjoyed with his episcopal colleagues will make little progress until we abandon that second presumption.

One can indeed argue that it is, in large part, owing to Possidius' efforts to codify Augustine's voice, as captured by the mountain of texts he dictated, that the literary and theological contributions made by other bishops, including himself, have become obscured. It is Possidius, too, who insisted on an episcopal collegiality to the point of muting any independence the other bishops may have possessed. He offers an opportunity worthy of pursuit, however, in that we can see, if only in glances, a literary landscape that differs from the one Augustine envisioned. It is the *Vita*, after all, that tries to wrest away from Augustine the kind of portrait he himself thought most edifying to share with the public. Simply stated, the writing of the *Vita* constitutes a deliberate entry into the conversation about the future of Augustine's legacy. With Augustine on one side and a reading audience on the other, Possidius' biography seeks to get between the two in order to mute or mitigate what some readers found objectionable, be it the kind of life he led or the books he wrote. Possidius takes on the role of mediator who tries to 'adjust' Augustine and his works to make them more like they 'should' be. Thus, the *Vita* offers a great deal of evidence about what it was like *not* to be Augustine, but instead a Catholic bishop living in Africa at the time of Augustine. Only Orosius' *Seven Books against the Pagans*, which has also experienced its share of harsh criticism, offers a similarly sustained opinion from one of Augustine's colleagues that dissents from the bishop's literary oeuvre.[12]

The engagement of textual evidence and allusion is Possidius' literary forte. The *Vita* offers few hints about the breadth of Possidius' acquaintance with books, but that is because the biography is reserved for only three kinds of citation: the scripture, imperial law, and Augustine. An emerging trend in the first decades of the 400s was to refer to the works of established authors, often bishops, as proof of theological correctness.[13] Here, in the *Vita*, the scripture and the words of Augustine refer to and support each other, while letters from provincial administrators and declarations by emperors offer external

---

[12] The classic article is Theodor E. Mommsen's 'Orosius and Augustine', in Eugene F. Rice, Jr. (ed.), *Medieval and Renaissance Studies* (Ithaca: Cornell University Press, 1959), 325–48. For context and discussion on the contributions of Orosius, see W. Frend, 'Augustine and Orosius on the End of the Ancient World', *AugStud*, 20 (1989), 1–38; and A. H. Merrills, *History and Geography in Late Antiquity* (Cambridge: Cambridge University Press, 2005), esp. 1–99.

The silence with which Paulinus of Milan's *Vita Ambrosii* was received (it was a work commissioned by Augustine) may indicate it landed wide of the mark in Augustine's estimation.

[13] Mark Vessey, 'Opus Imperfectum: Augustine and His Readers, 426–435 A.D.', *V Chr*, 52 (1998), 264–85, esp. 277–84.

affirmation. Possidius constructs an interdependent textual framework to defend Augustine's orthodoxy. At the same time, however, there is a great deal of manipulation going on. Possidius is at pains to prove that his version of Augustine is true, and he adopts the traditional view that to know Augustine was the best way to learn from him. Personal 'memories' were late antique literature's guarantor of narrative truth, but the ones in the *Vita* are largely constructed from Augustine's own texts.[14] Even when Possidius tells a story of how he himself was attacked by Donatists in the vicinity of Calama, he takes his material from Augustine's letters and treatises. The borrowing results in an ingenious refashioning: Augustine of the *Vita*, so often at odds with the one Augustine himself presented to the world, is actually made from sentences and phrases of Augustinian text. Possidius creates a 'new' Augustine by rendering his own words at variance with their intended meaning.

We know that the bishop of Calama liked to hunt for specific scriptural directives that he could pull out of an authoritative text, like plums, to guide the behavior of his congregation (*ep.* 245).[15] His was a life that revolved around the word, specifically scripture. He also believed that exegetical and literary works could contain truth as well as preserve historical moments and the imprints made on the world by holy lives. Possidius' complete investment in text comes through even at unlikely moments. Take, for example, the year 415, when Orosius traveled east armed with a dossier of documents supplied by the African bishops to protest the doctrines of Pelagius. While at Diospolis, he obtained relics of St Stephen and brought them back to Africa. They were distributed among many episcopal territories, including those overseen by Augustine and Possidius.[16] Both bishops usually resisted the incorporation of miracle stories into their writing; consequently, Book 22 of the *De civitate Dei* stands apart in Augustine's works for its catalogue of wonders that occurred at various shrines dedicated to St Stephen (22.8). Augustine compiled the list

---

As for Augustine, he subscribed to the idea of authorial consensus, as opposed to patristic authority, fairly late in his career. For discussion, see especially Éric Rebillard, 'Augustin et ses autorités: l'Élaboration de l'argument patristique au cours de la controverse pélagienne', Studia Patristica, 38 (2001), 245–63 and 'A New Style of Argument in Christian Polemic: Augustine and the Use of Patristic Citations', *JECS*, 8 (2000), 559–78. See also James J. O'Donnell, 'The Authority of Augustine', *AugStud*, 22 (1991), 7–35 and Robert Eno, 'Doctrinal Authority in Saint Augustine', *AugStud*, 12 (1981), 133–72.

[14] See, for example, Claudia Rapp, 'Storytelling as Spiritual Communication in Early Greek Hagiography: The Use of Diegesis', *JECS*, 6 (1998), 431–48 on the accentuation of text's veracity through eyewitness narration.

[15] See n. 9.

[16] On the further distribution of the relics to sees throughout Numidia, see Victor Saxer, *Morts martyrs reliques en Afrique chrétienne aux premiers siècles* (Paris: Éditions Beauchesne, 1980), 258–9.

from the local records of the African sees. Evodius only began recording what transpired at the shrine at Uzalis after Augustine's exhortation to care for their preservation.[17] The bishop of Hippo admits that many events occurring in his own city were now irretrievable since they were not written down. Possidius was frequently absent from Calama on account of episcopal business, but he maintained meticulous records ('Calamae vero...ipsa memoria...crebrius dantur'). Demonstrably 'more' miracles occurred at Calama than any other place precisely because Possidius ordered them to be written down and circulated.

A scripture-based faith fostered a privileged relationship with the written word, so it is not surprising that Possidius relied so extensively on text. Another issue, however, warrants consideration. It is not the same as scriptural citation or the kind of interpretive sweep that often entails, but may be detected in places like that dossier of documents, just mentioned above, that Orosius took with him to Jerusalem and Diospolis to argue against Pelagius. Much of the *Vita* is dedicated to Augustine's battles with heretics, and here the theological particulars that demarcate religious belief cede to the drama of public debate. This biography is not about dogma, but about law and the textual evidence required to win cases. The *Vita* is all about Augustine's books, but not the major theological treatises that medieval monasteries sought to acquire for their libraries and students of religion still read today. Possidius prefers to cite the conference of 411 and the 'abolition' of Donatism by imperial decree rather than to discuss a distinctly theological text like *On Baptism*. Or, instead of describing the circumstances surrounding the composition of *On Grace and Free Will*, Possidius treats his readers to a list of documents—signed by emperors and popes—that outlawed Pelagianism. Possidius is fixated on the legal aspects of theological controversies: arguments presented, the recording and distribution of transcripts, and the presentation of said transcripts to Roman administrators for review and adjudication.

Possidius was not the only one who paid close attention to the law. Many African bishops traveled to Italy and the court to tell the emperor news of Donatist 'unrest' and Pelagian 'connivance' in the hope of soliciting laws that favored Catholic interests. These men were acutely aware of the advantages the law provided in the pursuit of religious dominance. Debates, treatises, and epistles constituted evidence that could be shown to secular representatives, whose recognition of the Catholic party was crucial for proving orthodoxy (meaning, in this context, right-thinking). In the *Vita*, the rulings of secular

---

[17] Evodius was bishop of Uzalis, very close to Utica. He was one of Augustine's dearest friends and well known to Possidius from their days together in the monastery at Hippo. Subsequent contact between Evodius and Possidius included the Council of 411 and, around 418, the gift, perhaps, from Evodius to Possidius of relics of St. Stephen. See *PCBE Afrique*, 'Evodius', 366–73.

administrators largely determine theological soundness. It is for this reason that Possidius told the Donatists at the 411 conference that their assertions of correct belief had to be more than matters of opinion; they had to be proved (*Coll. Carth.*, II, 11 and III, 22). For Possidius, this meant the accumulation of imperial rulings, some of which he himself solicited, that declared his party the orthodox one.[18]

Possidius' decidedly legislative perspective helps explain what appears to be the *Vita*'s failure to attract much attention in the years after its 'publication'. Listing, prioritizing, and excerpting from the works of authoritative Christian authors, especially Augustine, in the fifth and sixth centuries became its own subgenre, with Possidius and Prosper of Aquitaine being among the first, if we do not count Augustine's *Retractationes*.[19] There is a distinct possibility that Possidius and Prosper met in Rome after the bishop's exile from Africa, and both men tenaciously defended the soundness of Augustine's doctrines, but neither Prosper nor later Augustinian commentators like Cassiodorus, Gennadius, or Eugippius followed Possidius in designating the same texts as quintessential.[20] The *Vita* is most interested in Augustine's legalistic texts, but Possidius also appended to the end of the biography an *Indiculum*, a list of all Augustine's treatises, letters, and sermons ordered according to subject. In explicitly linking the two texts together (Possidius speaks of the *Indiculum* within the life proper), he is merely following an established paradigm of prefacing literary collections with introductory biographies. This format

---

[18] Robert A. Markus, 'Africa and the Orbis Terrarum: the Theological Problem', in Pierre-Yves Fux, Jean-Michel Roessli, and Otto Wermelinger (eds.), *Augustinus Afer* (Fribourg: Éditions Universitaires Fribourg Suisse, 2003), 325, n. 21.

[19] For the possible relationship between Augustine's *Retractationes* and Jerome's *De viris illustribus*, see Vessey, 'Demise of the Christian Writer'. For discussion of 'canonization' of Christian writers and their works, see O'Donnell, 'The Authority of Augustine', 16–22. Much of Mark Vessey's work, beginning with his unpublished doctoral dissertation *Ideas of Christian Writing in Late Roman Gaul* (Oxford, 1988), deals with this phenomenon. See also his 'Peregrinus Against the Heretics: Classicism, Provinciality, and the Place of the Alien Writer in Late Roman Gaul', in *Cristianesimo e specificità regionali nel Mediterraneo latino sec. IV–VI* (Rome: Institutom Patristicum Augustinianum, 1994), 529–65, 'The Forging of Orthodoxy in Latin Christian Literature: A Case Study', *JECS*, 4 (1996), 495–513, and 'Opus Imperfectum'.

[20] For Prosper in Rome, see R. A. Markus, 'Chronicle and Theology: Prosper of Aquitaine', in C. Holdsworth and T. P. Wiseman (eds.), *The Inheritance of Historiography, 350–900* (Exeter: University of Exeter, 1986), 31–43.

See M. Vessey's introduction to the textual and legal worlds of Cassiodorus in *Cassiodorus: Institutions of Divine and Secular Learning of the Soul*, translated by James W. Halporn (Liverpool: Liverpool University Press, 2004), 3–101. Cassiodorus' library owned a copy of Possidius' *Indiculum* (1.16.4). Gennadius' brief entry for Augustine in his *De viris illustribus* picks out just a few works distinguished for their learning and piety, but he repeats Possidius' tag that nobody could have read all the works of Augustine. Eugippius' *Excerpta ex operibus S. Augustini* (CSEL 9.1) contain a lengthy assortment of biblical interpretations and entries of general knowledge, including those relating to morals and dogma.

should not have confused later readers, yet most of our extant manuscripts, the earliest of which dates to the ninth century, contain the life *or* the list. Rarely are they found together.[21] Posterity's refusal to follow Possidius' lead is a direct outcome of the *Vita*'s preoccupations. Whatever the merits of the biography, it is not strong on Augustine's philosophical and theological works. After the passing of Augustine's generation, and with it the historical concerns of fifth-century North Africa, Possidius' interest in the law and evidentiary dossiers did not translate well into territories that barely felt the impress of Donatism, one of the *Vita*'s primary concerns. The biography records the final days of a lost world. Later audiences were more interested in acquiring for their own libraries Augustinian texts listed in the *Indiculum* but not showcased in the biography. The book catalogue can function very well without the work that was initially designed to be its explanatory aid.

Modern readers have been even less kind to Possidius. Excellent work by Pellegrino and Bastiaensen on the bishop's use of Augustinian text has not significantly changed the trajectory of scholarship.[22] Much of it attempts to comment on or correct perceived errors in the biography.[23] Other studies analyze the *Vita*'s relationship with the genre of hagiography or try to pinpoint the author's intended audience.[24] The aim of this study is to discuss the accomplishments of the *Vita* by placing the work within its literary and historical contexts. The book is divided into two parts. Part I looks at the biography as a literary work: its aims, structure, and relationship to Augustine's literary oeuvre. Other commentators have had similar ambitions, but there still lingers the assumption that Possidius possessed a mind not capable of comprehending Augustine's intellectual breadth. The uncharitable pronouncement requires revision. This man governed a large Numidian see, twice visited the imperial consistory, cultivated alliances with the senatorial elite, was an architect of the 411 conference, and took it upon himself to make the definitive inventory of Hippo's library. Possidius' grasp on Augustine's oeuvre was as firm as

---

[21] A. Wilmart, 'Operum S. Augustini Elenchus a Possidio eiusdem discipulo Calamensi episcopo digestus: Post Maurinorum labores novis curis critico apparatus numeris tabellis instructus', in *Miscellanea agostiniana* (Rome: Tipografia Poliglotta Vaticana, 1931) ii, 149–233. For the manuscript history, see H. T. Weiskotten, *Sancti Augustini scripta a Possidio episcopo*.

[22] Michele Pellegrino, 'Reminiscenze letterarie agostiniane nella *Vita Augustini* di Possidio', *Aevum*, 28 (1954), 21–44 and Bastiaensen, *Vita di Agostino*.

[23] Pierre Courcelle, *Les Confessions de saint Augustin dans la tradition littéraire* (Paris: Études Augustiniennes, 1963), 612–13; A. Bastiaensen, 'The Inaccuracies in the *Vita Augustini* of Possidius', *Studia Patristica*, 16 (1985), 480–6, and, most recently, Serge Lancel, *Saint Augustine*, translated by Antonia Nevill (London: SCM Press, 2002), 476.

[24] Eva Elm, *Die Macht der Weisheit: Das Bild des Bischofs in der Vita Augustini des Possidius und anderen spätantiken und frümittelalterlichen Bischofsviten* (Leiden: Brill, 2003); and Louis I. Hamilton, 'Possidius' Augustine and Post-Augustinian Africa', *JECS*, 12 (2004), 85–105.

his awareness of the critical resistance to it, and he was confident enough to attempt necessary editorial revisions to ease tensions that he believed were endangering his mentor's legacy.

A study of Possidius' career will help to dismantle old prejudices. Character rehabilitation is one goal of Part II of this book, but a more specific ambition is to link Possidius' career with the structure of the biography. The narrative of the *Vita* is deeply entrenched in fifth-century legal procedure. In the 390s, the Donatists constituted the majority of Christians in Africa.[25] By 420, most had been absorbed, by imperial decree, into the Catholic fold. The political success has been squarely attributed to Augustine, but it has also been noted with surprise that it came without his stirring from Africa. He had not been in Italy since 388, but we know that successful solicitation of legislation from the imperial consistory required intense lobbying through repeated visits. How could Augustine achieve such success without the discomfort of overseas travel?[26] He once told his congregation that the body's senses (hearing, sight, taste, smell, and touch) could be compared to the constant arrival of messengers at court who delivered news to the emperor (*s.* 21.6). In employing such an image to describe a phenomenon Augustine pondered at length (e.g. *Confessions* Book 10), he may have had in mind the future careers of his colleagues. The bishops like Possidius, Theasius, Evodius, Fortunatianus, and Alypius were the ones who traveled and possessed the legal savvy necessary to engender support from the imperial authorities at court and in Rome. This was not just Augustine's show. His writing, which constitutes the majority of evidence we possess regarding Catholic political success in the first decade of the fifth century, is merely the expression, or manifestation, of a legally minded episcopal culture. The constant flow of embassies to the imperial court, the solicitation of favorable legislation from the consistory, and the efforts by all these bishops to enforce its implementation at the local level enabled Catholicism to rise as the preeminent religious voice.

There is a sixteen-year period in Possidius' life (395–411) where we can trace his legal activities with accuracy and detail. He himself describes this time with a kind of fulsomeness that the rest of the *Vita* lacks, and so it is to these years we turn in Part II of the book, when Possidius emerged from the monastery to take his place as the bishop of Calama. This was an era of heightened conflict with the Donatists. The friction was sometimes very intense, with strong words exchanged and episodes of violence, but it was above all a struggle to attain legal recognition from the imperial administration. We are most familiar with the picture fashioned by the Catholic bishops, including Augustine and Possidius:

---

[25] *v. Aug.* 7.2: 'rebaptizante Donati parte, maiore multitudine Afrorum'.
[26] O'Donnell, 'The Authority of Augustine', 14–16.

Donatist kidnappings, beatings, and the looting of churches and farms. We hear that in response Augustine and his disciples, patient and rational, called on the Donatists to convert by means of letters, treatises, and the courts. They continued to suffer violence until reason and the hand of the emperor ordered the Donatists into unity. The Catholic version of the story is convenient, and entirely misleading. The Donatists were just as sophisticated as the Catholics when it came to the nuances of Roman law. They, too, approached local and imperial administrations armed with precedents and transcripts to argue their cases. Their strategy for the conference of 411 was to cast doubt on the validity of the imperial rescript that convened the meeting, the hope being that they could force its dissolution on the basis of legal procedure. The important role of law for both sides convinces me to retain the admittedly compromising terms 'Donatist' and 'Catholic', because ownership of these names was a matter of adjudication in the secular courts.[27]

An investigation of Possidius' legal career during these years provides the context and perspective required to understand the *Vita*'s narrative content. For him, the mechanisms of Roman law burned away heretical dross to reveal pure, Catholic orthodoxy. The construction of such a relationship between religion and human law may seem odd at first, but Possidius was not alone in marking similarities between the two. The law played a large role in Christian or, more accurately, late antique imagination. Secular law, albeit an impoverished simulacrum, nevertheless reflected its higher, divine form.[28] We remember that *lex* was another word for scripture. The emperor's pronouncements as well as the Bible were ceremonially hailed as *sacrae litterae*.[29] An oft-repeated statement from Ulpian equated the work of jurists with the holy work of priests (*Digest* I.i.I.1). He was not thinking of Christian clergy, of course, but within a little more than a century, Catholic bishops returned the compliment by asserting that a concordance of opinion among religious authorities would, as in the case of jurists, carry the authority of truth.[30] Lactantius, a veteran of Diocletian's reign, which witnessed the first codification of Roman law

---

[27] Brent Shaw, 'African Christianity: Disputes, Definitions and "Donatists"' in Malcolm R. Greenshields and Thomas A. Robinson (eds.), *Orthodoxy and Heresy in Religious Movements: Discipline and Dissent* (Lewiston: Lampeter, 1992), 4–34. In his recent biography, *Augustine: A New Biography*, James J. O'Donnell eschews the names 'Catholic' and 'Donatist' to edifying effect.

[28] Helpful discussion regarding the view of jurists and intellectuals who read them in the late third and early fourth centuries may be found in Tony Honoré, *Ulpian*, 2nd edn. (Oxford: Oxford University Press, 2002) and Elizabeth Digeser, *The Making of a Christian Empire* (Ithaca: Cornell University Press, 2000), 46–63.

[29] See Mark Vessey, 'Sacred Letters of the Law: The Emperor's Hand in Late Roman (Literary) History', *An Tard*, 11 (2003), 345–58, esp. 353–4, where he and the works he reviews call attention to the similarities between legal and Christian culture.

[30] See supra n. 13. We see that clerics like Possidius, Orosius, and Evodius (see Chapter 1, n. 105) invested authority in Church councils, legal declarations, and the writings of Augustine.

since the Twelve Tables,[31] named his *Divinae Institutiones* after the textbooks that educated young men in secular law (1.1.12).[32] When Cassiodorus, praetorian prefect and consul under Theodoric, came to write his *Institutiones* more than two centuries later, he structured the first book by clustering lists of appropriate exegetical works around sequential books of the Bible.[33] As jurists wrote commentary on law, so theologians, vetted and approved as authoritative experts, now commented on Scripture. From at least the days of Cyprian, clergy patterned their own Church councils on meetings conducted by the Roman senate, including the verbatim recording of discussion.[34] By the time of Augustine, Catholic and Donatist bishops alike employed their own transcripts, as well as those made by the offices of local magistrates (*acta*), as evidence to present to provincial administrators or, when that did not suffice, the imperial consistory. Since the rule of Constantine, bishops enjoyed the right to conduct their own civil courts.[35] Lawyers, imperial bureaucrats, and clergy spoke the same language and observed similar protocols, so even for those bishops with no formal training in the law, the experience afforded by clerical office could be adequate preparation for arguing in front of town councils and proconsuls.

The long history of assimilated definitions and metaphorical similarity to divine precepts rendered secular law a sum greater than its parts. The documents and transcripts with which Possidius and his colleagues assembled arguments to define orthodoxy before government administrators became a means to truth. And not just any kind of truth: Possidius sought that which

---

[31] For the legal culture of the tetrarchic courts, see Simon Corcoran, *The Empire of the Tetrarchs*, rev. edn. (Oxford: Oxford University Press, 2000).

[32] Much has been written about Lactantius' relationship to the law, especially regarding his familiarity with Roman legal practice generally and with Ulpian and the jurists in particular. Contardo Ferrini, 'Die juristischen Kenntnisse des Arnobius und des Lactantius', *ZRG*, 15 (1894), 343–52, reprinted in Italian in *Opere di Contardo Ferrini*, ii (Milano: U. Hoepli, 1929), 467–86 traces Lactantius' use of Ulpian and the other Roman jurists. See also Eberhard Heck, ' "Iustitia Civilis— Iustitia Naturalis" a propos du jugement de Lactance conernant les discours sur la justice dans le "*de re publica*" de Ciceron', in J. Fontaine and Michel Perrin (eds.), *Lactance et son Temps* (Paris: Éditions Beauchesne, 1978), 171–84, and Francesco Amarelli, *Vetustas-Innovatio: Un'antitesi apparente nella legislazione di Constantino* (Naples: E. Jovene, 1978), 133–45. For a review of Amarelli's work that argues that perhaps the words and ideas Constantine and Lactantius share may be a function of broad cultural developments rather than a direct link between the two men, see Jean Gaudement, 'Costantino e Lattanzio', *Labeo*, 26 (1980), 401–5.

[33] Vessey, 'Introduction', *Cassiodorus*, 3–101.

[34] Pierre Battifol, 'Le Règlement des premiers conciles africains et le règlement du sénat romain', *Bulletin d'ancienne littérature et d'archéologie chrétiennes*, 3 (1913), 3–19 and Munier, 'La Tradition littéraire des canons africains'. See also Francis Dvornik, 'Emperors, Popes and General Councils', *DOP*, 6 (1951), 3–23 and Jill Harries, *Law and Empire in Late Antiquity* (Cambridge: Cambridge University Press, 1999), vii.

[35] James C. Lamoreaux, 'Episcopal Courts in Late Antiquity', *JECS*, 3 (1995), 142–67.

was divine, that is, the correct translation of God's wishes for human action and obedience to those directives.[36] We see, in a way, what the legal process means when we compare it to what goes on at the shrine of St Stephen at Calama. Here, the *proof* of the miracles' occurrence depended on their transcription. The accounting 'book' that was their guarantor therefore constituted more than a mere act of transference. Possidius, too, elevates his subject by 'monumentalizing' Augustine into a series of texts, most of them legal, which have demonstrably received approval from external (imperial) sources. The historical, and therefore changeable, Augustine, is diminished in importance. Certainly, his life had a beginning, a middle, and an end, and while Possidius recognizes growth and decline of the body in the biography's preface, he is anxious to 'overwrite' changes that have occurred within the Augustinian literary 'corpus'.[37] In the *Vita*, Augustine's books are more important, and more permanent, than the man who created them: permanent in terms of their physical longevity, but also permanent in their content. Possidius does not trace changes in Augustine's approaches to scriptural exegesis. In opposition to his mentor's method of intellectual review in the *Retractationes*, Possidius addresses Augustine's works in the biography and the *Indiculum* by subject, not chronologically. The books, thus 'frozen' for the sake of preservation, deliberately sidestep what was fundamental to Augustine, as a man and a bishop—the process of change, and, one hopes, growth. For the bishop of Hippo, these were desirable consequences for those who engaged their minds in the pursuit of understanding the divine word. Possidius, to the contrary, believed the explanatory texts had already been written. It was up to us to find, read, and *follow* them.

---

[36] Augustine's philosophical relationship with the law, like his relationships with all complex ideas, changed over the years. While he came to accept the use of coercion, he also grew more skeptical as to what the good secular governments could accomplish. Law and society as abstract concepts discussed especially in the *De civitate Dei* will not be addressed in this book, but see John M. Rist, *Augustine: Ancient Thought Baptized* (Cambridge: Cambridge University Press, 1994), esp. 203–55 and Robert Dodaro, *Christ and the Just Society in the Thought of Augustine* (Cambridge: Cambridge University Press, 2004).

[37] Possidius sets out to trace the parameters of Augustine's earthly life (*v. Aug. Praef.* 3): 'et exortu et procursu et debito fine.'

Part I

The *Vita Augustini*: Augustine's Life and Text According to Possidius

1

The *Vita Augustini*

Possidius' biography of the bishop of Hippo is much like Augustine's writings in that it stresses unanimity among Augustine's colleagues. Possidius' representation of the harmony persisting through theological and legal difficulties is so encompassing that the men surrounding the bishop of Hippo appear ill-defined and inconsequential. The biography does not name even one of Augustine's episcopal contemporaries.[1] His colleagues possess little intellectual independence, but are there to accompany Augustine to debates, agree with his actions, and collectively offer support. Their cohesiveness demonstrates unity within the Church, a unity defined and upheld by Augustine. As for the heretics and schismatics whom Augustine tries to persuade to return to the Church, their roles, too, look alike: they challenge Augustine and then lose to his theological correctness and forensic excellence. Opponents come and go in repetitive and predictable cycles.

The result, one may say, is a minimalist biography: a flat, anonymous background completely dominated by the overwhelming presence of Augustine.[2] This is just one of the criticisms leveled at the work. It suffers even more when compared to the *Confessions*. Augustine documented his own progress chronologically, and the reader travels with the author, missteps and all, along the circuitous path to the garden in Milan. In many of Augustine's later writings, and most dramatically in the *Retractationes*, the sense of change and progress first seen in the *Confessions* becomes a dominant current flowing through the entire oeuvre.[3] Possidius ignores Augustine's internal evolution in favor of

---

[1] Valerius and Ambrose, Augustine's mentors, are mentioned, but none from the circle of bishops who received their training at Hippo. Perhaps in imitation of the *Confessions*, Possidius names only those clerics instrumental in the development of Augustine's religious life.

[2] Cf. Neil B. McLynn, *Ambrose of Milan: Church and Court in a Christian Capital* (Berkeley: University of California Press, 1994), 371, who describes Possidius' ability to 'quicken' Augustine with intimate details, such as the latter's tears at his forced ordination to the priesthood or the penitential tears he wept on his death bed; but Possidius' hesitation to call upon the whirling universe of punish and reward that marks Paulinus of Milan's *Life of Ambrose* does not mean his Augustine is not equally 'artificial' and well constructed. Augustine's tears are just as public as Ambrose's.

[3] Mark Vessey, 'From *Cursus* to *Ductus*: Figures of Writing in Western Late Antiquity (Augustine, Jerome, Cassiodorus, Bede)', in Patrick Cheney and Frederick A. de Armas (eds.),

external consistency. There are reasons why Possidius chooses such a perspective, but readers have concluded that the answer probably lies in Possidius' inability to produce a sophisticated narrative.[4] What we know of his education (based on some letters of Augustine and the Latinity of the *Vita*) suggests to some a literacy attained after childhood and exposure to a limited number of books.[5] He was certainly familiar with the *Confessions*, but some readers question whether he understood them. These kinds of objections define most of the history of Possidian scholarship, and this is unfortunate, because his honest prose navigates through literary, legal, and theological issues that go a far distance to explain the workings of the North African episcopate.

This chapter analyzes the structure and purpose of the *Vita Augustini*, and is divided into three areas of discussion. First, Possidius wrote the biography to introduce and accompany Augustine's literary corpus.[6] He was very familiar with Augustine's work, keeping abreast of what Augustine wrote,[7] utilizing the collection at Hippo during his frequent visits, and having various items from it transcribed and sent to him at Calama (*ep.* 23*A.4). Possidius' relentless mining of Augustine's books for textual material results in a biography comprising

European Literary Careers: The Author from Antiquity to the Renaissance (Toronto: University of Toronto Press, 2002), 47–103. At 51–9 Vessey describes Augustine's progressive and corrective literary career as 'Augustinian cursive'. The degree of change in Augustine's career prompts Goulven Madec to argue that here is no one 'Augustinian dogma'. See 'Augustin évêque', in Goulven Madec (ed.), *Augustin Prédicateur (395–411): Actes du Colloque International de Chantilly (5–7 Septembre 1996)* (Paris: Institut d'Études Augustiniennes, 1998), 11–32.

[4] This belief is changing. See Eva Elm, 'Die *Vita Augustini* des Possidius: The Work of a Plain Man and an Untrained Writer? Wandlungen in der Beurteilung eines hagiographischen Textes', *Augustinianum*, 37 (1997), 229–40, and her book *Die Macht der Weisheit: Das Bild des Bischofs in der Vita Augustini des Possidius und anderen spätantiken und frümittelalterlichen Bischofsviten* (Leiden: Brill, 2003), esp. 105–59. See also Louis I. Hamilton, 'Possidius' Augustine and Post-Augustinian Africa', *JECS*, 12 (2004), 85–105.

[5] Augustine's *ep.* 101 to Memorius, the bishop of Eclanum (and the father of Julian of Eclanum). See also Peter Brown, *Augustine of Hippo: A Biography* (Berkeley: University of California Press, 1967; reprint 2000), 143. Conrad Leyser reminds us in *Authority and Asceticism from Augustine to Gregory the Great* (Oxford: Clarendon Press, 2000), 21, that Possidius remained a perennial outsider in regard to the rest of Augustine's intimate circle. He was not of that first generation of Augustine's friends, like Alypius, Evodius, and Severus, who were successful before joining the Church. These men, who were lawyers and officials before ordination, appear more legitimate than those who came after and whose success was grounded exclusively in Church careers. Leyser's list of this second generation contains two names, Possidius and Anthony of Fussala. Even if unintended, the guilt by association is inescapable.

[6] Serge Lancel, *Saint Augustine*, translated by Antonia Nevill (London: SCM Press, 2002), 476.

[7] See *ep.* 23*A, *BA*, 46B (Paris, 1987), with an English translation in Roland Teske, *The Works of Saint Augustine: A Translation for the 21st Century* (Brooklyn: New City Press, 2005). See also Marie-François Berrouard, 'L'Activité littéraire de saint Augustin du 11 septembre au 1er décembre 419 d'après la lettre 23*A à Possidius de Calama', in *Les Lettres de saint Augustin découvertes par Johannes Divjak: Communications présentées au colloque des 20 et 21 septembre 1982* (Paris: Études Augustiniennes, 1983), 301–27.

many of Augustine's own words and phrases.[8] The intellectual grasp he held on the oeuvre must have been dramatically underscored by the physical act of packing the contents of Hippo's library for shipment away from the city. Possidius compiled or copied an *Indiculum*, a catalogue of Augustine's treatises, letters, and sermons, which he then appended to the end of the *Vita*.[9] Early on in the manuscript tradition, the life and the index began to be copied separately, and some of the most recent editions of the *Vita* still do not include the *Indiculum*. The works should stand together.[10] The structure of the biography and the kind of person Possidius depicts Augustine to be are predicated on the organization and presentation of Augustine's written works.

Second, the *Vita* emerges from an historical context defined by the activities of the Catholic and Donatist bishops in the early fifth century. Debates, embassies, councils, circulated letters, and *notarii* (stenographers) recording every word exchanged between parties constituted the quotidian realities of episcopal purview in North Africa during Possidius' lifetime. Bishops were well attuned to Roman imperial law. They knew how to petition the local municipal councils, address the proconsuls, and manipulate extant law. If their exertions in Africa did not provide the desired results, they sent embassies to the emperor to solicit favorable legislation. The *Vita* expresses an unusual interest in transcripts and legal procedure, and while citation and verbatim report are usually associated with study and establishment of proof through scripture, the biography focuses on the written words of Augustine in order to verify historical moments and theological arguments. This is, in part, a function of

---

[8] Michele Pellegrino has done much of the work tracing Possidius references to Augustine in the *Vita Augustini*. See 'Reminiscenze letterarie agostiniane nella *Vita Augustini* di Possidio', *Aevum*, 28 (1954), 21–44 and Pellegrino's edition of the *Vita Augustini*: *Vita di S. Augustino* (Alba: Edizioni Padine, 1955). Pierre Courcelle analyzes several allusions Possidius makes to the *Confessions*: 'Emprunts et compléments de Possidius aux *Confessions*', in *Les Confessions de saint Augustin dans la tradition littéraire: Antécédents et postérité* (Paris: Études Augustiniennes, 1963), 609–21.

[9] I use 'Indiculum' as opposed to 'Indiculus'. The neuter spelling is attested in the manuscripts and is preferred by A. Mutzenbecher, 'Bemerkungen zum Indiculum des Possidius. Eine Rezension', *RÉAug.*, 33 (1987), 129–31 and Goulven Madec, 'Possidius de Calama et les listes des oeuvres d'Augustin, in Jean-Claude Fredouille et al. (eds.), *Titres et articulations du texte dans les oeuvres antiques* (Paris: Institut d'Études Augustiniennes, 1997), 427–45 at 427 n. 1.

[10] See A. Wilmart, 'Operum S. Augustini Elenchus a Possidio: Post Maurinorum labores novis curis editus critico apparatus numeris tabellis instructus', in *Miscellanea agostiniana* (Rome: Tipografia Poliglotta Vaticana, 1931), ii, 149, on the fact that most of our manuscripts of the *Vita* likewise do not include the *Indiculum*.

As for modern editions, the one by A. A. R. Bastiaensen, *Vita di Agostino* (Milan: Fondazione Lorenzo Valla, 1975) does not, nor does H. T. Weiskotten's *Sancti Augustini Scripta a Possidio Episcopo: Edited with Revised Text, Introduction, Notes and an English Translation* (Princeton: Princeton University Press, 1919), or M. Pellegrino's. The exception is P. Angelus C. Vega, *Opuscula Sancti Possidii Episcopi Calamensis: Vita Augustini et Indiculum Librorum eius* (Escoreal: Typis Augustinianus, 1934).

the biography's relationship to the subject's oeuvre: the *Vita* was designed to be an introduction to Augustine's books, some of which are discussed contextually within the biography itself. But Possidius' mind was, essentially, a legal one. Law and the petitioning necessary to effect its solicitation defined his episcopal career, and these consequently became the keys to Catholic, and his own, success. Possidius regularly dealt with Calama's municipal council and appealed to prefects and emperors. He placed his faith in secular law and believed that God's will manifested itself through rulings of the Roman government. It is for this reason that the preponderance of Augustine's works cited by name in the *Vita* are transcripts from public meetings, which, compiled in dossiers, could be presented as evidence in anti-heresy cases brought before imperial officials.

Third, the biography is, in large part, a defense of Augustine. Written as many as nine years after Augustine's death,[11] the *Vita* refutes numerous calumnies, some of which are more than four decades old. Many people, including a number of Catholic bishops, never liked the man who became bishop of Hippo. He had criticized the African clergy for personal shortcomings, but was perceived to have stretched the rules regarding his own promotion to priest and bishop. Megalius, the primate of Numidia, protested Augustine's episcopal appointment on the grounds of violation of Church protocol (his elevation occurred when the bishop of Hippo was still alive)[12] and his past heretical affiliations. Manichaean entanglements from Augustine's youth continued to be a matter of reproach. Catholics and Donatists called him a crypto-Manichaean, or simply a Manichaean, in the 390s and early 400s. Augustine's treatises on predestination written in the 410s and 420s elicited from the Pelagians fresh accusations that he held dualistic Manichaean beliefs, and he died while writing a lengthy treatise against Julian of Eclanum, wherein he repeatedly differentiated his views.[13] As is made clear by Prosper of Aquitaine, some Gallic theologians (the Massilians or the semi-Pelagians)

---

[11] We are not sure when exactly Possidius composed his *Vita*. Reference to Boniface as 'erstwhile' ('quondam' [*v. Aug.* 28.12]) may mean that the composition dates to after Boniface's death, in 432. A terminus of 439 is suggested on the grounds that Possidius refers to Carthage as a city that has not been sacked by the Vandals, and the city was taken and partially destroyed in 439.

[12] *v. Aug.* 8.3 and 8.5. Cf. Roland Kany, 'Der vermeintliche Makel von Augustins Bischofsweihe', *ZAC*, 1 (1997), 116–25.

[13] *Contra Julianum opus imperfectum* 6.41 (CSEL 85.1). The very last words of the unfinished treatise place Augustine on the side of Ambrose regarding Adam's sin as introducing the struggle between the flesh and the spirit, something very different from the Manichaean notion that the flesh is alien and always evil. In *ep.* 224, Augustine explains he had to interrupt the composition of the *Retractationes* in order to begin the work. For discussion, see Robert A. Markus, 'Augustine's *Confessions* and the Controversy with Julian of Eclanum: Manicheism Revisited', in B. Bruning, M. Lamberigts, and J. van Houtem (eds.), *Collectanea augustiniana 2: Melanges T.J. van Bavel* (Leuven: University Press, 1990), 913–25, esp. 923–4.

were still worried about Augustine's Manichaean ties during the years Possidius was probably writing his biography.[14] It was consequently crucial for Possidius to show Augustine as a worthy Catholic bishop whose appointment was visibly sanctioned by God.

The defensive strategy employed by Possidius necessitates the exaltation of the episcopate. Earthly authority certainly accompanies the title, and in the biography Augustine counts high-ranking Roman magistrates as his peers. The office itself, however, energizes the talents within the man, and consequently the persuasive power of Augustine's texts, speeches, and sermons rapidly accelerates upon his ordination. Possidius' ideas of episcopal prerogative have scriptural precedent and an important advocate in no less than the person of Cyprian,[15] but in the *Vita* they are largely informed by the controversy that surrounded Augustine's past.

Augustine was hesitant to claim any moral prerogative for himself because of the chair he occupied. He often told his congregation that clerical office made no man inherently good, and he had seen too many bishops commit personal and administrative blunders to conclude that he or his colleagues enjoyed any moral advantage.[16] On the other hand, later in life Augustine did speak of written agreement among bishops as means of establishing a basis

---

Prosper, *Chron.*, at 430 (1304): 'Aurelius Augustinus episcopus per omnia excellentissimus moritur V. kl. Sept., libris Iuliani inter impetus obsidentium Wandalorum in ipso dierum suorum fine respondens et gloriose in defensione Christianae gratiae perseverans.'

[14] Prosper's *Epistula ad Rufinum* 3 and 18, for example *PL* 51, 79, and 88. For Prosper's relationship to Augustine, the definitive work is Rudolf Lorenz, 'Der Augustinismus Propsers von Aquitanien', in *ZKG*, 73 (1962), 217–52. See also Georges de Plinval, 'Prosper d'Aquitaine interprète de saint Augustin', *RecAug*, 1 (1958), 339–55. For background on Gaul's reception of Augustine's works see Ralph W. Mathisen, 'For Specialists Only: The Reception of Augustine and his Teachings in Fifth-Century Gaul', in J. T. Lienhard, E. C. Miller, and R. J. Tesker (eds.), *Collectanea Augustiniana: Augustine presbyter factus Sum* (New York: Peter Lang, 1993), 29–41. A general study of the Massilian (or semi-Pelagian) controversy may be found in Rebecca Harden Weaver's *Divine Grace and Human Agency* (Macon: Mercer University Press, 1996).

[15] Cyprian's *De ecclesiae catholicae unitate*. For discussion, see Jean-Paul Brisson, *Autonomisme et christianisme dans l'Afrique Romaine* (Paris: Éditions de Boccard, 1958), 43–78. Brisson's insistence on claiming Cyprian for the Catholics to the detriment of the Donatists does not obscure the importance of *origo* for both (Augustine's *ep*. 53 is a good example), but cf. A. Mandouze, 'Encore le Donatisme: Problèmes de méthode posés par la thèse de J. P. Brisson', in *AC*, 29 (1960), 61–107.

[16] In a number of works, Augustine rejected the holiness of bishops or the power one has merely because one is a bishop. See, for example, Augustine's response to Petilian's letters *c. litt. Petil.* 3.34 (39) where he discusses a litany of crimes committed by 'respectable' clergy. See *s*. 137, 179.2, 355.2, *s. Guelferbytanus* 26.2, the new Dolbeau *s*. 10, as well as *s. Guelferbytanus* 32 (*de ordinatione episcopi*). This sermon, 32, may have been preached on the ordination of Anthony of Fussala. See also *ep*. 208 and discussion by Rémi Crespin, *Ministère et Sainteté: Pastorale du Clergé et Solution de la Crise donatiste dans la vie et la Doctrine de Saint Augustin* (Paris: Études Augustiniennes, 1965), 177–247.

for argument.[17] While no text could approach scripture as the touchstone of truth, agreement among bishops, whether through Church council records or textual citation from individual works, was an efficacious method of arguing for theological correctness, especially when one could trace ideas and associations back to the apostles, informed as they were by the Holy Spirit. Possidius' Vita employs an approximate idea. Once ordained bishop, Augustine's powers visibly increase, but they extend exclusively to the realms of text, argument, and persuasion. There are very few miracles in the Vita. Augustine healed the sick once, the only time he exercised this kind of power, when he himself was confined to bed with an illness. He told his petitioner that if he actually possessed special abilities, surely he would have already used them on himself.[18] While setting physical laws at defiance often defined holy lives written in the fourth and fifth centuries, events such as postmortem appearances and dominance over nature play no role in the Vita. The wonder of Augustine is that he returned the North Africans to Catholicism. His ability to *persuade*, as secured by his elevation, guaranteed his orthodoxy and acceptability as a bishop.

These three points of discussion—the Vita as catalogue raisonné, legal history, and personal defense—direct readers of the Vita to the place where Possidius wants them to go: Augustine's texts. Possidius acknowledges other biographies of holy men, which, like his, were written with the aid of the Holy Spirit.[19] He certainly was familiar with Paulinus' Vita Ambrosii and probably knew as well the lives of Cyprian and Martin of Tours. Possidius had comparanda available when he composed the Vita, and consequently many readers of the biography have tried to place the work within the context of other saints' lives written in the West in the fourth and fifth centuries.[20] Because the Vita so closely engages Augustine's works, however, it consciously departs from

---

[17] See *Contra Julianum*, Books 1 and 2, which places emphasis on the agreement among episcopal texts. Éric Rebillard argues in 'A New Style of Argument in Christian Polemic: Augustine and the Use of Patristic Citations', *JECS*, 8 (2000), 559–78, and 'Augustine et ses autorités: l'Élaboration de l'argument patristique au cours de la controverse pélagienne', *Studia Patristica*, 38 (2001), 245–63 that Augustine employs these citations for polemic and not as proof of ecclesiastical law.

[18] See *v. Aug.* 29.5: 'si aliquid in his posset, sibi hoc utique primitus praestitisset.' The story gives credence to Possidus' assertion that Augustine's death during the siege of Hippo was an answer to his prayer for release. For frequency of miracles, cf. Hamilton, Possidius' Augustine and Post-Augustinian Africa.

[19] *v. Aug. Praef.* 2: 'Id enim etiam ante nos factitatum fuisse a religiosissimis sanctae matris ecclesiae catholicae viris legimus et comperimus, qui, divino adflati Spiritu, sermone proprio atque stilo et auribus et oculis scire volentium dicendo et scribendo similia studiosorum notitiae intulerunt, quales quantique viri ex communi dominica gratia in rebus humanis et vivere et usque in finem obitus perseverare meruerint.'

[20] Elm's study *Die Macht der Weisheit* places the *Vita* in a broad literary context of saints' lives stretching from the third to ninth centuries.

other hagiographies, and attempts at close comparison eventually lose momentum. The *Vita* is best understood within the historical context of early fifth-century Africa, the episcopal experience shared by Possidius and Augustine, and, finally, Possidius' concerted efforts to demonstrate the efficacy and orthodoxy of Augustine's work.

POSSIDIUS DEFENDS AUGUSTINE

The Confessions

The biography begins with a promise to investigate the life and habits (*de vita et moribus* [*v. Aug. Praef.* 1]) of Augustine. The *Vita* broadly traces this two-step pattern, with the first eighteen chapters following a (roughly) chronological progression of his career (the *vita* part), from baptism through the conflicts with the heretics and culminating in his confrontation with the Pelagians, which occupied his final years.[21] In Chapter 19, diachronic narrative cedes to a synchronic portrayal of life within the monastery at Hippo (the *mores* part).[22] Glimpses of communal life among the clerics include the kind of food and drink served; how Augustine dealt with secular authorities and acted as judge; and how he handled household discipline, including matters of property, legacies, and accounting books. The concluding sections (Chapter 28 to the end) relate the circumstances surrounding Augustine's death. The kind of portrait that first progresses chronologically and then switches to analysis of character without reference to specific historical time has been labeled the quintessential pattern of biography as written by Suetonius.[23] Death scenes, too, are considered 'Suetonian' in nature. The imperial lives announced the portents presaging the emperors' demise, followed by the manner of death, last words,

---

[21] For the progression of heresies and their narrative placement in the *Vita*, see n. 170.

[22] The chapter headings were added by D. Joannis Salinas in his 1731 edition, published at Rome. Weiskotten keeps them, but other editors, including Bastiaensen, excise them. For discussion and review of how readers interpret the sections of the Life, see, Brigitta Stoll, 'Die *Vita Augustini* des Possidius als hagiographischer Text', *ZKG*, 102 (1991), 1–13 at 11–12.

[23] Suetonius' *Life of Augustus* is considered paradigmatic, and here he informs his readers that after having related the events in Augustus' early life, he will proceed to categories (*per species*), presented a-chronologically, which include, among other matters, Augustus' civil wars, foreign wars, governmental reforms, and domestic affairs. See 9.1: 'Proposita vitae eius velut summa, partes singillatim neque per tempora sed per species exsequar, quo distinctius demonstrari cognoscique possint'; and 61.1: 'Quoniam qualis in imperis ac magistratibus regendaque per terrarum orbem pace belloque re p. fuerit, exposui, referam nunc *interiorem ac familiarem eius vitam* quibusque moribus atque fortuna domi et inter suos egerit a iuventa usque ad supremum vitae diem' (italics mine). Citation from Henri Ailloud (ed.), *De vita Caesarum* (Paris: Les Belles lettres, 1967).

and final assessment. Aside from offering an enhanced narrative clarity, this kind of presentation allows for greater exactitude in moral evaluation.[24] As much as a man may be defined by his accomplishments, his value as a public figure can only be elicited by study of personal *characteristics*, which, in the end, adumbrate character.[25] Friedrich Leo's extraordinarily influential work on the classification of Greek and Roman biography and hagiography argued that the 'Suetonian' and 'Plutarchian' forms of biography became the standard templates for writing lives, including those for Christian holy men. His generic formulations are still prevalent in studies of late antique biography, and it is often argued that Possidius utilizes the 'Suetonian model' in his portrayal of Augustine.[26]

The assumption that Possidius relied on Suetonius is in itself problematic,[27] but more at issue is the value of this whole line of inquiry. The elicitation of the moral nature of the person observed is thought to be, in part, Suetonius'

---

[24] Andrew Wallace-Hadrill, *Suetonius: The Scholar and His Caesars* (New Haven: Yale University Press, 1983), 144.

[25] See Patricia Cox Miller, *Biography in Late Antiquity: A Quest for the Holy Man* (Berkeley: University of California Press, 1983).

[26] *Die griechisch-romische Biographie nach ihrer literarischen Form* (Leipzig: Teubner, 1901; reprint, New York: Georg Olms, 1990). Reassessment of Leo's work may be found in Arnaldo Momigliano, *The Development of Greek Biography* (Cambridge: Harvard University Press; reprint, 1993), 11. See also Cox, *Biography in Late Antiquity*, 54–5 and Wallace-Hadrill, *Suetonius*, 10, 70, and 144.

Shortly after Leo's work was published, Franz Kemper wrote his dissertation at the University of Münster on the lives of Western saints. He claimed that these, including Possidius' *Vita Augustini*, followed Suetonius' literary structure as articulated by Leo. The same argument has been defended, with variations, until today: *De vitarum Cypriani, Martini Turonensis, Ambrosii, Augustini rationibus: Commentatio Philologica quam consensu et auctoritate amplissimi Philosophorum ordinis in alma litterarum universitate regia monasteriensi ad summos in philosophia honores rite consequendos scripsit* (Münster: Manasterius Guestfalus, 1904), 36–40; see 41–3, for systematic comparisons between the saints' lives and imperial lives.

See also Weiskotten, *Sancti Augustini scripta a Possidio episcopo*, 20–1; Pellegrino (commentary), 20 ff.; Adolf Harnack, *Possidius Augustins Leben* (Berlin: Verlag der Akademie der Wissenschatten, 1930) 13 ff. H-J. Diesner, 'Possidius und Augustinus', *Studia Patristica*, 6 (1959–62), 350–65 responds to Pellegrino and Harnack at 350–2; Christine Mohrmann, 'Zwei Frühchristliche Beschofsviten: *Vita Ambrosii, Vita Augustini*, *Anzeiger*, 112 (1975), 321–2; Stoll, 'Die *Vita Augustini* des Possidius', 11; Elm *Die Macht der Weisheit*, 107–8 and 111–12; Georg Luck, 'The Literary Form of Suetonius' Biographies and the Early Lives of Saints', in *Ancient Pathways and Hidden Pursuits: Religion, Morals, and Magic in the Ancient World* (Ann Arbor: University of Michigan Press, 2000), 178–80. The original article, published in 1964 as 'Die Form der suetonischen Biographie und die frühen Heiligenviten', *Mullus*, 1, 230–44, criticizes imperfect associations made between Suetonius and lives of the saints, but Luck was persuaded that the second part of Possidius' *Vita* describing life at the monastery was a product of Suetonian influence.

[27] There is little evidence that Possidius had access to the lives of the emperors. Possidius was acquainted with other, later *vitae*, which may have acted as a conduit between the authors. Jacob Bernays' study on Sulpicius determined that he was familiar with Suetonius. See *Ueber die Chronik des Sulpicius Severus: Ein Beitrag zur Geschichte der klassischen und biblischen Studien* (Berlin: Wilhelm Hertz, 1861), 53 ff. or H. Usener (ed.), *Gesammelte Abhandlungen* (Berlin: W. Hertz, 1885), ii, 167 ff.

goal; to do so, he peeled apart and displayed, as much as possible, the private sides of a man. To think that Possidius shared this narrative objective may generate mistaken impressions. Is Possidius, in fact, trying to balance Augustine's public life with his private, and to elucidate the inner character of the man by focusing on the details of quotidian existence? A student of Suetonian biography may conclude, for example, that Possidius' description of Augustine's diet is designed to tell us as much or more about the man's inner heart than the books he wrote or the theological victories he enjoyed. Was Augustine a glutton? Did he have control over his physical nature?[28]

Possidius' narratological focus is elsewhere. The object of his attentions was the author of the *Confessions*, that book being the deepest meditation on character that survives from antiquity. The internally oriented Augustine of the *Confessions* continued throughout his career to speak of his life through sermons and treatises.[29] The chronological ordering of his books aimed to demonstrate to his readers where and how he erred along his route of inquiry. To the contrary, Possidius announces at the beginning of the *Vita* that the kind of interior examination to which Augustine had already subjected himself plays no part in his biography. He will not review what Augustine said before he received grace (i.e. baptism), for Augustine's books followed the precepts of Paul, which warn against thinking oneself worthy of more honor than the public was willing to bestow. The desire to remain humble ('humilitatis sanctae more') governed the writing of Augustine's *Confessions*, a stricture that was not applicable to Possidius' role as author.[30] The angel tells us that it is good to remain silent about the details of a king's earthly entanglements, but Possidius was speaking of the works of God.[31] We move from the interior world of the *Confessions* to the external manifestations of an accomplished life, and the *Vita* consequently cleans up the personal and theological complications

---

[28] Cf. *conf.* 10.31 on the tension between the usefulness and pleasure of eating and drinking. Where one left off, and the other began, remained problematic for Augustine.

[29] See James J. O'Donnell, *Augustine Confessions* (Oxford: Oxford University Press, 1992), xli–li, and R. Markus, 'Augustine's Confessions and Controversy with Julian of Eclanum', 913–25.

[30] Cf. with Augustine's reasons as to why he will not defend his *Confessions* after Petilian raised the issue of his 'past' life (at 3.10). He says he joins 'freely with all men in condemning and bearing witness against the whole period of my life before I received the baptism of Christ, so far as it relates to my evil passions and my errors, lest, in defending that period, I should seem to be seeking my own glory, not His, who by His grace delivered me even from myself.' Translations of the *Against the Letters of Petilianus* from *Nicene and Post-Nicene Fathers* (Grand Rapids: W. B. Eerdmanns, reprint, 1989).

[31] *v. Aug. Praef.* 7: 'Sacramentum igitur regis, ut angelica auctoritate prolatum est, bonum est abscondere; opera autem Domini revelare et confiteri honorificum est' (from Tob. 12:7). For other views of Augustine's humilty within the *Vita Augustini*, see Elm, *Die Macht der Weisheit*, 118–43.

of Augustine's internal meditations as he, Augustine, wrote of and defined them.[32] Aside from changes attendant to his conversion and subsequent elevation, Augustine of the *Vita* remains consistent in his person and his books. Possidius was familiar with the *Retractationes* and mentions them in the *Vita*, but in choosing a different method of cataloguing Augustine's books (by subject), he mutes Augustine's public reconsiderations, and renders the collection theologically more consistent, approaching the monolithic. The *Vita* could justifiably be called an 'anti-*Confessions*' or even an 'anti-*Retractationes*', in that it attempts to force an ever-evolving man to be still. Possidius' biography is not an armchair Suetonian exposé, and even less is it an attempt to portray someone he simply did not understand.[33] Possidius appreciates Augustine's literary and theological trajectories as well as the reactions these elicited from an international audience. In response, the *Vita* seeks to retrench his hero in theological stability. Possidius' ambition is to secure Augustine's legacy with a definitiveness that was lacking in the late 430s.

The most famous example of Possidius' efforts to 'clean up' Augustine is the 'reconsideration' he forces upon the *Confessions*.[34] Allusions to the *Confessions* can be found throughout Possidius' biography, but the first four chapters traverse the ground of Augustine's early life until his conversion and decision to return to Africa in 388. Possidius skims over these years, covering books one through nine of the *Confessions* in a single short chapter. Augustine quickly grows from infancy to an attendee of Ambrose's basilica in Milan. It is the first substantive look at events of Augustine's life in the biography, but the presentation is so condensed as to be incorrect. Books five through nine of the *Confessions* detail the struggle Augustine experienced before his baptism. Possidius ignores Augustine's encounters with Cicero's *Hortensius*, astrology, Neoplatonism, and even his mother Monica in favor of one decisive meeting between Augustine and Ambrose. Augustine arrives at Ambrose's church, eager for the bishop to speak 'vel pro ipsa vel contra' on Manichaeism, the religion

---

Compare *conf*. 10.4 (6): 'Hic est fructus confessionum mearum, non qualis fuerim sed qualis sim', with *v. Aug. Praef*. 5: 'Nec adtingam ea omnia insinuare...qualis ante perceptam gratiam fuerit qualisque iam sumpta viveret, designavit.' Augustine's trajectory is evolutionary: to know him now means to have learned him as he went along. For Possidius, the break between pre- and post-conversion (or pre- and post-Confessions), is absolute.

All citations of the *Confessions* from O'Donnell, *Augustine Confessions*.

[32] Petilian (3.10 [11]) and Julian of Eclanum (e.g. *Contra Julianum opus imperfectum* 1.25 and 1.68) criticized Augustine's life as he describes it in the *Confessions* for his Manichaean beliefs and his past behavior. Julian even insulted Augustine's mother.

[33] See H. J. Diesner, 'Possidius und Augustinus', 355.

[34] Ibid., 350–65; Courcelle, 'Emprunts et compléments', 609–21; A. Bastiaensen, 'The Inaccuracies in the *Vita Augustini* of Possidius', *Studia Patristica*, 16 (1985), 480–6.

to which he had dedicated himself. Through God's will, Ambrose did preach on the heresy, which, little by little (*paulatim*), Augustine learned to abandon. He was baptized at Easter by Ambrose and subsequently decided to adopt an ascetic lifestyle.[35]

The action in the conversion scene is construed as entirely passive. Ambrose's heart is touched by God, inspiring him to preach on the heresy.[36] Augustine's questions regarding God's law are resolved ('legis solverentur quaestiones') by the resulting sermons, and eventually the heresy is driven from Augustine's soul ('haeresis...ex animo pulsa est'). Ambrose's preaching constitutes the kind of accidents of speech one sees frequently in the *Confessions*. God works through human agency, and a sermon, a rebuke, or a casual remark can break embedded habits.[37] For Possidius, too, there is no such thing as chance. Despite this thematic correlation, almost all the detail in Possidius' version of Augustine's conversion departs from that found in the *Confessions*. We know that Augustine's dedication to Manichaeism faltered at Carthage and decreased further while he lived in Rome. When he began attending Ambrose's church, Catholicism remained 'unbeaten, but still not victorious'.[38] Once he resolved important issues regarding the Old Testament by aid of Ambrose's discussions on allegory, Augustine chose the Catholic doctrine.[39] Possidius simplifies Augustine's relationship with Manichaeism, making that religion a consistent and monolithic barrier to his conversion, and Ambrose the sole agent of his release.[40]

The reconstruction of the order of the events is also incorrect. Augustine adopted asceticism before being baptized or resigning his post as imperial rhetor at Milan, but in Possidius' version, conversion comes first, baptism second, the adoption of an ascetic lifestyle third, and then, finally, retirement. This chronological manipulation, like the stress unduly placed on Augustine's Manichaean past, is no mistake, as it clarifies Augustine's break from the heresy.

---

[35] For Courcelle's judgment of Possidius' narrative manipulation see 'Emprunts et compléments', 613: 'A mes yeux, ce récit de Possidius fausse gravement la suite des faits et prête à Augustin une évolution asses banale, alors qu'elle ne le fut pas dans la réalités.'

[36] *v. Aug.* 1.5: 'Et provenit Dei liberatoris clementia sui sacerdotis cor pertractantis.'

[37] See Henry Chadwick, 'History and Symbolism in the Garden at Milan', in F. X. Martin and J. A. Richmond (eds.), *From Augustine to Eriugena: Essays on Late Antique Thought and Culture in Honor of R. A. Markus* (Washington: Catholic University of America Press, 1990), 42–55.

[38] *conf.* 5.14 (24): 'ita enim catholica non mihi victa videbatur, ut nondum etiam victrix appareret.'

[39] *conf.* 6.5 (7) 'Ex hoc tamen quoque iam praeponens doctrinam catholicam.' The intention is not to take away from the importance of Ambrose's sermons, which Augustine himself credits in the *Confessions* for clarifying crucial issues. The point is that Possidius has excised all other influences.

[40] Stoll, 'Die *Vita Augustini* des Possidius', 6.

By cutting out much of the detail, Possidius makes the story of renunciation decisive by its narrative clarity and its dependence on Ambrose. Possidius also stresses that it was Catholicism and baptism that prompted Augustine's embrace of asceticism. Emphatically, the predilection for bodily discipline did not come from Manichaean teaching. Practices considered now typical of monastery life were largely unfamiliar in the West in the late 300s and early 400s, and some people accused the residents at the monastery of Hippo, several of them former Manichaeans, of engaging in practices that could be traced to the heresy. These included restrictions on food and sexual behavior.[41] Possidius carefully traces the biblical passages that exhort communal living and the sharing of goods.[42]

The *Confessions* never reveals that it was Ambrose who performed Augustine's baptism, perhaps because Augustine did not want to call attention to the external acts that constituted the ceremony, including its administering bishop.[43] For Augustine, baptism was more about internal conversion than what the Donatists would consider the key component: the worthiness and legitimacy of the bishop who performed the sacrament. The name of Ambrose, however, is clearly announced by Possidius,[44] and the shift speaks to evolving developments in North Africa, wherein the arguments against the Donatists were now considered secondary to the requirements of Augustine's larger audience, especially in Gaul and Italy, where Pelagianism had students and sympathizers. Ambrose's presence, crucial to the *Vita*, became likewise more frequent in Augustine's own anti-Pelagian treatises written in the 420s. Pelagius had used the works of Ambrose for support on doctrinal matters, and Augustine, in turn, repeatedly cited Ambrose, 'my teacher', in exchanges with

---

[41] Augustine, Profuturus, and Severus, all residents of the monastery at Hippo, were also former Manichaeans. There is also the connection to Romanianus, the uncle of Alypius, a friend and supporter of Augustine. He may have returned to Manichaeism around 408. Aimé Gabillon, 'Romanianus alias Cornelius: Du nouveau sur le bienfaiture et l'ami de saint Augustin', *RÉAug*, 24 (1978), 58–70; and for the date of 408, see Dom De Bruyne, 'Les anciennes Collections et la chronologie des lettres de saint Augustin', *RBén*, 43 (1931), 284–95.

See Terrence G. Kardong, 'Monastic Issues in Possidius' *Life of Augustine*', *American Benedictine Review*, 38 (1987), 159–77 at 163 and 174. See also Bastiaensen's commentary, 413, where he says that the biblical quotations Possidius uses in discussion of food are those used by Augustine in his works against the Manichaeans: *Contra Fortunatum* 22; *C. Faust.* 6.7 and 14.11; *De natura boni* 84; *De moribus* 1.33.72.

[42] Luke 12:32–3; Matt. 19:21, and 1 Cor. 3:12. Augustine had to defend the monks, some of whom, he admitted, were not of the highest caliber, to his own congregation. See, for example, *en. Ps.* 132.

[43] Henry Chadwick, 'Donatism and the *Confessions* of Augustine', in Glenn W. Most, Hubert Petersmann, and Adolf Martin (eds.), *Philanthropia kai Eusebeia: Festschrift für Albrecht Dihle zum 70. Geburtstag* (Göttingen: Vandenhoeck & Ruprecht, 1993), 23–35.

[44] As noticed by Courcelle, 'Emprunts et compléments', 612.

Julian of Eclanum to claim the advantage.[45] The connection between Ambrose and Augustine precluded ownership by the Pelagians. At the same time, the Ambrose of Possidius' *Vita* possesses religious authority to a degree that Augustine's Manichaean 'cure' should be secure for the *Vita*'s readers—those readers, perhaps, knowing that the Pelagians and the Massilians were voicing their doubts. Finally, and this is particular to the *Vita*, Ambrose as bishop passes to Augustine his spiritual gifts: wisdom, orthodoxy, and the ability to persuade.

We see how bishop empowers bishop when the reader is brought back to Augustine's conversion much later in the biography (*v. Aug.* 15).[46] Manichaeism is the only heresy in the *Vita* that makes separate, reoccurring appearances, an assurance that Augustine's orthodoxy rejects the former allegiance. Years have passed since the momentous encounter with Ambrose. The bishops Augustine and Possidius, and other residents of Hippo's monastery, are sitting together at table after church, and Augustine asks the company if they noticed he lost track of his place in the sermon and detoured into questions on Manichaeism. They agree that he never returned to conclude his main points, the impression being this was not one of Augustine's best performances, but God was once again working through what appeared to be random occurrence.[47] A day or two later, Firmus, a local merchant and attendee of Augustine's church, came to the monastery and told the company

---

[45] *Contra Julianum* 1.10.1 'But again, listen to another excellent steward of God, whom I reverence as a father, for in Jesus Christ he begat me through the Gospel, and from this servant of Christ I received the laver of regeneration.' Translation by Roland J. Teske (Brooklyn: New City Press, 1998).
See O'Donnell, 'The Authority of Augustine', *AugStud*, 22 (1991), 11. Augustine's reliance on, and allusions to, Ambrose began in earnest during the Pelagian controversy. As for Augustine's solicitation of Paulinus to write the *Vita Ambrosii* see A. Paredi, 'Paulinus of Milan', *Sacris Erudiri*, 14 (1963), 206–30, and Émilien Lamirande, *Paulin de Milan et la Vita Ambrosii: Aspects de la religion sous le Bas-Empire* (Paris: Les Éditions Bellarmin, 1983).

[46] Manichaeism appears in Chapters 1, 6, 15, and 16 of the *Vita*.
The readings suggested in the *Vita Augustini* are, more often than not, shorter works (like the *Contra Fortunatum* and the *Gesta cum Emerito*). One of the lengthier treatises mentioned is the *Contra Felicem*, which was a debate held at the basilica at Hippo in December of 404. It is here that Felix *and* Augustine disavowed their allegiance to Manichaeism (*Contra Felicem* 2.22): 'Augustinus ecclesiae catholicae episcopatus iam anathemavi Manichaeum et doctrinam eius et spiritum, qui per eum tam execrabiles blasphemies locutus est, quia spiritus seductor erat non veritatis, sed nefandi erroris ipsius.'
For discussion see Richard Lim, *Public Disputation, Power, and Social Order in Late Antiquity* (Berkeley: University California Press, 1995), 99–102.

[47] *v. Aug.* 15.3: 'in cuius manu sunt et nos et sermones nostri', which is taken from book of Wisdom 7:16 and used frequently by Augustine (see, e.g., *s. Guelferbytanes* 30.2).
The passage in the *Vita* (15.6) echoes the sentiments of Augustine: 'admirantes et stupentes, glorificavimus sanctum eius nomen et benediximus, qui cum voluerit et unde voluerit et quomodo

that Augustine's sermon had convinced him to abandon the heresy.[48] Firmus quit his occupation, became a monk, and was later forced by the people in his town to be their priest, which is exactly what had happened to Augustine after his encounter with Ambrose.[49] Thus, Augustine has become Ambrose and Firmus is now the Augustine figure. The repetition underscores Augustine's rejection of Manichaeism in that the story of Augustine's conversion has, essentially, been told twice, but Possidius also demonstrates that Augustine, a bishop and conduit of God's will, is the direct successor of Ambrose. Augustine has become Ambrose's equal.

Failure

To Possidius' thinking, bishops give orthodoxy to others through teaching, preaching, and writing. Theological persuasion, that is, the physical act of making someone change his mind, is proof positive that it is God empowering the relationship between teacher and student. God's spirit flows through acceptable vessels, so if you cannot convince, you are not advocating orthodox belief. Possidius draws a distinct line between who is and is not capable of persuading others to correct belief. The heretics in the face of Augustine's arguments do not have this power, despite their deployment of a variety of rhetorical strategies, many of which are cunning and unethical. Those who do persuade are Ambrose, Augustine, and, as we shall see later, Possidius. The lines are drawn clearly: Catholic clerics on one side and heretics on the other.

---

voluerit, et per scientes et per nescientes, salutem operatur animarum.' Cf. with *Quaestiones in Heptateuchum* 7.49 and *conf.* 6.7.12: 'ut aperte tibi tribueretur eius correctio, per me quidem illam sed nescientem, operatus es...Sed utens tu omnibus et scientibus et nescientibus ordine quo nosti...de corde et lingua mea carbones ardentes operatus es.' At the beginning of *en. Ps.* 138, Augustine remarks that he had prepared to preach on a different psalm. He interpreted the reader's mistake in reciting this psalm as a command from God to follow where the error led him.

[48] *v. Aug.* 15.5: 'ac se in ecclesia Dei misericordia fuisse eius tractatibus nuper correctum atque catholicum factum.'

[49] We are not certain about the identity of this former Manichee Firmus. One person we know he is *not* is the Firmus who asked Augustine for a copy of the *De civitate Dei*. See 1*A in the Divjak collection, first published by Lambot in 1939 and listed as *ep.* 231A in the Maurist catalogue. Augustine's *ep.* 2* makes it clear that this Firmus was married and unbaptized.

As for the possibility of this Firmus being the priest who acted as courier between Augustine and his correspondents, especially Jerome, see *PCBE Afrique*, 'Firmus 2', 458–9 and Yves-Marie Duval, 'Julien d'Éclane et Rufin d'Aquilée. Du Concile de Rimini a la répression pélagienne: L'intervention impériale en matière religieuse', *RÉAug*, 24 (1978), 246–7.

Surprisingly, even acceptable vessels 'purged onto honor'[50] can sometimes be ineffective if they do not hold clerical office.[51] Consider the *agens in rebus* episode in the *Vita*. When Augustine returned to Africa from Italy, he lived in his hometown of Thagaste, but soon felt compelled to go to Hippo Regius because he had received report of an *agens in rebus* who, on the verge of adopting an ascetic life, sought Augustine's company and reassured him that he would give up the world gladly if only he could hear salutary words from Augustine's lips.[52] Augustine arrived at Hippo and spent his time with the officer; every day Augustine was told a decision was imminent, but it never came.[53] Augustine could not persuade the man. This is a strange moment in the biography, especially because just few lines before, Possidius emphasizes that Augustine possessed grace (3.1).[54] Rarely, if ever, does failure make an appearance in saints' lives, and I am inclined to say that the explanation for Augustine's stumble ultimately resides in his nonclerical status.

Cyprian spoke of episcopal prerogative as an expression of apostolic power. The fire of Pentecost and its gifts (preaching, healing, and administration of sacraments) flowed on to the disciples' successors. Legitimate bishops, the heirs of Christ's apostles, enjoyed the privileges established immediately after Christ's ascension. Catholicism and the unbroken progression of the lineage, from origin to contemporary time, preserved that inaugural apostolic force in its entirety. Cyprian's articulation of the episcopate was very influential among African Christians, Catholic and Donatist alike, and some of Cyprian's notions about apostolic power may be playing a part in Possidius' narrative.[55] Augustine himself paid little attention to such arguments when it came to assessing his

---

[50] *v. Aug.* 3.5: 'Sed vacare utique et inane esse non potuit quod per tale vas mundum, in honore, utile Domino, ad omne opus bonum paratum, in omni loco divina gerebat providentia.' This is from 2 Tim. 2:21, and see Rom. 9:21–3. The use Augustine made of this statement, for anti-Pelagian arguments, is paramount.

[51] Notice *v. Aug.* 29.4 that Augustine was able to help men possessed with demons only when a presbyter and bishop: 'Novi quoque eumdem et presbyterum et episcopum...daemones ab hominibus recessisse.'

[52] A. Mandouze, *Saint Augustin: L'Aventure de la raison et de la grâce* (Paris: Études Augustinennes, 1968), 204–12 on the monastery at Thagaste. See also George Lawless, *Augustine of Hippo and His Monastic Rule* (Oxford: Clarendon Press, 1987), 45–62 as well as his 'Augustine's First Monastery: Thagaste or Hippo?' *Augustinianum*, 25 (1985), 65–78.

[53] *v. Aug.* 3.5: 'Ac se ille de die in diem facturum pollicebatur, nec tamen in eius tunc hoc implevit praesentia.' Cf. Pierre Courcelle, *Recherches sur les Confessions de saint Augustin* (Paris: Éditions de Boccard, 1950), 183, n. 4, who interprets the passage to mean that Augustine's bid was ultimately successful, which is, of course, correct if the *agens in rebus* here is Possidius.

[54] Cf. Brigitta Stoll, 'Einige Beobachtungen zur Vita Augustini des Possidius', *Studia Patristica*, 22 (1989), 344–50 at 347.

[55] J. Pintard, 'Sur la succession apostolique selon saint Augustin', in *Forma future: Studi in onore del cardinale Pellegrino* (Torino: Bottega d'Erasmo, 1975), 884–95 and Robert B. Eno, 'Doctrinal Authority in Saint Augustine', *AugStud*, 12 (1981), 150–1.

own performance. The office he held neither granted nor guaranteed who he was this day and who he would be tomorrow.[56] He readily admitted that there were good bishops and bad bishops.[57] Office did not make a better person. If anything, the temptations accompanying the honors and privileges could chip away at a man's integrity. On many occasions, he told his congregation that being bishop offered him no spiritual advantage over anyone else. He performed biblical exegesis, but he reminded his readers in the *Confessions* that Christ, not a bishop, was the intercessor between man and God (10.43). His longing to study Holy Scripture and the time spent doing so did not guarantee he would be able to explain, truthfully, the Bible's *opaca secreta*. Augustine must call upon Christ, the intercessor and word made flesh, 'in whom are his all the treasures of wisdom and knowledge', to illuminate the pages (11.2).[58]

Augustine also believed that one's occupation never determined the capacity to act as a conduit for God. Divine ability to move the will expressed itself through all kinds of people and situations. One thinks of the slave girl who mocked Monica for her tippling in the *Confessions* (9.8). The impetus arose merely from a child's cruelty, yet the sting precipitated Monica's lifelong abstemiousness. Such correctives, random as they are, allow humans to live and love correctly,[59] and they can come from anywhere at any time. To the contrary, the changes that occur in the hearts of those populating the *Vita* are limited to theology and conversion as accomplished by Catholic clerics, notably bishops.

Ordination

Augustine's meeting with the *agens in rebus* immediately precedes his attendance at the basilica of Hippo, where the Catholics took hold of him and made him their priest. We possess another version of Augustine's arrival at Hippo from his own sermon 355, where he tells the congregation he was well aware

---

[56] Supra n. 16.

[57] See *s. Guelferbytanus.* 32.6 (*PL* Supplementum 2): Bad bishops retain their titles, but they are not true bishops: 'Quid ergo dicemus? Sunt episcopi mali? Absit, non sunt: prorsus audeo dicere, non sunt episcopi mali; quia si mali, non episcopi.'

[58] O'Donnell, *Augustine Confessions,* iii, 229–31.

[59] Augustine's beliefs on God's working through unwitting human conduits who 'delight and stir the mind' as to change behavior and lives, began to emerge in the *Ad Simplicianum* and always remained with him. See, for example, *On Rebuke and Grace,* 45. For discussion, F. Edward Cranz, 'The Development of Augustine's Ideas on Society before the Donatist Controversy', *HThR,* 1 (1954) 255–316, at 281–2 and Paula Fredriksen, 'Beyond the Body/Soul Dichotomy: Augustine on Paul against the Manichees and the Pelagians', *RecAug,* 23 (1988), 88–114 at 94–8.

that his name was known among African Catholics, and he feared being seized. He consequently resisted entering any city that was in need of a bishop.[60] Augustine confirms that he went to Hippo to recruit one of his friends for his monastery at Thagaste, but he felt no uneasiness being there because Hippo already had a bishop. He does not disclose, like Possidius, that his attempt at conversion was not a success.[61] Despite Augustine's stated lack of concern upon entering Hippo, Possidius' pointed reference to the call from the *agens in rebus* means that Augustine's attendance at church was purely an accident and not a function of his *ambitio*. Augustine was not scheming for a clerical appointment. There are discrepencies, however, when we place the *Vita* next to Augustine's version of events. We know that when the congregation demanded that Augustine be ordained as their priest, he began to weep. Augustine felt obliged to explain his reaction to the bishop Valerius (*ep.* 21), and Possidius thought repetition was necessary more than forty years later, but each man reveals a different impetus for the emotion. In Augustine's letter to Valerius, the tears constitute recognition of punishment, even derision, by God for having criticized other Catholic clerics and their bad deeds ('peccata' [*ep.* 21.2]).[62] Members of the congregation encouraged him with kind words, but they did not fathom the real reason for his emotional state and so their attempts to comfort were ineffectual. Augustine does not record the substance of these blandishments, but Possidius writes that some people believed his tears were prompted by the humiliation at being appointed presbyter. He was expecting, they thought, to be named bishop, so they tried to reassure him that while he was too good for the priesthood, he still had some way to go before being counted worthy of the episcopate.[63] Possidius repeats Augustine's statement that his comforters misread his reaction, and says that Augustine later intimated to him that the tears were prompted by cognizance of the challenges of administering the Church and the dangers implicit in the responsibilities accompanying oversight of its resources. In short, Possidius says that Augustine feared for his soul, and that

---

[60] See the annotated translation of *s.* 355 and 356 by Goulven Madec, *La Vie communautaire* (Paris: Institut d'Études Augustiniennes, 1996); the Latin may be found at *PL* 5.2.1568–81: 'Usque adeo autem timebam episcopatum, ut quoniam coeperat esse iam alicuius momenti inter Dei servos fama mea, in quo loco sciebam non esse episcopum, non illo accederem' (355.2).
  Possidius, as he will often do, says that Augustine personally told these things to him. *v. Aug.* 4.1: 'solebat autem laicus, ut nobis dicebat, ab eis tantum ecclesiis, quae non haberent episcopos, suam abstinere praesentiam.'
[61] 'Veni ad istam civitatem propter videndum amicum, quem putabam me lucrari posse Deo, ut nobiscum esset in monasterio; quasi securus, quia locus habebat episcopum' (355.2).
[62] Cf. *De moribus ecclesiae catholicae et de moribus Manichaeorum* 1.32.69 (dated to 388–9) where bishops and leaders of the Church are lavishly praised.
[63] *v. Aug.* 4.2: 'quia et locus presbyterii, licet ipse maiori dignus esset, propinquaret tamen episcopatui.'

is why he cried.[64] He has avoided any mention of prior invective lodged against Catholic clergy. Moreover, the source of Augustine's emotions is confirmed by Possidius' use of the *Confessions* by alluding to the tears Augustine shed when his mother died. At Hippo, those who saw him cry misread his reaction ('nonnullis quidem lacrimas eius...*superbe interpretantibus*'). At Ostia, alone in his room and after his recitation of *Deus creator omnium*, Augustine cried legitimate tears on his pillow into the ears of God, and not to those who would mistake them for something else ('ibi erant aures tuae, non cuiusquam hominis *superbe interpretantis* ploratum meum' [*conf.* 9.12.{33}]). A reader of the *Vita* should not doubt the appropriate trepidation with which Augustine entered his new and unwelcome appointment.

Elevation from layman to bishop in a metropolitan area was rare in real life and the stuff of legends in literature.[65] Augustine admitted he stayed away from towns that needed bishops in fear of being forced to occupy an empty episcopal throne. The residents of Hippo reassured their new priest that the appointment, while not what Augustine had hoped for, was appropriate. If word had it that Augustine was confident he would be asked to assume the office of bishop, his presumption may have generated hostility, especially among Catholic bishops who had been objects of his criticism. We know that some bishops did not like him personally. That information is from a later time, after he was made presbyter, but Augustine had given ample opportunity for the bishops to distrust him. The criticisms launched from Thagaste against the African clergy followed his days as a Manichaean debater, when he had bested a number of Catholic opponents, some of whom were bishops.[66] These men also found objectionable many practices employed at Hippo's basilica. Augustine preached while presbyter, for example, but the responsibility of

---

[64] *v. Aug.* 4.3: 'cum ille homo Dei, ut nobis retulit, et maiori consideratione intellegeret et gemeret, quam multa et magna suae vitae pericula de regimine et gubernatione ecclesiae inpendere iam ac provenire speraret, atque ideo fleret.'

[65] It is true that Numidia and Byzacena had numerous bishops, many more per capita than Italy or perhaps even Asia Minor. That should be kept in mind, but as opposed to a *villa* or *castella*, Hippo was a large port city. For the numbers of bishops in Africa, see Leslie Dossey's forthcoming work (circulated as 'Bishops Where No Bishops Should Be: The Phenomenon of the Village Bishopric in Augustine's Africa', Group for the Study of Late Antiquity, Princeton University, February 2004). Cf. Mandouze, *Saint Augustin*, 137, who says that promotion from layman to bishop was common, but perhaps that only seems so because such occasions are celebrated in lives of holy men. These are no measures for what is 'ordinary'. We have an inventory of Catholic and Donatist bishops from the 411 conference: *Coll. Carth.*, I, 112–215.

[66] *conf.* 4.26 and 9.11 as well as *s.* 51.6. See Henry Chadwick, 'On Re-reading the Confessions', in Fannie Lemoine and Christopher Kleinhenz (eds.), *Saint Augustine the Bishop: A Book of Essays* (New York: Garland Publishers, 1994), 145.

addressing congregations was reserved exclusively for the bishop.[67] A number of Catholic bishops complained about this.[68] The changes that Augustine introduced to Africa early in his clerical career, especially the demand that his subordinates who were training to be clerics adopt ascetic practices, must have generated mistrust, if not open hostility, among some other African bishops whose lifestyles, albeit perfectly respectable, came under direct or implied criticism from Hippo.[69]

At the end of August 392, Augustine stood before the Manichaean presbyter Fortunatus and announced to the audience that he, too, had once held Manichaean beliefs as true. Just fourteen months later (October 393), he appeared at the general council of African bishops, and although only a presbyter at the time, delivered to them a declaration of Catholic faith (*De fide et symbolo*), an explication of the Nicene creed—which all the bishops had just recited together.[70] How much the speech was designed for the edification of the bishops as opposed to offering reassurance regarding his own adherence to, and understanding of, the orthodox creed is an important question, especially when Possidius was still defending Augustine's monastic way of life in the late 430s. The bishops at Hippo in 393 were gauging the merits of the new presbyter, and this sermon may have been a test.[71]

Augustine's appointment as bishop, or co-bishop (Valerius was alive when Augustine received his office), also met with resistance. Opposition based on the protocols of the Nicean Council, which determined the rules for appointment of a new bishop when the old one was still alive, may have been a matter of legitimate concern.[72] But we know at this time that Megalius, the bishop of Calama and primate of Numidia, accused Augustine of being a Manichaean

---

[67] Cf. Possidius' light imagery in describing the benefits of Augustine's preaching with Augustine's letter to Aurelius (*ep.* 41) at the news Aurelius will now allow his priests to speak to his congregation.

[68] *v. Aug.* 5.3: 'unde etiam nonnulli episcopi detrahebant.'

[69] *c. litt. Petil.* 3.48. The Donatists, too, find monastic life suspect: 'In the next place, he [Petilian] has gone on, with calumnious mouth, to abuse monasteries and monks, finding fault also with me, as having been the founder of this kind of life.' See *ep.* 22, written in the first days of his priesthood, asking Aurelius to stop the long-standing celebrations at African gravesides, the *laetitiae*. See the precepts of the Council of 393, which enumerated monastic expectations, especially on commerce with women and ownership of property. *Concilia Africae, Breviarium Hipponense* (pp. 30–46).

[70] *retr.* 1.16.1; *Concilia Africae, Breviarium Hipponense* (pp. 30–1).

[71] Cf. *ep.* 22 with Augustine's warm and cooperative relationship with the bishop of Carthage, Aurelius, as seen especially at the beginning of Augustine's career.

[72] *v. Aug.* 8.5. The Catholic Chuch at Hippo possessed a copy of decisions made at Nicea, the original of which was brought back to Africa by Caecilian. *Concilia Africae, Concilium Carthaginense anni 419*, p. 94, lines 162–6. See Monceaux, *Histoire littéraire de l'Afrique chrétienne*, iii, 218–20.

and of administering drugs, or perhaps a kind of love philter, to an older woman while her complacent husband looked on.[73] These are allegations lodged against opponents whose reputations and careers you want to destroy. Megalius later apologized for his comments,[74] but the vitriol may have been representative of, not exceptional to, clerical sentiment. Augustine's elevation to the episcopate was a very unpleasant episode. Possidius tells us only that Megalius was invited to Hippo by Valerius so that the latter could share his wishes with the primate of Numidia in the presence of Hippo's congregation. The burden of accepting or declining the office in the narrative is placed on Augustine, who, as presbyter, feels compelled to reject this irregular invitation.[75] At the 411 conference, however, we see the unease with which Possidius reacted to questions regarding Augustine's ordination. He and his colleagues protested the Donatists' repeated demand that Augustine state publicly the name of the bishop who ordained him. Augustine stated Megalius' name with additional words and in a tone that anticipated ridicule. The impetus of the question did not come from Donatist suspicions regarding the 'purity' of Calama's former bishop, but from the fact that Megalius had embarrassed Augustine with his insults.[76]

---

[73] *C. litt. Petil* 3.16 (19); *Cresc.* 3.80 (92); *Coll. Carth.*, III, 247. See also Lim, *Public Disputation*, 70–108.

[74] *C. litt. Petil.* 3.16 (19): 'quod autem a sancto concilio de hoc quod in nos ita peccavit, veniam petivit et meruit.'

[75] *v. Aug.* 8.3–4: 'episcopatum suscipere contra morem ecclesiae suo vivente episcopo presbyter recusabat...compulsus atque coactus succubuit et maioris loci ordinationem suscepit.'

[76] *Coll. Carth.*, III, 243–7. Augustine's response is at III, 247: 'Megalius me ordinavit, primas ecclesiae Numidiae catholicae, eo tempore quo ille me potuit ordinare. Ecce respondi. Prosequere, profer quae praeparas, ibi etiam calumniosus appareas. Ecce dixi ordinatorem meum; profer iam calumnias tuas.'

ep. 38, sent by Augustine to his friend and fellow bishop Profuturus, was written twenty-four days after the burial of Megalius, when Augustine was sick and confined to bed. The subject of the letter was the need to find a replacement for Megalius and the attendant difficulties of that need: scandal (*scandala*), griefs (*maerores*), and anger (*ira*) are words Augustine uses to describe a process barely underway. Profuturus, the bishop, may have faced stiff resistance from the people at Calama, and his courier, Victor, seems to have expressed reservations about returning to Calama, although he had promised Augustine that he would do so. Several commentators have attributed Augustine's remarks on the destructive power of anger to his lingering bitterness about what Megalius had said about him. Augustine in this letter, however, discusses the difficulties posed by events now that Megalius is dead. This anger is not about Augustine's personal feelings regarding Megalius, but instead the frustration felt by Augustine, Profuturus, and, perhaps, Severus (all bishops, all men who had lived at Augustine's monastery), at trying to appoint an episcopal successor for a town possibly hostile to Augustine and his 'cronies'. Calama may have wanted to appoint one of Megalius' presbyters and tried to resist external pressure from other Catholic interests. Nectarius, a wealthy and influential Christian in town, did not want to enter into negotiations with Augutine about a successor. Nectarius will be discussed in a later chapter.

The Agens in Rebus

Augustine's sermon 355 offers no clue as to the identity of the acquaintance who prompted Augustine to leave Thagaste for Hippo.[77] The *Vita* identifies him as an *agens in rebus* and adds the brief detail that he was 'bene Christianus Deumque timens': a good Christian who feared God.[78] I wonder if this brief description of a nameless bureaucrat who pops out dramatically from the narrative constitutes a kind of inside joke, the story of how Possidius once vacillated before his expectant mentor. Many readers of the *Vita* have commented that Possidius maintains a low profile in the biography. Possidius never refers to himself by name, nor does he claim credit for the important missions he was sent on in pursuit of imperial action against pagans and heretics. But the truth is that Possidius appears everywhere in the *Vita*. The heresy debates often feature Possidius as an audience member or primary participant. A reader knows that it was Possidius who successfully lobbied the proconsul of Africa and the emperor to place Donatists under the legal category of heresy. Possidius also anointed himself protector and heir of Augustine's literary heritage. In his own anonymous way, Possidius always claims his proper credit, and the understanding that he likes to write himself into Augustine's biography—we shall see more of this later—propels my assertion that this *agens in rebus* may be no other than Possidius himself.

One would think that such a proposal precludes narrative complications due to Augustine's nonclerical status. Possidius may have no deeper point here if he is recording his own hesitations that, obviously, were eventually resolved. The suggestion is a guess, but even if true, the episode still poses problems for a reading audience because of Augustine's past relationships with *agentes in rebus* which had been singularly successful. Evodius was one, but he abandoned his job for communal life with Augustine (*conf.* 9.8.1).[79] More importantly, Possidius' introduction of this noncommittal *agens* in the *Vita* ('ex his, quos dicunt agentes in rebus') is taken from Book 8 of the *Confessions* (8.6.15) where two of these officers search a house belonging to

---

[77] *s.* 355.2: 'Veni as istam civitatem propter videndum amicum, quem putabam me lucrari posse Deo, ut nobiscum esset in monasterio.'

[78] Possidius may be giving us a clue in this unidentified man's epithet, *Deum timens*. It is repeated two more times in the *Vita*, both times referring to 'bishops': once to refer to bishop Valerius (*v. Aug.* 5.2) and the other to a dying bishop, a old man and a good friend of Augustine, whose wisdom belied his lack of formal education (*v. Aug.* 27.10: 'Deum quidem timentem').

[79] Cf. Augustine's description of Faustinus as having been recruited from the *militia* in *s.* 356.4. His poverty indicates that he was probably a soldier of not very high rank. See *PCBE Afrique*, 'Faustinus 10', 388.

Christians.[80] They find a copy of *Life of St. Anthony*, and one of them takes it, reads it, and immediately decides to give up his career for a Christian life; he easily convinces his companion, who has not even had the benefit of looking at the text (although he would have heard it if read aloud), to do the same.[81] Augustine became very upset while listening to Ponticianus' story about the *agentes*' sudden turn. 'Look at them', he told Alypius, 'these unlearned men rise and grasp heaven while we, for all our learning, are still caught up in flesh and blood' ('surgunt indocti et caelum rapiunt, et nos cum doctrinis nostris sine corde, ecce ubi volutamur in carne et sanguine' [8.8{19}]). The anger that he feels for himself, for his own failure, begins to push him into the garden and a new life. It is a cascading series of stories: Anthony's ascetic life nudges the *agens in rebus*, who in turn convinces his friend; upon hearing the tale, Augustine turns to Alypius and says: 'Why not us?' Possidius' introduction of his own story with its allusion to this scene in the *Confessions* invites the sequence of conversion to spill over into the *Vita*. The *agens in rebus* should have had his moment in Hippo. That he does not pulls up on the narrative like the force of inertia.[82]

And so we return to clerical status. As a layman (Possidius never calls Augustine a catechumen),[83] Augustine had grace, and meditated on the Scriptures day and night,[84] yet he failed to win over someone on the very cusp of surrender. As a priest, he won the right to preach, a practice which was at first deplored, but then adopted, by other African bishops. Catholics as well as heretics began to read his treatises with delight, and the Church began to gain in strength, bolstered by new adherents.[85] The victories for orthodoxy won

---

[80] *conf.* 8.6.15: quam legere coepit unus eorum et mirari et accendi, et inter legendum meditari arripere talem vitam et relicta militia saeculari servire tibi. *Erant autem ex eis quos dicunt agentes in rebus*' (italics mine).

[81] Pierre Courcelle, *Recherches sur les Confessions de saint Augustin* (Paris: Éditions de Boccard, 1950), 175–202 on the connections between the story as told by Ponticianus and the conversions of Augustine and Alypius. Augustine read his *sors biblica* in silence.

[82] Jacobus de Voraigne used Possidius' *Vita* for Augustine's entry in the *Golden Legend*, but this turn of events with the *agens* was considered worthy of excising. 'Eodem tempore apud Hypponem erat quidam vir magnarum opum, qui Augustino misit, quod, si ad eum accederet et verbum ex ore suo adiret, saeculo renuntiare posset. Quod Augustinus ubi comperit, illuc concitus ivit, audiens autem Valerius Hypponensis episcopus famam eius, ipsum plurimum renitentem in ecclesia sua presbiterum ordinavit.'

[83] Bastiaensen, 'Inaccuracies', 482.

[84] *v. Aug. Praef.* 5 ('qualis ante perceptam gratiam') and 3.1 ('percepta gratia'). *v. Aug.* 3.2: 'in lege Domini meditans die ac nocte'. For Augustine's use of this phrase see O'Donnell, *Augustine Confessions* iii, 256–7.

[85] *v. Aug.* 7.2: 'Atque Dei dono levare in Africa ecclesia catholica exorsa est caput, quae multo tempore illis convalescentibus haereticis praecipueque rebaptizante Donati parte, maiore multitudine Afrorum seducta et pressa et obpressa iacebat.'

by Augustine while a priest dramatically increased upon his elevation to the episcopate.[86] The office of bishop carried with it great power: upon ordination, Augustine became unstoppable.[87]

One final note about the authority of the Catholic cleric and specifically the Catholic bishop: Possidius was aware that Augustine's views on grace and predestination were objects of scrutiny in the 420s and in the years following his death. Augustine's critics suggested that his earlier works were more theologically acceptable than the ones composed after he took up the episcopate.[88] Desire to explain the shifts in thought over the years, shifts that he considered necessary and justified, prompted Augustine to write the *Retractationes*.[89] Promotion to the bishopric was not the actual impetus that fostered changes in Augustine's ideas on grace and predestination. The writing of the *Ad Simplicianum* followed his rereading and study of Paul, and it is in these responses to the newly appointed bishop of Milan that Augustine entered another stage of his thinking.[90] The *Ad Simplicianum* was the first book of Augustine's episcopate, and the elevation offered a convenient chronological demarcation: it is with this work that Augustine begins the second of two books of *Retractationes*. After having read Augustine's treatise *De gratia et libero arbitrio*, Prosper began to describe Augustine's intellectual evolution, as Augustine himself

---

[86] *v. Aug.* 9.1: 'Et episcopus multo instantius ac ferventius, maiore auctoritate, non adhuc in una tantum regione, sed ubicumque rogatus venisset'.

[87] Notice however, that Possidius tempers Augustine's power by juxtaposing the external victories with an unknowable internal life. In his final days, Augustine pasted penitential psalms of David on his walls and wept while asking for forgiveness (*v. Aug.* 31.1: 'dicere nobis inter familiaria conloquia consueverat, post perceptum baptismum etiam laudatos Christianos et sacerdotes absque digna et competenti paenitentia exire de corpore non debere').
Ambrose had offered himself as the guiding example: 'I have not so lived that I should be ashamed to live among you, yet do I not fear to die, for we have a Lord who is good' (*v. Aug.* 27.8). Augustine was particularly fond of this saying as it took into account the deeds 'which men can judge about a fellow-man', but the following clause neither presumes upon the divine mind nor ignores interior lives which remain unknown to all save God. 'But as for his judgment by the divine justice, he trusted rather in the Lord who is good and whom he also said in the daily prayer: "Forgive us our trespasses"'.

[88] See, for example, *ep.* 226, written by Hilary to Augustine, and *On Grace and Predestination* 3 (7). The criticism continued after Augustine's death. Cassian suggested that Pope Celestius' mention of Augustine's earlier works, to the exclusion of those written after 411, meant that he disapproved of Augustine's later ideas on grace and predestination, a suggestion 'prosper vigorously denied. *Liber contra collatorem* 21. 2-3 (*PL* 51, 272) Translated as Against Cassian' by P. de Letter in *Prosper of Aquitaine: Defense of St. Augustine* (Westminster: Newman Press, 1963).

[89] See Augustine's letter to Marcellinus, *ep.* 143, wherein he says he wants to review and correct all his works. The interest in securing copies of the *Retractationes* was notable: Hilary asked Augustine if he could read the book while it was still in draft form (*ep.* 226). Augustine urged readers to reread his works so that they could follow the history of his thought. See *On Grace and Predestination* 3(7)-4(8).

[90] Robert A. Markus, 'Conversion and Disenchantment in Augustine's Spiritual Career (the Saint Augustine Lecture 1984)', in *Sacred and Secular* (Norfolk: Variorum, 1984) section xviii.

had done, as a case of what came before, and after, his episcopal appointment. Before he was made bishop, Augustine's views on predestination and grace were incorrect. He learned after becoming part of the Church's hierarchy.[91]

> It may be conceded that [Augustine's] inexperienced views of the first years after his conversion would favor the heretics more than the truth he came to know during his episcopacy could profit the Catholics. It is therefore with good reason that the holy doctor censors severely those who take this false pretext to rest content with opinion he had abandoned years ago; though they took pains to study the whole of his teaching, they refused to follow him in the progress of the truth.[92]

Possidius, too, uses Augustine's appointment as bishop as a marker to distinguish between his 'correct' authority as bishop and the incorrect beliefs from before.

The Monastery

Chapters 19–27 of the *Vita* bring readers inside the monastery at Hippo, and we see its day-to-day workings, with Augustine acting as host, judge, friend, leader, and landlord. This section has been called an imitation of the Suetonian *interior ac familiaris vita*.[93] Augustine's actions recorded here, including his diligent hearing of legal cases that occasionally detained him without supper into the evening, as well as his refusal to accept legacies in favor of the relatives of the deceased are indeed the hallmarks of both 'good' philosophers and emperors.[94] But convergence with literary demonstrations of paradigmatic behavior as found in other ancient biographies should not obscure the fact that every reason for which Augustine could have been (and was) criticized during his career is addressed and justified in this section: violation of Church council protocol,[95] his management of monastery funds,[96] commerce

---

[91] *Resp. Gen.* PL 51, 191. The translation, *Answers of Extracts of Genoese*, is by P. de Letter in *Prosper of Aquitaine* (Westminster: Newman Press, 1963), 51: 'Before he had understood the true doctrine on grace and before he was appointed to govern the Church, he has unwittingly erred by holding that opinion.' Cf. *On Grace and Predestination* 3 (7) and *On the Gift of Perseverance*, 21.55.

[92] *Contra collat.* 21.3 (PL 51, 272).

[93] Supra n. 23. See, for example, Diesner, 'Possidius und Augustine', 356.

[94] It was proper for philosophers and emperors to refuse inheritances when blood relations of the deceased were living. Edward Champlin, *Final Judgments: Duty and Emotion in Roman Wills 200 B.C.–A.D. 250* (Berkeley: University of California Press, 1991).

[95] *v. Aug.* 21.2: 'consuetudinem ecclesiae sequendum arbitrabatur.' See also *v. Aug.* 8.6 on the illegality of election while Valerius was still alive: 'Therefore [Augustine] endeavored to have it decreed by the councils of bishops that the rules governing all the priests should be made known by the ordaining bishop to those about to be ordained and those already ordained.'

[96] Augustine was criticized for using the gifts given by parishioners and patrons to the Church and its clerics to support dependents (*s.* 356).

with women,[97] reliance on secular courts for legal protection, dietary oddities that might be construed as Manichaean practices, refusal to write letters of introduction to imperial officials on behalf of his clientele, distribution of Church valuables to questionable recipients,[98] (im)proper conduct in matters of inheritances, and finally, legacies and rights of usufruct.[99] Augustine himself told his congregation that what went on at his monastery at Hippo must be transparent for all to see,[100] and the issues that preoccupied him, as articulated by Possidius and listed above, are matters of political, religious, and public import. Again, it is no accident that Ambrose's name is brought to the reader's attention here to guide Augustine's actions, as the bishop of Milan offers an acceptable precedent and defense.[101]

An example frequently cited of Possidius' determination to reveal Augustine's inner character is his description of the food and drink served at the monastery. The residents ate meat on occasion in order to accommodate guests, and wine was a regular item at the table. One interpretation erases any doubts that Augustine was either too parsimonious or too gluttonous: 'That man, as I have said, maintained the middle way, leaning neither to the right nor the left.'[102] It is perfectly appropriate to arrive at such a conclusion, as Possidius wants to underscore the rational moderation that governed the monastery, but the

---

[97] As Possidius points out, Augustine's contact with women (only visiting under very special circumstances with an escort, and choosing not to have female relatives live with him) is more stringent than the rules set forth by the bishops during the Catholic Council of 393. There were, however, many cases that Augustine had to investigate regarding monks and clergy who were thought to have had improper relations with women. See, for example, *epp.* 65, 75, 13*, 18* and 20*.5.

[98] *v. Aug* 24. 15–17, where Augustine broke down and melted precious Church vessels for the ransoming of captives. The anger he elicited required an explanation and reference to the authority of St. Ambrose, who did the same. For discussion of this episcopal topos and the unease that always accompanied it, see William Klingshirn, 'Charity and Power: Caesarius of Arles and the Ransoming of Captives in Sub-Roman Gaul', *JRS*, 75 (1985), 183–203, esp. 185–6.

[99] In *s.* 355 we learn of the priest Januarius, who made a will illegally disposing his property to the Church. The understanding was that as resident of the monastery at Hippo, all his property would be removed from Januarius' jurisdiction and placed aside for when his two children, a girl and a boy, came of age. Their father disinherited them at his death in favor of the Church. The unease of the congregation stemmed from the fact that Augustine refused the inheritance.

Cf. *v. Aug.* 24. 4–6 with *s.* 355. Augustine tells us that Aurelius returned the inheritance of a childless man given to the Church with the understanding that the man would enjoy the right of usufruct while he lived. Afterwards, the man fathered two children and Aurelius returned the inheritance to him, unasked. See also *s.* 392.2.

[100] *s.* 355 1.1: 'Credo autem ante oculos vestros esse conversationem nostram: ut et nos dicere fortassis audeamus, quamvis illi multum impares, quod dixit Apostolus: Imitatores mei estote, sicut et ego Christi. Et ideo nolo ut aliquis de nobis inveniat male vivendi occasionem.' See also *s.* 356.12: 'Ante oculos vestros volo sit vita nostra.'

[101] Courcelle, 'Emprunts et Compléments', 617–21.

[102] *v. Aug.* 22.1: 'at iste, ut dixi, medium tenebat, neque in dexteram neque in sinistram declinans.' Taken from Prov. 4:27.

impetus eliciting this statement comes, I believe, from external criticism. We know that some regarded Augustine as too strict in the administering and disciplining of monks, and Possidius employs several scriptural citations and a quote from the *Confessions* to justify Augustine's eating habits. That is one angle of the defense.[103] Another addresses a readership that may need more convincing that Augustine was not Manichaean, as Manichaeans touched neither meat nor wine.[104] A third speaks to the Pelagians. Augustine once quoted these very words of Solomon about maintaining the middle way to the monks of Hadrumentum, some of whom were disturbed by his writings on grace and free will. Florus, a resident of this monastery, had made a copy of one of Augustine's books he had found in Evodius' library at Uzalis, and when his brothers read it at Hadrumentum, they were surprised at what they concluded to be Augustine's rejection of the possibility that humans exercised free will as direct means to their own salvation. A letter requesting clarification was sent to Evodius, who answered with admonitions that the books in his library written by the learned teachers of the Church must be read with piety, not with an eye to contest. It is pride not to wish to accept Augustine's treatises on divine will, 'and what must be avoided at all costs, not to wish to accept the approved decisions of the Church councils as regards this matter.'[105] A delegation from Hadrumentum subsequently arrived at Hippo to see Augustine, and he offered them a more fulsome exposition. One of the precepts he taught them was 'Make straight the paths for thy feet, and direct all thy ways; decline not to the right hand nor to the left.' The left, as everyone knew, was the side of evil. Why, then, keep away from the right, the side of righteousness? 'But he will make thy course straight; he will bring forward thy ways in peace.' Whoever declines to the right attributes good works to his own will. The center path is for those who do not trust their own strength, but rely on the grace of God to lead them to the correct way (*ep.* 215.5–8). The items on the table at Hippo's monastery are about correct belief, and one can even argue that the meat and wine Possidius serves in the *Vita* take aim against Pelagian self-confidence. But they are not there to expose the workings of a man's internal, and personal, life.

---

[103] *s.* 335.4–6. See Crespin, *Ministère et sainteté*, 177–206.

[104] *On haer.* 46 ('Nam et vinum non bibunt, dicentes [f]el esse principum tenebrarum). See Pellegrino's commentary, 218 ff. who says that this diet may have been published abroad to combat rumors of the monks' Manichaeanism. See supra n. 41.

[105] See *ep.* 216. We know that letters were sent to the monks by Evodius, Januarius, and a priest by the name of Sabinus (*ep.* 216.3), but the last does not survive. For the letters that Evodius and Januarius, see G. Morin, 'Lettres inédites de s. Augustin et du Prêtre Januarien dans l'affaire des moines d'Adrumète', *RBén*, 18 (1901), 241–56 (these texts may also be found at *PL Supplementum* 2, 331–4). For recent suggestions for variant readings in the letter from Evodius, see Yves-Marie Duval, 'Note sur la letter à l'abbé Valentian d'Hadrumète', *RÉAug*, 49 (2003), 123–30.

LEGAL HISTORY

Catholic Bishops and the Secular Courts

Paul admonished Christians not to seek justice in the secular courts (1 Cor. 6:1–6 [see *v. Aug.* 19.1]), and the *Vita* is a good source for learning about the *audientia episcopalis* because Possidius emphasizes the bishop's role as arbiter of Christian, not imperial, law (*v. Aug.* 19).[106] Augustine, he said, conducted correspondence pertaining to private legal matters,[107] but he never wrote letters of introduction or intercession to officials on behalf of his friends. He maintained this was best, since the powers bestowing favors often became oppressive ('plerumque potestas, quae petitur, premit' [*v. Aug.* 20.1]). Possidius offers only one example of an appeal to imperial authority in the form of letters exchanged between the bishop and Macedonius, vicar of Africa (Cf. *epp.* 152–155). Macedonius was impressed by Augustine's books (he had been sent the first three books of *De civitate Dei*) and the reasonable letter that accompanied them, so he congenially complied with Augustine's request to show mercy to condemned criminals: 'You do not insist, like most men in your position, on extorting all that the suppliant asks. But what seemed to you fair to ask of a judge occupied with many cares, this you advise with an accommodating modesty (subserviente verecundia) which is most efficacious in settling difficulties among good men.'[108] In the *Vita*, Augustine is someone who could have pressed authority to his own advantage, but did not.[109]

In reality, Augustine was as accomplished at utilizing secular power to make heretical opponents return to orthodoxy as he was at writing appropriately mannered letters. Macedonius' favorable—and in terms of the etiquette of exercising power, impeccable—reply to Augustine's first approach (the section reproduced in the *Vita*) is answered by the bishop (*ep.* 155) with a philosophical

---

[106] For the so-called *audientia episcopalis*, see M. Rosa Cimma, *L'episcopalis audientia nelle costituzioni imperiali da Costantino a Giustiniano* (Turin: G. Giappichelli, 1989), and John C. Lamoreaux, 'Epsicopal Courts in Late Antiquity', *JECS*, 3 (1995), 143–67. For use of new evidence specifically regarding Augustine's role as judge, see Noel Lenski 'Evidence for the *Audientia Episcopalis* in the New Letters of Augustine', in Ralph W. Mathisen (ed.), *Law, Society, and Authority in Late Antiquity* (Oxford: Oxford University Press, 2001), 83–97.

[107] *v. Aug.* 19.6: 'Rogatus quoque a nonnullis in eorum temporalibus causis epistulas ad diversos dabat.'

[108] *v. Aug.* 20.5: 'Non enim instas quod plerique homines istius loci faciunt, ut quodcumque sollicitus voluerit extorqueas; sed quod tibi a iudice tot curis obstricto petibile visum fuerit, admones, subserviente verecundia, quae maxima difficilium inter bonos efficacia est.'

[109] *v. Aug.* 20.2: 'tam id honeste ac temperate agebat, ut non solum onerosus ac molestus non videretur, verum etiam mirabilis exstitisset.'

meditation on happiness, which, with the social groundwork having been laid for an epistolary friendship in the previous letter, invites Augustine's right of free speech (the *parrhēsia* of the bishop-philosopher) to engage and criticize Macedonius as a figure of authority.[110] Augustine's *verecundia* showcases the mannered 'polish' of a gentleman who knows how to approach peers in this world.[111] His are not the guileless protestations of a 'humble' bishop.[112] Augustine well understood the strategic advantages offered by the implementation of imperial law favorable to the Church's interests. He and his colleagues deliberately sought its promulgation, soliciting the authorities whom they knew would impose harsh sentences with the intention of having the decreed punishments reduced or dismissed through intercession.[113] We do not know the circumstances surrounding the crime committed by those for whom Augustine pleads, but there is every likelihood that they were Donatists who had been involved acts of violence against Catholic clergy. The Catholic bishops, with Augustine's knowledge, may very well have initiated the prosecution that convicted them.[114]

---

[110] Macedonius' role as public authority may help bring to his subjects happiness in the safety and the wholeness of their bodies, but this is not a virtue. 'Yours are no true virtues and theirs no true happiness. That respectful attitude of mine which you praised with kind words in your letter should not prevent me from speaking the truth' (*ep.* 155.11).
Éric Rebillard, 'Augustin et le ritual épistolaire', in É. Rebillard and C. Sotinel (eds.), *L'Évêque dans la cite du IVe au Ve siècle* (Rome: École Française de Rome, 1998), 127–52 at 142–4; and Madeline Moreau, 'Le Magistrat et l'evêque: Pour une lecture de la correspondence Macedonius-Augustine', *Recherches et Travaux*, 54 (1998), 105–17.

[111] Robert Kaster, 'Macrobius and Servius: *Verecundia* and the Grammarian's Function', *HSCP*, 84 (1980), 219–62.

[112] Elm, *Die Macht der Weisheit*, 136.

[113] *ep.* 153.19: 'There is good, then, in your severity which works to secure our tranquility, and there is good in our intercession, which works to restrain your severity.'

[114] See 'Macedonius 2', *PCBE Afrique*, 659–61. The letters were written in 413 or 414 and Augustine cites Macedonius for having issued laws of unity against the Donatists, wherein the secular law was employed to good ends: 'So it is clear that, though you wear the girdle of an earthly judge, you are thinking for the most part of the heavenly country' (*ep.* 155.17). See J. Sundwall, *Weströmische Studien* (Berlin: Mayer & Müller, 1915), 98 n. 283 who believes this letter was 'gengener der Donatisten'.
I do not think the tone of Macedonius' letter betrays impatience with Augustine or indicates that the vicar believes the bishops have overstepped their bounds. Macedonius' letter is an invitation to Augustine to begin a philosophical dialogue, or, expressed in a different way, Macedonius expects Augustine to 'talk him down', with agreeable ideas and pleasant discourse, from his judicial ruling. Peter Brown, *Power and Persuasion in Late Antiquity: Towards a Christian Empire* (Madison: University of Wisconsin Press, 1992), 3–70. For discussion of Macedonius' 'anger' and arguments that Augustine's correspondence with Macedonius has as its focus the role and function of the episcopal courts, see Kauko Raikas, 'The State Juridical Dimension of the Office of a Bishop in Letter 153 of Augustine to Vicarius Africae Macedonius', *Vescovi Pastori in Epoca Teodosiana, Studia Ephemeridia Augustinianum* 58 (Rome: Institutum Patristicum Augustinianum, 1997), 683–94; Peter Iver Kaufman, 'Augustine, Macedonius, and the Courts', *AugStud*, 31 (2003), 67–82.

Documents

Possidius was an effective legal tactician. He, with other bishops like Alypius, Evodius, Theasius, and Fortunatianus, spent years pressing authorities for legislation against religious opponents, and they learned how to compile documents and transcripts that constituted evidence in secular courts. Possidius' preoccupation with law consequently governs the choice of texts he includes in the *Vita*. It is also why the Donatist and Pelagian heresies are falsely represented as coming to a precipitious end upon the issue of imperial edicts.[115] These groups continued to function and sometimes thrive after 411 and 419—these being the dates of condemnation to which Possidius refers—but for Possidius, promulgation of legislation at the highest level constituted the precise moments of victory. One can argue that because the chapters in the first half of the *Vita* are arranged by heresy (Manichaeism, Donatism, Manichaeism again, Arianism, and Pelagianism), it only makes sense that the books Possidius mentions follow the narrative contours adumbrating commerce with Catholicism's opponents. Even so, one expects works very different from those described. For example, it is reasonable to anticipate reference to something like the *De Genesi ad litteram* (On the Literal Meaning of Genesis) when Possidius speaks against Manichaeans, or the *De baptismo* (On Baptism) when discussing the Donatists, and the *De Trinitate* (On the Trinity) regarding the Arians.[116] Certainly one could expect in a discussion about Pelagianism, mention of one of Augustine's many later treatises on grace and predestination. Instead, Possidius prefers transcripts from face-to-face encounters and documents comprising evidentiary dossiers.

Possidius mentions a few Augustinian texts by name: *Confessions*, *Retractationes* (called the *De recensione librorum* in the *Vita*), and the *Speculum*.[117] The

---

[115] Augustine argued with the Pelagians, Possidius says, for about ten years ('per annos ferme decem'). Twenty years is the more accurate number, but 'nearly ten' is perfectly adequate when one considers, within the context of Possidius' narrative, 411 as the beginning when Marcellinus directed Augustine's attention to Pelagius' writings and then accepts the conclusion to be the condemnation of Pelagianism as a heresy by Honorius in 419. See comments by Bastianensen, 'Inaccuracies', 483.

[116] See Lancel, *Saint Augustine*, 216–17 and 377–80 on the writing of the *De Trinitate*. This work was composed over the course of fifteen years and not intended to be, exclusively, an anti-Arian treatise. Books 5, 6, and 7 are directed to that specific audience.

[117] See Bastiaensen's commentary, 429. Augustine himself and the manuscript history exclusively use the term *Retractationes*. Possidius' title probably comes from the prologue of the *Retractationes*, where Augustine uses the verb *recenseo*. It is interesting that here Augustine states that he wants to review his books with a 'judicial severity' ('cum quadam iudiciaria severitate recenseam').

other works described well enough to be easily identified by those somewhat intimate with Augustine's work are: *Contra Fortunatum* (*v. Aug.* 6); *Gesta cum Emerito* (*v. Aug.* 14); *Contra Felicem* (*v. Aug.* 16); the collection of letters between Pascentius and Augustine (*epp.* 238–41), which may have been planned as two separate works; the *Contra supra scriptos Arrianos ad Pascentium liber unus* and the *Duae [litterae] ad eundem contra questiones diversas* (*v. Aug.* 17);[118] and finally, the *Collatio cum Maximino Arianorum* (*v. Aug.* 17). The transcript of the 411 conference (as discussed in *v. Aug.* 13) is not listed in the *Indiculum*, but one finds there the *Breviculus conlationis* and the *Ad Donatistas post conlatione*.[119] It is not clear whether Possidius expected his readers to be familiar with the transcript of the court proceedings involving Manichaeans questioned by Ursus, the *procurator regiae* (*v. Aug.* 16), or if he assumed they would recognize the episode from Augustine's *De haeresibus* 46 (*PL* 8.36).

Excepting the first three works in this list (*Confessions, Speculum*, and *Retractationes*) these are all transcripts from debates, recollections of debates not recorded over the objections of the Catholics (the Pascentius letters), or descriptions of examinations conducted by imperial officials. The Catholics used these kinds of records to help establish argument and proof for subsequent encounters with opponents as well as to appeal to Roman authorities to pursue legal action against heretics.[120] While the *Vita* presents these meetings as dramatic moments between flesh and blood adversaries—Augustine on one side and a heretic on the other—we must remember that these lively scenes resided in Augustine's library as evidentiary documentation.

Text versus speech

Given Augustine's strength in forensics, it comes as no surprise (in the *Vita*) that most people (save the Pelagians) express great reluctance to join Augustine in debate. Fortunatus the Manichaean was well acquainted with Augustine's abilities. He tried, then failed, to decline a meeting, and was subsequently so embarrassed by the Catholic presbyter that he left Carthage, never to return

---

[118] See *Indiculum* VIII. 6–7 and the notice by G. Madec, 'Possidius de Calama et les listes des oeuvres d'Augustin', 441.

[119] Listed in the *Indiculum* as the *Breviationes gestorum de conlatione facta contra supra scriptos donatistas* (VI. 15) and the *Post conlationem contra supra scriptos donatistas liber unus* (VI. 16).

[120] Caroline Humfress, 'Roman Law, Forensic Argument and the Formation of Christian Orthodoxy (III–VI Centuries)', in S. Elm, É. Rebillard, and A. Romano (eds.), *Orthodoxie, Christianisme, Histoire* (Rome: École Française de Rome, 2000), 125–47. For more in-depth discussion, see the same author's *Forensic Practice in the Development of Roman and Ecclesiastical Law in Late Antiquity, With Special Reference to the Prosecution of Heresy* (Ph.D. dissertation, Cambridge University), 236–45.

(*v. Aug.* 6). The Arian Pascentius refused to have stenographers present at his meeting with Augustine on the grounds that the written record would make him vulnerable to prosecution under heresy laws.[121] The result was what Augustine had feared: distortion of the proceedings because of oral recapitulation (*v. Aug.* 17.1–6).[122] The exchange of letters that followed (three letters from Augustine and one from Pascentius) reveal a dismissive Pascentius whose curtness, Possidius implies, poorly obscures his complete inability to defend himself. Maximinus, an important Arian bishop who also debated Augustine, had extensive experience with Church councils and documentation, but the reader of the *Vita* is impressed with Maximinus' inability to win his argument by fair means.[123] Mention of this encounter with Augustine comes directly after the meeting with Pascentius, but Maximinus employs a kind of reverse tactics, speaking so much that he exhausts all the time allotted. Maximinus' excessive, wandering loquaciousness, as Possidius and Augustine later called it, prevented Augustine from arguing his points fully. Maximinus returned to Carthage with the boast that he had beaten the old bishop at his own game. For Possidius, verbosity revealed weakness as readily as silence.[124]

---

[121] Augustine scoffed at Pascentius' reticence and his fear that a recorded debate would lead to prosecution, especially since the audience, filled with important government leaders, were those whom Pascentius had personally invited. When Pascentius first accused Augustine of wanting *notarii* to record for the express purpose of legally cornering him, Augustine was so taken aback that he let slip out insulting words that he immediately regretted (*ep.* 238.7). Pascentius did have a point. The Catholic bishops were not shy about bringing heretics to the attention of authorities when it suited their purposes.

[122] Compare Possidius' description of the encounter with Augustine's (*v. Aug.* 17.2): 'cuiquam posset liberum forte dicere, nullo scripturae documento, se dixisse quod forte non dixerit, vel non dixisse quod dixerit,' and Augustine's *ep.* 238.2: 'ne quisquam...diceret ab aliquo nostrum aut non esse dictum, quod dictum erat, aut dictum esse, quod dictum non erat.'

[123] For background, see 'Maximinus 10', *PCBE Afrique*, 731. Maximinus ministered to the Gothic soldiers under the command of Count Sigisvult, who had been sent to Africa to deal with Boniface. He enjoyed a colorful and lengthy career (Ralph W. Mathisen, 'Sigisvult the Patrician, Maximinus the Arian, and Political Stratagems in the Western Roman Empire c.425–40', *Early Medieval Europe*, 8 [1999], 173–96). For Maximinus' familiarity with councils and his acumen in debate, see Neil McLynn, 'From Palladius to Maximinus: Passing the Arian Torch', *JECS*, 4 (1996), 477–93. Maximinus published a commentary on extracts from the Council of Aquileia (which occurred in 381), where Ambrose had defeated, in front of a court that clearly leaned in his favor, the prominent Arian clergy Palladius and Secundianus. The commentary may be found in R. Gryson (ed.), *Scolies Ariennes sur le councile d'Aquilée*, Sources Chrétiennes 267 (Paris: Éditions du Cerf, 1980).

[124] But, as McLynn points out in 'From Palladius to Maximinus', it seems to have been the opinion that Maximinus did win this debate as Augustine felt compelled to follow up their meeting with two lengthy books of refutation.

As for loquaciousness, Augustine said that if many words were required to speak the truth, so be it. Empty words deployed for their own sake with little attention to God's truth needed to be eschewed. He says in the prologue of the *Retractationes*: 'Ex multiloquio non effigies peccatum.' Possidius admonished the Donatists with the same scriptural tag at the 411 conference (*Coll. Carth.*, II, 29).

As for the Donatists, Possidius emphasizes their inability to formulate convincing arguments (he speaks repeatedly of their *diffidentia*, a word he borrows from Augustine and Catholic Church councils).[125] They angrily refused to send anything in writing to Augustine: 'Augustine sought to make known to all their lack of confidence in their own cause, and when they met in public conferences they did not dare to debate with him.'[126] Instead, they spoke furiously among themselves and preached to their congregations that Augustine's murder would be a welcome event. Possidius juxtaposes the Catholic world of transcripts that connote certainty and truth with the Donatist world of orality that prevaricates and lies. Prosper of Aquitaine once voiced a similar sentiment: people may angrily whisper about, and against, Augustine all they wish, but the calumnies dissipate in the presence of those massive, authoritative texts.[127] Possidius shows Augustine patiently writing pleas to unity and peace.[128] These pictures of measured charity alternate with jarring scenes of irrational violence perpetrated by the Donatists: the throwing of acid in the faces of Catholic clerics and attempts on the lives of Catholic bishops. Possidius' comparison of the competing strategies between Catholics and heretics, which accurately reflects the way Augustine himself portrayed the struggles in his own writings, remains the dominant image among historians and theologians.

It is important to remember, however, that documentation and imperial law were of equal importance to the Donatists. Stenographers recorded the proceedings of their councils, excerpts from which Augustine occasionally read to his own congregation.[129] The Donatists wrote and circulated books.

---

[125] *Concilia Africae, Registri Ecclesiae Carthaginensis Excerpta* 92 and *Cresc.* 3.45 (49). Possidius uses the word three times in the *Vita* (9.4 twice and 14.7) and should be understood as lack of confidence or an awareness of one's own ineptitude. The Donatists accuse the Catholics of displaying the same attribute at the conference of 411.

[126] *v. Aug.* 9.4: 'Et ut eorum causae diffidentia cunctis innotesceret elaboravit, et publicis gestis conventi, non sunt ausi conferre.'

[127] See *Epistula ad Rufinum* 4 (*PL* 51, 79–80.) 'But does not everybody know why they whisper their chagrin in private and on purpose keep silent in public? Desirous of taking pride in their own justice, rather than glorying in God's grace, they are displeased when when we oppose the assertions they make in many a conference against a man of the highest authority. They know full well that whenever they raise a question on the matter, whether in some meeting of prelates or in some gathering of other people, we could put before them hundred of volumes of Augustine.' Translation by P. de Letter (Westminster: Newman Press, 1963), 24.

[128] *v. Aug.* 9.2: 'aut eadem responsa ad sanctum Augustinum deferebantur, eaque comperta patienter ac leniter et, ut scriptum est, cum timore et tremore salutem hominum operabatur, ostendens quam nihil referre illi voluerint ac valuerint, quamque verum manifestumque sit, quod ecclesiae Dei fides tenet ac dicit; et haec diebus ac noctibus ab eodem iugiter agebantur.' The juxtaposition between a calm Augustine and violent and calumnious Donatists may not be entirely fictional. See, for example, *c. litt. Petil.* 1.12 (19) where, in contradiction to what Possidius says, no one wanted to give to Augustine a complete copy of Petilian's scathing letter.

[129] *en. Ps.* 36.2 for example, where Augustine reads out minutes from 24 June 393 meeting of the Maximianist bishops in Cebarsussa.

They submitted cases to local magistrates in attempts to protect their financial and legal interests, and sent embassies to the imperial consistory. Donatist bishops knew very well the importance of evidentiary dossiers. Their strategy at the 411 conference not only looked to legal documents to make their case, but also looked forward to the use of the recording of the present proceedings as evidence in future appeals.

As the Donatists predicted, the Catholics were declared the orthodox party at the 411 conference, and the *coup de grâce* came a few months later when the emperor Honorius rejected the Donatist bid to have the emperor overturn Marcellinus' verdict. The *Vita*'s postscript to the meeting in 411 consists of a final confrontation in Caesarea in 418 between Catholic bishops and Emeritus, who was one of the most eminent Donatist bishops and, along with Petilian, the most eloquent (Possidius would say loquacious) disputant at the conference of 411.[130] Since the meeting's conclusion, Possidius writes, Emeritus had protested that Marcellinus, the imperial magistrate sent by Honorius to oversee the 411 conference, had been unduly prejudiced in his verdict: the trial had been unfair and the decision should consequently be ruled invalid.[131] In 418, Augustine invited Emeritus to speak his mind in a public forum before stenographers, assuring him that he need not fear reprisal from the imperial authorities.[132] Possidius asserts that Augustine admonished Emeritus to ground his arguments on the transcripts of the conference proper. Thus constrained by legal records that had been certified and signed by both parties, he was left with nothing to say except: 'Those records of what was done by the bishops at Carthage contain the proof of whether we were victors or vanquished.' The written word curbs and controls the loose nature of that which is spoken. Cornered and embarrassed (Possidius' word, again, is *diffidentia*), Emeritus crumbled. Emeritus had indeed been rebuked by Possidius in 411 for speaking too much.[133] In 418, he was metaphorically gagged by the very transcript he wanted to challenge. That, anyway, is the impression upon reading of the episode in the *Vita*.[134]

---

[130] Emeritus wrote the denunciation of the Maximianists composed for the Council of Bagai. From what remains of it, the language is expressive and full of scriptural images.

[131] *v. Aug.* 14. 4 and *retr.* 2.46: The lost work, *Ad Emeritum episcopum Donatistarum post collationem liber unus*, is ascribed to the year 416 and addressed Emeritus' complaints as to the bias affecting the outcome of the conference of 411.

[132] Notice that the *Gesta cum Emerito* begins like a legal proceeding, with date and time indicated: 'Gloriosissimis imperatoribus, Honorio duodecimum et Theodosio octavo consulibus, duodecimo kalendas octobres Caesareae in ecclesia maiore.'

[133] *Coll. Carth.*, II, 31: 'in multiloquio numquam fuit sapientia.'

[134] Corruption in the manuscripts of the *v. Aug.* makes it unclear whether Possidius repeated Emeritus' order to the *notarii* as we have it in the *Gesta cum Emerito*: 'Write that "Fac"' after Augustine asked him: 'Requiro quare veneris. Hoc non quaererem, si non venisses.' Augustine

The *Gesta cum Emerito* tells a different story. Possidius was with Augustine at Caesarea when they met Emeritus in the town square, and he heard these very words the Donatist bishop said upon entering the basilica where he and the Catholics were to speak: 'I cannot disagree with what you want, but I can wish what I want.'[135] Emeritus' silence was not tacit surrender, but a determination to stay loyal to his party and his beliefs. The one comment he makes—that they should all consult the records to see who was victor in June of 411—is incomplete as reported in the *Vita*. Possidius left out the final remark that for Emeritus the records would reveal 'if I was conquered by truth or oppressed by authority' ('si veritate victus sum, aut potestate oppressus sum'). Emeritus *wanted* the transcripts of the proceedings read out to the assembled crowd. This would have taken hours, if not more than a full day. Expectation of Donatist acquiescence in 411, especially in light of Emperor Honorius' uncompromising letter that governed the conference, proved that the meeting's conclusion had, in fact, been predetermined.[136]

The Pelagians

That the *Vita* is fixated on documentation emerges most forcefully in the chapter on the Pelagians. Augustine wrote numerous treatises against them, some of which were sources of great contention among Christians. Possidius' discussion of Pelagianism is brief, and with the possible exception of the *De gestis Pelagii*, he does not discuss any specific Augustinian treatise as found in the *Indiculum*. Instead, the history of the confrontation is mainly represented as a catalogue of documents (*v. Aug.* 18.1–5).[137]

---

goes on: 'Emeritus episcopus partis Donati dixit notario qui excipiebat: Fac.' Possidius tells the story in much the same way (*v. Aug.* 14.7) with Pellegrino reconstructing the Latin as: 'et alio loco, dum a notario ut responderet admoneretur, ait "Fac"; et cum reticeret, facta eius cunctis manifestata diffidentia.' Bastiaensen renders the sentence in the following way, leaving the 'Fac' out: 'Et alio loco, dum a notario ut responderet admoneretur, ait; et cum reticeret, facta eius cunctis manifestata diffidentia.'

[135] *Sermo ad Caesariensis ecclesiae plebem* 1 (CSEL 53): 'Non possum nolle quod vultis, sed possum velle quod volo.' See discussion in James J. O'Donnell, *Augustine: A New Biography* (New York: Ecco, 2005), 256–8.

[136] Alypius read out to the assembled congregation a copy of the Catholic bishops' letter to Marcellinus before the trial, the one that informed him that if the Donatists won, the Catholics would happily accept correction and assimilate into the new faith (*Emer.* 5). They sent it knowing that their chances of winning were overwhelming. For background, see Émilien Lamirande, 'L'Offre conciliatrice des Catholiques aux Donatistes relativement à l'épiscopat (Gesta collationis carthaginiensis I.16)', *L'Église et Théologie*, 2 (1971), 285–308.

[137] See Mark Vessey, 'Ideas of Christian Writing in Late Roman Gaul' (dissertation, Oxford University, 1988), 206–7, and J. Patout Burns, 'Augustine's Role in the Imperial Action Against Pelagius', *JTS*, n.s., 29 (1978), 67–83.

> Against the Pelagians also, new heretics of our time and skillful debaters, who wrote with an art more subtle and noxious, and spoke whenever they could, in public and in homes—against these he labored about ten years, writing and publishing many books and very frequently arguing in the church with people of that error. When they perversely tried through their flattery to persuade the Apostolic see of their false doctrine, it was most positively resolved by several African councils of holy bishops first to convince the venerable Innocent, the holy pope of the city, and his successor, the holy Zosimus, that this sect ought to be abominated and condemned by the Catholic faith.[138] And the bishops of that great see at various times (*suis diversis temporibus*) censured them and cut them off from the membership of the Church, and in letters sent to the African churches of the West and to the churches of the East decreed that they should be anathematized and shunned by all Catholics. When the most pious Emperor Honorius heard all of this judgment which had been passed upon them by the Catholic Church of God, influenced by it, he in turn decreed that they should be condemned by his laws and should be regarded as heretics.[139]

There is no mention here of Pelagius or Julian, the men who repeatedly challenged Augustine, but the intensity and effectiveness of their arguments are acknowledged through reference to their hot, clever speech. Pelagian eagerness for confrontation is a singular attribute in the *Vita*. As we have seen, others try to avoid commerce with the bishop of Hippo.

Possidius' involvement in this particular debate spanned two decades, and may have even included meeting Pelagius on his visit to Rome in 408–9. We know that one of Augustine's episcopal colleagues argued with Pelagius over the oft-repeated line from book ten of the *Confessions*, 'Da quod iubes et iube quod vis.' Pelagius, Augustine says, was so upset by the ensuing conversation that he appeared on the verge of striking the bishop.[140] The redating of

---

[138] Cf. *retr.* 2.76: 'Contra Pelagium et Caelestium de gratia Christi et de peccato originali ad Albinam, Pinianum et Melaniam libri duo.'

[139] 'Adversus Pelagianistas quoque, novos nostrorum temporum haereticos et disputatores callidos, arte magis subtili et noxia scribentes et, ubicumque poterant, publice et per domos loquentes, per annos ferme decem elaboravit, librorum multa condens et edens et in ecclesia populis ex eodem errore frequentissime disputans. Et quoniam iidem perversi sedi apostolicae per suam ambitionem eamdem perfidiam persuadere conabantur, instantissime etiam conciliis Africanis sanctorum episcoporum gestum est, ut sancto papae urbis, et prius venerabili Innocentio et postea sancto Zosimo eius successori, persuaderetur quam illa secta a fide catholica et abominanda et damnanda fuisset. At illi tantae sedis antistites suis diversis temporibus eosdem notantes atque a membris ecclesiae praecidentes, datis litteris et ad Africanas et <ad> occidentis et orientis partis ecclesias, eos anathemandos et devitandos ab omnibus catholicis censerunt. Et tale de illis ecclesia Dei catholicae prolatum iudicium etiam piissimus imperator Honorius audens ac sequens, suis eos legibus damnatos inter haereticos haberi debere constituit.'

[140] *De dono perseverantiae* 20.53.

Pelagius' *De natura* between the years 405 and 410 puts this encounter within that same time frame.[141] It is true that many African bishops traveled to Italy in these years, but attention in pursuit of an identification has focused on Evodius and Possidius, with the former, who was in Italy in 404–5, considered the more likely candidate because of his support of the African denunciations of Pelagius in the 410s.[142] Possidius, however, whose trip to Italy in late 408 lasted well into the following year, was no less involved. Possidius also knew his *Confessions*. Citation and explanation would have come easily.[143] The section of *De dono perseverantiae* that contains this story (20.52–3) defends Augustine's textual record against claims that his doctrine of predestination was without precedent. Several works written before the arrival of the Pelagians, he states, proleptically refute their beliefs, including the *Confessions* (hence the 'da quod iubes' quotation). But Augustine again puts his finger on the moment when he began to have 'fuller knowledge of the truth'. The first book of his episcopacy, the treatise to Simplician (*Ad Simplicianum*), asserted correctly that the beginning of faith was a gift from God. Possidius used the same divide for somewhat different purposes: the chronological coincidence in Augustine's intellectual development became an indicator of episcopal effectiveness.

Pelagius and his colleague Caelestius came to Africa after the sack of Rome in 410, and Caelestius, while seeking ordination, was charged with heresy by Paulinus of Milan, the author of *Life of Ambrose*.[144] Pelagius meanwhile proceeded east and successfully defended himself in Jerusalem and Diospolis against charges of heresy leveled against him by Spanish and Gallic clerics.[145] The acquittals were forwarded to the pope. The African Councils of Carthage and Milevis, which both met in the summer of 416 after news of Pelagius' success reached Africa,[146] wrote to Pope Innocent warning him about the dangers of this new heresy. Possidius signed both the declaration from the Council of

---

[141] Yves-Marie Duval, 'La Date du "De natura" de Pélage', *RÉAug*, 36 (1990), 257–83.

[142] O'Donnell, *Augustine Confessions* iii, 201. Duval prefers Evodius: 'La date du "De natura"', 283 n. 178. Lancel, *Saint Augustine*, 326, agrees.

[143] Paulinus of Nola was on friendly terms with both Pelagius (*ep.* 186.1 and *De gratia Christi* 1.35 [38]) and Julian of Eclanum (*Carmen* 25), smoothing the way for an introduction as Possidius visited Paulinus in 408. For a concise description of the intersecting social circles, see Elizabeth A. Clark, *The Origenist Controversy: The Cultural Construction of an Early Christian Debate* (Princeton: Princeton University Press, 1992), esp. 33–5.

[144] Lamirande, *Paulin de Milan*, 16–19.

[145] Paul Orosius brought the charges in Jerusalem and the bishops Heros and Lazarus faced Pelagius at Diospolis.

[146] *ep.* 175 in the Maurist catalogue (Augustine does not sign the letter, but it is attributed to him): 'after we had gathered in solemn conclave in the church at Carthage, according to our custom, and were holding a synod on various subjects, our fellow priest Orosius brought us a letter from our holy brothers and fellow priests, Heros and Lazarus.'

Milevis (*ep.* 176), and then a second letter (*ep.* 177, sent by the select group of Augustine, Aurelius, Alypius, Evodius, and Possidius), which more carefully articulated the theological faults in Pelagius' teaching. Innocent was convinced by the arguments made by the Africans, and he responded to the bishops in a series of letters (*epp.* 181–83).[147] Pope Innocent died in early 417, and Caelestius appealed to his successor, Pope Zosimus. This appeal, as well as Pelagius' declaration of faith sent by letter to Zosimus and other Italian bishops, resulted in a setback for the Catholics. Paulinus of Milan was called to Rome as he himself was now charged with heresy. Heros and Lazarus, the men who had challenged Pelagius at Diospolis, were excommunicated, and Zosimus admonished the African bishops for their ill-informed denunciation. Augustine and his colleagues responded by compiling a dossier that, point by point, demonstrated Pelagius' prevarications, even dishonesty, at Diospolis.[148] Zosimus' subsequent retraction of his earlier support for Pelagius and Caelestius coincided with a decree from Honorius declaring these men heretics.[149] A little before 9 June 419, Honorius issued a letter condemning Pelagianism.[150]

Possidius' version of events, focused on decisions made rather than theological ideas defended, offers a degree of historical clarity that simplifies the ardent debate between Augustine and his Pelagian opponents. Church councils, popes, and an emperor agreed that Pelagianism was incorrect. This was a powerful assertion, especially in light of the sophistication of the tactics engaged, and the works written by Pelagius and Julian. Possidius followed the strategy Augustine had recently employed. Arguments need not be exclusively scriptural and answers to questions need not always lie within the purview of doctrinal proof. The bishops were accomplished advocates, so much so that in this particular episode, they may have appealed to the emperor for the express purpose of forcing Zosimus' hand to retract his support for Pelagius.[151]

---

[147] The pope's declarations called for Pelagius and Caelestius to be refused communication until they disavowed their claims, and he also refused to acknowledge the records from the meeting at Diospolis. Lancel, *Saint Augustine*, 338, and Brown, *Augustine of Hippo*, 360, stress the mildness with which Innocent tried to temper these men.

[148] The *Contra gesta Pelagii* as listed in the *Indiculum*, but more commonly known as the *De gestis Pelagii*. See Robert F. Evans, 'Pelagius' Veracity at the Synod of Diospolis', in John R. Sommerfeldt (ed.), *Studies in Medieval Culture* (Kalamazoo: Medieval Institute, Western Michigan University, 1964), 21–30.

[149] Possidius' reference to the popes condemning the heresy at various times ('suis diversis temporibus') is not chronological imprecision, but indicates that they circulated separate pronouncements during their respective rules.

[150] The text of the law is lost, but *ep.* 201 in the Augustinian corpus is addressed to Aurelius from Honorius and Theodosius II announcing that such a law has been issued. Possidius' version of events indicates that the Catholics did not solicit the emperor's aid, but it is clear from the surviving evidence that they did.

[151] Patout Burns, 'Augustine's Role in the Imperial Action Against Pelagius'.

More to the point, the history of Pelagianism as narrated by Possidius utilizes material constituting the contents of a dossier assembled by Augustine to be read to, and then sent back home with, the monks from Hadrumentum who stayed over at Hippo during Easter of 426 (*ep.* 216).[152] Along with *De gratia et libero arbitrio* (not mentioned in Possidius' narrative), Augustine collated the following documents for the monks' edification: the transcript of the councils of Carthage and Milevis (summer of 416), the letter sent subsequent to the Council of Milevis signed by the five bishops (Augustine, Aurelius, Alypius, Evodius, and Possidius [*ep.* 177]), Pope Innocent's answers (*epp.* 181–183), Pope Zosimus' conciliatory letter to the African bishops and his empire-wide denunciation of Pelagius and, finally, the report of the council of African bishops held at Carthage on 1 May 418 (*ep.* 215).[153] Possidius depicts the Pelagian conflict in large part as the very documents that Augustine considered appropriate reading for the monks. Augustine may have also sent this dossier to others who made inquiries at Hippo. Prosper of Aquitaine worked with similar materials (probably all in hand by 426), including the acts of the Council at Diospolis, the letters the African bishops sent to, and received from, Pope Innocent, the bishops' correspondence with Pope Zosimus, as well as a copy of Honorius' decree.[154] For Augustine and Possidius, documents proved the Catholics right. They made for a new and effective kind of theology.

THE *VITA AUGUSTINI* AS CATALOGUE RAISONNÉ

Body and Corpus

In a sermon preached at Carthage celebrating the martyrdom of Cyprian (*s. Guelferbytanus* 26 [*PL Supplementum* 2]), Augustine likened the saint to myrrh in that its rich scent reaches far beyond the area of the brazier on which it is burned. Likewise, Cyprian's 'dispersal' through the Christian world (the word for myrrh is *cyprus*) is effected by circumstances that transcend the

---

[152] Supra n. 105.
[153] For discussion, see Mark Vessey, 'Opus Imperfectum: Augustine and His Readers, A.D. 426–35', *V Chr*, 52 (1998), 269–70; Giovanni Maschio 'L'argomentazione patristica di s. Agostino nella prima fase della controversia pelagiana', *Augustinianum*, 26 (1986), 459–79; and Otto Wermelinger, *Rom und Pelagius: die theologische Position der römischen Bischöfe im pelagianischen Streit in den Jahren 411–432* (Stuttgart: A. Hierscmann, 1975), 147–8, for a list of the documents used by Augustine.
[154] Vessey, 'Opus Imperfectum', 276 and for more detail, see his *Ideas of Christian Writing*, 206–8.

burning of his body in martyrdom: 'Whatever region in the world is able to be found where his eloquence is not read, his doctrine not praised, his charity not loved, his life not preached, his death not venerated, the festival of his martyrdom not celebrated?' What follows is a list of Cyprian's books, with Augustine's enumeration of the titles taking up at least one-fifth the sermon's length. Augustine then tells his congregation: 'Many people everywhere have in their possession the large body of his written works. But we give greater thanks to the Lord, because we have merited to possess the sainted body of his limbs.'[155] Cyprian's body renders the prayers of Carthage effective, and his martyred limbs offer grace to the people privileged to be living closest to them.[156]

With Augustine dead, the Vandals having taken Hippo, and Possidius perhaps no longer in Africa at the time he wrote the *Vita*, the body of Augustine's texts, not the body made of flesh, becomes the efficacious inheritance the saint bequeaths to his heirs. Notice how brief a description Possidius offers of Augustine's internment. The reader has little feel for what his tomb is like, and there are no miraculous events transpiring subsequent to burial that tell us Augustine's body nourishes the land that received it. Instead, all the ways through which a dead saint succors the living—remembrance, edification, and intercession—reside in the books Possidius exhorts people to read. Thus, we find the epitaph at the end of the *Vita*, a clichéd one that most ancients and modern classicists have seen in one form or another, but a complete surprise coming from the pen of a Catholic bishop living in fifth century North Africa: 'Vivere post obitum vatem vis nosse viator? Quod legis, ecce loquor, vox tua nempe mea est.'[157]

To read Augustine plucked him out from the number of the dead, but it is more important to acknowledge that consultation of Augustine's texts taught orthodoxy in a way appreciably similar to experiencing the bishop in person when he convinced and converted North Africa. The assertion that the text can approach the efficacy of its author is underscored by the physical act of reading: out of one's mouth comes the bishop's own voice. Conjuring the bishop of Hippo, however, required great care and deliberation. So many things were dictated and written by him that it was difficult, even for the *studiosi*, to know

---

[155] 'Multi usquequaque habent magnum corpus librorum eius. Sed nos uberiores gratias domino agamus, quod habere meruimus sanctum corpus membrorum eius.'

[156] See Peter Brown, *The Cult of the Saints: Its Rise and Function in Latin Christianity* (Chicago: University of Chicago Press, 1981), esp. 23–49.

[157] *v. Aug.* 31.8. 'Passerby, do you wish to know how poets still live after death? These words you read, behold I speak! Your voice is very much mine.' See Bastiaensen's commentary (447) for the popularity of this phrase and those similar to it.

or read all of his works.[158] In order to negotiate Augustine's corpus profitably, Possidius provides the necessary guides: the *Vita* first, and then the index of Augustine's works, his *Indiculum*. Possidius is only one writer of many literary or philosophical biographies that detailed the lives and deeds of men as preface to a description of their works or, in other cases, collected editions of their books. The placement of a biography before some sort of presentation (whether a list, a description of the actual books, or an edition) constituted a regular method of introducing a philosopher's or poet's work to students.[159] Tradition dictated that one had to know the man, if only second hand, in order to 'know' the books.[160] There is a good chance Possidius would have been familiar with Rufinus' translation of Eusebius' *Ecclesiastical History*, with its life of Origen and descriptive bibliography, as a copy resided at Augustine's library in Hippo.[161] Possidius could also have been aware of Jerome's *De viris illustribus*, wherein brief descriptions of authors' lives preceded lists of the books they

[158] *v. Aug.* 18.9: 'Tanta autem ab eodem dictata et edita sunt, tantaque in ecclesia disputata, excepta atque emendata, vel adversus diversos haereticos, vel ex canonicis libris exposita ad aedificationem sanctorum ecclesiae filiorum, ut ea omnia vix quisquam studiosorum perlegere et nosse sufficiat.'

For this comment—one that many authors used in reference to Augustine, but Jerome said of Eusebius, and Augustine said of Varro—see Mark Vessey, 'The Demise of the Christian Writer and the Remaking of "Late Antiquity" from H.-I. Marrou's Saint Augustine (1938) to Peter Brown's Holy Man (1983)', *JECS*, 6 (1998), 377–411. For repetition of the saying that Augustine wrote more than anyone could possibly read, see Gennadius, *De viris illustribus* 35; Eugippius *Epistula ad Probem* 2.19 and Isadore of Seville (*PL* 83, 1109). This is not proof that these authors knew Possidius' *Vita* and/or the *Indiculum*, but Isadore's salute to Augustine comes very close to Possidius' inclusion of that classical epitaph: 'He lies who claims that he has read all of you. And what reader is able to possess all your works? Augustine, you shimmer in your thousands of volumes. The books are your testament, because I myself speak of you. Although knowledge from the books of many authors is pleasing, if Augustine is with you, he alone is sufficient.'

[159] Erich Bethe, *Buch und Bild im Alterum* (Amsterdam: A. M. Hakkert, 1964), 84–98 and 138–43; Jaap Mansfeld, *Prolegomena: Questions to Be Settled before the Study of an Author, or a Text* (Leiden: Brill, 1994), 108–47.

[160] Loveday Alexander, 'The Living Voice: Scepticism towards the Written word in Early Christian and in Graeco-Roman Texts', in D. J. A. Clines, S. E. Fowl, and S. E. Porter (eds.), *The Bible in Three Dimensions: Essays in Celebration of Forty Years of Biblical Studies in the University of Sheffield* (Worcester: Billing & Sons Ltd, 1990), 221–47.

[161] See Paulinus of Nola's *ep.* 3, addressed to Alypius. Paulinus of Nola had sent a copy of Eusebius to Africa around 395; he had secured this copy from Domnio and sent it to Aurelius at Carthage with instructions that the bishop of Carthage should have it copied and sent on to Alypius, who Paulinus believes was staying at Hippo. The original he asked to be sent back to its owner.

Eusebius also wrote a life of Pamphilius in three books. We do not know if episcopal centers in Africa had access to it, but it is interesting to note that Eusebius included in it a list of works by Origen and other authors Pamphilius had drawn up for the contents of his library in Caesarea. For discussion, see Anthony Grafton and Megan Williams, *Christianity and the Transformation of the Book* (Cambridge, MA: Belknap Press of Harvard University Press, 2006), 180–3.

The Vita Augustini

wrote. The work ends with Jerome cataloguing his own treatises.[162] Arranging an author's works, including one's own, was certainly not unknown,[163] and Augustine's experience in the schools and commerce with the philosophically oriented company he once kept at Milan—without accounting for specific authors he may or may not have read—could mean that creating book catalogues as a cultural, literary practice was familiar to the bishop of Hippo and his colleagues.[164] We have already seen Augustine list all of Cyprian's books in a sermon he gave to the people of Carthage.[165] There are many ways Possidius could have learned that biographies and catalogues go together.

The Indiculum

More specifically, Augustine had a list of his own books drawn up in the 420s, which he consulted while writing the *Retractationes*. He, likewise, called his index of books an *indiculum*.[166] To what extent does Possidius' catalogue look

---

[162] Jerome's method of presenting these men may have suggested to Augustine the writing of the *Retractationes*; see Mark Vessey, 'The Demise of the Christian Writer', 382–3. For Jerome, P. Nautin, 'La Date du *viris inlustribus* de Jérôme, de la mort de Cyrille de Jérusalem, et de celle de Grégoire de Nazianze', *Review d'Histoire Ecclésiastique*, 56 (1961), 33–5 and P. Nautin, 'La Liste des oeuvres de Jérôme dans le *De viris inlustribus*', *Orpheus*, n.s., 5 (1984), 319–34.

[163] Some well-known examples: Donatus and Servius began their Vergilian commentaries with lives of the poets. Galen wrote a bibliographical autobiography, explaining where he was living and under what conditions he wrote his books. He returned to the subject in his subsequent *The Order of My Own Books*, which gives instructions to his readers as to which of his works people should consult in order to address specific questions. The argument has been made that Porphyry's *Life of Plotinus* was written to mirror the lives of philosophers Plato and Aristotle and thus mimics the probably common procedure of presenting the works of authors with a biography followed by a catalogue or complete edition. In fact, we know from Diogenes Laertius that Thrasyllus wrote about the lives of Democritus and Plato, and he inserted a catalogue of books following their biographies. Ernst Robert Curtius, *European Literature and the Latin Middle Ages* (Princeton: Princeton University Press, 1953; reprint 1990), 221; Galen's *My Own Books* and the *Order of My Books* have been translated into English by P. N. Singer in *Selected Works* (Oxford: Oxford University Press, 1997), 3–29. Mansfeld, *Prolegomena*, 108–16. For Porphyry, cf. Mansfeld's arguments to H. D. Saffrey, 'Pourquoi Porphyre a-t-il édité Plotin?' in *Porphyre: La Vie de Plotin II* (Paris: E. de Boccard, 1992), 31–64.

[164] Pierre Courcelle, *Late Latin Writers and Their Greek Sources*, translation by H. E. Wedeck (Cambridge: Harvard University Press, 1969), 148–223, discusses the Greek works and their translations that may have been accessible to Augustine. For Latin and Greek non-Christian literature Augustine did, or did not, read, see O'Donnell, 'Augustine's Classical Readings', in *RecAug*, 15 (1980), 144–75.

[165] G. Morin, 'Une Liste des traités de saint Cyprien dans un sermon inédit de saint Augustin', *Bulletin d'ancienne littérature et d'archéologie chrétienne*, 4 (1914), 16–22.

[166] And like Augustine, who calls the works listed in his *Indiculum* 'opuscula': see *retr. Prolo.* and 2.67 ('in opusculorum meorum indiculo'). Possidius gives the same diminutive to his *Vita*. It was not uncommon to refer to literary works in this way. Mark Vessey, 'From *Cursus* to *Ductus*', 83. See also E. Arns, *La Technique du livre d'après saint Jérôme* (Paris: E. de Boccard, 1953), 193–5 and Madec, 'Possidius de Calama', 430.

like the one Augustine compiled?[167] Possidius' *Indiculum* could be an exact copy of Augustine's, but if so, it is difficult to explain some of its oddities. For example, some titles are placed under categories where they do not belong.[168] Other entries bear names that vary greatly from what Augustine called them. There are a few errors so egregious that it is difficult to posit Augustine as their author, the most famous being the identification of *De ideis* (as found in *De diversis quaestionibus octaginta tribus* 46) as a *quaestio de iudaeis* which was placed in the section of the index for works on the Jews. These discrepancies prompt some to conclude that the *Indiculum*, as adopted by Possidius, was probably compiled by a resident of the monastery who worked in the library.[169] This would explain the 'mistakes' that are difficult to assign to Augustine.

It has also been argued, in contradiction to the above, that Augustine's *indiculum* shared no resemblance to the one we now possess thanks to Possidius. At some point, perhaps during the seige of Hippo when Possidius had months of time on his hands, he consulted the list of Augustine's books and then arranged them in the categories we now see in the *Indiculum*. This suggestion may account for the perceived errors in the catalogue, although Possidius should have known enough to avoid such mistakes, but it does explain why the extant *Indiculum* departs so radically from the *Retractationes*. Works are listed by subject rather than chronologically, and the division into sections seems to follow instead the contours of the *Vita* proper, wherein Augustine's life moves according to the heresies confronted, and not always presented in strict chronological order.[170] That suggestion, however, suffers under the scrutiny of François Dolbeau, who noticed that there are two strata within the *Indiculum*. The register is segregated by topic (against Jews, Pagans, Manichaeans, Arians,

---

[167] It has been suggested the number of discrepancies in the *Indiculum* made an Augustinian or Possidian authorship impossible. Instead, the *Indiculum* as we have it is the product of a monastery library in Gaul or Italy, and which would have been compiled before the time of Cassiodorus. This is the thesis of Dagmar Luise Ludwig, *Der sog. Indiculus des Possidius. Studien zur Entstehugs und Wirkungsgeschichte einer spätantiken Augustin-Bibliographie* (unpublished dissertation, Georg-August-Universität zu Göttingen, 1984). Her work generated fruitful discussion. For response, see Almut Mutzenbecher, 'Benerkungen zum Indiculum des Possidius. Eine Rezension', *RÉAug*, 33 (1987), 129–31.

[168] *De haeresibus* is listed under the heading of treatises against the Arians. While Arianism is mentioned in this particular work, it is only one of eighty-eight heresies discussed; Pelagianism receives far more attention here than the other heresies.

[169] François Dolbeau, 'La Survie des oeuvres d'Augustin: Remarques sur l'*Indiculum* attribué à Possidius et sur la bibliothèque d'Anségise', in Donatella Nebbiai-Dalla Guarda and Jean-François Genest (eds.), *Du copiste au collectionneur: mélanges d'histoire des textes et des bibliothèques en l'honneur d'André Vernet* (Turnhout: Brepols, 1998), 3–22, esp. 11.

[170] The debate with Felix the Manichaean (*Contra Felicem*), for example, took place in December 404, but in the *Vita* it is placed in the narrative after the section on the Donatists, the last entry regarding them being Augustine's debate with Emeritus which took place in 418.

Donatists, Pelagians, and so on), and within these topics the works are further arranged by books, letters, and sermons. Under several topic headings, items have been tacked on at the end where the sermons are listed, but these 'add-ons' are not sermons and do not belong there. The majority of these items were written in, and after, the mid-420s, subsequent to the time we know Augustine's *indiculum* was collated.[171] What we have, then, are two visible 'layers' of a catalogue. It is therefore unlikely that Possidius was responsible for compiling the *Indiculum* we possess. Instead, we should postulate the existence of an *indiculum* before 426 (Augustine's list) to which Possidius or, more likely, someone else made additions.[172]

As for the relationship between the catalogue and the biography, the *Indiculum* Possidius relied on predated the writing of the *Vita*. This simple observation is fundamental to understanding the construction of the biography: the catalogue informs the life and not the other way around. Most scholarship on the *Vita* attempts to articulate a 'structure' within the work, and there is broad agreement that the biography seems to come in three fairly distinct pieces: Augustine's efforts to raise the Catholic church to preeminence in Africa (otherwise known as the career section comprising Chapters 1–18), his conduct as bishop (or personal life, Chapters 19–27) and his preparation of death amidst the chaos of the Vandal invasions (Chapters 28–31). We should not think of Suetonius' tripartite pattern so much as Possidius' promise, given in the preface and consisting of Augustine's own words, to trace the rise, conduct, and demise of his friend and colleague. We should also take note that trips to the library at Hippo serve as codas to each of these sections. At the end of the 'career' section (Chapter 18), Possidius announces the appending of the *Indiculum* to the end of the biography and exhorts interested parties to inquire at Hippo for the best copies of works. In Chapter 28, after discussion of Augustine's 'daily life', we learn how the bishop went to great lengths to prepare the library and organized his books. Shortly before his passing ('ante proximum vero diem obitus sui' [28.1]), Augustine revised his books and corrected their errors, paying special regard to those texts he wrote or dictated early on in his career and were consequently prone to theological error. At the end of the biography, in Chapter 31, Possidius vouches for the security of the library's contents. Augustine's planning and Possidius' personal protection

---

[171] Dolbeau, 'La Survie des oeuvres d'Augustin', 7–9.

[172] Including placing the treatise *On Heresies* under the heading for the Arians. It is to this work that Possidius may be referring when he discusses the interrogation of several women by Ursus, an imperial official, on the grounds that they had been engaging in Manichaean practices (*v. Aug.* 16). While everyone agrees Augustine would have known better, Possidius would have, too.

ensure the collection's permanence.[173] There are three separate visits, then, to the library at Hippo, all of them conclusions to the major sections of the biography. Might we, think of these distinct pieces of the biography (rise, episcopal conduct, and preparation of death), which in themselves constitute allusion to Augustinian text, as being strongly linked to the the contents of the library at Hippo? The first eighteen chapters of the biography are occupied, in large part, with the events recorded in Augustine's books (*libri*). Chapters 19–27 take as their focus the monastic life as defended in two famous sermons of Augustine's *s*. 355 and 356, the texts of which Possidius relies on heavily. Chapters 29–31 are dominated by a lengthy letter (*epistula*) (in Chapter 30) to Honoratus, the bishop of Thiabe, on how clergy should behave in the face of the Vandal invasion.[174] Of course, neither the *Indiculum* nor the *Retractationes* follow the arrangement as such, with books (*libri*), followed by sermons (*tractatus*), and then letters (*epistulae*). Instead, the *Indiculum* and *Retractationes* list Augustine's books first, with the letters coming next, and the sermons catalogued last. One detects, however, deliberation in Possidius' (mis)representation because he twice adopts the erroneous order (books, sermons, and letters) when he speaks of the appended *Indiculum*. In Chapter 18, and then at the end of the *Indiculum* itself, Possidius lists the categories of Augustine's writings in the way he follows them in the biography.[175]

Death and Vandals

Possidius even subjects Augustine's *Retractationes* to historical reconsideration. The review and correction of all of Augustine's works, claims Possidius, was a labor undertaken in anticipation of Augustine's approaching death.[176] This is not true. The *Retractationes* were conceived as a project as early as 412 (*ep.* 143) and written in 427 (*ep.* 224), three full years preceding Augustine's death. The bishop of Hippo admitted that their 'publication' was a matter of

---

[173] *v. Aug.* 31.6: 'Ecclesiae bibliothecam omnesque codices diligenter posteris custodiendos semper iubebat.'

[174] Possidius' placement of the letter offers some indication as to how we are to understand the function of Augustine's writing. Chapter 29 sees an approaching Vandal army and a sickness settle on Augustine that we are told will prove fatal ('et illa ultima exercebatur aegritudine'). Possidius then interrupts the narrative for this letter to Honoratus. Here is the calm, strong voice offering advice and direction. Augustine's withdrawal and death are, if not erased, then tempered with the words he leaves behind.

[175] 'Deo praestante in huius opusculi finem etiam eorumdem *librorum, tractatuum* et *epistularum* indiculum adiungere' (*v. Aug.* 18.10); and at the end of the *Indiculum*: '*libros, tractatus, epistulas* numero mille triginta' (italics mine).

[176] *v. Aug.* 28.1: 'Ante proximum vero diem obitus sui a se dictatos et editos libros recensuit.'

urgency (*ep.* 224.2), but the work resulted from Augustine's need to demonstrate to his polarized audience how one should read his books. While the corrections are as wide-ranging as the topics he wrote about, Augustine was particularly concerned that some of his early works would be interpreted as advocating that the will toward God was within the purview of human ability. For Augustine, intellectual evolution, which included habitual reappraisal of one's beliefs and admitting to the commission of errors, was a good and necessary part of an examined life.[177] Possidius acknowledges that Augustine's *Retractationes* were, in part, for the correcting of theological inconsistencies stemming from the days when he was not as familiar with ecclesiastical rule, but he clearly attributes their reaction as a function of his approaching end.[178] Possidius mutes Augustine's rigorous self-correction in favor of a *Retractationes*, paired with his *Speculum*, that predominantly function as tools enabling the learned and unlearned to navigate collections of texts. Both books anticipate Augustine's absence. They are the gifts from a man determined to ensure his powers of edification after he dies.[179]

Augustine's prescience of his own demise is closely linked to the Vandal invasion. 'By divine will and command', the invaders proceeded east along the coast of North Africa. Augustine, sick with fever, retired to his room, whose walls had been pasted with the short penitential psalms of David. He wept in prayer and repented the wrongs he had committed in this life.[180] Augustine was dying. The Vandals were ravaging Africa. We are witness to what can only be called an implosion of Augustine's life work. The final chapters of the *Vita* terminate the continual expansion Augustine enjoyed at the height of his career.

---

[177] For discussion as to the scope of change in Augustine's thought and its chronological progression, the standard works are Cranz, 'Development of Augustine's Ideas', 255–316; Markus, 'Conversion and Disenchantment' in *Sacred and Secular* (Norfolk, 1984), Section xviii Variorum.

[178] *v. Aug.* 28.1: 'et quaecumque in his recognovit aliter quam sese habet ecclesiastica regula a se fuisse dictata et scripta, cum adhuc ecclesiasticum usum minus sciret minusque sapuisset, a semetipso et reprehensa et correcta sunt' ('And in those works which he had dictated or written while he was as yet not so well acquainted with ecclesiastical usage and had less understanding, whatsoever he found not agreeing with the ecclesiastical rule, this himself he censured and corrected').

Notice that the corrections are reserved for his early career. Late clarifications are necessitated by his fellow clerics distributing his books before Augustine had a chance to revise them (*v. Aug.* 28.2).

[179] Vessey, 'Opus Imperfectum', 264–7.

[180] Ambrose's presence is felt here too in Augustine's final penance. In his last hours, Ambrose reassured his grieving friends (one of them Stilicho), 'I have not so lived that I should be ashamed to live among you, yet I do not fear to die, for we have a Lord who is good.' Augustine liked to repeat this phrase in Possidius' presence, with the added (anti-Pelagian) annotation that Ambrose relied on the forgiveness of God rather than confidence in his own purity. It is with meditations like these that Augustine prepared for his own passing. See Éric Rebillard, *In hora mortis: Évolution de la pastorale chrétienne de la mort aux IVe et Ve siècles* (Rome: École Française de Rome, 1994), 213–14.

Spreading further outwards, his influence reached ever further, across Africa and the sea. His texts had circulated all over the Roman world; for many years, his trained clerics emerged from Hippo's monastery ready to take up clerical posts in Africa, where they, in turn, established their own monasteries. At the end of the *Vita*, however, everything collapses inwards, seeking safety back within the walls of Hippo. As the Vandals make their way along the coast, Possidius and other clergy who had fled their basilicas find themselves besieged within the monastery. Churches across Africa burn. Some priests and bishops suffer torture and death. The invaders destroy monasteries; the nuns and monks suffer from abuse and hunger. Hymns are not sung, and the sacraments are no longer performed. The regular saying of mass is disrupted. Augustine, who excelled all in wisdom, is particularly aggrieved by these events, as he knows that more than 'wood and stones' are of issue.[181] Souls will be lost because clerics are not performing the necessary sacraments for their congregations.

Upon the heels of this dire news comes Possidius's final announcement that Augustine left behind a healthy church, one with a 'sufficient body of clergy and monasteries of men and women with their continent overseers'. The world Augustine laboriously built is crashing down in a most dramatic fashion, and Possidius' sudden shift in assessment strikes the reader as inappropriate and at odds with his own story. The incongruence between the narrative and final declaration must be attributed to Possidius' personal situation. Modern archaeology has never uncovered the burn layers and destruction levels Possidius vividly, if economically, describes.[182] Africa's clerical and monastic infrastructure likewise fared better than indicated in Possidius' initial report, although it probably suffered considerable financial strain from Vandal requisitions.[183] Possidius exaggerates the damage and disruption. Augustine's deepest

---

[181] For Augustine's quoting Plotinus see Pierre Courcelle, 'Sur les dernieres paroles de saint Augustin', in *RÉA*, 46 (1944), 205–7; Brown, *Augustine of Hippo*, 425–6 and now James J. O'Donnell, 'The Next Life of Augustine', in William E. Klingshirn and Mark Vessey (eds.), *The Limits of Ancient Christianity: Essays on Late Antique Thought and Culture in Honor of R. A. Markus* (Ann Arbor: University of Michigan Press, 1999), 215–20.

[182] Edward Gibbon, *The History of the Decline and Fall of the Roman Empire*, J. B. Bury (ed.) (London: Methuen & Co., 1909; reprint, New York: AMS Press, 1974), iii, 429, and Christian Courtois, *Les Vandales et l'Afrique* (Paris: Arts et Métiers Graphiques, 1955), 165–6. More recent studies arrive at the same conclusion. Frank M. Clover, 'Carthage and the Vandals', in J. H. Humphrey (ed.), *Excavations at Carthage 1976 Conducted by the University of Michigan* (Ann Arbor: University of Michigan Press, 1982), 1–14, and H. R. Hurst and S. P. Roskams, *Excavations at Carthage: The British Mission* Vol I, 1: The Avenue Habib Bourguibe Salambo (Sheffield: British Academy and Sheffield University, 1984).

'Victor of Vita', in M. Petschenig (ed.), *Historia persecutionis africanae provinciae*, CSEL 7 (1881) and Caprelus, *ep.* 1 (*PL* 53,845) also describe the displacement caused by the Vandals arrival as extreme.

[183] Y. Modéran, 'L'Établissement territorial des Vandals en Afrique', *An Tard* 10 (2002), 87–122.

fear was that human souls would be lost because of clerical flight; consequently, his colleague's escape from Calama demands justification. The overblown portrayal and, conversely, its cheerful resolution sanctions Possidius' departure. Augustine's letter to Honoratus, inserted into the biography when Augustine first begins to feel his fever, enumerates concerns for those whose salvation depends on the sacraments now denied to them, but weighed against these is the exhortation to avoid false martyrdom. Fortitude was one thing, Augustine said, but determination to the point of placing oneself and one's own congregation in danger was quite another. As Possidius describes the invasion, his decision to seek the walls of Hippo was only prudent. He did not abandon his congregation. More importantly, Possidius made the trip to Hippo because that was where the books were. It was the bishop of Calama's responsibility, as Augustine's heir and successor, to protect them. Augustine had no written will and, as was appropriate, left nothing to his relatives.[184] The basilica at Hippo and its goods were placed in the care of his successor, Eraclius. Augustine's preoccupation, however, was not with the buildings and the accoutrements, but the safety of the library. The books were his bequeathal to future generations, and he asked that all precautions be taken for their preservation.[185] The books guaranteed the future health of the Church, and Possidius had to be at Hippo to receive them.

---

[184] Again, the shadow of scandal: the monks were supposed to hold everything in common. If Augustine had heirs, that would have meant he violated the rules of the monastery as discussed in *s.* 355 and 356.

[185] See supra n. 173.

2

The Literary Possidius

As the curator of Augustine's library, Possidius was best qualified to comment on the state of the collection. He exhorted his readers to send to Hippo for whatever texts they required, for it was there that the best copies could be found.[1] Possidius also offered guides (the *Vita Augustini* and *Indiculum*) for navigation through a corpus so large that few people could know of all the books Augustine wrote, let alone read them (*v. Aug.* 18.9).[2] The biography and catalogue thus lodge themselves between Augustine's oeuvre and audience in the imposition of a selective (and, as we have seen, edited) context for introduction. Augustine habitually tested the soundness of his theological beliefs, and in later years critiqued and corrected the manuscripts in his library. He chose to review his works chronologically so that people could learn of his mistakes and observe what he hoped was progress towards the truth. Possidius manipulates the events in Augustine's career in contradiction to the way the bishop of Hippo wrote about them, and insists on a man whose well-demarcated stages of life were both few and, once passed through, irretrievable.[3] Having been appointed bishop, Augustine remains static in his doctrines and actions. Likewise, through the organization of Possidius' biography and the *Indiculum*, Augustine becomes an author of texts categorized by type, not chronology, and so he loses that sense of progress as demonstrated in his own books, letters, and sermons. The bishop of Hippo, whose character as adumbrated in the *Vita* maintains an unwavering consistency, has been turned inside out. The meditative and evolving man has become a public and perfected one.

---

[1] That Possidius invites requests from the library at Hippo be accompanied with payment ('qui magis veritatem quam amant divitias'), see Jürgen Scheele, 'Buch and Bibliothek Bei Augustinus', in *B&W*, 12 (1978), 63. Cf. Berthold Altaner, 'Die Bibliothek Augustins', in *Kleine Patristische Schriften* (Berlin: Akademic Verlag, 1967), 174–8 for the argument that a regional library at Hippo (Klosterbibliotheken der Diözese Hippo), not the basilica complex, held Augustine's books.

[2] See Chapter 1, n. 158.

[3] This is in direct opposition to Augustine, who understands his character as a cumulative experience. See Chapter 1, n. 31.

Possidius applied a great deal of pressure to Augustine's life and books. The push was intentional. We have seen in Chapter 1 that Possidius' 'reconsiderations' were inspired, in part, by an eagerness to defend the man, but some narrative manipulations can also be attributed to the bishop of Calama's literary ambitions. The *Vita* is rarely praised for its style or poetics, but the author successfully plays with the genres of biography and holy lives, as much as they had been established by the mid-430s, in order to secure himself a place within the history of Augustine's life and in the nascent world of Augustinian scholarship. The bishop Possidius as a character in the *Vita* enjoys relationships with Augustine and Ambrose that transcend issues of remembrance and discipleship. The part Possidius plays renders him a third-generation descendant in a 'genealogical' progression that flows from Ambrose to Augustine to himself. In turn, Possidius as an author attempts to secure Augustine's legacy by imposing a separate order on his life and books, and using the *Vita* to induct students into correct methods of approaching the master.

Certainly the most striking literary tactic Possidius employs is to alter the relationship between a teacher and his literary works. Tradition had it that knowledge gained through personal discipleship always superseded whatever could be gleaned through book study alone. Possidius seems to agree with the sentiment and makes declarations to that effect.[4] The biography itself, however, is constructed—literally—from hundreds of bits and pieces of Augustine's written works (textual borrowing accounts for over one-half of the *Vita*).[5] Even in those historical instances when we know Possidius was standing at Augustine's side, the *Vita*'s descriptions come, in large part, from Augustine's own textual record. Possidius' claim of narrative superiority through autopsy demands scrutiny when in fact his 'eyes' convey words written by his subject. The primary goal of this text-oriented biography is to guide the *studiosi* to Augustine's books, but in doing so, Possidius collapses the distance between the man and his written works. Augustine *was* what he wrote. Possidius thus tries to join that which tradition had long separated by defending the notion that the benefits accrued from listening to the master firsthand may not outweigh the edification granted by reading texts from afar.[6]

---

[4] *v. Aug. Praef.* and 31.9.

[5] This includes the lengthy letter sent by Augustine to Honoratus and inserted in the *Vita* by Possidius as a salutary example of how clerics should act in the face of the Vandal invasion (*ep.* 228 in the Maurist catalogue).

[6] Possidius follows here Augustine's lead in portraying a life as the books one has written, which is why Augustine wrote the *Retractationes*. See James J. O'Donnell, *Augustine: A New Biography* (New York: Ecco, 2005), 317–19, as well as Mark Vessey, 'Jerome's Origen: The Making of a Christian Literary Persona', *Studia Patristica*, 28 (1993), 135–45 for a discussion of the presentation of Origen's and Jerome's lives as writers. This is not quite the same as a life defined by that which one has written, but Jerome's *De viris illustribus* may have served, in part, as inspiration to Augustine.

POSSIDIUS TAKES THE STAGE

Readers of the *Vita* may be impressed by the degree to which its Catholic bishops, including Possidius, exude humility. He does not refer to himself by name (he gives very few names, in fact, of Catholic clerics), and there are moments where the credit for action due to Possidius is given to Augustine instead. Possidius even begins the biography with traditional admonitions designed to dampen a reader's expectations: the author will do his best with his limited powers neither to offend God nor the truth.[7] When one removes the blushing veneer from the *Vita*'s preface (or any other part of the biography), however, one discovers that a very self-confident author resides just beneath the surface. The *Vita Augustini*'s very first sentences announce that this is a work inspired by the Holy Spirit, and it stands in competition with other lives of saints whose authors were likewise filled with the divine breath.[8]

Augustine as portrayed in the *Vita* sustains the life of African Catholicism. He is orthodoxy's guarantor, and as such, Possidius reins in the other players, including himself, lest the hero become obscured. It is true, however, that Possidius' 'anonymity' as a character and 'modesty' as an author create large areas in the biography through which Possidius can freely wander. It is as if Possidius were 'flying under the radar'. His very unobtrusiveness allows him to claim for himself the same advantages of episcopal prerogative that Augustine enjoys: the conversion of others to Catholicism, claim over the books that reside at Hippo's library, and the right to edit and rewrite Augustine's life. Possidius' character remains strangely ambivalent: anonymous and liminal, yet imperative and central.

We see best where Possidius' actions undercut impressions of unimportance in those sections of the *Vita* occupied by the Catholic confrontation with the Donatists (Chapters 9–14). Possidius spends more time on the Donatists than other religious opponents and reveals a great deal about his own role in the affairs of the African Church. His narrative is a rich mix of history, biography, and personal memoir. The Donatist chapters balance the opposing parties, with each description functioning as a comment on

---

[7] Tore Jansen, *Latin Prose Prefaces: Studies in Literary Conventions* (Stockholm: Almquist, 1964).

[8] *v. Aug. Praef.* 1–2: 'Inspirante rerum omnium factore et gubernatore Deo…studens…de vita et moribus praedestinati et suo tempore praesentati sacerdotis optimi Augustini, quae in eodem vidi, ab eoque audivi, + minime reticere + . Id enim etiam ante nos factitatum fuisse a religiosissimis sanctae matris ecclesiae catholicae viris legimus et comperimus, qui, divino adflati Spiritu, sermone proprio atque stilo…studiosorum notitiae intulerunt.'

the behavior and comportment of the other.[9] Augustine, recently appointed bishop (9.1),[10] calmly writes letters and pamphlets to the Donatists on the necessity for unity while the opposition speaks calumnies and preaches the virtues of assassination. The Donatist bishops refuse to debate with Augustine, but exhort their followers to commit acts of violence against the Catholics. Some proceed to beat and terrify innocents across North Africa, all the while 'going about under a profession of continence' ('sub professione continentium ambulantes'). These men 'hated peace' ('oderant pacem'), and tried to intimidate those speaking in its favor. Amidst all the disruption, a few Africans began to turn against the violence. They broke with the Donatist clergy and decided to adhere to the unity and peace of the Church ('paci atque unitati ecclesiae'). Circumcellion attacks increased in inverse proportion to the declination of Donatist numbers, and they eventually resorted to the torture, disfigurement, and murder of Catholic clergy. Possidius' language here closely follows that of Augustine: 'those who hate peace' was one of Augustine's definitions for heretics, and used especially in his works against Donatists.[11]

Precisely at this moment, Possidius introduces the residents of Hippo's monastery. Men ordained by Augustine begin to accept appointments as bishops and clergy in cities throughout Africa (v. Aug. 11.1).[12] They subsequently establish their own monasteries patterned after the one at Hippo and train priests who, in turn, eventually leave to administer other churches. Augustine's

[9] Something that Augustine had done before. See *en. Ps.* 132.3–6, wherein the Catholic monks—temperate, circumspect, stable, community dwellers—are compared to the drunken, reckless, fanatic, and vagrant circumcellions. See also *en. Ps.* 101.9, ex. 2.

[10] *v. Aug.* 9.1: 'Et episcopus multo instantius ac ferventius, maiore auctoritate, non adhuc in una tantum regione, sed ubicumque rogatus venisset, verbum salutis aeternae alacriter ac gnaviter pullulante atque crescente Domini ecclesia praedicabat.'

[11] See, for example, *De laude pacis* (*s.* 357.3), delivered in mid-May 411: 'Odit pacem haereticus.' *C. litt. Petil.* 2, 96 (218): 'For in fact it is dissention and division that make you heretics, but peace and unity make men Catholics.' See also *en. Ps.* 39.20–8 (*PL* 36, 446), Dolbeau *s.* 63, *ep.* 140. 17 as well as *en. Ps.* 132, the sermon in which Augustine discusses 'how good it is for brothers to dwell together in unity'.

'Pax et unitas' was a Catholic phrase for orthodoxy, especially in the context of the Donatist controversy (Cyprian's *De ecclesiae catholicae unitate* being a major source of contention between the parties). From Chapters 10–18 of the *Vita Augustini*, the words *pax* and *unitas* together or *pax* alone appear eight times (10.3, 10.4, 11.2, 12.4, 12.5, 13.1 [twice], and 18.7). The words make their appearance only after Augustine is consecrated bishop, and all appear in the Donatist chapters.

For further discussion, see N. Duval, 'Notes d'épigraphie chrétienne III: Episcopus unitatis,' *Karthago*, 9 (1958), 137–49 and Mireille Labrousse (ed.), Optat de Milève *Traité Contre les Donatists* (Paris: Éditions du Cerf, 1995), 117–21.

[12] See *ep.* 20*.5 for an idea how people from Augustine's monastery were farmed out to African churches. There were correct and incorrect ways in which residents at Hippo's monastery (including *notarii*) should be distributed to African churches.

initial foundation begets more clergy and monasteries to at least the third generation. The thrust is outward, with these clergy progressing further away from a geographic center. It is a fact, however, that several of these men had left Hippo years ago, some having received their appointments as early as the mid-390s. In other words, Possidius' placement of Augustine's episcopal cadre here in the Donatist narrative is about a decade too late, as the kind of attacks against Catholic clergy Possidius describes did not occur until 403–4. The men enjoy their debut now because they provide a clear counterweight to the Donatist clergy and their violent disciples. The circumcellions, educated by evil teachers ('malis doctoribus'), were as a consequence disruptive, unchaste, and unsuccessful in maintaining Donatist numbers. Augustine trained his own cadre of about ten men ('nam ferme decem'),[13] and as he was a teacher who taught true things, his students were genuinely celibate and learned.[14]

With the introduction of the clerics from Hippo's monastery, conversion to Catholicism begins on a greater scale. Augustine has qualified colleagues who make gains through preaching and conversion. 'Your servants were peaceful with those who hated peace and when they spoke, those who hated peace were willingly overcome by them.'[15] These are unambiguous terms—those who are peaceful and those who hate peace—identifying orthodox Catholics in the act of turning Donatists away from their old loyalties. We remember that the *Vita* is at pains to show Augustine as the successor of Ambrose; the former receives orthodoxy, and thus legitimacy, from the bishop of Milan. The salutary persuasion that loosened Augustine's adherence to Manichaeism was present years later when Augustine unconsciously broke the hold that same heresy exercised on Firmus. The gift from God first bequeathed by Ambrose to Augustine has passed to the next generation. The men trained and ordained by Augustine are able to convince, bringing to 'unity' those who had previously remained unmoved.

---

[13] As for the ten, we know many of their names, and most of them went on to be important bishops in Africa. That number is probably more of philosophical than of historical import, as it harks back to the *Confessions* and Augustine's first attempt to establish a philosophic community in Italy. A group of nearly ten men ('decem ferme homines' [*conf.* 6.14{24}]) eagerly made plans to live together and as in the later arrangements at Hippo, hoped to share their resources. The plan was thwarted by the objections of some of the men's wives. The monastery at Hippo constituted the fulfillment of Augustine's dream. Pierre Courcelle, *Les Confessions de Saint Augustin dans la Tradition littéraire: Antecédents et Postérité* (*Appendice iv: Emprunts et compléments de Possidius aux Confessions*) (Paris: Études Augustiniennes, 1963), 612, believes that Possidius concluded that Cassiciacum was not a monastic life proper.

[14] *v. Aug.* 11.3: 'Nam ferme decem, quos ipse novi, sanctos ac venerabiles viros continentes et doctos beatissimus Augustinus diversis ecclesiis, nonnullis quoque eminentioribus, rogatus dedit.'

[15] *v. Aug.* 11.6: 'servi autem tui, ut dictum est, cum his qui oderant pacem erant pacifici, et cum loquerentur, debellabantur gratis ab eis' (Ps. 119:7).

Possidius' own experience offers explicit illustration as to how Augustine's successors inherited his episcopal authority. While the Donatist violence against Catholic clerics increased, the *Vita* tells us that Augustine narrowly escaped an ambush. He was on his way to preach in a diocese outside of Hippo, and a gang of Donatists lay in wait to intercept him along his anticipated route. Augustine's guide took the wrong road—here again is Providence working through human action and error—and the party arrived at its destination, unharmed (*v. Aug.* 12.2). This is a true story. Augustine himself spoke of this near miss, and more chronological detail has emerged since the discovery of the Mayence sermons in 1990.[16] We now know that within six months of this attempt on Augustine, the Donatists likewise set upon Possidius, but the bishop of Calama was not as fortunate as Augustine.[17] While traveling with an entourage in the diocese of Calama, Possidius was ambushed by a Donatist gang. The bishop and his escort ran away, leaving pack animals and baggage behind. Possidius hid in a farmhouse, but was discovered, dragged from upstairs, and badly beaten. The similarity of the attacks on Augustine and Possidius takes on theological and political importance when Possidius initiates efforts to prosecute his Donatist rival, Crispinus, in front of Calama's magistrates. In Possidius' view, the attack was not a question of battery so much as a matter of heresy, and it should be judged as such: 'de qua re, ne pacis amplius ecclesiae provectus inpediretur': again, *pax*, like *unitas*, being words that connote Catholic claims to orthodoxy.

Crispinus was a formidable opponent: wealthy, popular, the owner of a sizable estate, and well educated.[18] He had been a bishop in Calama long before Possidius took up residency in the town, and clearly considered his rival someone he could intimidate: Crispinus was the one who had ordered Possidius to receive this drubbing in the first place. He scoffed at the charge of heresy. Possidius' initial bid came to nothing, and we may gauge from this local decision the disparity of authority that existed between the two bishops. Crispinus had the upper hand, and continued to enjoy that position when the proconsul subsequently ruled, too, in his favor. Augustine insisted that the proconsul listen to Possidius and Crispinus debate. This was a crucial meeting, says Possidius, and the Christians in Carthage and in all of Africa

---

[16] Augustine mentions the episode in *Enchiridion* 17.5, and the Dolbeau *s*. 26 *Contra Paganos* puts the attack as having occurred in 403. See F. Dolbeau (ed.), *Vingt-six sermons aux peuple d'Afrique* (Paris: Institut d' Études Augustiniennes, 1996), 345–417.

[17] Aside from the *Vita*, information on the attack against Possidius may be found in Augustine's *Contra Cresconium* and *ep*. 185.

[18] *v. Aug.* 12.5: 'Crispinus, qui iisdem Donatistis in Calamensi civitate et regione episcopus fuit, praedicatus scilicet et multi temporis et doctus.'
See *ep.* 51 and *c. litt. Petil.* 2. 83 (184) for the nature and extent of Crispinus' estate.

eagerly awaited the outcome.[19] The proconsul was ultimately convinced, and he declared Crispinus a heretic. Possidius won.

Historically, the legal categorization of Donatists as heretics came down to a case argued by Possidius, but in the *Vita*, Augustine always remains the central focus. Possidius does not actually refer to himself at any point in this story, nor does he declare that he won the case, but instead reports in the passive voice that the Donatist bishop was pronounced a heretic by the African proconsul.[20] It is Augustine who arranges the meeting. The bishop of Hippo likewise seeks, and obtains, the emperor's pardon for Crispinus after the emperor rejects the Donatists' subsequent appeal. Augustine is credited in the chapter's concluding sentence for fostering the growth of the Church, a direct outcome from having managed this affair.[21]

Possidius' muting of his particular role in the confrontations with the Donatists continues (Chapter 13), when he bequeaths to Augustine the palm of victory for securing the unity of peace within the Church ('pacis unitas'). This was accomplished at the conference of 411. The biography constructs that meeting as having been conducted exclusively by Augustine. His bishop-colleagues are there to offer support.[22] Possidius has just glided over another personal achievement of historical import, in that he and three other bishops traveled to Ravenna in 410 to ask the emperor to convene this conference. He also neglects to mention that the rules governing the debate required each delegation, Donatist and Catholic alike, to select seven representatives who would be responsible for making arguments. Augustine was not alone at Carthage; six of his colleagues helped carry the Catholic side, one of whom was Possidius. That Augustine always remains the force of unity and peace within the Church is demonstrated both by the alliance he enjoys with the bishops and his successful efforts to incorporate former heretics into the Catholic fold. The other bishops, including Possidius, remain in the background.

All the attention devolves on Augustine, but attributing Possidius' narrative muting to humility or some other emotion connoting a lack of interest in his literary persona is, in the end, at odds with the *Vita*'s ambition to vindicate Augustine (as well as the author himself) through the bequeathal of episcopal power to his disciples. Possidius compares himself to Augustine through shared experience with Donatist attacks, but more important, he

---

[19] *v. Aug.* 12.7: 'magna populorum Christianorum multitudine causae exitum et apud Carthaginem et per totam Africam exspectante.'

[20] 12.7: 'atque ille est Crispinus proconsulari et libellari sententia pronuntiatus haereticus.'

[21] 12.9: 'et Domino adiuvante perfectum est. Qua diligentia et sancto studio multum crevit ecclesia.'

[22] *v. Aug.* 13.5: 'Per sanctum illum hominem, consentientibus nostris coepiscopis et pariter satagentibus, et coeptum et perfectum est.'

ranks himself among the youngest of an elite whose membership previously included Ambrose and Augustine. He beat Crispinus, successfully defended orthodoxy, and converted Donatists. Possidius' travails and ultimate victory secured for him a place in a very special genealogy. By extension, his inheritance and its attendant prerogatives must apply to the importance of the biography he wrote. What he says about the spirit's inspiration in the *Vita*'s preface does not constitute idle remarks.

It is clear that Possidius conceives of the office of bishop in a way fundamentally different from Augustine. In the *Vita*, a kind of informed power stronger than grace alone fills a recipient upon appointment to the office. It is as if these men are 'plugged in' to an unearthly source of energy. They become arbiters of truth, and a conduit through which others come to understand the divine. What Ambrose has, he gives to Augustine: this possession Augustine in turn passes on to the bishops he himself has ordained. Possidius' abilities, which may be traced to the bishop of Milan, have their ultimate origin with the apostles at Pentecost. Ambrose, of course, did not appoint Augustine to the episcopate, but Possidius compensates by eliding the men's careers with a literary doublet. As Ambrose did for Augustine, so Augustine did for Firmus, the Manichaean who converted upon hearing Augustine preach. Possidius, one of about ten bishops trained by Augustine, came next. His given power allowed him to engage the law, convert Donatists, and write the definitive biography of his mentor. The same kind of power, bequeathed but never lessened, filled them all.[23] They *were* the Church.[24] Heretical or schismatic bishops, such as the Donatist Emeritus or the Arian Maximinus, did not possess the same gifts. Wrong belief separated them from the source. They had the gift of interminable talk, but in the end, they could not persuade.

The emphasis Possidius places on his descent from Ambrose and Augustine bolsters his literary and historical authority. It makes sense for the bishop of Calama to invest his words with certainty in light of his efforts to secure Augustine's legacy. On the other hand, one notices that Possidius' views of the episcopate, which had their origins in the writings of Cyprian, were also espoused by the Donatist clergy. Augustine believed that being bishop, even an orthodox Catholic one, was no guarantee of a lock on the truth, and even if one was fortunate enough to grasp it in some way, office or status was by no means

---

[23] Notice, however, that they have right (and need) to correct each other. Ambrose's correction of Augustine's faulty beliefs led him to true faith. In turn, Augustine edited a statement of Ambrose's lest he appear too confident of salvation, and thus too 'Pelagian'. Augustine once rebuked Possidius for his loose tongue. As we have seen, Possidius frequently applies gentle 'correction' to Augustine's literary persona.

[24] See Cyprian's *epp.* 66.8 and 59.7 on the bishop as the personification of the Church.

the sole means of access. Augustine would have been deeply skeptical of Possidius' faith in an episcopal genealogy. The anniversary sermons he preached to celebrate Cyprian's martyrdom emphatically situated Christ, not Cyprian, as the mediator between human and divine.[25] Likewise in his letters, sermons, and, most famously, the *Confessions*, Augustine kept 'Donatist' assumptions about episcopal power at arm's length. What is at issue is the extent to which Augustine's thoughts constituted those of the larger Catholic episcopate. Modern readers continue to discover just how different from his contemporaries Augustine could be in his thought and writing. Rather than argue that the urgency to endow Augustine with authority in the 430s forced Possidius to embrace beliefs he himself would have held as erroneous, it is more likely that Possidius' view of the episcopate was that of a more 'mainstream' Catholic bishop. Similarly as with his career and his books, Possidius was here applying pressure *on* Augustine to situate the man, his beliefs, and his oeuvre within parameters necessary to ensure their acceptance and authority.

'VOX TUA NEMPE MEA EST': AUTOPSY AND ALLUSION

Assistance of the divine kind allows for innovation and surprise, such as Possidius' blurring of distinctions between eyewitness reporting and written-source citation. To anyone with a degree of familiarity with Augustine's works, it is quickly apparent that Possidius was present at many of the debates between Augustine and his opponents as re-created in the biography.[26] Possidius' frequent, if silent, presence shifts historical perspective to give an even stronger impression—we may even say the illusion—that Possidius was Augustine's constant companion. This narrative filter through which he coaxes the life compromises the assumption that Possidius aspired to remain unnoticed to the reading audience. On the other hand, one can argue that the fact that Possidius records events to which he was a witness merely fulfills the promise to his readers that the contents of the *Vita* constitute the things he saw of, and

---

[25] See especially *s. Guelferbytanus* 29, preached against the Donatists.
Augustine regarded the succession of bishops as crucial in the context of continuity and authority. In the face of innovation, episcopal and ecclesiastical succession provided reliable guides to correct belief. See Robert Eno, 'Doctrinal Authority in Saint Augustine', *AugStud*, 12 (1981), esp. 150–1 and Jacques Pintard, 'Sur la succession apostolique selon saint Augustin', in *Forma futuri: Studi in onore del cardinale Michele Pellegrino* (Turin: Bottega d'Erasmo, 1975), 884–95.

[26] The debate with Crispinus, the meeting with Emeritus in 418, the 411 conference, the councils to condemn Pelagianism, and perhaps the meetings with Pascentius (Possidius testifies to the presence of bishops) and Maximinus.

heard from, Augustine.[27] Like many biographers before him, he declares that hearing the man speak was by far a better thing than reading his books, but it was best to know him personally.

> From his writing assuredly it is manifest that this priest, beloved and acceptable to God, lived uprightly and soberly in the faith, hope, and love of the Catholic Church in so far as he was permitted to see it by the light of truth, and those who read what he wrote about divine scripture profit thereby. But I believe that they were able to derive greater good from him who heard and saw him as he spoke in person in the church, and especially those who knew well his manner of life among men. For not only was he a 'scribe instructed unto the kingdom of heaven, which brings forth out of his treasure things new and old', and one of those merchants who 'when he had found the pearl of great price, sold all that he had and bought it', but he was also one of those of whom it is written: 'So speak and so do', and of whom the Savior said: 'Whoever shall so do and teach men, the same shall be called great in the kingdom of heaven.'[28]

This statement is consonant with the sensibilities of a contemporary audience, first of all, because it positions the author advantageously whereby he can impart knowledge thought to be inaccessible to readers at large. Possidius knew Augustine personally, and thus it is assumed that the information provided will be richer and more reliable.[29] The biographies of great men functioned, in part, as a substitute for the opportunity to learn from the teachers themselves. Books written by a master were not necessarily the distilled statements that best articulated the contents of a great mind, but a consolation whose edificatory effectiveness, albeit sound, was inferior to knowledge gleaned from having sat at his knees. Partial remedy was available in the form of reminiscences and character descriptions from those who had enjoyed precisely that kind of relationship.[30] In having been a friend and colleague, Possidius was

---

[27] *v. Aug. Praef.* 1: 'quae in eodem vidi ab eoque audivi, + minime reticere +.'

[28] *v. Aug.* 31.9–10: 'Et in suis quidem scriptis ille Deo adceptus et carus sacerdos, quantum lucente veritate videre conceditur, recte ac sane fidei, spei et caritatis catholicae ecclesiae vixisse manifestatur, quod agnoscunt qui eum de divinis scribentem legentes proficiunt. Sed ego arbitror plus ex eo proficere potuisse, qui eum et loquentem in ecclesia praesentem audire et videre potuerunt, et eius praesertim inter homines conversationem non ignoraverunt. Erat enim non solum eruditus scriba in regno caelorum, de thesauro suo proferens nova vetera, et unus negotiatorum, qui, inventa pretiosa margarita, quae habebat venditis, comparavit, verum etiam ex his ad quos scriptum est: "Sic loquimini, et sic facite:" et de quibus Salvator dicit: "Qui fecerit et docuerit sic, hic magnus vocabitur in regno caelorum."'

[29] Claudia Rapp, 'Storytelling as Spiritual Communication in Early Greek Hagiography', *JECS*, 6 (1998), 431–48.

[30] It is important to remember in this context Cassian's *Conferences*, which stress the importance of oral learning from masters. Cassian prefers the dialogue as means of instruction over the study of text, yet delivers that precept in the form of a book.

better situated to guide the reader in study in that he could guarantee that as Augustine wrote, so he lived.

Possidius intimates that the 'things that he saw and heard' comprise the contents of the *Vita*, and that autopsy is the superior method by which one learns. That much is clear. How seriously, then, are we to take Possidius' epitaph for Augustine: 'What you read, I speak'?[31] Shaping his written words with spoken ones, in the act of reading, cuts through the distance and time separating teacher from student. That is how Possidius suggests one may conjure Augustine. He remains a living and vibrant presence through the reading of his books. Moreover, although Possidius defers to autopsy, in fact the *Vita* largely consists of stitched-together phrases, sentences, and paragraphs from Augustine's written works. Possidius' presence, vaunted in the text as guarantor of the narrative's veracity, becomes, arguably, obscured by the fact that these 'personal' reminiscences have been filtered through Augustinian text. Possidius has just had his way with the prevalent literary tradition, and there is no better example to illustrate his manipulations than an episode already discussed: the debate between Possidius and Crispinus. Separate rulings from the proconsul and emperor, that is, securing a shift in legal attitudes toward the Donatists marked historical occasions whose import did not elude Possidius. At such a moment, however, Possidius describes the scene using words and phrases taken from one of Augustine's letters (*ep.* 105) and the *Contra Cresconium*.[32] These are Possidius' own experiences from what must have been exhilarating times. Authors may recommend autopsy as a rule, but this occasion in the *Vita* almost demands its employment. The self-conscious decision to render a personal experience dependent on another's text demonstrates the 'bookishness' of the *Vita*. Autopsy is traditionally considered the best security for truth within a narrative, as well as a means of getting closer to the hero's character, but here veracity and knowledge are redirected through Possidius' eyes and back to Augustine's text. Possidius' personal 'sight' are books that can be read by anyone, and it is these books that become the best witness to Augustine's character. Possidius again pushes his readers into the interior of Augustine's library.

That Possidius binds what is considered the superior perspective of a first-hand account closely to Augustine's written works, draws tighter the two

---

[31] 'Quod legis, ecce loquor, vox tua mea nempe est.' See Chapter 1, n. 157.

[32] *v. Aug.* 12.5: 'ad multam teneri aurariam publicis legibus contra haereticos constitutam.' Cf. *Cresc.* 3.47 (51), which, in turn, alludes to Theodosius' law of 392 against heretics. See the comments of A. Bastiaensen in his commentary *Vita di Agostino* (Milan: Fondazione Lorenzo Valla, 1975), 377: 'malgrado la sua esperienza personale, Possidius dipendo qui de Agostino'. See also Bastiaensen, 'The Inaccuracies in the *Vita Augustini* of Possidius', *Studia Patristica*, 16 (1985), 480, n. 2.

sets of texts: Possidius' biography and Augustine's books. If the versions offered by Possidius' 'autopsy' and Augustine's books remain consonant, the former confirms the latter. That seems clear, but the rub is that the *Vita* deliberately alters many episodes in Augustine's life, from his conversion as presented in the *Confessions* to the debate in 418 with Emeritus. Possidius departs from Augustine on the details about his appointment to the episcopate, the bishop's intellectual evolution, and the degree to which he consulted the secular courts and imperial administrators. The discrepancies between what Augustine wrote and how Possidius chose to represent his life are, I think, successfully resolved by the fact that Possidius' 'reconsiderations' of Augustine's life find their sources in Augustine's work. The *Vita* employs words and phrases written by a man who would disagree with much of what was in the biography. Possidius thus has it both ways: faithful to his source, but determined to tell a different story.

'HE HIMSELF TOLD ME'

The narrative tension Possidius creates when passing text for autopsy is greatest in those moments when Possidius insists that information he conveys comes directly from Augustine's mouth. Several times Possidius assures his readers regarding some statement that: 'he himself told me' ('ut nobis dicebat' or some close variant).[33] Such specific assurances occur six times in the biography, but most of these can be traced to texts written either by Augustine or by Ambrose and Paulinus of Milan (in his *Vita Ambrosii*). Here is an example: Augustine prepared for his approaching death by sharing with Possidius and others edificatory stories about how other bishops faced their final days.[34] The first he told was about the dying Ambrose, who reassured his grieving visitors (one of

---

[33] *v. Aug.* 4.1, 4.2, 4.3, 24.17: 'ut nobis dicebat'; 'nobis ipse retulit', 'ut nobis retulit', and 'nobis aliquando retulerat'. This last from the notice that Ambrose has melted down the silver liturgical fittings in order to pay ransom for captives and that Augustine had done the same (*De officiis* 2.28.136), as discussed in Courcelle, 'Emprunts et compléments', 617–21. See also *v. Aug.* 31.1: 'dicere nobis inter familiaria conloquia consueverat...absque digna et competenti paenitentia exire de corpore non debere', a sentiment that Augustine shared with his congregation in *s*. 351.3 (4) and 352.3 (9).

[34] As noticed by Bastiaensen, the story as taken from Ambrose contains explicit criticism of Pelagian attitudes. The story of the bishop's fear of death is taken from Cyprian's *De mortalitate*, a text which appears in some of Augustine's anti-Pelagian works (such as *ep*. 217.6, *Contra Iulianum*, 2.8.25 and *De praedestinatione sanctorum* 14.26). See Bastiaensen, 'Inaccuracies', 484–5.

whom was Stilicho): 'I have not so lived that I should be ashamed to live among you, yet I do not fear to die, for we have a Lord who is good.' These words come directly from Paulinus of Milan's *Vita Ambrosii* (45.2).[35] There has been some debate as to whether Possidius has recalled a phrase he heard from Augustine directly or if he (accidentally) transposed a written text to the realm of speech and remembrance,[36] but that question is easy to answer when one turns to Possidius' other declarations that the information he passes along comes from Augustine's lips. A burst of these—'as he told us'—comes in Chapter 4, with three closely placed within one paragraph.[37] This section of the *Vita* details Augustine's seizure at Hippo and his forced ordination to the priesthood. As we have seen, the historical episode is problematic, first because some thought Augustine was canvassing to be appointed bishop, and second, because he had to come to terms with having previously criticized African clerics. We know that Possidius took pains to edit history so as to render Augustine's ordination as smooth and linear as possible; he consequently lards the narrative with three emphatic pledges in order to make this, his version, the official one: whatever else one has heard, *this* is what Augustine told me. Possidius' efforts to mold the story do not impel him to distinguish between what he heard firsthand and what one could read in a text. Here, Augustine personally told Possidius he stayed away from towns in need of bishops, but this information may be found in *s.* 355. The overlap is not a coincidence, as Possidius utilizes that sermon extensively in the *Vita*. Likewise, the residents of Hippo did not understand why Augustine began to cry when they asked him to be their priest, but this is not privileged information: Augustine writes about those misunderstood tears in a letter to bishop Valerius in *ep.* 21. The final 'ut nobis retulit' involves Augustine's deep understanding of the dangers to his own life ('suae vitae') that would come from holding clerical office. The phrase undoubtedly alludes

---

[35] Cf. Possidius' phrase: 'Non sic vixi, ut me pudeat inter vos vivere; sed nec mori timeo, quia bonum Dominum habemus', with that of Paulinus of Milan: 'Non ita inter vos vixi, ut pudeat me vivere; nec timeo mori, quia Dominum bonum habemus.'

[36] P. Courcelle, 'Emprunts et compléments', 435. Cf. Pellegrino, 'Reminiscenze letterarie agostiniane nella *Vita Augustini* di Possidius', *Aevum*, 28 (1954), 28, and Bastiaensen, 'Inaccuaracies', 485.

[37] *v. Aug.* 4.1–3: 'solebat autem laicus, *ut nobis dicebat*, ab eis tantum ecclesiis, quae non haberent episcopos, suam abstinere praesentiam—eum ergo tenuerunt et, ut in talibus consuetum est, episcopo ordinandum intulerunt, omnibus id uno consensu et desiderio fieri perficique petentibus magnoque studio et clamore flagitantibus, ubertim eo flente: nonnullis quidem lacrimas eius, *ut nobis ipse retulit*, tunc superbe interpretantibus et tamquam eum consolantibus ac dicentibus quia et locus presbyterii, licet ipse maiori dignus esset, propinquaret tamen episcopatui; cum ille homo Dei, *ut nobis retulit*, et maiori consideratione intelligeret et gemeret, quam multa et magna suae vitae pericula de regimine et gubernatione ecclesiae inpendere iam ac provenire speraret, atque ideo fleret' (italics mine).

to the heavy responsibilities he feared would interfere with his own spiritual well-being.[38] Augustine knew well the unwanted pull of duty on those who were trying to live the life of the gospel, but in this particular instance, I believe Possidius is using his position as eyewitness to mute admissions on the part of Augustine that he wept in recognition of the punishment meted out to him for having criticized God's servants, of whom he was now, unwillingly, one. In other words, the manipulation of citation as autopsy has its inspiration from attempts to defend Augustine. When Possidius recalls 'his own' experiences, they accord with, yet manage to shift, Augustine's writings.

While it is certainly possible to create a portrait of a man with borrowed words and phrases, it is another matter entirely to do it well. Even more difficult is to do it by assembling textual pieces in a way that contradict the sentiments held by the person who initially wrote them. Modern commentators employ many adjectives to describe Possidius' *Vita*, many of which are not complimentary, but the ones seen most often are the following: simple, artless, naïve, and guileless. It is an indication of the artistic competency Possidius commands that he could 'quicken' Augustine by using a framework within which textual borrowing dominated.[39] Possidius successfully brings Augustine closer to his readers, not in the intimation of new information previously available only to students, but in the collapsing of the distance between the man and his reading audience. Augustine has become, and remains, essentially, his books. His books, that is, as Possidius wants us to read them.

A LIFE AS A CITY AS HISTORY AS A BOOK

If Augustine's life as represented in the *Vita* is the sum of his books, we need to return to Possidius as the self-appointed curator of the library at Hippo. The bishop of Calama situated himself within the biography as the spiritual descendant of Ambrose and Augustine. As the author of the life, he places himself in front and at the center of Augustine's literary legacy, not only in the collection's protection, but in its interpretation. That Possidius organized and edited Augustine's books for use by filtering them through the *Vita* is clear, but the preface shows the extent to which Possidius' rendering of Augustine's life is

---

[38] For discussion of the anxieties posed by earthly obligations, see Philip Rousseau, *Ascetics, Authority, and the Church in the Age of Jerome and Cassian* (Oxford: Oxford University Press, 1978), 58; Derwas J. Chitty, *The Desert A City* (Oxford: Basil Blackwell, 1966), 23; Owen Chadwick, *John Cassian* (Cambridge: Cambridge University Press, 1968), 68.

[39] See Chapter 1, n. 2.

deliberately textual. He says: 'I have undertaken to set forth the rise and career and the destined end of this venerable man, those things which I have learned and experienced, living with him in friendship for so many years.'[40] Personal friendship and the knowledge gleaned from that relationship determine the shape and direction of the biography—that is the claim to autopsy again—but the phrase 'et exortu et procursu et debito fine' which he employs to trace the trajectory of Augustine's life is one of Augustine's own phrases.[41] Augustine used it many times, once to mark the transience of all that which is created,[42] but the others as a programmatic statement describing the narrative structure of the second half of the *De civitate Dei*—the rise, progression, and ultimate destiny of the two cities. The phrase appears at the close of the first half of the *De civitate* and it opens the second (10.32 and 11.1), wherein Augustine describes the contents of Books 11–22 with the three evolutionary steps, each comprising four books.[43] Augustine uses this phrase again to describe the second half of the *De civitate* in the *Retractationes*,[44] and the reason for the emphasis is, in large part, Augustine's concern that the entire piece be read correctly. He asked that the work be copied in the arrangement reflective of its narrative structure (*epp*. 231A and 1*A),[45] and he admonished his 'editor'[46] that if the *De civitate* must be divided, he found only two acceptable ways of doing it: either to make two volumes, with Books 1–10 in the first and 11–22 in the second, or to break it into five volumes with Books 1–5 in the first, 6–10 in the second, and the remaining twelve books divided into three volumes of four books each (discussing in the three volumes respectively the rise, progression,

---

[40] *v. Aug. Praef*. 3: 'De praedicti venerabilis viri et exortu et procursu et debito fine, quae per eum didici et expertus sum, quamplurimis annis eius inhaerens caritati, ut Dominus donaverit, explicandum suscepi.'

[41] Christine Mohrmann, 'Zwei Frühchristliche Bischofsviten: *Vita Ambrosii, Vita Augustini*', *Anzeiger* 112 (1975), 325, and H. J. Diesner, 'Possidius und Augustinus', *Studia Patristica*, 6 (1962), 351. See also Elena Zocca, 'La figura del Santo Vescovo in Africa da Ponzio a Possidio', in *Vescovi e pastori in Epoca teodosiana: Studia ephemeridis augustinianum*, 58 (Rome: Institutum Patristicum Augustinianum, 1997), 469–92, and Louis I. Hamilton, 'Possidius' Augustine and Post-Augustinian Africa', *JECS*, 12 (2004), 102–3.

[42] *conf*. 4.10.15: 'ad illud autem non sufficit [i.e. sensus carnis], ut teneat transcurrentia ab initio debito usque ad finem debitum.'

[43] Also at *civ. Dei* 1.35.15 and 18.1.1.

[44] *retr*. 2.69(43): 'Duodecim ergo librorum sequentium primi quattuor continent exortum duarum civitatum, quarum est una dei altera huius mundi, secundi quattuor excursum earum sivi procursum, tertii vero qui et postremi debitos fines.'

[45] C. Lambot, 'Lettre inédite de S. Augustin relative au *De civitate Dei*', *RBén*, 51 (1939), 109–21; B. V. E Jones, 'The Manuscript Tradition of Augustine's *De civitate Dei*', *JTS* n.s., 16 (1965), 142–5; Henri-Irénée Marrou, 'La technique de l'édition à l'époque patristique', *V Chr*, 3 (1949), 217–24.

[46] A man by the name of Firmus, not the same as our converted Manichaean from the *Vita*. See Chapter 1, n. 49.

and ultimate destiny of the two cities). Therefore, the 'rise, career, and end' describes a progress within a narrative, but also defines the tripartite shape of two actual books, Augustine's *De civitate* and Possidius' *Vita Augustini*.[47]

In Augustine's view, this second half of the *De civitate* constituted the core of the project. One hundred years earlier, Lactantius wrote the *Divinae Institutiones*, the first three books of which acted as a kind of extended preface that refuted pagan religion and philosophy that was necessary before getting to the real purpose of the work. It is not until Book 4 that Lactantius began to speak of Christianity as the correct fusion of religion and wisdom.[48] Augustine's opening decade similarly dedicates its energies to refuting pagan systems. The twelve books remaining define and explain God's interaction with the world. That Possidius would use this phrase and speak of Augustine as 'predestined long ago and presented in his own time' ('praedestinati et suo tempore praesentati') means that he is a representative, or a microcosm, of Christianity as it is present in the world. The biography reflects upon all of history as experienced in the life of one man.[49]

Possidius places the *Vita* next to the second half of the *De civitate Dei* as texts to be compared. Augustine thought the *De civitate* to be his most ambitious work, as it sifted through much of the literary accomplishments of the pagan and Christian traditions. Augustine's ready use of source material was designed to sway and stagger his pagan readership. Augustine relied heavily on the works of Varro, a man, Augustine said, who read so much that he must have had no time to write, and who wrote so much that scarcely anyone could read it all.[50] The point is that Augustine had read it all, and it was at his disposal for explanation or refutation. Possidius, in turn, had Augustine's texts under his command, and that is why he repeats the compliment Augustine had paid to Varro: 'And so many things were dictated and published by [Augustine] and so many things were discussed in church, written down and amended,

---

[47] See Chapter 1, n. 173.

[48] Peter Garnsey, 'Lactantius and Augustine', in Alan K. Bowman et al. (eds.), *Representation of Empire: Roman and the Mediterranean World* (Oxford: Proceedings of the British Academy, 2002), 153–79, at 154.
See also *ep.* 184A, where the pattern of book segments emerges as Augustine approaches the completion of Book 14. The divide between Book 10 and what follows is crucial. 'We do not wish to give the impression of being satisfied with refuting the views of others without setting forth our own in this work.'

[49] Possidius repeats Augustine in the belief that the life of a human being retells the history of all mankind. See discussion in O'Donnell, *Augustine: A New Biography*, 303–307.

[50] *civ. Dei* 6.2: 'tam multa scripsit [Varro] quam multa vix quemquam legere potuisse credeamus.' Here in 6.2, Varro is lauded at length as the most erudite of Romans. It is through his books that he tried to save the gods, who were at risk of disappearing because of Roman indifference. See Paul C. Burns, 'Augustine's Use of Varro's Antiquitates Rerum Divinarum in his *De Civitate Dei*', *AugStud*, 32 (2001), 37–64.

whether against various heretics or expounded from the canonical books for the edification of the holy sons of the Church, that scarcely any student would be able to read and know them all' (*v. Aug.* 18.9).[51] Possidius grasped the width and breadth of the Augustinian corpus, and the *Vita* functioned as the passage into which initiates entered a larger textual world. The reference to Augustine's life as akin to the progress of the two cities says as much about Possidius' attitude toward the importance of his biography, as it does about Augustine as the embodiment of Christianity. For Possidius, the *Vita* was the inaugural moment for Augustinian studies.

[51] See Chapter 1, n. 158.

Part II

Possidius and the Legal Activities of North African Episcopate

The Life and Career of Possidius

The majority of the *Vita Augustini*'s modern reading audience is composed of those who study Augustine or the genre of hagiography. Both constituencies in the past have found Possidius' biography inadequate, whether in substance or accuracy. The history of Possidian scholarship is largely defined by the articulation or absolution of the author's perceived shortcomings. The dominant chord that still sounds expresses doubt whether Possidius was able to grasp Augustine's intellectual accomplishments, and if not, whether he ill-served his teacher with a recollected life that planed away his texture and depth. The consequent trajectory of scholarship, even for those trying to end the conversation, bends toward a discussion of Possidius the man: his education, his limitations, his capacity to understand. I have argued that Possidius wrote the *Vita* with deliberation. The changes imposed on Augustine's career as well as his interference with Augustine's way of seeing life as a cumulative experience constitute reactions to external criticism. The solutions Possidius offers may rightly be considered inferior to those preferred by Augustine, but of greater concern are the reasons behind his choices. Possidius is responding to the reception of Augustine's work during the first decades of the fifth century, and it was his opinion that Augustine's life and corpus needed stiffening.

An ambition for this book is to extricate the *Vita* from areas of analysis that have run their course. Questions of authorial competence can be dismissed by the use of evidence from the *Vita* itself, but only a review of his career will lay to rest any remaining assumptions that Possidius was a mediocre representative of the Catholic episcopate who must somehow be 'got round' when studying Augustine. It is indeed true that a man of stellar professional skills does not necessarily make a good biographer. One can also argue that another study of Possidius' life constitutes merely a homeopathic remedy to the others that have attributed the obscurities of the *Vita* to what are assumed to be the author's intellectual shortcomings. A story of a smart and successful bishop now replaces other views of the same man which arrive at different, and less flattering, conclusions. In this case, however, discussing the connection between the author and his creation is warranted. In establishing Possidius as a central figure in Catholic negotiations against opponents, the law and its solicitation become the basis for evaluating the thematic preoccupations of the *Vita*. From there, we can proceed from Possidius the individual to Possidius the representative of an episcopal culture that well understood legal processes and the documentation they required. It is by these that the Catholics, as well as the Donatists, tried to prove to representatives of the imperial government that they were the legitimate religion.

The Donatists were African Catholicism's primary focus in the late fourth and early fifth centuries. The Catholics often said that the scripture prophesied its own dissemination throughout the world, and that the party of Donatus occupied only one of the earth's corners. The Catholics, actively cultivating alliances with Christian communities outside Africa, believed that exclusivity in the face of scriptural promise refuted Donatist claims to be the true Church. Thus, the Catholics made a theological point when seeking to solicit support from the emperor. But the imperial court also constituted unpleasant historical and political realities for the Donatists, whose close affiliation with local and provincial magistrates had insulated them, politically and religiously, from external meddling for the past several decades.

The most famous of the Donatist allies are Firmus and his brother Gildo, the Moorish princes, who in succession commanded the armies of Africa. Gildo, for example, remained loyal to Emperor Theodosius while Maximus pushed for control of the west in 387–8, and was rewarded with rule over the African provinces. The Donatist episcopate, especially Optatus, the bishop of Timgad, enjoyed good relations with Gildo and his administration. As the Catholics would do in the first decade of the fifth century, the Donatists in the last decade of the fourth century capitalized on their alliance with the provincial government to pressure schismatic churches—including those we call Catholic, Rogatist, and Maximianist—into unity. Coercion applied either by the Donatist Church or by the African administration enforced the law. Gildo's subsequent unsuccessful revolt from Rome in 398 resulted in his execution and a sharp, and as it turned out, permanent drop in political stock for the Donatists.[1] Bishop Optatus died while in custody, and many of Gildo's followers lost the positions, land, and perks that had been the rewards for their support.

The tone of the surviving ancient evidence encourages modern readers to describe the time of Gildo and Optatus as a 'reign of terror', wherein local opportunists separated themselves from distinctly Roman administrative paradigms and randomly abused the representatives of a more civilized society, including landowners and clergy. This interpretation merely reproduces a picture of the world as conservative Catholic bishops were determined to have us

---

[1] Y. Modéran, 'Gildon, les Maures, et l'Afrique', *MÉFRA*, 101 (1989), 821–72.

see it.[2] Force exercised by the Donatists, including deployment of circumcellions acting under the orders of clergy, was well organized and, at the height of Donatism, sanctioned by provincial authorities.[3] The Donatists, recognized by the local courts as the true Catholics, applied pressure to possess the churches and the loyalty of those they considered schismatic Christians. Augustine's vituperation against Donatist 'outrages' often describes actions that, when the law finally turned in their favor, were equally pursued by the Catholics. When thinking about Gildo, and how he has been presented in the ancient literature, it is salutary to remember that a mere fifteen years after his fall, Heraclian, the *comes Africae* and an ally of the Catholics, also revolted against the emperor Honorius. Heraclian was defeated and killed. In the subsequent purges, two good friends of Augustine's, Flavianus Marcellinus and his brother Apringius, were arrested. One wonders if thoughts of Bishop Optatus, the disgraced friend of Gildo, entered Augustine's mind as he visited Marcellinus in prison. Bishops allied with the fallen could fall too, and, in the right circumstances, so the churches they represented. Augustine, a regular visitor to Carthage since the year of his ordination, rarely left Hippo after Marcellinus was executed in September 413.[4]

The point is that the Donatists and Catholics courted government authorities and utilized similar methods to gain access and influence. Donatist relations with the government were not limited to African personnel. They successfully presented cases before at least four different proconsuls in the 390s, one of them being the son of consul Mallius Theodorus, the very man who may have introduced Augustine to Neoplatonism in the late 380s. The Donatists sent embassies to the emperor, too, before and after having been declared heretics.[5] They well understood the ways of the world and were quite willing to call

---

[2] W. H. C. Frend, *The Donatist Church: A Movement of Protest in Roman North Africa* (Oxford: Clarendon Press, 1951; reprint 1971), 208–26; Serge Lancel, *Saint Augustine*, translated by Antonia Nevill (London: SCM Press, 2002), 170, and Michael Gaddis, *There Is No Crime for Those Who Have Christ: Religious Violence in the Christian Roman Empire* (Berkeley: University of California Press, 2005), 108.

[3] Leslie Dossey, 'Judicial Violence and the Ecclesiastical Courts in Late Antique North Africa', in Ralph W. Mathisen (ed.), *Law, Society, and Authority in Late Antiquity* (Oxford: Oxford University Press, 2001), 98–114.

[4] Peter Brown, *Augustine of Hippo: A Biography* (Berkeley: University of California Press, 1967; reprint 2000), 337–8 and James J. O'Donnell, *Augustine: A New Biography* (New York: Ecco, 2005), 225.

[5] One should not underestimate what personal contact with the emperor could accomplish, as by tradition they liked to make exceptions and bestow favors. The Donatists may have been aware that Constantine's threats against heretics did not apply to the Novatians because the emperor esteemed Acesius, their bishop in Constantinople (Soz. 2.32). Despite Theodosius the Great's rulings against heretics, he acknowledged a plea from Luciferians who petitioned him (see infra n. 13). For discussion of Donatist hopes to persuade the emperor of the rightness of their cause, see James S. Alexander, 'Count Taurinus and the Persecutors of Donatism', *ZAC*, 2 (1998), 247–67, esp. 249–51.

upon the administrative apparatus. Their expansively bureaucratic outlook, however, is rarely credited them. Stories of violent attacks by circumcellions, which are flavored by Augustine's forceful and repetitive rhetoric, become for modern readers their sole means of persuasion. We follow Augustine when we state that the Donatist episcopate—excitable, backwards, and reactionary—did not know, exactly, what to do in the face of Roman law. At the 411 conference, seven Donatist bishops spoke on behalf of their Church, and their performance is judged by the scholarship as it is by Augustine. They wasted time in efforts to mislead the listening public. Possessed of no sound legal knowledge, they pressed points that had little bearing on the case. It is Augustine who must provide explanations and 'corrections' to their bizarre tactics and muddled confusion.[6]

If the strategy the Donatists employed was the same as that of the Catholics, the question is why the Donatists eventually lost out. The political backlash after Gildo's downfall in 398 is an important event, but it is telling that one of the most powerful Donatist bishops who went before the African proconsul in 404 was surprised when the ruling went against him. The Catholic episcopate, which was not always unified about how to react to Donatist resistance, agreed that bypassing provincial authorities and appealing directly to the emperor offered the best course of action. They sent so many embassies to Rome and the court that the pope asked African bishops to set limits on how many of their number could approach him.[7] Circumnavigating the local enclaves of support the Donatists had cultivated was too effective to honor Pope Innocent's request. The key was to seek recognition beyond Africa: the scripture's ignorance of geographical borders worked in tandem with the emperor's secular rulings. These, too, applied to all Romans. Catholic appeals to court, which resulted in decrees and threats of punishments, eventually forced provincial administrators to retract their support from the Donatists. The Donatists, neither incompetent nor uncomprehending, resisted in kind, but were overwhelmed by the Catholic success in exposing Africa to outside authority.

---

[6] Cf. Caroline Humfress, 'A New Legal Cosmos: Late Roman Lawyers and the Early Medieval Church', in Peter Linehan and Janet L. Nelson (eds.), *The Medieval World* (New York: Routledge, 2001), 557–75, esp. 565, who recognizes the Donatist facility with law at the 411 conference. See also Maureen A. Tilley, 'Dilatory Donatists or Procrastinating Catholics: The Trial at the Conference of Carthage', *Church History*, 60 (1991), 7–19, who argues for deliberation in the Donatist arguments.

[7] *Concilia Africae, Registri Ecclesiae Carthaginensis Excerpta* 94. In August 405, at the Catholic bishops' meeting in Carthage, a letter from Pope Innocent was read out asking the bishops not to make trips to court so frequently on such light pretexts: 'ut episcopi ad transmarina pergere facile non debent.'

It is not without irony that Possidius has much the same kind of reputation for slowness and incomprehension that is still borne by the Donatists. His career, treated as an appendage of his mentor's, is thought to have been successful in that he followed orders well. Once alone and without direction after Augustine's death, he supposedly misinterpreted both the texts and the man who wrote them. In reality, the bishop of Calama was a successful tactician for the Catholic side and respected by the bishops in Augustine's circle. That he received a diocese in a predominantly Donatist area overseen by a highly popular and long-standing bishop, Crispinus, indicates the level of confidence his colleagues invested in him. Possidius preached to his congregation on doctrine and articulated the errors of Donatism, paganism, and Pelagianism. We have little idea of what his style of address was like, as not one of his sermons survives, but he must have been a polished speaker—quick-witted and fluent with scriptural citation. From the limited verbatim statements we possess, he also had a rough, confrontational edge. He traveled around Calama's environs and, as an evidence of his bold style, exhorted those in predominantly Donatist areas to convert. We know he ran his own monastery based on the rules governing the one at Hippo, and although he visited Augustine frequently and consulted the library there, his requests for material to be sent to him at Calama probably means the collection at his own basilica was respectable.[8] Possidius presided over his own court of civil law (the so-called *audientia epsicopalis*), provided food and shelter for the poor, and managed land that the Church owned in Calama's vicinity. He traveled to Carthage for annual Church councils and attended regional conferences overseen by the primate of Numidia. He was an important man who went about with an entourage, received and returned visits from Calama's municipal leaders, and could hold his own in any theological discussion.

His quotidian responsibilities as a bishop in a large town are of secondary importance to us, and perhaps to him, because the extant evidence, much of which he provides, delineates the unusual events in his life. Aside from writing letters to popes and helping to organize the 411 conference, Possidius went to the imperial court, where he met the praetorian prefect and Emperor Honorius. In 408, he visited Bishop Memorius, the father of Julian of Eclanum, and

---

[8] *ep.* 23*A. It is circumstantial evidence that marks Possidius as the recipient of this letter, but the argument as first put forward by Marie-François Berrouard and augmented by Serge Lancel is convincing. See Berrouard, 'L'Activité littéraire de saint Augustin du 11 septembre au 1ᵉʳ décembre 419 d'après la lettre 23*A à Possidius de Calama', in *Les Lettres de Saint Augustin découvertes par Johnannes Divjak: Communications presentees au colloque des 20 et 21 Septembre 1982* (Paris: Études Augustiniennes, 1983), 301–27 and Serge Lancel, 'Saint Augustin et la Maurétanie Cesarienne (2): L'affaire de l'évêque Honorius (automne 419–printemps 420) dans les nouvelles Lettes 22*, 23*, et 23* A', *RÉAug*, 30 (1984), 251–62.

Paulinus of Nola. That same trip may have occasioned his introduction to the contemporary and former consuls, Anicius Auchenius Bassus and Mallius Theodorus, respectively, both men good friends of Augustine's from their days together in Italy.[9] There is a distinct possibility that Pope Innocent accompanied Possidius to Ravenna in 410. He also seems to have been on friendly terms with Volusian, the uncle of Melania the Younger (*ep.* 137). As a bishop whose tenure spanned more than thirty years, Possidius experienced his share of unpleasantness, but adverse circumstances provided the occasions to make acquaintances with the greats of the world. Possidius was a resilient person whose stubbornness—the Romans would call it *instantia*—turned resistance to political advantage.

The next four chapters offer a partial reconstruction of Possidius' life between 395 and 411. His legal and diplomatic achievements during this time represent only a fraction of his life's activities, but the state of the evidence requires the focus to remain there. Limiting the chronological scope of inquiry is historically—and, for our purposes, literarily—felicitous, in that these years constitute bookends of the legal campaign against Donatism, and so their study can present Possidius' career and, more broadly, episcopal strategy in a comprehensive, sensible manner. We can see Possidius' accomplished handling of the law, and the crucial role it played in promoting Catholic ascendancy in the early fifth century. Looking back at Possidius through this kind of historical lens reveals to what extent the law informed his portrait of Augustine in the *Vita*. Concomitantly, the Donatists also emerge as legally minded tacticians, whose approach to imperial administrators, especially in the 390s, functioned as the pattern which the Catholics successfully copied.

In 403, the Catholics believed the magnitude of their disagreement with the Donatists was still of a provincial scale. They asked the African proconsul, Serenus, to help them arrange a conference with the Donatists in hopes that episcopal delegates chosen by their respective Churches could meet and settle the century-old differences.[10] It was a long history everyone knew, although the sides had different opinions about it. When the bishop of Carthage, Mensurius, died in around 308, his deacon, Caecilian, was elected as his replacement and ordained by three bishops, one of whom was Felix of Abthungi. Caecilian was not universally esteemed in Africa, and had rivals. There were also persistent

---

[9] Erika T. Hermanowicz, 'Book Six of Augustine's *De musica* and the Episcopal Embassies of 408', *AugStud*, 35 (2004), 165–98.

[10] Before this, the Catholic bishops had invited Donatist counterparts to public, one-on-one discussions. We know at least one occurred, with Fortunius, bishop of Thiave. The outcome was amiable but inconclusive (*ep.* 44). Several Donatist bishops turned down similar invitations, either for personal meetings or the public exchanges of letters (including Proculianus, bishop of Hippo [*ep.* 33] and Crispinus, bishop of Calama [*ep.* 51]).

rumors that Felix of Abthungi had cooperated with the Roman officials during Diocletian's persecution. If true, this would mean for many clergy that his efficacy in performing sacraments, including that of ordination, had been compromised. A group of about seventy bishops met and canceled Caecilian's election. They elevated in his place one of the former bishop Mensurius' lectors, Majorinus.

In the ensuing confusion as to just who was now the bishop of Carthage, those who rejected the election of Caecilian appealed to Constantine. The emperor, who was known to dislike what he considered unimportant quibbles over ecclesiastical procedure, ruled on the side of simplicity by upholding the election of Caecilian. In several subsequent hearings, Caecilian and Felix of Abthungi were declared innocent of any wrongdoing. Rebaptism, which for the Catholics in Possidius' day was a major point of theological disagreement between the two Churches, was not as controversial an issue in the first decade of the fourth century. African bishops often repeated the baptisms of those thought to require it. It was the pro-Caecilian group who at this point began to follow the practice of other areas in the empire by insisting that there must only be one.[11] By 403 the Catholics, as we now call them, were still employing versions of the two-pronged argument against the Donatists that had emerged from the earliest days of the conflict. The first was theological, wherein they argued that humans did not have the power to compromise God's efficacy in the performance of sacraments. Thus, one baptism was sufficient. The second was historical. Whatever the arguments put forward about the crimes committed by Caecilian and Felix, they had been declared innocent by the emperor, a council held at Rome, and an episcopal tribunal at Arles comprised of thirty-three bishops. Moreover, the figure of Caecilian and the complaints about him to Constantine countered any Donatist objections to Catholic requests for imperial intervention. The Donatists had gone to the authorities first.

Such were the arguments that the Catholics planned to employ in their debate in 403, but the Donatists refused to meet with them.[12] Proconsul Serenus, who had served in Africa for many years, and was perhaps sympathetic to the Donatist Church (or, more accurately, loyal to the men who served that Church), did not insist. The parameters of the subsequent conference in 411

---

[11] See J. Patout Burns, 'On Re-Baptism: Social Organization in the Third Century Church', *JECS*, 1 (1993), 387–403, and Robert A. Markus, 'Africa and the Orbis Terrarum: The Theological Problem', in Pierre-Yves Fux, Jean-Michel Roessli, Otto Wermelinger (eds.), *Augustinus Afer: Saint Augustin, Africanité et Universalité: Actes du Colloque International, Alger-Annaba, 1–7 Avril 2001* (Fribourg: Éditions Universitaires Fribourg Suisse, 2003), 323.

[12] See *Concilia Africae, Registri Ecclesiae Carthaginensis Excerpta* 92, where the Catholic invitation to the debate declares that they should talk about 'what separates your communion from ours' so that this 'rusty old error may receive its end'.

were identical, save this time the members of a Catholic embassy that included Possidius asked the emperor to ensure Donatist attendance. Both sides were again invited to choose delegates to present arguments. The Catholics also anticipated that the debate would follow those two distinct lines already mentioned, the first being a theological argument (identified by the Catholics as the *causa ecclesiae*) as to what constituted the Church: its boundaries, its purity, how sin affected its well-being. The second (dubbed by the Catholics the *causa Caeciliani*) was historical. Reminders of the rulings on Caecilian's innocence accompanied the insistence that the Donatists were the first to appeal to the emperor. The Catholic rebuke that the Donatists first subjected the Church to the scrutiny of outside parties was quite audacious, as the crucial difference between 403 and 411 was the Catholic recognition that external rulings hurt the Donatist position, prompting their consequent efforts to involve Honorius in the dispute. The historical argument was also extraordinarily effective. The conference of 411 was clearly a legal hearing, convened by a rescript and overseen by a judge. The Donatists certainly saw themselves embroiled in a court case and came prepared to defend themselves accordingly. The Catholics, already supported by the emperor and his rescripts, ingeniously protested that the conference was about history, not law. History allowed them to accuse the Donatists of being the instigators of the entire conflict. Argument by law would have revealed the Catholics as plaintiffs, as they were the ones who asked the emperor to issue the rescript that convened this particular conference. Honorius obliged the Catholics in that he not only gave them the authority to haul up the Donatists in front of a judge, but also allowed them to escape the undesirable appellation of prosecutor, and by extension, Christian persecutor.

Despite their arguments from history, it was the promulgation of legislation in the catholics' favor that separated the disappointment of 403 from the success at the conference of 411. The strategy the Catholics developed and refined between these years consisted of seeking heresy convictions against Donatists by asking for confirmation of laws that had been previously promulgated, but at the same time requesting that they be widened in scope and applied anew. The Catholics constructed their petitions by taking laws, including those that were not specific to the Donatists, editing and excerpting them, and then resubmitting them as part of a request to have them 'reissued' to account for their Donatist opponents. Roman law was actually very flexible in solicitation and enforcement. We know that in the age of Theodosius the Great many kinds of legally designated 'heretical' Christians presented themselves to judges as Nicene orthodox while accusing rivals of deviating from true belief. After Theodosius demanded that all his subjects observe Catholic rites, many representatives from various groups approached local and provincial judges armed with Theodosius' laws. They sought legitimacy for themselves as well as directives that could be used to push local governments to aid them in the requisitioning of property, churches, and adherents from other churches.[13] It was a matter of fitting themselves to the text of the law and then pointing out the errors—whether true or not—practiced by others. Rules as to what qualified as evidence to prove their points were surprisingly liberal. We know that the Donatists presented transcripts from their own councils to African judges who based their rulings on the self-proclaimed assurances that they, the Donatists, and not their rivals, the Maximianists, were the Catholic party. The records of debates between Augustine and Manichaeans, Donatists, and Arians are precisely dated so that they could serve as evidence in court. A bishop's record of dealings with his own congregants (*acta*) likewise qualified (see *Ep.* 22*), as did theological treatises, such as Augustine's work *On Baptism*.[14]

Within ten years of the initial attempts to make the law speak on their behalf, the Catholics had a slate of legislation at their disposal for use against the Donatists. On the whole, one could argue that they were fairly careful in its use, especially as laws emerging from the consistory carried heavy fines for heresy and promises of physical punishment for those who attacked clergy. The Catholics learned how to negotiate at all levels: to solicit the imperial consistory to issue laws they wanted, threaten their opponents with their implementation, but negotiate with local and provincial magistrates in order to mitigate the force of the punishments. We know that during these years Augustine was not interested in corporal aspects of the law, and he told his friends in the African administration that other bishops, too, would be hesitant to prosecute when they knew that those whom they brought to court might be beaten or condemned under a capital sentence.

The bishops' advertised temperance, however, obscured the amount of room they allowed for hard-line bishops to pursue Donatists more aggressively. For years, the Catholics tried to activate Theodosius' law on heretics against the Donatists. Augustine made repeated assurances that this law was

---

[13] See the letter of Marcellinus and Faustinus to Emperor Theodosius (CSEL 35.1), called the *Libellus precum* and dated to 384. These presbyters were what we call Luciferian Christians, but they complained that numerous members of other, heretical, churches were claiming themselves to be Catholics in order to take possession of churches ('nihilominus hi omnes de vestris gloriantur edictis et sibi ecclesias vindicant'). These included Origenists, Apollinarists, and Anthropomorphites.

For discussion, see Neil B. McLynn, '"Genere Hispanus": Theodosius, Spain, and Nicene Orthodoxy', in Kim Bowes and Michael Kilikowski (eds.), *Hispania in Late Antiquity* (Boston: Brill, 2005), 77–120, esp. 108–11.

[14] Caroline Humfress, Forensic Practice in the Development of Roman and Ecclesiastical Law in Late Antiquity with Special Reference to the Prosecution of Heresy (dissertation, Cambridge University, 1998), 243. See also E. Volterra, 'Appunti intorno all'intervento del vescovo nei processi contro gli eretici', *BIDR*, 42 (1934), 453–68.

to be invoked only when Catholic clerics became the victims of attacks; that is, as it was part of a strategy to reduce violence, only the Donatist bishops in dioceses where assaults had taken place would be brought to court and charged. In 404, Possidius submitted such a case to the African proconsul after he had been assaulted in small hamlet outside Calama. The incident was also brought to the attention of the emperor. Honorius ruled that the Donatists were indeed heretics, subject to Theodosius' law of 392, and thus their clergy were liable to heavy financial penalties. The stipulations, Augustine said, which were necessary to invoke this law, however, constituted no part of Honorius' renewed decree. Despite explicit assurances as to the limited circumstances under which the law was to be activated, the fact was that now any Donatist bishop (or Donatist, for that matter) could be called forth on a charge of heresy at any time. The Catholics were careful to temper execution of sentences, but they reserved for themselves a great deal of flexibility so that they could respond in stronger terms if they deemed them advantageous.

Augustine and his episcopal allies shied away from soliciting laws forbidding repetition of baptism. These had been promulgated as early as the 370s and entailed fines and property restrictions against all those who practiced or witnessed baptismal reiteration. As stated earlier, additional baptisms had long been part of the two-pronged attack on Donatism, so Catholic hesitation here may seem surprising. Augustine himself said that he wanted to rouse laws that would target only Donatist clergy, not the general population. Extant laws against rebaptism affected laypersons, while the legislation against heretics that interested Augustine focused on bishops. This serves as a partial explanation for the preference, but it remains unsatisfactory in light of the fact that the Catholics wanted Donatism declared heretical. That would mean that all anti-heretical legislation promulgated in the past could be used as leverage against the general population. We can point to this as another example of the maneuverability which the Catholic bishops liked to reserve for themselves, but one may also speculate that Augustine and his colleagues were not interested in laws against rebaptism because they had proven ineffective in the past. Augustine's letters, sermons, and treatises are replete with scriptural explanations as to why the Donatists adhered to wrong belief and practice, but it is striking that these theological arguments were not central to the Catholic pleas in the courts. Instead, the argument became one about stubbornness. The Catholics argued that those in the Church who disagreed over personnel and administration (technically schismatics) should be considered heretics if the quarrel remained unaddressed and unresolved for too long.[15] This new approach underscores the

---

[15] *Cresc.* 2.7(9). The idea was adopted by the emperor and employed as his explanation for promulgating the Edict of Unity (*CTh.* 16.6.4).

intensity of the Catholic desire to force the Donatists into debate, and indicates the Donatists had remained unassailable on theological grounds. The success in adopting this new tactic, including a definition of heresy that differed from all those previous, also reveals the extent of the law's flexibility. Heresy had no set definition, and could accept any number of interpretive accretions.

The Catholics secured several victories, especially the promulgation of the Edict of Unity in early 405, after they began to frequent the imperial court. The success they enjoyed was often resisted at the local level. African denizens and administrators alike tried—sometimes successfully—to ignore legal pressures exerted on them by Catholic interests. A prime example involves Possidius' unfortunate experiences in his own town. The residents of Calama were celebrating in the streets on 1 June 408. When Possidius tried to stop them, they rioted. They set his basilica on fire and murdered one of his clerics. Possidius turned to the local magistrates for vindication, but they ignored him and the law he invoked. Coincident with the unrest in Calama was an upsurge in anti-Catholic violence across Africa. News arrived that the western administration had been purged and that Stilicho was now dead. The Donatists anticipated the cancellation of Stilicho's legislation, including those measures directed against them. In the heady days of rumor and hope for release, two Catholic bishops were murdered and three others were seriously wounded. Although the Catholics had at their disposal several laws, including one that had been very recently posted in Carthage that renewed extant laws against heretics (including Donatists), the Catholic bishops thought it best to send Possidius to inform the imperial consistory of events in Africa and to receive new laws from the emperor. He was not disappointed and came away with a new declaration of a capital sentence against those who dared to lay violent hands on Catholic bishops.

Possidius returned to Africa after March 409, but soon boarded another ship for Italy when news arrived that Honorius had issued a new law guaranteeing people the right dedicate themselves to whatever form of Christianity they thought best.[16] Honorius' seemingly inexplicable reversal was more likely an exception he made for those at court who were not Catholic, but whose services he valued.[17] Like the Catholics, the Donatists regularly intercepted news coming from Ravenna. They interpreted this particular ruling broadly, as applicable to *them*. This was only correct, as Honorius seems

---

[16] *Concilia Africae, Registri Ecclesiae Carthaginensis Excerpta* 107: 'lex data est, ut libera voluntate quis cultum christianitatis exciperet.'

[17] A. C. De Veer, 'Une mesure de tolérance de l'Empereur Honorius', *Revue des études byzantines*, 24 (1966), 189–95, and Monceaux, *Histoire Littéraire de l'Afrique Chrétienne depuis les Origins jusqu'a l'Invasion Arabe* (Paris: Éditions Ernest Leroux, 1912–1923; reprint Brussels: Culture et Civilization, 1966), iv, 261. For discussion, see Chapter 6, 190.

to not have specified that it was meant to be an isolated declaration. The Donatists disseminated copies of the law around Africa and, as in the past, probably appeared before local magistrates and the proconsul in order to reclaim confiscated basilicas and property. In response, Possidius and three other bishops sought another audience with Honorius, and they asked him to appoint a moderator for an official conference between the Catholics and Donatists that would put an end, finally, to the controversy. The emperor commissioned Marcellinus to oversee this meeting, whose purpose, he openly proclaimed, was to suppress the Donatist heresy. Despite the sound efforts by the leading Donatist bishops to deflate the victory promised to the Catholics at the conference of 411, the legal injunctions that predetermined the winner proved insurmountable.

In fewer than ten years, the Catholic episcopate broke Africa's majority Christian religion. The Donatists certainly did not disappear.[18] In some areas, they received support from patrons who protected them from the scrutiny of imperial administrators.[19] Catholic bishops continued to cajole, and occasionally congratulated each other over conversions achieved without recourse to physical means.[20] Even the *Vita* allows the story to continue with a reunion between Augustine and the Donatist bishop Emeritus in 418 (*v. Aug.* 14). Emeritus still rejected Marcellinus' ruling, but the law bid him to remain silent now. Possidius' point was that Augustine worked in conjunction with both scriptural and secular law to affirm orthodoxy. Residual antipathy was of minor consequence in the face of imperial rulings.

As we proceed from the first literary–critical section of this book to the second section, which investigates the legal activities of Possidius and the North African episcopate, it is important to remember that the law comprises more than portions of the biography's linear narrative. What happened in the courts and the effect of the emperor's decrees occupy several chapters of the *Vita*, but the law functions on another, deeper level of the biography, giving the whole

---

[18] See, for example, Robert A. Markus, 'Country Bishops in Byzantine Africa', in Derek Baker (ed.), *The Church in Town and Countryside* (Oxford: B. Blackwell, 1979), 1–15.

[19] *ep.* 28*.1: Augustine to Novatus, the bishop of Sitifis in Mauretania Sitifensis, dated to the year 418. Augustine here congratulates Novatus on the Catholic reclamation of formerly Donatist churches, along with most of their congregations. 'The only exceptions were a small number of officials whom an intervention of the judge made more recalcitrant and alienated, as it were, from the constraints of the law.' Augustine goes on to recommend to these holdouts a reading of the proceedings of the 411 conference so that they may become aware of eternal *and* secular law.

[20] See C. Lepelley, 'Trois Documents méconnus sur l'Histoire sociale et religieuse de l'Afrique romaine tardive, retrouvés parmi les *Spuria* de Sulpice Sévère', *AntAfr*, 25 (1989), 235–62, esp. 252–7 and Peter Brown, *Authority of the Sacred* (Cambridge: Cambridge University Press, 1995), 43–4.

purpose and shape. To explain, I want to go back again to Orosius' experiences in the East (last mentioned in this book's introduction) when he presented the bishops a dossier of documents which had been compiled by the African episcopate.[21] These included letters and treatises from Augustine as well as the transcripts from the Catholic council of 411 (not to be confused with the conference of 411) that articulated the deficiencies in Pelagius' beliefs. When presented with these papers, Pelagius asked: 'But who is Augustine to me?'[22] Augustine is too important an arbiter of doctrine to be dismissed so abruptly, so the question seems rather strange to us, but Pelagius' bemusement is perfectly reasonable. As far as he was concerned, the matter was between him and the tribunal he faced. That Augustine's writings or those of another nonscriptural author should be introduced as authorities through whose aid Pelagius could be judged, was an unfamiliar practice. John, bishop of Jerusalem, who ran the proceedings, was equally perplexed. He answered Pelagius' question by saying: 'I am Augustine', which, for him, meant his presence carried the greatest authority among those gathered. Orosius believed that this kind of personal *auctoritas* only could skew the proceedings. He responded: 'If you assume the person of Augustine, follow the opinion of Augustine.'[23] This is an interesting moment of cultural dissonance where identifying the locus of power ranges between human and textual agents. Orosius insisted that Augustine was what he wrote, and that his textual opinion could stand alone as the accusing party in this hearing. John of Jerusalem found this equally strange: since it was Orosius who stood before the bishops, it was Orosius who should clarify and present accusations, if accusations were to be made (4–5). Orosius instead pointed to the documents he carried. He did not need to say anything. The words of Augustine, Jerome, and the transcripts of the synod of Carthage that ruled against Pelagius' protégé, Caelestius, were enough: 'These fathers, whom the universal church of the world approves, whose communion you rejoice to belong, has declared that these beliefs are worthy of condemnation. It is right that we hearken to these judges. Why do you ask their sons what they think when you can hear what the fathers have decided?' (5.3)[24]

---

[21] Orosius presented these at the diocesan synod at Jerusalem on 30 July 415.

[22] 'Et quis est mihi Augustinus?' Orosius, *Liber apologeticus* 4.1 (CSEL 5). Orosius says that Pelagius' question shocked the audience ('universi acclamarent blasphemantem in episcopum'), but this does not tally with the reaction of Bishop John of Jerusalem who paid little attention to the African dossier. 'Universi' probably means Orosius and those who accompanied him.

[23] '"Augustinus ego sum", ut scilicet persona quasi praesentis assumpta liberius ex auctoritate eius qui laedebatur ignosceret et dolentium animos temperaret. Cui mox a nobis dictum est: "si Augustini personam sumis, Augustini sequere sententiam."'

[24] 'Patres, quos universa per Orbem Ecclesia probat, quorum communioni vos adhaerere gaudetis, damnabilia haec esse dogmata decreverunt: illis probantibus nos oboedire dignum est. Cur interrogas filios quid sentiant, cum patres audias quid decernant?'

Possidius and Orosius were at the forefront of a new cultural phenomenon. Council decisions had always been of great importance, but in the decades following Augustine's death, the consultation of 'canonical' writers and the weighing of their collective opinion became essential in making theological arguments. The emerging dialogue among texts is an outcome, at least in part, of the legal activities of the Catholic Church. Aside from the use of the scripture, to determine what constituted truth now required the collection and comparison of documents, an understanding of precedent, and recognition that while some theologians were more authoritative than others, to speak in unison constituted the best position. A consensus of texts as proof of doctrine is not far removed from the assembling of historical and councilor dossiers for arguing in court. What constituted legitimate evidence, including treatises, letters, as well as council and debate transcripts (i.e. the contents of a bishop's library) renders even closer the connection between the textual and legal cultures.

The *Vita* memorialized Augustine as a body of texts. In Possidius' opinion, the collection was too unwieldy and too inconsistent if left to stand on its own, so in order that the books make a presentable defense for Augustine, they had to be properly assembled and simplified. Once this was done, the edited texts remained unchanged, suspended above the events they depicted as well as the author who wrote them, as it was these that were received by external parties to act as edifying arbiters of truth. The *Vita* functions like a well-ordered catalogue of documents. Possidius presents to us a narrative that is built from texts, a collection of evidence whose acceptance confirms our understanding of right belief.

3

Donatists, Catholics, and Appeals to the Law: 392–404

In the early months of 404, Possidius persuaded the proconsul of Africa to rule that Crispinus, the Donatist bishop of Calama, was a heretic. This is the first time a representative from the imperial government declared that the Donatists were subject to heresy laws, as well as the first time since the reign of Julian that the Donatists sent a delegation to the emperor to appeal a provincial verdict.[1] Their antipathy for secular law is well known. They exhorted all to obey the scripture, not the legislation promulgated by emperors.[2] Their anti-imperial stance, however, was, and still is, exaggerated. Donatists and Catholics alike sought the support of the government. Both knew the benefits of imperial recognition as well as the advantages gleaned from solicitation of favorable laws. Prior to 404, the Donatists had enjoyed liberal treatment from African administrations, and the bishop's success against Crispinus may be attributable, in part, to the lessons in law the Catholics had received from watching the Donatists in action during the 390s.

The kind of pressure Possidius exerted on Crispinus is only one episode in a series of attempts by both sides to engage the law. Donatist and Catholic posturing, especially in the years 403 and 404, resulted in numerous councils, aborted negotiations, an increase in violence, and embassies sent to the imperial court. Heightened diplomatic and physical struggle with the aim of receiving affirmation from external authority ultimately proved to the Catholics' advantage, and Possidius' victory can be understood as a culmination of these efforts. What came before, however, were repeatedly unsuccessful attempts by the Catholics to gain what the bishop of Calama at last attained.

The majority of evidence we have about the Catholics' legal relationship with the Donatists is from Augustine's writings, and it is well known that

---

[1] *en. Ps.* 36.2.18; *c. litt. Petil.* 2.92.203.
[2] See, for example, *s. Denis* 19, where Crispinus, the bishop of Calama, is quoted by Augustine as exhorting the proconsul to judge according to the laws of the scripture, not of emperors. For the passage, see infra n. 68.

his willingness to apply coercion against them hardened over time.[3] In 417, Augustine wrote that a decade ago he believed that Donatists should not be forced: conversion or transference should be a deliberate act prompted by individual conscience. He had since changed his mind (*ep.* 185). Forced unity, he concluded, was a sound practice, and best achieved through financial pressure as stipulated by imperial law. Donatist bishops, along with their congregations, could be made subject to the Catholic Church through threats of monetary penalties.

The bishop of Hippo is one of the few writers in antiquity whose surviving works, composed throughout a long life, allow one to follow the shifts in his personal beliefs. Modern readers therefore often regard Augustine's discussions about coercion as a distinct feature of his personal character, and a matter of private struggle. Here, however, Augustine's own ethical perspective cedes to the construction of a larger historical picture. Coercion, one of its forms being the promulgation of laws against religious rivals, was integral to the episcopal culture of North Africa as Donatists and Catholics repeatedly sought legitimacy through external recognition. The image of the bishop of Hippo as a lone figure on an empty landscape shaping, for better or worse, the future of inquisition is set aside to accommodate the numbers of bishops—Augustine's friends, colleagues, *and* opponents—whose respective efforts to protect the interests of their parties necessitated the solicitation of local and imperial support.

In tracing the establishment of legal relationships between center and periphery, I want to begin with two points of clarification. First, Roman law as promulgated by the consistory was brutal in its threats and punishments. Some readers who study the Theodosian Code, for example, may think that corporal punishment followed convictions of heresy, and that consequently Augustine tried to halt executions and beatings on behalf of those Donatists who were convicted of heresy *alone*. This is not true. For the years discussed here (392–411), it should be understood that Donatist allegiance, when recognized as heretical, was punished by fines.[4] Religious tensions sometimes resulted in violence, and many Catholic bishops wanted legislation enacted that would target entire Donatist congregations in order to stop it. Augustine

---

[3] *ep.* 185.25. Peter Brown, 'St. Augustine's Attitude to Religious Coercion', *JRS*, 54 (1964), 107–16 remains the definitive work. Emilien Lamirande offers an overview of the scholarship in *Church, State, and Toleration: An Intriguing Change of Mind in Augustine* (Villanova: Villanova University Press, 1975), 7–28. See now Frederick H. Russell, 'Persuading the Donatists: Augustine's Coercion by Words', in W. Klingshirn and M. Vessey (eds.), *The Limits of Ancient Christianity* (Ann Arbor: University of Michigan Press, 1999), 115–30.

[4] Slaves, of course, were an exception, as well as, after 405, some procurators and lessees on private and imperial land, but my point is that Donatist clergy were not punished corporally for being Donatist clergy.

favored financial penalties only against the bishops in whose dioceses violence occurred. For those who committed acts of battery and murder, he interceded on behalf of the convicted to thwart severe penalties. He asked the courts not to use corporal punishment specifically in cases of violence against Catholic clerics. He later admitted, however, that the only way some people could be curbed was through salutary beating.[5] For these kinds of measures he asked that punishment be imposed with restraint.[6]

Second, it is also important to keep in mind that the court of the bishops, the so-called *audientia episcopalis*, plays almost no role in the present discussion.[7] The attacks against Catholic clergy could constitute grounds for charges of *iniuria* and *vis* (both of these prosecutable in criminal courts) and although the *audientia* was reserved for civil cases, bishops could hear criminal cases when actions of clergy were in question.[8] But this is all beside the point. The Donatists, like the Catholics, operated their own courts at this time, but neither Church would have consented to being judged by a bishop of another party (i.e. Donatists settling the matter with a Catholic bishop presiding, Catholics

---

[5] See *ep.* 9*.2 where a prominent layman raped a nun in church, was discovered by some monks, and then was beaten by them. He protested his treatment to the pope who, apparently not working with full information, ordered the monks to be punished. Augustine was angry: 'What, then, is a bishop or what are other clerics going to do in the case of such crimes and not just any sins of human beings? We must, first, ask this of those who think that no corporal punishment at all should be imposed on anyone, especially on account of the sort of persons who do not have the least care about ecclesiastical communication at all, either because they are not Christians or Catholics or because they live such lives that they might as well not be.'

[6] See *ep.* 133, where Augustine writes to Marcellinus about what should be done about the Donatist gang, led by clerics, who murdered the Catholic priest, Restitutus, and badly wounded another priest, Innocentius. Here, Augustine seems to be endorsing penal work (the mines?) as punishment, but hopes that no death sentences will be carried out. This letter is interesting for another reason: it is one of the few places where we are told it was local law enforcement, and not Catholic clergy, who brought the charges.

[7] There never was any indication that any legal proceedings between Catholics and Donatists would be heard in the bishop's court (called by modern scholars the *audientia episcopalis*), the exception being when Crispinus, the Donatist presbyter, was subject to discipline for beating the Catholic bishop, Possidius. Crispinus, the bishop, wanted to keep any disciplinary measures confined to the oversight of the Donatist Church. For general discussion, see Noel Lenski, 'Evidence for the *Audientia Episcopalis* in the New Letters of Augustine', in Ralph W. Mathisen (ed.), *Law, Society, and Authority in Late Antiquity* (Oxford: Oxford University Press, 2001), 87–97.

[8] In Justinian's *Digest* 47.10.11, *iniuria*, while it can be a criminal offence, was most often considered a delict (a misdeed prosecuted through a private lawsuit—a civil case) that fell under the jurisdiction of the *lex Aquilia*. Such attacks as organized by the Donatists—coordinated and for specific purposes—could technically fall under the criminal charge of *vis* as well as the criminal charge of *iniuria* (as outlined by Sulla's *lex Cornelia de iniuriis*) because of the extent to which these Donatist attacks were designed to humiliate the victim. See Bruce Frier, *A Casebook on the Roman Law of Delict* (Atlanta: Scholars Press, 1989), 195; and O. F. Robinson, *The Criminal Law of Ancient Rome* (London: Duckworth, 1995), 41–51.

being heard and judged by a Donatist bishop, or some combination thereof). In the end, it was paramount to have these cases heard in government courts. Any change in law, or conversely, its preservation, needed to be elicited from, or validated by, imperial officials, optimally the emperor himself. While Catholic strategy demanded imperial recognition, the Donatist response required protection against Catholic infringement on their legal status.

Despite our reliance on him for information, Augustine is not the focus of this chapter, nor is justice as it was exercised in episcopal courts. Our attention turns to Roman law and the clerical hierarchy that sought to utilize it. Catholic and Donatist bishops were highly litigious, but so much evidence has been lost on the Donatist side that it is difficult to do them justice. We know that both parties circulated letters publicly, recorded their debates, coordinated responses, utilized documentation as proof to inquirers, and sent embassies to the emperor.[9]

In order to solicit the promulgation of general legislation against the Donatists, the Catholics argued to have extant general laws expanded in definition and category, and they also manipulated and exploited imperial rescripts, which technically could not be used as precedents when they were serving as personalized answers or favors to individuals. Catholics engaged in systematic application of two laws in particular. Neither initially had anything to do with the Donatists—as these laws targeted heretics and the Donatists did not fall under that category—but by forced association, manipulation of meaning, and rhetorical persuasion, the Catholics convinced imperial representatives to make the Donatists subject to these laws.[10] Catholic success was, therefore, largely attributable to the inherent malleability of Roman law and the tenacity of the group determined to shape it. In the struggle for souls among the residents of North Africa, the Catholics did not mind stretching either the law or the truth.

ATTEMPTING TO ROUSE THE LAW

Augustine continually impressed upon his audience that the Catholics always had numerous legal options to prosecute the Donatists. The assertion

---

[9] For Augustine's influence on the decisions rendered at the annual Catholic councils, which could have legal implications because of subsequent decisions to send council representatives to the court, see C. Munier, 'L'influence de saint Augustin sur la législation ecclésiastique de son temps', in Pierre-Yves Fux, Jean-Michel Roessli, and Otto Wermelinger (eds.), *Augustinus Afer: Saint Augustin, Africanité et Universalité: Actes du Colloque International, Alger-Annaba, 1–7 Avril 2001* (Fribourg: Éditions Universitaires Fribourg Suisse, 2003), 109–23.

[10] Caroline Humfress, 'Roman Law, Forensic Argument and the Formation of Christian Orthodoxy (III–VI Centuries)', in S. Elm, É. Rebillard, and A. Romano (eds.), *Orthodoxie, Christianisme, Histoire* (Paris: École Française de Rome, 2000), 125–47.

is false. In the late 390s and early 400s, the Catholics asked many times that their rivals be subject to imperial heresy laws, but their efforts were unsuccessful. Augustine's claims to have the law on his side only began to appear, it is important to note, when Catholics garnered their first successes against the Donatists.[11] In the *Contra epistulam Parmeniani*, recently re-dated from 398–400 to 404 or even 405,[12] Augustine said that no one was ignorant of the numerous imperial laws which could be applied against the Donatists.[13] In about 406, Augustine wrote to the Donatist grammarian, Cresconius, that the Catholics had no lack of laws; they simply remained quiet in their hands.[14] These treatises (*Contra epistulam Parmeniani* and *Contra Cresconium*) look back from a perspective of triumph: the Edict of Unity of early 405 (which Augustine would know of while writing the *Contra Cresconium*); the episcopal embassy sent to Honorius in June 404, which had prompted the promulgation of the 405 legislation; and, finally, the judgment in favor of Possidius against Crispinus in 404. Augustine's boast is that the Donatists were always liable to a slate of laws, but that the Catholics refrained from pressing charges.

To the contrary, all other evidence indicates that before 404, each time the Catholics attempted to prosecute the Donatists (or threaten prosecution), they referred to two laws only: either the law of 381 that restricted property rights of Manichaeans (this will be discussed later), or the Theodosian law against heretics issued in 392 (we know it in the *Theodosian Code*

---

[11] Emin Tengström, *Donatisten und Katholiken: soziale, wirtschaftliche und politische Aspekte einer nordafrikanischen Kirchenspaltung* (Göteborg: Elanders Boktryckeri Aktiebolag, 1964), 102–4, who in disagreeing with Frend, argues that during 395–401, there were no legal victories by Catholics over the Donatists.

For more examples of Augustine's claims to legal backing, see *ep*. 88.6: 'De nobis ergo quid queramini, non habes et tamen ecclesiae mansuetudo etiam ab his imperatorum iussionibus omnino conquieverat, nisi vestri clerici et Circumcelliones per suas immanissimas inprobitates furiosasque violentias quietam nostram perturbantes atque vastantes haec in vos *recoli et moveri coegissent*' ('You have no complaint to make of us, and the mildness of the Church would even have allowed these decrees of the emperors to remain inactive, if your clerics and circumcellions had not forced their *revival and renewal* against you'). See also *s. Denis* 19, *Cresc.* 3.44 (48), and 3.43 (47) for statements regarding numerous legal means in Catholic possession, but which carry no factual weight, whatsoever.

[12] Alfred Schindler pushes the date to late 404–early 405, 'Die Unterscheidung von Schisma und Haresie in Gesetzgebung und Polemik gegen den Donatismus', in Ernst Dassman and K. Suso Frank (eds.), *Pietas: Festschrift für Berhard Kötting* (Münster: Aschendorffsche Verlagsbuchhandlung, 1980), 227–36, esp. 231–3. Dolbeau and Hombert are more cautious, preferring the early months of 404. See François Dolbeau, *Vingt-six Sermons au Peuple d'Afrique* (Paris: Institut d'Etudes Augustiniennes, 1996), 358–9 and Pierre-Marie Hombert, *Nouvelles Recherches de la Chronologie Augustinienne* (Paris: Institut d'Etudes Augustinienne, 2000), 89–91.

[13] 1.12.19: 'Aliorum autem imperatorum leges quam vehementes adversus eos latae sint quis ignorat?'

[14] *Cresc.* 3.47 (51): 'leges quae non deerant, sed quasi deessent in nostris manibus quiescebant.'

as 16.5.21).[15] The challenge was to obtain the assent of Roman administrators that the Donatists were, in fact, heretics. They were the dominant Church in Africa and had proved themselves in several proconsuls' courts as deserving the name 'Catholic'. In urging the law to take under its jurisdiction a group not intended for inclusion at the time of promulgation, the Church that we now call Catholic engaged in a forceful rhetoric designed to shape in the minds of all parties that previously separate categories were now synonymous.[16] The laws were not sleeping in Catholic hands. The bishops, in fact, had tried very hard to rouse them, but they did not have legal options when it came to prosecuting Donatists on the basis of religious infractions, specifically heresy. The gap between the intent of the law and how (and against whom) the Catholics wanted that law applied necessitated intense rhetorical persuasion, a legal swimming against the current. Repeated reference to the law, presented as fact but working as rhetorical possibility, corrects Augustine's assurances that the Catholics were given optimal legal freedom but operated with restraint. It took much time and effort for them to gain a footing against the Donatists.

THEODOSIUS' LAW OF 392

Theodosius' law of 392 stipulated that heretical clergy—those who had been ordained and had the power to ordain—were subject to a fine of ten pounds of gold.[17] Landowners and procurators of imperial estates who knowingly allowed heretics to conduct services on those estates would pay the same fee.

---

[15] When I refer to laws in the *Theodosian Code* as well as the Sirmondian Constitutions, it should be understood that the people described in this chapter are not posting, distributing, and reading these texts per se. The Constitutions and the *Code* constitute collections of imperial laws and letters gathered and edited after the events of which we speak. For the *Theodosian Code*, see Tony Honoré, 'The Making of the Theodosian Code', ZRG, 103 (1986), 133–221 and John F. Matthews, *Laying Down the Law: A Study of the Theodosian Code* (New Haven: Yale University Press, 2000), esp. 55–84 and 200–53.

For background and discussion of the Sirmondian Constitutions which will receive attention in Chapter 5, see Mark Vessey, 'The Origins of the *Collectio Sirmondiana*: A New Look at the Evidence', in Jill Harries and Ian Wood (eds.), *The Theodosian Code* (Ithaca: Cornell University Press, 1993), 178–99.

[16] Caroline Humfress, 'Roman Law, Forensic Argument and the Formation of Christian Orthodoxy', 125–47.

[17] As has been noticed by Paul Monceaux, *Histoire Littéraire de l'Afrique Chrétienne depuis les Origins jusqu'a l'Invasion Arabe* (Paris: Éditions Ernest Leroux ; reprint, Brussels: Culture et Civilization, 1966, 1912–23), iv, 254–60; Tengström, *Donatisten und Katholiken*, 102–4; Rémi Crespin, *Ministère et Sainteté: Pastorale du Clergé et Solution de la Crise Donatiste dans la Vie et la Doctrine de Saint Augustin* (Paris: Études Augustiniennes, 1965), 71.

A lessee (*conductor*) also paid the stipulated amount unless of servile status, in which case he would be beaten with clubs and then deported.[18] We will be referring to the law of 392 several times, so I include the text here:[19]

> [Emperors Valentinian, Theodosius, and Arcadius] Augustuses to Tatianus Praetorian Prefect:
> In the case of heretical false doctrines, We decree that if it should appear that any persons *have ordained clerics or should have accepted the office of cleric, they shall be fined ten pounds of gold each. The place in which forbidden practices are attempted shall by all means be added to the resources of Our fisc,* if it should become clear that the offense was committed with the connivance of the owner. But if it should appear that the landowner was unaware of such misdeed, inasmuch as it was done secretly, We direct that the chief tenant of such estate, if he should be freeborn, shall pay ten pounds to Our fisc, if he should be descended from servile dregs and should despise the penalty of monetary loss because of his poverty and low degree, he shall be beaten with clubs and condemned to deportation. Furthermore, We especially provide that if such place should be an imperial villa or a villa subject to any public right, and if the chief tenant and the procurator should give permission for the assembly, each of them shall be fined ten pounds of gold in accordance with the penalty as herein set forth. But if those persons who have been found to perform such mysteries at the same time be revealed to usurp for themselves the title of cleric, We command that each of them shall be fined ten pounds of gold and such fine shall be paid.
> Given on the seventeenth day before the calends of July at Constantinople in the year of the second consulship of Arcadius Augustus and in the consulship of Rufinus.—15 June 392 (italics mine).[20]

---

[18] Notice that *procuratores* and *conductores* on imperial estates were subjects to fines but not beatings. We will return to this topic when we discuss the promulgation of the Edict of Unity in 405.

[19] Idem AAA. Tatiano PPO: 'In haereticis erroribus quoscumque constiterit vel ordinasse clericos vel suscepisse officium clericorum, denis libris auri viritim multandos esse censemus, locum sane, in quo vetita temptantur, si coniventia domini patuerit, fisci nostri viribus adgregari. Quod si id possessorem, quippe clanculum gestum, ignorasse constiterit, conductorem eius fundi, si ingenuus est, decem libras fisco nostro inferre praecipimus, si servili faece descendens paupertate sui poenam damni ac vilitate contemnit, caesus fustibus deportatione damnibitur. Tum illud specialiter praecavemus, ut, si villa dominica fuerit seu cuiuslibet publici iuris et conductor et procurator licentiam dederint colligendi, denis libris auri proposita condemnatione multentur. Verum si quos talibus repertos obsecundare mysteriis ac sibi usurpare nomina clericorum iam nunc proditum fuerit, denas libras auri exigi singulos et inferre praecipimus. DAT XVII KAL.IUL. CONST(ANTINO)P(OLI) ARCAD(IO) A. II ET RUFINO CONSS.'

[20] All Latin citations of the *Codex Theodosianus* are from *CTh*. All English translations of the *Theodosian Code* are from Pharr (Princeton: Princeton University Press, 1952).

A passage of the *Contra epistulam Parmeniani* (1.12.19) confirms Augustine's familiarity with law in claiming that it was successfully used by the Catholics in order to chastise the Donatists:

> Among them there is one general law against all who wish that they be called Christians; indeed, they have no communion with the Catholic Church, but instead they are gathered, apart, amongst their own groups; *the law stipulates the following: that the one who ordains clerics or himself is ordained will be punished with a fine of ten pounds of gold: the property itself on which the unholy separatist movement gathers will be remitted to the imperial fisc.*[21]

Without question, Augustine is referring to Theodosius' law of 392, as the words and their order are directly taken from that imperial letter.[22] The re-dating of *Contra epistulam Parmeniani*,[23] along with a lack of factual information regarding the particulars by which the Catholics called forth this law, makes it difficult to determine to which episode, exactly, Augustine is here referring. In any event, his knowledge of the law is certain.[24] The first attempt by the Catholics to activate it occurred around 395. We are not sure of the date.[25] At this time, the Donatist Church in general, and Optatus, the bishop of Timgad, in particular, enjoyed the support of the imperial administrators in North Africa. Gildo, the highly popular count (*comes*) of Africa who was killed in 398, while engaged in a revolt against Emperor Honorius, and Seranus, once vicar of

---

[21] 'In quibus una generalis adversus omnes, qui se christianos dici volunt et ecclesiae catholicae non communicant, sed in suis separatis conventiculis congregantur, id continet, *ut vel ordinator clerici vel ipse ordinatus denis libris auri multentur: locus vero ipse quo impia separatio congregatur redigatur...in fiscum*' (italics mine).

[22] *CTh.* 16.5.21: 'vel ordinasse clericos vel suscepisse officium clericorum, denis libris auri viritim multandos esse censemus.'

Lenski 'Evidence for the *Audientia Episcopalis* in the New Letters of Augustine', 88–90 lists other imperial constitutions collected by Catholic bishops, namely Augustine and Anthony of Fussala. A point of clarification regarding Augustine's discussion of this particular law in *c. ep. Parm.*: W. H. C. Frend, *The Donatist Church: A Movement of Protest in Roman North Africa* (Oxford: Clarendon Press, 1952; reprint 1971), 249, with Gerald Bonner following, *St. Augustine of Hippo: Life and Controversies* (Philadelphia: Westminster Press, 1963), 260, believe that Augustine is referring to a later law, issued to the vicar of Africa in June 399 (*CTh.* 16.2.34) wherein heretics or such men ('vel ab haereticis vel ab huiuscemodi hominibus') doing anything against the Church are fined five pounds of gold. The penalty—ten pounds vs. five pounds—does not tally, and the verbal associations between Augustine's words and *CTh.* 16.5.21 disqualify from consideration this *Code* entry 16.2.34 with its five pounds' penalty.

[23] See supra n. 12.

[24] Hombert, *Nouvelle recherches*, 570–1, among others, believes that the law was currently effective against the Donatists, but we have seen Augustine refer to this law in place as early as 395 and, as we shall shortly see, in 402. Referring to Theodosius' law of 392 as fact does not offer definitive proof that it was indeed used (or usable) against the Donatists.

[25] Serge Lancel, *Saint Augustine*, translated by Antonia Nevill (London: SCM Press, 2002), 275.

Africa and later made proconsul, consistently sided with Donatist interests.[26] Asserting their position as the officially recognized Church (i.e. Catholic) in Africa, the Donatists pushed hard against the Maximianists and Catholics, utilizing their legal status to take over or repossess churches. Augustine informs his readers that armed bands under the command of Optatus harassed numerous Catholic churches (*c. litt. Petil.* 2.83.184),[27] including one at Asna, which was occupied and its altar broken (*ep.* 29.12).[28] The Catholics appealed to Serenus, vicar at the time, that he apply the Theodosian heresy law of 392 against Optatus. This first attempt to activate Theodosius' law was unsuccessful. Augustine concedes that as to the fine of ten pounds, 'none of you have ever paid to this very day' (*c. litt. Petil.* 2.83.184). This clearly means that the Catholics lost their case against Optatus, if in fact Serenus agreed to hear it.[29]

Crispinus, the Donatist bishop of Calama, was well known to the Catholics before Possidius defeated him in court. He had received a previous warning from Augustine that he was liable for punishment under Theodosius' law. In around 402 (the date of Augustine's *ep.* 66), Augustine rebuked the Donatist bishop of Calama for rebaptizing eighty residents of a village close to Mappala whose lands, recently purchased, he held by emphyteusis.[30] Augustine told

---

[26] Augustine *epp.* 51, 53, 76.3, 87; *c. litt. Petil.* 2.92.209 (*CSEL* 52 [1909]). Claude Lepelley, *Les Cités de l'Afrique romaine au Bas-Empire*, 2 vols. (Paris: Études Augustiniennes, 1979–81), ii, 472–3, nn. 108 and 109. See commentary on *Contra Cresconium* by A. C. De Veer (*BA* 31, 1968), 781–3.

In numerous treatises and letters, Augustine represents the close relationship between Gildo and Optatus as vicious, seditious, and suspect. Brown, *Augustine of Hippo: A Biography* (Berkeley: University of California Press, 1967; reprint 2000), 230 rightly points out that there is convenience in Augustine's emphasis on the political (and amicable) connection here. Gildo's reputation as traitor and betrayer was used to great effect to demonstrate the inherently anti-Roman character of his friend, bishop Optatus. See Claudian's *De bello Gildonico* I (e.g. 1.161): 'pars tertia mundi unius praedonis ager'. Cf. Tengström, *Donatisten und Katholiken* 75–7, 84–90.

[27] 'Ipsa ecclesia catholica solidata principibus catholicis imperantibus terra marique armatis turbis ab Optato atrociter et hostiliter oppugnata est.'

[28] See *ep.* 29.12: 'At Asna, where brother Argentius is the priest, the circumcellions raided our basilica and shattered the altar. The case is now being tried.' We do not know where Asna is located and nothing of Argentius save Augustine's reference here (*PCBE Afrique* 'Argentius 1', 91). Notice that as the case is being tried, Augustine is still a priest; he identifies himself (*presbyter*) as such in the greeting to the recipient of this letter, Alypius.

[29] 'Quae res coegit tunc primo adversus vos allegari apud vicarium Seranum legem illam de decem libris auri, quas nullus vestrum adhuc pendit, et nos crudelitatis arguitis.'

See *Cresc.* 48–50 (58–60); *PCBE Afrique*, 'Seranus', 1060–1.

[30] Land holding by emphyteusis (use of imperial land to the possession, enjoyment, mortgage, and bequest to heirs) was quite common in Africa. Frend, *Donatist Church*, 40–2.

See *c. litt. Petil.* 2.83.184: 'Quid nuper, quod ipse adhuc lugeo? nonne Crispinus vester Calamensis cum emisset possessionem et hoc emphyteuticam, non dubitavit in fundo catholicorum imperatorum, quorum legibus nec in civitatibus esse iussi estis, uno terroris impetu octoginta ferme animas miserabili gemitu mussitantes rebaptizando submergere?'

Crispinus that according to civil law, he was subject to a fine of ten pounds of gold.[31] He emphasized Crispinus' rebaptism of those who lived in a hamlet under imperial ownership. The act occurred on lands owned by *Catholic* rulers, and in Theodosius' law, the emperor took particular exception to heretics performing religious services and rites on imperial estates.[32] We do not know if Possidius tried to bring charges against Crispinus at the local level, but if so, they were not received well, as we hear nothing more about them.

We get a better idea of how the Catholics brought cases in front of local administrators when Augustine writes about Restitutus, a presbyter from Victoriana villa, which was a hamlet located about thirty miles from Hippo.[33] Shortly before August 403, Restitutus, a former Donatist who had voluntarily rejoined the Catholic Church, was dragged from his house during the day by some Donatists, beaten with clubs, and then taken to another farm hamlet ('proximum castellum').[34] There he was held prisoner for almost two weeks. No Catholic dared try to approach the *castellum* (*Cresc.* 3.48 [53]). Ritualistic humiliation rather than lethal harm seems to have been the aim.

---

[31] This would have been the opportune moment to press charges pursuant to laws from the 370s that survive to us in the *Theodosian Code* including one certainly addressed to the proconsul of Africa, Julianus, in 373 (16.6.1), which forbade rebaptism and declared that the cleric performing the act was not worthy of his office. Augustine and the Church did not pursue these laws. They always favored the heresy law of 392. See Chapter 4, n. 37.

[32] *CTh*.16.5.21: 'Tum illud specialiter praecavemus, ut, si villa dominica fuerit seu cuiuslibet publici iuris et conductor et procurator licentiam dederint colligendi, denis libris auri proposita condemnatione multentur.'

[33] Augustine *epp.* 105.2, 88.6, and *Cresc.* 3.48 (53). See also *PCBE Afrique*, 'Restitutus 6', 972.

[34] Augustine clearly indicates that the attack against Restitutus occurred before imperial legislation was promulgated in 405 (*CTh.* 16.5.38 known as the Edict of Unity, issued on 12 February 405, which ordered the Donatists to rejoin the Catholics), because that presbyter made the decision of his own accord ('Restitutus quidam in regione Hipponiensi vester presbyter fuit, qui cum ad catholicam pacem, antequam istis imperialibus legibus iuberetur, veritiatis ratione permotus manifesta voluntate transisset', *Cresc.* 3.48 [53]). Augustine narrows the time frame in *ep.* 88.7, wherein he states that the case of Restitutus and subsequent negotiations between the Catholics and Donatists over the beating directly led to the convening of the church council: 'Nec tamen de his iniuriis et persecutionibus, quas ecclesia catholica in regione nostra tunc pertulit, imperatoribus questus est episcopus noster. Sed facto concilio placuit, ut pacifice conveniremini'. So, we have mention of the Restitutus incident, then a calling of the conference, and finally the invitation to the Donatist bishops, including Proculianus, to engage the Catholics in debate. Clearly, Augustine is putting the attack against Restitutus *before* the Council of 403.

In the *Contra Cresconium*, a description of the attack against Restitutus is situated at the conclusion of the recapitulation of the Crispinus affair, when the Donatist bishop was brought up on charges by Possidius in late 403 or early 404, but it is in *ep.* 88 that we seem to have a sure chronological link between Restitutus and the convening of the August 403 conference in Carthage. *ep.* 88 and *Contra Cresconium* are documents contemporary to each other, but the Restitutus story is placed in very different parts of the respective narratives. It comes much later than it should in the *Contra Cresconium*. For dating, see Hombert, *Nouvelles recherches*, 196–200.

The Donatists rolled Restitutus in mud, tore off his clothes, wrapped him in a reed mat and repeatedly paraded him in public. The bystanders did not interfere, but Augustine tells us that while some people were horrified at what was happening, others laughed and cheered (*Cresc.* 3.48 [53]). Proculeianus, the Donatist bishop of Hippo, eventually arranged for Restitutus' release because the Catholic bishops had informed him that they would press charges unless he resolved this matter (*ep.* 105.3).[35] Even after Restitutus was freed, the Catholics still addressed complaints about this attack to the authorities. As Victoriana villa was under the jurisdiction of the municipal council of Hippo, the case was referred to this administrative body.

See PCBE Afrique, 'Restitutus 6 and 7', 972–3, and 'Restitutus 18', 976–7. Augustine's *ep.* 249 (date uncertain) is addressed to another Restitutus who is seeking answers on ways to deal with difficulties posed by the Donatists, including what seems to be violence against Catholic clergy. Augustine exhorts Restitutus to read the works of the Donatist Tyconius: 'It seems to me, however, that he has dealt vigorously with this question, and has solved it; namely, how the bond of unity is to be preserved if we have to tolerate abuses and even accursed deeds which, perhaps, we are not able to correct or stamp out.' This Restitutus is clearly a deacon and more than likely not the same man. There was a Catholic priest in the diocese of Hippo named Restitutus who was murdered some time between June 411 (after the conference of 411) and February 412. The murder, committed by Donatists, was well planned, as Restitutus apparently walked into an ambush. The same men who killed Restitutus then dragged a priest, called Innocentes, from his home. They beat him, cut off one of his fingers, and gouged out one of his eyes. Although this Restitutus was a priest who served in the diocese of Hippo, we are not sure if this is the same priest who was attacked before August 403.

[35] PCBE Afrique, 'Proculeianus 1', 924–6. Before the death of Augustine's episcopal predecessor—Valerius—Proculeianus and Augustine (at that time a priest of Hippo) made overtures to each other about the possibility of a public debate. Augustine's *ep.* 33 is an exhortation to Proculeianus that this debate might occur with stenographers present, and he asks the bishop to forgive Augustine's friend Evodius for having treated Proculeianus rudely when the latter expressed willingness to meet with Augustine. The debate never took place.

Clerical defection, as we saw with Restitutus, remained fluid even after stringent legal measures against Donatists were enacted. While the Conference of 404 was meeting at Carthage in June, Augustine wrote to his parishioners asking them to restrain their recent vaunting over Proculeianus' flock, as recently two Donatist deacons had joined the Catholic Church: 'Some had insulted the flock of Proculeianus, boasting about ours, as if nothing of the sort ever happened among the clerics of our flock. Whoever of you did this, I confess to you, you did not do well' (*ep.* 78.8). He may have had in mind Maximianus of Bagai (who will appear later in this chapter as a besieged Catholic, but he had previously been relieved of his episcopal duties in August 402 when he became a Donatist [*ep.* 69]).

Defection went both ways. Cresconius mentions a Candidus and a Donatus, both of whom left the Catholic clergy for the Donatists in 401(*Cresc.* 2.10 [12]). A Catholic subdeacon in the mid-390s became Donatist after being defrocked because of inappropriate behavior with nuns (*ep.* 35), and we also know about a priest who threatened to go over to the Donatists after being reprimanded for beating his mother (*epp.* 34, 35). See also *epp.* 106–8 on Macrobius' rebaptism of Rusticianus (Macrobius was the Donatist bishop of Hippo, the successor of Proculianus). Also in *ep.* 108, we learn that Proculianus had some time before rebaptized an unnamed Catholic deacon who had been excommunicated for unspecified reasons.

Augustine, as bishop of Hippo, was the one who issued the formal protest.[36] Proculeianus and his staff, called before the municipal council, requested that the investigation be waived, especially now that Restitutus was at liberty. The leaders of Hippo agreed, and Proculeianus went home. As far as the Donatist bishop was concerned, the matter was closed. Not for Augustine: he tried 'again and again' to summon Proculeianus before the council (*ep.* 88.6: 'et iterum continuo'). Proculeianus had nothing more to say; he simply referred Augustine to the municipal *gesta* that had recorded the dismissal of the case. The authorities at Hippo did not press in Augustine's favor, and the bishop later informed his readers that he considered taking the case to the imperial court, but refrained from doing so in order to maintain a calm dialogue among the local parties (*ep.* 88.7).

The authorities at Hippo were clearly not sympathetic to Augustine's petition. They had no reason to be, as Augustine did not have legal grounds to pursue Proculeianus in alleging a direct association with the kidnapping and beating of Restitutus.[37] Augustine continued, however, to press Hippo's municipal council regarding the Donatist bishop because the plan was to argue that Proculeianus, rather than Restitutus' kidnappers, was the legally responsible (and thus liable) party. Prosecution based on the delict itself was not Augustine's aim. Here, too, he was likely planning to use (or try to have implemented) Theodosius' law against heretics. Augustine was not successful.

CRISPINUS AND POSSIDIUS, THE BISHOPS OF CALAMA

It was Possidius who succeeded in convincing the authorities that the Donatists should be considered heretics under Theodosius' law. The bishop's legal

---

[36] Augustine refers to himself in the third person in *ep.* 88.6: 'Proculeianus was summoned by our bishop' ('unde conventus...a nostro episcopo Proculeianus'), but states it quite plainly in *Cresc.* 3.48 (53): 'hoc episcopo vestro Hipponiensi Proculiano ipse sum questus gestis sane municipalibus.'

[37] Generally, in cases dealing with free adult peoples removed from the context of the *familia* (the extended household), the law stipulated that a leader of an organization, religion, or institution was not responsible for infractions perpetrated by his subordinates. For example, in the *Theodosian Code*, heresy laws predating the Restitutus case clearly indicate that the owners of property were not liable to punishment (in this case, fines) if they did not know that their tenants were engaging in illegal activities (see *CTh.* 16.5.21, dated 15 June 392 and 6.5.34, dated 4 March 398).

Roman law of *iniuria*, under which category such a treatment of Restitutus would fall, deemed culpable not just those who performed a violent deed, but those who were complicit in it. Thus, there was room to prosecute and convict if the Catholics could allege that the Donatist bishop, namely Proculeianus, had procured the beating of Restitutus; he could also be considered liable if he had merely used persuasion (rather than tangible remuneration) to solicit the attack.

efforts began with the annual council of August 403, when the Catholic bishops spoke out with acclamations for a debate between themselves and their Donatist counterparts. The Catholics assured the Donatists that they could choose their own delegates as well as the time and places convenient for meeting. The goal, they said, was to secure the religious well-being of ordinary Africans whose lack of familiarity with the finer points of theology might endanger their souls.[38] If the Donatists refused the terms of the offer, the Catholics would assume they were conceding the victory.[39]

Diffidentia was not the reason for the Donatist refusal. They had no interest in a meeting of this kind, as they were still the majority party in Africa and felt they had nothing to gain from discussion with those whom they considered outside the true Church. The Catholic council of 403, which had issued the invitation, was not attended by a quorum of bishops (there was unrest in Numidia on account of a rebellion among army recruits)[40] and so its resolutions, one could argue, did not reflect the sentiments of the Catholic Church anyway. Nor did the Catholics call upon any external authority as leverage to facilitate a gathering. After a month, when the bishops received no response from their Donatist colleagues, the Catholics sent a request to the proconsul, Septiminus, asking him to provide the necessary aid (*copia*)

---

[38] *Concilia Africae, Registri Ecclesiae Carthaginensis Excerpta* 92: 'cum pace discutiant, et tandem aliquando, adiuvante Domino Deo nostro, finem veternosus error accipiat, ne, propter animositatem hominum, infirmae animae et ignari populi sacrilega dissensione dispereant.'

That unlettered and uneducated parishioners added to the chances of the true Church becoming a victim of untrue belief was a sentiment repeatedly expressed in Possidius' *Vita*. In the following year at the council of 404 the language used by the Catholics became much stronger: *infirma anima* and a *populus ignarus* we see in 403 cedes to a people afflicted with *imperitia* and *pertinacia*. See Peter Brown, 'Augustine and a Practice of the *Imperiti*', in Goulven Madec (ed.), *Augustin prédicateur (395–411): Actes du Colloque International de Chantilly (5–7 Septembre 1996)* (Paris: Institut d'Études Augustiniennes, 1998), 372–3.

[39] 'Si autem hoc facere nolueritis, *diffidentia* vestra facile innotescet' (*Concilia Africae, Registri Ecclesiae Carthaginensis Excerpta* 92). See also *Cresc.* 3.45 (49): 'saltem *diffidentia* eorum non frustra illis, qui hoc a nobis poposcerant, appareret. Factum est, conventi sunt, recusarent: quibus verbis, quo dolo maledictione amaritudine plenis, nunc longum est demonstrare.'

Diffidentia is a word Possidius uses three times to describe the Donatists in the *Vita* and should be translated not as a sense of distrust or diffidence, but as lack of confidence based on ineptitude or an awareness of one's own shortcomings (*v. Aug.* 9.4—twice—and 14.7).

[40] Alypius says that only he, Augustine, and Possidius were able to come from Numidia. *Concilia Africae, Registri Eccclesiae Carthaginensis Excerpta* 90: 'Nos quidem de Numidia venimus, ego et sancti fratres Augustinus et Possidius, sed de Numidia legatio mitti non potuit, quod adhuc tumultu tyronum episcopi propriis necessitatibus in civitatibus suis aut impediti aut occupati sunt.' The primate of Numidia, Xanthippus, had written to say that it was impossible to attend because of the disturbances caused by the recruits. He lived at Thagura, which is only about thirty kilometers to the south and east of Thagaste, Alypius' see. It is clear that messages were getting through from the hinterland to the coast, but Possidius and Alypius may have been with Augustine at Hippo or Carthage when the unrest began.

to make sure that these discussions took place. Septiminus assented with a letter, dated 13 September 403, that called for a convening, with words expressing eagerness for a restoration of a unified calm as manifested by respect for the law.[41] All or most of the Donatist and Catholic bishops would have received this letter, and in a few cases, we know about the Donatist reaction to it.[42]

Proculeianus, the Donatist bishop of Hippo, informed the Catholics while standing before Hippo's magistrates that he needed to consult with his episcopal colleagues about the possibility of such a meeting.[43] The Donatists convened and agreed that a council of the two churches was neither advantageous nor necessary. Proculeianus returned home and for some time the Catholics were unaware of what the Donatists had decided, for Augustine reports that he had to call Proculeianus again before the magistrates of Hippo in order to elicit a response. Proculeianus indicated that the Donatists were not interested in a meeting.[44] The proposed debates fizzled out, as the actual weight backing the invitation may have been inconsequential. The Catholics wanted *copia*. We are not sure to what extent Septiminus obliged them. It also seems that the local governments were not very interested in pursuing the Donatists. Municipal administrators did succeed in calling forward the Donatist bishops so that they might respond to the proconsul's letter (we know that this happened with Crispinus, Proculeianus, and Primian, Donatist bishop of Carthage).[45] Perhaps

---

[41] Both the request to Septiminus and his (partial) response are preserved in the transcripts of the 411 conference between the Donatists and Catholics in Carthage (*Coll. Carth.*, III, 174–5). The text of Septiminus' answer follows: 'In quolibet loco antistibus legis venerabilis ob quietem imperii gestorum conficiendorum tribuitur facultas, hoc etiam tenore huius praeceptionis limitato ut intellegant se deviae plebis magistri salubriter petentibus propriae persuasionis ratiocinia persolvere ut, rebus in medio prolatis, amica legis moderatio servetur, superstitione supplosa.'

For *superstitio* as indicating heresy, see discussion by Lancel, *Actes de la Conférence de Carthage en 411* (Paris: Les Éditions du Cerf, 1972), Vol. 1, 25 n.1; and Brown, *Imperiti*, 372. For the history and meaning of the word, see J. Sheid, 'Le Délit religieux dans la Rome tardo-républicaine', in *Le Délit religieux dans la cité antique*, Collection de l'École française de Rome 48 (1981), 130–66.

[42] See Lancel, *Actes de la Conférence*, Vol. 1, 32–4 regarding methods by which dispatchers were sent to the bishoprics to announce the meetings and deliver letters.

[43] Augustine tells us that his response was recorded in the public records (*ep.* 88.7).

F. Van der Meer, *Augustine the Bishop: The Life and Work of a Father of the Church*, translated by Brian Battershaw and G. R. Lamb (London: Sheed and Ward, 1961), 87, asserts that we should think of these exchanges as occurring through depositions given to the magistrates' *notarii*, who recorded the *gesta*. The Donatists may have refused to appear with the Catholics, and thus the parties may have stood before the council members at different times. This is, indeed, what happened in the case of Primian, bishop of Carthage, but as we see later in the exchange between Possidius and Crispinus, Possidius and the Donatist bishop stood near each other as Possidius responded to Crispinus' refusal to engage him further.

[44] *ep.* 88.7: 'recusans pacificam conlationem.'

[45] *ep.* 88 (Proculeianus); *Cresc.* 3. 48 (50) (Crispinus); and infra n. 48 (Primian).

administrators exhorted adherence to Septiminus' letter, but they either were not in a position, or of the will, to force the Donatists to comply.[46]

The particulars of Proculeianus' refusal are lost, but the Donatist bishops were agreed as to the responses they should use to decline participation in the debate. Primian, the Donatist bishop of Carthage, was the man likely responsible for organizing the meeting of Donatists and their choreographed defense.[47] He informed the people and administrators of Carthage by letter, which was delivered by one of his deacons that 'it was unworthy that the sons of the martyrs and the children of the traitors come together'.[48] We learn more about the refusal from Crispinus. The Donatist bishop of Calama, one of the most important in Africa, enjoyed a reputation as a praiseworthy and learned man.[49]

The Catholics had for several years expressed interest in meeting the Donatists, and Augustine had known Crispinus since 398 or 399, when the two men exchanged messages as preliminary to meeting for a public discussion. When Crispinus retreated from promises to join Augustine in Carthage (*ep.* 51), Augustine sent Crispinus a letter in the hope that the Donatist bishop would circulate responses to several questions, one of them addressing the role of the Roman state in their long-standing disagreement.[50] Augustine's subsequent letter of *c.*402 regarding the rebaptism of eighty residents of Mappala has

---

[46] *ep.* 76 was written to the Donatists after they rejected the invitation.

[47] See *PCBE Afrique*, 'Primianus 1', 905–13. In *en. Ps.* 36.2.18, which was preached at Carthage probably in late September 403, right after the conference and the circulation of the proconsul's letter, Augustine indicates that Primian has called for a meeting of Donatists: 'Qualis tu, tales et ceteri. Nam merito talia verba omnibus misisti; abundare voluisti societate mendacium, ne tu solus erubesceres de mendacio.'

For a discussion of the dates, see Dolbeau, *Vingt-six sermons* 323; Monceaux, *Histoire littéraire*, vi, 131; Frend, *Donatist Church*, 259; and Lancel, *Saint Augustine*, 287–8.

[48] 'Indignum est quidem ut in unum conveniant filii martyrum et progenies traditorum' (*c. Don.* 1,1; see also *Coll. Carth.* III, 116). As to the method of delivering this message, see *c. Don.* 1.1: 'Primianus hoc scriptum magistratui Carthaginis dedit et a diacono suo dicendum apud acta mandavit.' There is an indication that Primian's message to the magistrates of Carthage also criticized the Catholics for relying on the 'divinity' (*sacras*) of imperial legislation while the Donatists put their trust in God's word alone (*c. Don.* 31.53): 'ubi sunt verba Primiani apud acta magistratus Carthaginiensis expressa: illi portant multorum imperatorum sacras, nos sola offerimus evangelia'? See Crispinus' response to the proconsular ruling against him (infra n. 68).

See also Jean-Louis Maier, *Le Dossier du Donatisme*, 2 vols. (Berlin: Akademik Verlag, 1987–9), ii, 124–6.

[49] *v. Aug.* 12.5: 'praedicatus scilicet multi temporis et doctus'. See *PCBE Afrique*, 'Crispinus 1', 252–3. He was named eleventh on the list of twelve episcopal supporters of Primian who condemned the partisans of Maximianus on the 24 April 394. See *Cresc.* 3.53 (59); 4.10 (12).

[50] 'Ad hanc epistolam responde, si placet, et fortasse sufficiet non solum nobis sed et eis, qui nos audire desiderant, aut, si non sufficiet, scripta atque rescripta, donec sufficiat, repetantur. Quid enim nobis commodius poterit exhibere urbium, quas incolimus, tanta vicinitas? Ego enim statui nihil de hac re agere vobiscum nisi per litteras, vel ne cui nostrum de memoria, quod dicitur, elabatur, vel ne fraudentur talium studiosi, qui forte interesse non possunt' (*ep.* 51.1).

already been discussed. Called forward by the magistrates of Calama to answer the letter of summons from Proconsul Septiminus in 403, Crispinus likewise responded that he was obliged to confer with his colleagues.[51] As Proculeianus had been at Hippo, Crispinus was subsequently entreated to submit a formal answer to the Catholic invitation, and he apparently appeared only after several weeks had elapsed following the Donatist conference.[52] He defended his refusal to meet the Catholics with an abundance of scriptural citation. Augustine, as he repeats some of Crispinus' phrases, turns the bishop's defense into a series of facile platitudes, but we should be wary of this simplified recapitulation.[53] Here is what we know of the specific contents, as told to us by Augustine, which formed the basis for Crispinus' refusal:

> And then after some time, with the meeting once again having been sought, he responded on record: 'May you not have feared the words of a sinning man'; And again; 'Beware what you have uttered into the ears of the rash man lest when he hears you, he laughs at your discerning speech'; Finally, I restrict this response of mine to the language of a patriarch; let the impious depart from me. I do not wish to know their ways.[54]

The Donatists had been saying such things for years, and Possidius was ready for them. Possidius' counterarguments immediately followed Crispinus' remarks and were delivered in front of Calama's people, magistrates, and the Donatist bishop himself. Crispinus, as Augustine describes him, was *inanis*, shouting *maledicta* that did nothing for the Donatist cause except elicit the laughter of Calama's residents, learned and unlearned alike.[55] Possidius was the *tiro*,[56] a novice who, facing his opponent, served up his own remonstrance.

> To be sure, of that man saying that he did not fear the words of a sinning man, to whom he scarcely dared to respond, and that he did not wish to utter anything into the ears of a rash man, as if he were accidently about to entrust something secret to the ears of a rash man, when the the things which he did say many discreet people were able to hear, for the sake of whom, in fact, Christ the Lord spoke about such things to the Pharisees, Ever so much rash men; and that he did not wish to know their ways of

---

[51] *Cresc.* 3.48 (50).

[52] 'Deinde post non parvum tempus repetita conventione rursus apud acta respondit' (*Cresc.* 3.46 [50]). In Augustine's *ep.* 88.7 we learn that Proculeianus had to be called by the Catholics in front of the magistrates before he would give a response to the summons for debate.

[53] Cf. Lancel, *Saint Augustine*, 288.

[54] 'Deinde post non parvum tempus repetita conventione rursus apud acta respondit: 'verba viri peccatoris ne timueris' (2Macc. 2:62). Et iterum: 'in aures imprudentis cave quicquam dixeris, ne cum audierit inrideat sensatos sermones tuos' (Prov. 23:9). Postremo 'hanc responsionem meam patriarchali sermone definio: recadant a me impii, vias eorum nosse nolo' (Job 34:27).

[55] 3.46 (50): 'docti indoctique riderent.'

[56] As once Augustine described himself in relation to Proculianus (*c*.396–7). See *ep.* 34.6.

wickedness, as if those whom he thought wicked wished to teach him their ways, an not it rather that he, if he held fast to the ways of God, ought to teach even the wicked, just as it was written: I shall teach the unjust your ways and the wicked will return to you.[57]

When imagining Possidius responding with these rebukes, a rapt and at times participatory audience, which included local magistrates, should be prominent in our minds. Possidius was not being gratuitously rude, nor should we trust Augustine's portrait of Crispinus as an old man uttering inanities. These were two skilled professionals. Crispinus' public vows to shun the 'unclean sinner' placed Possidius and the Catholics in the roles of the prosecutor and persecutor, all to the advantage of the Donatists. Conversely, Possidius' ridicule placed Crispinus in a very difficult position, wherein to ignore the taunts of the Catholic bishop intimated a kind of acquiescence and silent acceptance of the Catholic rebuttal. For Crispinus to speak, however, even if in unmeasured tones, meant engaging in exactly what the Donatists wanted to avoid: a debate. Crispinus could not respond and remain faithful to decisions reached by the majority of bishops. The harder Possidius pushed, the better for the Catholics. Either Crispinus would answer, in which case the Catholics would get, in the end, a discussion, or Crispinus would retreat from the field, maintaining his silence, but to the residents of Calama appearing overwhelmed.

Possidius' rebukes may not seem particularly cutting to a modern audience, but Crispinus' embarrassment was extreme and the subsequent response was equally so. Only a few days passed when a Donatist band attacked and seriously wounded Possidius.[58] Crispinus' presbyter, also named Crispinus and perhaps a relative of the bishop, organized a 'hit' on Possidius.[59] Possidius was traveling with baggage and a small retinue to Figulina (fundus Figulinensis) on a preaching campaign to exhort Donatists to join the Catholics (*ep.* 105.4; *v. Aug.* 12.4). Crispinus the presbyter had gathered a group of armed men together to ambush the Catholic bishop. At the last minute Possidius learned that an attack had been planned against him, so he changed course and headed for Oliveta, another farm in what may have been Donatist hands. The Donatists followed and stole his pack animals and baggage, all of which

---

[57] 'Quippe hominis dicentis verba viri peccatoris se non timere, cui respondere minime auderet, et in aures imprudentis nolle se aliquid dicere, quasi aliquod secretum fuerat imprudentis auribus temere commissurus, cum ea quae diceret multi possent prudentes audire, qualium causa et dominus Christus tanta Pharisaeis quamvis inprudentibus loquebatur, et nolle se nosse vias impiorum, quasi vias suas eum docere vellent, quos impios putabat, ac non potius ipse, si teneret vias dei, etiam impios docere deberet, sicut scriptum est: doceam iniquos vias tuas et impii ad te convertentur' (*Cresc.* 46 [50]).
[58] 3. 46 (50): 'post paucos dies.'
[59] 3. 46 (50): 'alius Crispinus eius presbyter et ut perhibetur propinquus.'

Possidius and attendants had abandoned in flight. Possidius ran into a farmhouse for safety, but the place was immediately surrounded and pummeled with rocks and incendiaries. The attackers were attempting to gain entrance to the house when the tenants of Oliveta appeared, terrified by the potential consequences for them if a crime were committed on the premises. None dared to resist Crispinus with physical force, but, according to Augustine, some begged the attackers to spare Possidius while others busied themselves putting out the flames spread by the burning projectiles. Crispinus ignored the farmers' pleas and broke down the door. The Donatists entered, wounded the oxen that were housed on ground level, and then went upstairs, where Possidius was hiding.[60] They dragged him downstairs, probably rolled him in the dung and the blood of the animals, insulted him, and beat him. Just when things were looking bleak for the bishop, Crispinus put a stop to the abuse. Augustine says that the presbyter pretended to heed to the entreaties of the resident farmers at Oliveta, but in reality, he feared that there were too many witnesses to the crime of murder (*Cresc.* 3.46 [50]). To the contrary, Crispinus' timely halt to the beating means that the attack was not a spontaneous display of outrage, but a well-timed and well-placed message. The aim was to discourage and intimidate, but inflict no permanent physical damage.

When news reached Calama that Possidius had been attacked by the presbyter Crispinus, all the townspeople waited to see what the Donatists would do. Augustine tells us that from feelings of fear or shame ('vel timore vel pudore'), Bishop Crispinus reported the attack to the municipal council with the understanding that he would handle the discipline through ecclesiastical channels ('ecclesiasticam vindictam'). Crispinus never exercised punitive measures, and Possidius soon concluded that nothing more would happen without the involvement of external parties, so he decided to bring charges of heresy

---

[60] Colder weather, which comes later than November in areas of North Africa close to sea level, may account for the oxen being in the house in which Possidius was attacked. Granted, some farmers kept their animals inside when not out to pasture or otherwise employed, but the housing of these animals suggests that the attack occurred in late fall or early winter of 403/4. This makes sense. The proconsul Septiminus published his letter exhorting a meeting between the two churches in mid September 403. The time between its release and Possidius' beating must be at minimum two months. Augustine says (*ep.* 88) that after Septiminus' directive, Proculeianus was called in front of the magistrates to answer the invitation, and he told them that a meeting with his colleagues was necessary before he could give an answer (*en. Ps.* 36.2.18). See also *Cresc.* 3.46 (50) for Crispinus' similar response: 'ad concilium vestrum primo distulerat, pollicens cum collegis suis ibi se visurum, quid respondere deberet.' We need to tabulate the time necessary to arrange a meeting of the Donatist bishops, hold that meeting, and then accommodate Augustine's notice that a significant amount of time had elapsed between the council and the Catholic summons of the Donatist bishops to force them to announce their decision (cf. Serge Lancel, who believes the Donatists could not have met for their meeting until at least the beginning of 404 [*Actes de la Conférence de Carthage en 411*, Vol. 1, 16, n. 4]).

against Crispinus. Augustine presented the legal situation as one of enemies of the Church who were to be prosecuted not according to 'heretical presumption with the circumcellions raging away in their rebellious fury', but 'according to prophetic truth with the guiding yoke of the Lord God, with the kings of this world present to lend their aid'. The Old Testament, the New Testament, and the Roman emperors came together as the fundamental principles and preservers of law. Augustine continues:

> Crispinus was therefore brought forward, and because he had denied it to the proconsul asking him what he was, he was easily 'proved to be a heretic'; he was not compelled to pay the ten pounds of gold, the punishment the emperor Theodosius the Great had established against all heretics, because Possidius interceded on his behalf.[61]

When we turn to the *Vita*, we see that success in employing Theodosius' law of 392 was not as effortless as Augustine contends.[62] Possidius tells us, too, that when challenged by the *defensor ecclesiae* at the local level, Crispinus denied he was a heretic and therefore was not subject to Theodosius' heresy law. Crispinus went willingly in front of the proconsul of Africa.[63] The bishop denied that he was liable to a fine of ten pounds, as he was certainly not a heretic, but a bishop of the true Catholic Church.[64] Crispinus had just *legal* cause to make this assertion, and we should not be too surprised that the proconsul agreed. Possidius next tells us that the *defensor ecclesiae*, who had the charge of the case at Carthage, was dismissed (*v. Aug.* 12.7). The Catholic bishops then regrouped and Augustine made an ardent request to the proconsul that he listen to the two bishops, Crispinus and Possidius, debate over the nature of their disagreements. This was a closely watched event, and the crowds in Carthage waited for the outcome with great anticipation (*v. Aug.* 12.7). Possidius must

---

[61] *Cresc.* 3.47 (51): 'Neque enim aliter innotesceret, quid adiutorio Christi ecclesia catholica in suos inimicos posset et nollet, non secundum haereticam praesumptionem privato furore circumcellionibus saevientibus, sed secundum propheticam veritatem iugo domini dei subditis regibus. Exhibitus igitur Crispinus et, quod se esse proconsuli quaerenti negaverat, facillime convictus haereticus decem tamen libras auri, quam multam in omnes haereticos imperator maior Theodosius constituerat, intercedente Possidio non est compulsus exsolvere.'
Cf. *ep.* 88.7 where Augustine says: 'The case was heard and *Proculianus was pronounced a heretic* along with Crispinus.'

[62] Neil McLynn, 'Augustine's Roman Empire', *AugStud*, 30 (1999), 29–44, esp. 36–7.

[63] *Cresc.* 3.48 (52): 'cum Crispinus maluerit Carthaginem pergere.'

[64] *s. Denis* 19: 'Quid dixisti in iudicio proconsulis? Catholicus sum. Vox est ipsius: de gestis recitatur' (*Miscellanea Agostiniana* [Rome: Tipografia poliglotta vaticane, 1931] i, 108). *Cf.* Possidius *v. Aug.* 12.6: 'quoniam, si ab eodem dissimularetur, forte catholicus episcopus ab ignorantibus haereticus crederetur, illo se quod erat negante, atque ita ex hac desidia infirmis scandalum nasceretur.' See Frend, *Donatist Church*, 318, n. 1.

have been very convincing in his arguments because the proconsul of Africa declared Crispinus a heretic and fined him the stipulated amount of ten pounds of gold.[65]

The penalty itself was actually of little importance for the Catholics. An appeal for its recension demonstrated Catholic mercy, but what they now possessed would open the way for the unification of the two churches: the means to apply external pressure on the Donatists. The proconsul agreed to waive the fine at Possidius' request, but Crispinus' dissatisfaction with the court ruling prompted him to appeal to Honorius (*ep.* 105.4 and *v. Aug.* 12.8), an action that earned censure from Possidius and Augustus. Both men called him *ingratus*: had Crispinus simply accepted the decision, the Catholics would have seen to it that the fine was waived and that would be the end of it (*Cresc.* 3.48 [52]). But Crispinus and the Donatists had no choice but to appeal. Aside from theological considerations and the understandable rejection of the appellation 'heretic', acceptance of the ruling gave the Catholics the precedent they needed to pursue all Donatist bishops and landowners with heavy monetary fines. The importance of this case is underscored by the fact that the decision to appeal was not made at Crispinus' basilica at Calama, but was an expression of collective opinion among the Donatist hierarchy.[66]

From *sermo Denis* 19, preached at Carthage and dated to the first half of 404,[67] Augustine offers insight into Crispinus' reaction to the proconsul's ruling. It is here that we get the strongest indication that the Donatist bishop had welcomed the confrontation with Possidius and was surprised that the decision had gone against him.

> In the end, Crispinus was adjudged a heretic. But what did he say? 'Was I defeated by a sentence as rendered from the gospel?' Then, he insisted that he was not vanquished because it was the proconsul who judged against him, not Christ. If, therefore, he considers the judgment of a man to be of such little consequence, why did he appeal from the proconsul to

---

[65] *v. Aug.* 12.7: 'ad controversiam ambo illi Calamenses episcopi venerunt, et de ipsa diversa communione tertio conflictum secum egerunt, magna populorum Christianorum multitudine causae exitum et apud Carthaginem et per totam Africam exspectante, atque ille est Crispinus proconsulari et libellari sententia pronuntiatus haereticus.'

'Proconsulari et libellari sententia': for 'libellaris, e', see *Thesaurus Linguae Latinae* or *TLL* (Leipzig: Teubner, 1900–), v, 7.2, 1261 ('libello compositus et divulgatus'). Possidius may be one of the first writers to use this word. It may also be found in the minutes of the Council of Toledo (400) in the judgment of Priscillian as a heretic ('Episcopi libellarem direxere sententiam').

[66] *Cresc.* 3. 47 (51): 'quod displicuisse vestris omnibus dicebatur.'

[67] Othmer Perler and J. L Maier, *Les Voyages de Saint Augustin* (Paris: Études Augustiniennes, 1969), 249–55, esp. 250–1; 448–9. See also A. Kunzelmann, 'Die Chronologie der Sermones des HL. Augustinus', in *Miscellanea Agostiniana* (Rome: Tipografia poliglotta vaticane, 1931) ii, 440.

the emperor? He himself insisted upon the judgment of the proconsul; he himself said: 'Hear me. I am not a heretic.' The one whose judgment you sought, is that judgment displeasing to you? Why? Because he judged against you? If he had judged in your favor, he would have judged well; because he judged against you, he judged poorly. Before he rendered his decision, he was a good judge, to whom you said: 'I am not a heretic. Hear me.' But the proconsul judged, you said, according to the laws of the emperors, not according to the laws of the gospels. That's just what he did, the proconsul judged according to the laws of the emperors. If, therefore, the emperors judged poorly against you, why are you appealing to their judgment regarding the proconsul's decision? For those were indeed the laws of the emperors against you, or were they not? If they were not, the proconsul pronounced against you not according to them. But if they were, do you think the emperors are going to judge in your favor against their own laws?... It is clear as day and cannot be denied, that here are a multitude of imperial laws against you.[68]

The emperor's ruling on Crispinus' appeal (v. Aug. 12.9) brought even more surprise. Honorius declared first that Crispinus and the Donatists were accountable to the laws established against heretics. Crispinus was ordered to pay the stipulated fine, but so too were the proconsul and his staff for not enforcing their previous judgment.[69] The proconsul was undoubtedly displeased with this result; he had been forced by the Catholics to listen to the debate and then punished by the emperor for showing leniency, at the bishops' behest, toward the man the Catholics themselves hauled up before him.[70] The proconsul would be even more displeased if it had been his predecessor who made the decision and the new administration, with no direct connection to case, received the fine. We would very much like to know the identity of the proconsul listening to the debate between Possidius and Crispinus, but there

---

[68] s. Denis 19.8: 'Iudicatus est modo Crispinus haereticus. Sed quid ait? Nunquid evangelica sententia superatus sum? Inde se asserens victum non esse, quia proconsul contra illum iudicavit, non Christus. Si ergo iudicium hominis parvi pendit, quare a proconsule ad imperatorem appellavit? Ipsius proconsulis iudicium ipse flagitavit; ipse dixit: Audi me, non sum haereticus. Cuius iudicium flagitasti, eius iudicium displicet tibi? Quare? Quia contra te iudicavit, Si pro te iudicaret, bene iudicaret: quia contra te iudicavit, male iudicavit. Antequam iudicaret, bonus iudex erat, cui dixisti: Non sum haereticus, audi me. Sed iudicavit proconsul, inquit, secundum leges imperatorum, non secundum leges evangelii. Ita fecerit, secundum leges imperatorum proconsul iudicaverit: si ergo male contra te iudicant imperatores, quare a proconsule ad eorum iudicium provocasti? Iam erant leges imperatorum contra te, an nondum erant? Si nondum erant, non secundum ipsas proconsul iudicavit. Si iam erant, numquid pro te imperatores contra leges suas iudicaturi sunt?...Manifestum est enim, et non negatur, multas imperatorum leges esse adversus illos.'
[69] See Christopher Kelly, Ruling the Later Roman Empire (Cambridge: Harvard University Press, 2003), 98 on the existence of collective funds maintained to pay fines levied on entire departments and their staffs.
[70] McLynn, 'Augustine's Roman Empire', 37.

are no entries in the law codes addressed to the proconsuls of Africa at this time. We know that in mid September 403, Septiminus was presiding in Carthage, but our sources do not pick up again until 5 March 405, when we know that Diotimus held that office.[71] In any case, Possidius reports that efforts by Catholics to relieve the provincial staff were intense and immediate.[72] Honorius agreed to the request, and the fines were eventually suspended.

An extract from an imperial letter reminding the African proconsul Diotimus that penalties leveled against Donatists had to be enforced is preserved in the *Theodosian Code* as 16.5.39: 'We decree that heretics of the Donatist superstition, in any place whatever, shall pay to the full the due penalty without delay, if they should either confess their crime or should be convicted with due observance of the provisions of the law.' The date on the letter is 8 December 405.[73] Some believe that this is Honorius' response to Crispinus' appeal, but to have received an answer at the end of 405 is very late, about two years after Possidius' beating and more than one and a half years after we think a Donatist embassy visited the emperor to appeal the proconsul's ruling. If we unhook this letter from the case against Crispinus, it becomes an evidence indicating that after the application of Theodosius' law against heretics and after the publication of the Edict of Unity (February 405),

---

[71] For Septiminus at Carthage in September 403, see *Coll. Carth.*, III, 174–7; for Diotimus holding office in March 405, see *CTh.* 16.11.2.

It is worth reviewing the career of Caecilianus, who was the vicar of Africa in 404 and into 405 (*CJ* 1.51.4 [Ad Caecilianum vicarium]). In letter 86 (dated to shortly after the promulgation of the Edict of Unity), Augustine seems to indicate that Caecilianus was the proconsul at the very time of the Possidius–Crispinus affair, but McLynn 'Augustine's Roman Empire', 37–8, interprets Augustine's trust in Caecilianus' ability to enforce imperial laws around Hippo and other towns in Numidia as prodding to have the laws enforced everywhere, including Africa proconsularis, not under the jurisdiction of the vicar. Cf. *PLRE* 2.244–6. Caecilianus had links to Symmachus in the 380s and was appointed *legatus senatus* in late 408 or early 409. He was sent as an envoy to Honorius by the senate with Attalus and Maximianus during Alaric's first siege of Rome. The trip from Rome to Ravenna would have coincided with Possidius' progress north (Zos. 5.44.1). He was appointed praetorian prefect to succeed Theodorus (Zos. 5.44.1–2) and took office just days after the issue of Sirmondian Constitution 14. See Augustine *ep.* 151, the bishop's letter to Caecilianus after the execution of Marcellinus.

[72] *v. Aug.* 12.9: 'Sed protinus opera data est per catholicos episcopos, praecipue per sanctae memoriae Augustinum, ut illa omnium condemnatio principis dimitteretur indulgentia.'

[73] 'Donatistae superstitionis haereticos quocumque loci vel fatentes vel convictos legis tenore servato poenam debitam absque dilatione persolvere decernimus.'

A. C. De Veer in his commentary *BA* 31, 377, n. 4 asserts that this is the official response to Crispinus' appeal. Lancel in *Actes de la Conférence de Carthage in 411* says that this date is far too late to be related to the Crispinus affair (Vol. 1, 18, n. 1), but in *Saint Augustine* (288), he believes that this is the response generated by the Crispinus appeal. Maier *Le Dossier du Donatisme*, ii, 146, n. 1 objects on the grounds of the time elapsed, but also because this decree is applicable to all ('quocumque loci') and is thus not a response to a particular suit or embassy (a rescript).

the Donatist and Catholic bishops continued to appeal the classification of Donatists as heretics and the punishments prescribed against them.[74] We can suggest several scenarios to which this letter may be fitted. First, local administrations and the proconsul(s) may have resisted levying fines against convicted Donatists, and the Catholics took their complaints to the emperor (we have no evidence for this from the Church council minutes, but they are very abbreviated for 405 and 406). Second, this letter may have been written in response to a Donatist appeal. The Catholics publicized a Donatist visit to the emperor in 406, when, after the Edict of Unity was circulated, they claimed (falsely, as we will see) that the Donatists asked the emperor to arrange a debate with the Catholics.[75] We do not have any evidence for an embassy of Donatists to court in 405, but that does not preclude the possibility that the Donatists launched a campaign after Crispinus' visit to push back this new legislation against them. Here, Honorius stated that the penalties would remain in place.

The third, and in my mind most likely, possibility is that the Catholics were requesting the proconsul(s) that Donatists subject to fines be released from punishment. Whatever unpleasantness occurred when the proconsul and his staff were fined during the Crispinus–Possidius affair, this did not deter the Catholics from pursuing the same tactic: lobby for prosecution and then appeal in order to relieve the imposed penalties. As Augustine informs us, the way these laws worked was that the Catholics bore the onus of bringing charges against the Donatists when they thought it necessary to apply pressure, especially as a method to control violence. Existence of a law itself was not enough to provoke the local and regional administrations to pursue its enforcement. Passive governmental bodies were roused to action once notified of infractions by outside parties. The Catholics called the attention of the local governments to violations and submitted charges accordingly. That Honorius addressed Diotimus with such a letter meant: (a) that the Catholics were proceeding with prosecutions and (b) that if we judge this scenario from previous experience, fines as levied by the proconsul's office may have been the object of Catholic bids for clemency. If the proconsuls

---

[74] Monceaux, *Historire littéraire*, iv, 74, argues that this letter is more to the promulgation and enforcement of the Edict of Unity. Once the edict reached Africa (according to the *Liber genealogus*, 26 June 405), Carthage was rapidly brought to unity (by late August of the same year, according to the Church council minutes of 405) with mass conversions and the confiscations of basilicas. The transition was not so smooth in the rest of Africa. The letter to Diotimus, according to Monceaux, is an imperial exhortation that Donatists be fined everywhere to expedite the drive to Catholic unity. For *Liber genealogus* see T. Mommsen (ed.), *MGH Chronica Minora I* (Berlin: Weidmann, 1892), 196.

[75] *Coll. Carth.*, III,141, an assertion the Donatists denied but to which they offered no detailed refutation. See discussion in Chapter 6, 201–2.

denied the Catholic requests, the bishops may have appealed to the emperor and received a negative answer.[76]

THE LAW OF 381 AGAINST THE MANICHAEANS

It took almost a full decade of Catholic action for the imperial authorities to recognize the Donatists as subject to Theodosius' heresy law. The Catholic bishops tried the same tactic with only one other law, and the story of its eventual success is interesting for what it tells us about how the Roman legislative process worked. A nobleman fought to retain his sister's property, although at her death she bequeathed it to the Donatist Church. Augustine said that the law indicated that the property *should* remain ('restituerentur') with her brother. It was suggested that the Donatists would react violently to a decision that contradicted the sister's wishes, and this prompted the emperor to act. He ruled in favor of the brother.

> There are other general laws, in which the ability of making wills or of transferring something through gifts is forbidden, as is the ability of accepting anything as gifts or from wills. For in a certain case, a noble man went as suppliant to the emperors because when his sister, who was a member of the Donatist sect, died, she bequeathed most of it to heaven knows, what persons of her community, with the greatest amount going to Augustine, some bishop of theirs. From that general law it was commanded that all of her estate should be respond to the brother. Furthermore, as soon as mention of circumcellions was made, in case they, according to their custom, violently resist, they would be warded off with armed protection and other support. Indeed, they were so well known and proven by so many battles that when the brother went as *supplex* about these matters to the emperor, the emperor was not able to remain silent.[77]

---

[76] We do know that episcopal correspondence and embassies were frequent during this year. In the Church Council of August 405, the pope asked that the African Church stop sending so many emissaries to Italy. The African bishops agreed. They also agreed that same day to send more letters to the emperor and an embassy of two to thank for anti-Donatist legislation promulgated that year. *ep.* 88.9 indicates that after the promulgation of the Edict of Unity, there was continued episcopal intervention on behalf of those accused of Donatist violence against Catholic interests.

[77] *c. ep. Parm.* 1.12.19: 'Sunt et aliae iussiones generales, quibus eis vel *faciendi testamenta* vel per *donationes aliquid* conferendi *facultas* adimitur *vel ex donationibus aut testamentis aliquid capiendi*. Nam in quadam causa cum homo nobilis imperatoribus supplicasset, quod soror eius, quae de parte Donati fuerit, cum defungeretur, in nescio quos communionis suae ex maxime in quendam

One may take these words literally, but Augustine here is probably employing rhetorical skill to the detriment of fact. The first point is that since the brother appealed to the emperor, we may conclude he lost his case at the local level. This is underscored by the man's designation as *supplex* ('homo nobilis imperatoribus supplicasset'), as *supplicatio* constituted a specific kind of petition based on perceived unfairness of the trial or appeals process.[78] When the petition reached the consistory, Augustine tells us that the emperor was not able to remain silent. That does not tell us much, however, as to the *nature* or the *extent* of the victory. We need not assume that the man's victory in the final arrangement of his sister's property was due to a conviction of heresy.[79] Property owned by women, regardless of religious affiliation, was highly regulated—officially and unofficially—in matters of testaments and bequeathal. The brother of the deceased would have solid grounds to appeal his sister's will simply by reason that a woman's property, and in this case we assume it was substantial, was subject to a number of restrictions, including limitations on amounts that could be distributed outside the family. Women, as once decreed by Theodosius (*CTh*. 16.2.27), did not have the right to bequeath their property to a church or a cleric when she had living relatives by marriage or by blood. If the woman had been a Catholic and had given her property to Augustine's church at Hippo, the brother would have had just as much right to protest her will.[80]

Augustine presents the case of the man and his sister's property in terms of a victory over the Donatists as proven heretics. That is, at least, the impression one gets while reading Augustine's description, but there is nothing here—no word 'heretic'—indicating that religion lay at the center of the dispute. There is also the social status of the brother to consider. He will have enjoyed influence in the community and, perhaps, ties of sympathy with people close to the

---

Augustinum episcopum eorum plurima contulisset, ex illa generali lege praeceptum est, ut omnia fratri restituerentur; ubi etiam circumcellionum mentio facta est, si more suo violenter obsisterent, quo genere auxiliorum et amminiculis repellerentur. Sic enim noti, sic multis proeliis probati sunt, ut de his et supplex imperatoris et imperator tacere non posset' (italics and underlining mine).

[78] William Turpin, 'Imperial Subscriptions and the Administration of Justice', *JRS*, 81 (1991), 101–18 at 117.

[79] Something done by Frend, *The Donatist Church*, 249–50, Bonner, *St. Augustine of Hippo*, 270, and Hombert, *Nouvelles recherches*, 570–1.

[80] *CTh*. 16.2.27 was issued in June 390. The law was repealed a couple of months later (see *CTh*. 16.2.28), but Jerome indicates in a letter of 394 (*ep*. 52.6) that the law remained active ('Pudet dicere: sacerdotes idolorum, mimi et aurigae et scorta hereditates capiunt; solis clericis et monachis hoc lege prohibetur et prohibetur non a persecutoribus, sed a principibus Christianis'). See A. Arjava, *Women and Law in Late Antiquity* (Oxford: Clarendon Press, 1996), 157–62, esp. 160, and Judith Evans Grubbs, 'Virgins and Widows, Show Girls and Whores: Late Roman Legislation on Women and Christianity', in Ralph W. Mathisen (ed.), *Law, Society, and Authority in Late Antiquity* (Oxford: Oxford University Press, 2001), 220–41.

court. That he publicized, truthfully or not, that pressure from the Donatists included threats against his person should have been enough to galvanize support for his cause, and would have served as legal justification for his designation as *supplex*. Elites guarded their physical sovereignty, and threats made against a nobleman by those, we assume, of lower status (circumcellions) would not have been tolerated.[81]

The words Augustine employs to describe the brother's grounds for protest allude to a law promulgated in 381 by the emperors Gratian, Valentinian, and Theodosius, which was aimed exclusively at the Manichaeans.[82] This law forbade Manichaeans to bequeath property or to accept inheritances. Confiscated goods and estates were to be absorbed by the imperial fisc. Unlike most Roman laws, this one was applied retroactively. The emperors realized that this was an unusual procedure and defended their decision on the basis of the severity and the entrenchment of the heresy: 'We recognize by our sense of just inspiration what an inveterate obstinacy and a pernicious nature deserve.'[83]

> If any Manichaean man or woman, from the date of the law as previously and originally issued by Our Fathers, has transmitted his own property to any person whatsoever, by the execution of a testament or under any title of liberality whatever or any kind of gift, or if any one of the aforesaid persons has become enriched by the bestowal, through any form whatever, of an inheritance upon which he has entered, inasmuch as We forthwith deprive the aforesaid persons under the perpetual brand of just infamy of all right to make a will and to live under the Roman law, and since We do not permit them to have the right to bequeath or to take any inheritance, the whole of such property, after due investigation conducted by Our fisc, shall be appropriated to its resources.[84]

---

[81] Peter Brown, *Power and Persuasion* (Madison: University of Wisconsin Press, 1992), 54. See also Leslie Dossey, 'Judicial Violence and the Ecclesiastical Courts in Late Antique North Africa', in Ralph W. Mathisen (ed.), *Law, Society, and Authority in Late Antiquity* (Oxford: Oxford University Press, 2001), 108–12, for a discussion of Donatist and Catholic use of violence against the upper classes and the outrage such action elicited from the imperial government. In Augustine's *ep.* 9* a man of high social rank was caught in the act of raping a nun and beaten by clerics. He brought charges of *iniuria* against them as they had no right to hit a man of his position.

[82] What we know as *CTh*. 16.5.7, as noted by Munier in *Concilia Africae, Registri Ecclesiae Carthaginensis Excerpta*, 93, n.1. Cf. Hombert, *Nouvelles recherches*, 571, n. 53.

[83] 'Quid consuetudo obstinationis et pertinax natura mereatur ... sanctione iustae sensu instigationis agnoscimus.'

[84] Compare with Augustine's words at supra n. 77. 'Si quis Manichaeus Manichaeave ex die latae dudum legis ac primitus a nostris parentibus in quamlibet personam condito *testamento* vel cuiuslibet titulo liberalitatis atque specie *donationis* transmisit proprias *facultates*, vel quisquam ex his aditae per quamlibet successionis formam conlatione ditatus est, quoniam isdem sub perpetua inustae infamiae nota testandi ac vivendi iure Romano omnem protinus eripimus *facultatem* neque eos aut <u>relinquendae aut capiendae alicuius</u> hereditatis habere sinimus *potestatem*, totum fisci nostri viribus inminentis indagatione societur' (italics and underlining mine).

Augustine and the Catholic bishops must have known this particular law well. Augustine used its language when speaking of the brother's property case, and it shows up again in the minutes of the Catholic council convened at Carthage in June 404.[85] What this means is that the Catholics referred to an imperial law issued against the Manichaeans in order to push for the restriction of property inheritance among Donatists. This is interesting. There was no justification for an emperor to rule against Donatists by use of a general law promulgated against the Manichaeans. If the nobleman won his case on the basis of the emperor's equating Donatism with Manichaeism, the emperor stretched the law well beyond its intended meaning. But that is almost certainly impossible. No subsequent legislation that we know of (until 405) indicates that Manichaeism and Donatism were assimilated in the eyes of the law, and continued efforts by the Catholics to prove the Donatists heretics through the use of Theodosius' law of 392 rule out the possibility of lost evidence to the contrary. Of course, the brother could have challenged his sister's will on the grounds that his sister was, in fact, a Manichaean. Shrewd (mis)use of the law in order to secure a victory was considered standard strategy by some late antique authors.[86] Although there is no evidence that Donatists were generally confused with Manichaeans, it is true that people practicing forms of asceticism were sometimes—from mistake or for convenience—taken for Manichaeans.[87] The noble brother

---

[85] The Catholic bishops commissioned Evodius and Theasius to go to court and ask the emperor to reissue the law (*repetatur*) restricting transferal of property inheritances of heretics. The request contains a transposition of words from Augustine's treatise, but also shows direct traces of the *Code* entry of 381: 'Petendum etiam, ut lex quae haereticis, *vel ex donationibus vel ex testamentis, aliquid capiendi aut relinquendi* denegat *facultatem*, ab eorum quoque pietate hactenus repetatur: ut eis relinquendi vel sumendi ius adimat, qui pertinaciae furore caecati in Donatistarum errore perseverare voluerint' (*Concilia Africae, Registri Ecclesiae Carthaginensis Excerpta* 93). 'Vel ex donationibus vel ex testamentis' is a phrase also found in the section quoted above of Augustine's *c. ep. Parm.*, but 'aliquid capiendi aut relinquendi' is much closer to the text of the law of 381 and does not appear in Augustine's passage.

The verbal associations between *c. ep. Parm.* and the Council of Carthage in 404 argue for this particular episode with the noble brother to have occurred before June 404. If Schindler is right in believing that *c. ep. Parm.* was penned as late as 405, the inheritance case *itself* predated the enactment of the Edict of Unity, when Manichaeans and Donatists technically came under the same heresy restrictions. We can be less sure about which passage came first, Augustine's or the statement of the Church council. If Hombert is correct in his dating, the bishops at the Council of 404 (including Augustine) were adopting language from Augustine's *c. ep. Parm.*

[86] Ammianus Marcellinus, *Res Gestae*, 30.4.8–20, esp. 30.4.11, he describes the kind of advocate who manipulates legal texts, whether valid or not, to build his cases.

[87] Priscillian is the most famous example. See Humfress, 'Roman Law', 137–9, who discusses the law of 381 in terms of its gathering of some Christian ascetic groups under the rubric of Manichaean heresy, and G. Barone Adesi 'Eresie "sociali" e inquisizione Theodosiano' in

and his lawyers may have referred to the general law of 381 when presenting their appeal, but the substance of the law is not what secured the sister's estate. We still do not know on what grounds the brother won.

Augustine carefully underscored the fact that the emperor's decision in *this* property case rested on the principles laid down in the law of 381: notice that he twice calls it 'general' ('Sunt et aliae iussiones generales and ex illa generali lege'), which indicates that the law applied always and in all territories of the empire. But Augustine was eliding, or blurring, use of the law as a precedent to argue a case in court with the methods by which the emperor rendered this particular decision. The brother, for whatever reason—dissatisfaction with a preliminary ruling, search for personal favor on the grounds of connection with the court, or threat of violence—applied to the emperor for intercession. The emperor's response was in the form of a rescript. Rescripts did not always constitute general law and could act as singular, nonpermanent, legal answers that could contradict general laws, but not affect their ontological status. In other words, the emperor's reply here was probably a mark of favor and not a recognition that the law itself was in need of a change. As such, the emperor was free to base the decision on any one of several reasons already mentioned: personal favor, acknowledgment of alliances through friends or family, social status, protection of elites from violence, or recognition of rights of familial heirs. Although these kinds of rescripts were not allowed to serve as precedents in other court cases, we have ample evidence that people used them to seek favorable decisions.[88] This seems to be one of those instances, as the Catholics subsequently petitioned the emperor that he issue a law limiting the property rights of Donatists using this specific rescript as a precedent.

THE JUNE COUNCIL OF 404

In June 404, the bishops convened in Carthage for their annual council. The extant minutes ask Honorius for aid in these times of violence. The previous

---

Atti dell'Accademia romanistica costantiniana VI Convegno internazionale (Perugia: Studium Generale Civitatis, 1986), 119–66. Emperor Magnus Maximus ordered the execution of Priscillian based on his conviction that the bishop was a sorcerer and a Manichaean; see *Coll. Avell.*, 40 (CSEL 35.1), p. 91, l.22–4.

[88] Jill Harries, *Law and Empire in Late Antiquity* (Cambridge: Cambridge University Press, 1999), 26–31. In 398, Emperor Arcadius revised the rescript system. Now rescripts answering legal questions were added to rescripts dealing in personal benefactions as applicable only to the cases to which they specifically referred.

For a discussion of how we think precedent was used in local courts, see Ranon Katzoff, 'Precedents in the Courts in Roman Egypt', *ZRG*, 89 (1972), 256–92.

year (August 403), the Catholics had requested a meeting with the Donatists, but they maintained silence, the Catholics said, due to their awareness of their own inferiority (*diffidentia*). Their eventual answer consisted of violent attacks against Catholic bishops, clerics, and laypersons. They were now sending the bishops Evodius and Theasius to the emperor to tell him that the solution to the current problem was to issue legislation that would force the Donatists to stop these attacks. The bishops did not ask for the issue of new laws, but for the reissue of the anti-Manichaean law of 381 and the heresy law of Theodosius of 392.

> Simul etiam petendum est, ut illam legem quae a religiosae memoriae eorum patre Theodosio de auri libris decem in ordinatores vel ordinatos haereticos seu etiam in possessores, ubi eorum congregatio deprehenditur, promulgata est, ita deinceps *confirmari praecipiant*: ut in eos valeat, contra quos propter eorum insidias catholici provocati contestationem deposuerint, ut hoc saltem terrore a schismatica vel haeretica pravitate desciscant, qui consideratione aeterni supplicii emendari corrigique dissimulant.
> Petendum etiam, ut lex quae haereticis, vel ex donationibus vel ex testamentis, aliquid capiendi aut relinquendi denegat facultatem, ab eorum quoque pietate hactenus *repetatur*: ut eis relinquendi vel sumendi ius adimat, qui pertinaciae furore caecati in Donatistarum errore perseverare volverint.[89]

The first paragraph, of course, refers to the law of 392 with its penalty of the equivalent of ten pounds of gold. The proconsul's ruling against Crispinus established the precedent. Now the Catholics were looking for its applicability against Donatists to be confirmed ('confirmari'). The second paragraph, which takes its language from the anti-Manichaean law of 381, works on the same principle, but the claim on this law for the Catholic arsenal constitutes more of a stretch. There are enormous gaps between a general law and a personal rescript, between a Manichaean and a Donatist. The Catholics were asking Honorius to reissue ('repetatur') legislation that had never been promulgated in the form the Catholics claimed it to have been. The emperor once rendered a decision favoring a brother in a property dispute with Donatist clerics. His appeal involved, however ephemerally, the law of 381 against the Manichaeans. Once the association was made, however, the Catholics pushed further by requesting that the individualized ruling be now considered generally applicable. The pieces were all there. What connected them was the request for 'reissue'. There was no change in language, but the law as the Catholics now envisioned it had grown to embrace Donatists and heretics in general, not just Manichaeans.

---

[89] *Concilia Africae, Registri Ecclesiae Carthaginensis Excerpta* 93.

THE DONATISTS AND THE LAW

The ruling against Crispinus by the African proconsul constituted a dramatic reversal for the Donatist Church. The initial findings of Calama's municipal council and the decision first rendered by the proconsul were more in line with the experiences of the past decade. Constantine's verdicts in favor of Caecilian's bid for the bishopric of Carthage and the later embassy of Paul and Macarius which turned violent, it is true, had made for unpleasant memories of rejection and persecution, but as of the 390s, the legal effects from these early years had to a large degree dissipated. The power of laws eased with desuetude, and the emperors were continuously asked to clarify or reissue laws because the most recent rulings carried the greatest authority.[90] Since the reign of Julian, numerous verdicts on both the provincial and imperial level assured the Donatists legal recognition.[91]

Much of what we know of the African administration under Gildo and his alliance with Optatus, the bishop of Timgad, who, in turn, supported the case of Primian against Maximian, is informed by epideictic speeches of Claudian lauding the defeat of rebels such as Gildo and, likewise, the hostile words of Catholic bishops criticizing rivals, namely Optatus. That is the nature of the surviving evidence. One reads about Africa being subject to violence and anarchy in the 390s, but it is important to recognize beyond the rhetoric that the Donatists solicited the support of the African officials by taking cases before them, including proconsuls. They sought, and received, recognition as the Catholic party in Africa.

The Maximinianist controversy offers then a good view of Donatist legal strategy. When Parmenian, the Donatist bishop of Carthage, died (in 391 or 392), his successor, Primian, was challenged by one of his own deacons, Maximian. Primian's conduct, considered morally and theologically questionable among the supporters of Maximian, became grounds for the bishops to come to that city for consultation.[92] Primian refused to recognize the meeting's legitimacy and held no communication with its attendees (Augustine applauds this action, as Caecilian, too, had refused to recognize those who objected to his election).[93] Then he had the meeting broken up using guards provided by provincial officials.[94] It is believed that this episode occurred at the end of 392.

---

[90] Harries, *Law and Empire in Late Antiquity*, 82–8.
[91] See *CTh*. 16.5.37. The Donatists continued to use Julian's letter of recognition as proof of standing until Honorius sought to invalidate it in late February 405, the same time the Edict of Unity was promulgated.
[92] *en. Ps.* 36.2.19.   [93] Ibid. 36.2.19.   [94] Ibid. 36.2.20.

In June 393, a council of bishops who supported Maximian gathered at Cebarsussa (in southern Tunisia). Their meeting was recorded by *notarii*; Augustine owned a copy of the transcript, and read excerpts to his congregation. The bishops lodged complaints against Primian and then voted to remove him from his bishopric. Maximian was installed in his place by bishops who ruled that the rest of the clergy had six months to separate themselves from the deposed Primian.

The supporters of Maximian, whom we now call the Maximianists, underestimated Primian. He responded with a council of his own on 24 April 394. The meeting at Cebarsussa had about one hundred bishops in attendance, but Primian's was more than three hundred strong. Again, *notarii* recorded the meeting. The transcript served as evidence in several proconsuls' courts, and Augustine himself quoted from it in his treatises.[95] The bishops who convened in the Numidian town of Bagai declared that Maximian and his closest supporters were excommunicated. Clerics now had until the end of the year to separate themselves from *him*. The eventual resolution to the Maximianist controversy constitutes the main point of interest for Augustine. That Maximian and his supporters, once condemned as schismatics, were eventually welcomed back into the Church without having to undergo rebaptism, undercut, Augustine claimed, the theological and logical grounds by which the Donatists refused communion with the Catholics. The Maximianists had broken with the Donatists; since then, according to Donatist views, their performance of the sacraments should have been inefficacious, and yet they were received again without remedying the fundamental break they had created in the flow of spiritual gifts. For Augustine, this one fact cracked the entire Donatist edifice.

Of paramount interest for us, however, are the methods employed by the Donatists to coerce the supporters of Maximian. The extant excerpts from the transcripts inform us that the Donatists (those who supported Primian) referred to their opponents as schismatics. In order to apply pressure to the Maximianist bishops and threaten them with the loss of their basilicas, the Donatists and their lawyers approached municipal councils, vicars, and proconsuls equipped with specific imperial laws against heretics, which they wanted to have applied to the Maximianists.[96] They argued that as their opponents were heretics, according to the law their churches and property should to cede to the

---

[95] As much of the transcript that survives from several of Augustine's works has been collated in the *PL* 11, 1183–9.

[96] *c. litt. Petil.* 2.58.132 and *en. Ps.* 57.15. Augustine says specifically that the proceedings of the Council of Bagai were inserted into municipal and proconsular *acta*, indicating that the Donatists brought their requests to local and then provincial officials.

orthodox Catholics, that is, themselves. When asked for evidence, the Donatists produced the transcript of the Conference of Bagai and read out the decree of the bishops condemning Maximian. 'It had thus been established that the Maximianists being condemned as heretics, had no right to possess the basilicas, and the proconsul announced his decision in conformity with the law. But what law? The law passed against heretics.'[97]

Augustine asks an interesting question: *But what law?* We do not know which one the Donatists brought before the provincial government, but they made their case soon after Christmas of 394. An imperial letter written to the vicar of Africa, Hierius, and dated 23 March 395, confirms previous statues regarding the rights and privileges of churches, and it is quite possible that the Donatists or the vicar had requested confirmation of ownership.[98] The Donatists presented their case against Maximianist rivals to several proconsuls over at least three years.[99] At each hearing, the proconsuls ruled in favor of the Donatists as the orthodox, Catholic party. Augustine claims that the Donatists deliberately deceived provincial administrations with the lie that they were Catholics, but this is just more rhetoric. They always had assumed, and argued, that they were the 'true Church'. There *was* dissimulation, but it came in the form of a request that the supporters of Maximianus be recognized as heretics under imperial law. The condemnation of the Maximianists as schismatics in Donatist councils became a charge of heresy in front of imperial administrators because this would apply the necessary level of coercion to force the Maximinianists back into, or permanently out of, the fold. The same legal duplicity later allowed the Catholics to bring charges of heresy against the Donatists.

Prior distinctions between schismatics and heretics made by Catholics were relatively infrequent and a matter of theological substance. Neither term (*haereticus* or *schismaticus*) is prominent in the early minutes of Catholic councils in Africa, nor do distinctive definitions separate them. Cyprian, for example, tended to use the terms indiscriminately.[100] Much more prevalent in the Church councils were broad, but formulaic, statements as to what the

---

[97] *en. Ps.* 57.15.

[98] *CTh.* 16.2.29: 'We direct that whatever statutes were enacted by Our Fathers at different times with respect to the sacrosanct churches shall remain inviolate and unimpaired. None of their privileges, therefore, shall be altered, and protection shall be granted to all those persons who serve the churches, for We desire that reverence shall be increased in Our time rather than that any of the privileges which were formerly granted should be altered.'

[99] Herodes was proconsul in March 395; Theodorus was proconsul in December 396, and in, perhaps, 397 Seranus was proconsul (*Cresc.* 4.48 [58]). Augustine says (*en. Ps.* 21.31 and *Cresc.* 4.3[3]) that the Donatists appeared before at least four proconsuls.

[100] See, for example, *De unitate* 3 and 10. For an historical review of Cyprian's understanding of the terms, see Geoffrey D. Dunn, 'Heresy and Schism According to Cyprian of Carthage', *JTS*, 55 (2004), 551–74.

Catholic Church accepted (*item placuit*) or rejected ('anathema sit').[101] It is in the late 390s and early 400s that the clarity of terms becomes a matter of urgency, and the crystallization should be understood in the context of legal strategy.[102] It is difficult to pinpoint the date when the Catholics first tried to employ Theodosius' law of 392 in efforts to curb the bishop of Timgad, Optatus, because the dates of Serenus' tenure as vicar of Africa are obscure. There is a very good chance that they brought their plea after the first half of 395, which means that they copied the example of the supporters of Primian when they lodged heresy charges against the Maximianists. The strategy which eventually allowed the Catholics to force the Donatists into unity may have originated within the Donatist Church.

HERESY AND SCHISM

It can be persuasively argued that all parties (Catholic, Donatist, and Maximianist) understood their fundamental disagreements as procedural, not doctrinal. On the Catholic side, the first substantive discussion of heresy and schism in regards to the Donatist situation is by Optatus of Milevis (1.11–12). He argued that the Donatists were schismatics. Schism was a separation from the mother church, engendered by discordant sentiments, bitterness, rivalry, and feuds. The separation was rooted in divisions among men and had nothing to do with theological tenets approved and held by the Church. The people might be in disagreement, but that disagreement was not rooted in belief. 'Nor are they [the schismatics] able to do anything new or anything else, except what they have long since learned from their own mother' (1.11). Heretics, on the other hand, deviated in established creed. They also preached their beliefs to others, deceiving the unlearned and endangering the souls they seduced (1.12). I am simplifying some of the argument's finer points,[103] but Optatus' distinction remains within the confines of traditional exegesis and interpretation of the scripture; that is, heresy implied an individual choice

---

[101] Wilhelm Geerlings, '*Haeresis* und *Schisma* in den Canones der nordafrikanischen Konzilien von 345 bis 525', in André Gabriels and Heinrich J. F. Reinhardt (eds.), *Ministerium Iustitiae: Festschrift für Heribert Heinemann zur Vollendung des 60. Lebensjahres* (Essen: Ludgerus Verlag Hubert Wingen, 1985), 161–7.

[102] Caroline Humfress, *Forensic Practice in the Development of Roman and Ecclesiastical Law in Late Antiquity with Special Reference to the Prosecution of Heresy* (Ph.D. dissertation, Cambridge University), 236–45.

[103] For a more detailed discussion, see A. C. De Veer commentary in *BA*, 31, 759–64. See also S. L. Greenslade, *Schism in the Early Church* (London: SCM Press, Ltd., 1953), 15–34.

in theological belief alien to those held by others. Schism, on the other hand, was akin to a tear in clothing and involved dissention or disagreement among those who held the same theological tenets.[104] Tertullian, Jerome, Tyconius, and Faustus the Manichaean, the latter of whose definition of both words is preserved in Augustine's *C. Faustum*,[105] all offered identical meanings for 'heresy' and 'schism'. When Cresconius, the grammarian, wrote to Augustine, he too distinguished heresy and schism on the grounds of the nature of the disagreement. He denied that the Donatists were heretics. Donatists and Catholics may disagree, but they shared theological tenets, especially on the nature of Christ (*Cresc.* 2.3–4 [4–6]). What lay between the Donatists and Catholics was not a *secta*, but *separatio*. Cresconius draws a traditional line of demarcation. We remember that in the bid to pressure the Maximianists, the supporters of Primian pursued their rivals on heresy charges, and did so in order to affect the outcome of judicial cases. Cresconius' arguments may reach back to earlier definitions because at the time of composition the Donatists were facing imperial pressure from having recently been ruled heretics themselves.

In response to Cresconius, Augustine argued that it was not a matter of intellect or theology, but intractability over time: 'heresy is inveterate schism' ('haeresis autem schisma inveteratum', *Cresc.* 2.7 [9]).[106] Schism and heresy both arose out of disagreement among Church members. The substance of that disagreement did not determine which category one belonged, but the stubbornness with which one held on to mistaken ideas. All schism, every split within the Church, became heresy if it continued for too long. This is new.[107] Augustine

---

[104] For discussion of the words as they appear in the Bible (esp. 1 Cor. 11:18–19) and Christian writers' various interpretations and translations, see H. Pétré, 'Haeresis, schisma et leurs synonymes latin', *RÉL*, 15 (1937), 316–26.

[105] Jerome (*ep. ad Tit.* 3.11): 'inter haeresim et schisma hoc esse arbitrantur quod haeresis perversum dogma habeat, schisma propter episcopalem dissentionem ab ecclesia separetur.' For Faustus (*C. Faust.* 20.3): 'schisma, nisi fallor, est eadem opinantem atque eodem ritu colentem quo caeteri, solo congregationis delectari discidio.'

[106] See also *c. litt. Petil.* 1.27.29.

[107] Those whom modern readers refer to as African Catholics (like Augustine) often called the Donatists schismatics, but their language became more strident as they sought legal means to combat them. Likewise, Emperor Honorius called the Donatists schismatics, but in the past tense, only after he placed them in the category of heretics in early 405. In terms of imperial law, the definition of heresy that survives to us is in *CTh.* 16.5.28, dated to September 395: 'Those persons who may be discovered to deviate, even in a minor point of doctrine, from the tenets and the path of the Catholic religion are included under the designation of heretics' ('Haereticorum vocabulo continentur et latis adversus eos sanctionibus debent subcumbere, qui vel levi argumento iudicio catholicae religionis et tramite detecti fuerint deviare').

See also Augustine *en. Ps.* 57.15., dated to September 403; Augustine may have made a direct allusion to this law: 'Si tu haereticus non es, falsae sunt illae leges; ab his enim imperatoribus latae sunt, qui non sunt communionis tuae; omnes qui non sunt communionis eorum, legibus suis haereticos vocant.'

broke with the long-term, accustomed definitions which he himself had once held.[108] He now formulated his own. It has been argued that these new classifications formed in Augustine's mind early on in the 390s; his attempts in that decade and the early 400s to apply heretical law to the Donatists constituted a direct result of Augustine's new beliefs about the meaning of these words.[109] That statement requires two adjustments. First, Augustine's writing reflects the efforts of the entire Catholic episcopate, and we should not be surprised if Possidius' argument before the proconsul defined Donatist heresy as separation without an attempt at reconciliation. Second, the statement that Catholic theology precedes legal strategy should be turned around. The bid to control the Donatists by appealing to imperial law informed the evolution of Catholic definitions, and their emergence was due, in part, to watching the Donatists work the courts, and the repeated attempts to activate their own dossier of laws promulgated against heretics. Who was a heretic and who was a schismatic, especially on theological grounds, was of secondary consideration to the more pressing matter of convincing the emperor that the Donatists had to be coerced.[110] To articulate these definitions as Augustine and the bishops construed them effectively cut through theological entanglements. Distinctions between theology and personality, *secta* and *dissentio*, collapsed into a simplex concept of intractability. When Honorius wrote in early 405 that the Donatist heresy was born of a schism (*CTh.* 16.6.4 'ut haeresis ex schismate nasceretur'), the genesis of that statement was attributable to Catholic efforts to stretch the law, and beyond that, to stretch the definitions that determined that law's jurisdiction.

---

[108] See *De fide et symbolo* 10, where Augustine maintains that heretics hold false notions and schismatics engage in unlawful separation.

[109] Schindler, 'Die Unterscheidung von Schisma und Haresie', 231–3.

[110] The language in the Catholic petition of June 404 offers a clue suggesting that the answer to Crispinus' appeal was not available when the bishops met at Carthage in June 404. The Catholics requested that Theodosius' law be confirmed so that they might have protection against the Donatists who planned *insidias* against the Catholics. With this law exercising its terror, the Donatists would at last abandon their schismatic or heretical wickedness ('ut hoc saltem terrore a schismatica vel haeretica pravitate desciscant'). In terms of legal argument, we have seen how much was at stake in attempting to shift the Donatists to the category of heretics. If Honorius' rescript proclaiming Crispinus subject to Theodosius' law of 392, and thus a heretic, had been available to read, the Catholics probably would not have prevaricated on the terminology or described the Donatist actions with so flexible a definition as 'schismatica vel haeretica'. They would have called the Donatists heretics. I am inclined to think that news of Crispinus' appeal had not reached Africa by mid June 404.

Notice the distinction Augustine makes (*Cresc.* 3.47 [51]): 'nos autem usque adeo saevos persecutores esse arguat, ut nec *post imperiale rescriptum* aurum illud fisco Crispinus expenderit, indulgentiam illi catholicis episcopis impetrantibus, et *nunc inter ipsas etiam recentissimas leges* proscriptionem vestris episcopis comminantes in re propria securus sedeat et catholici clerici inter manus circumcellionum clericorumque vestrorum domos, victum, salutem ac lumen corporis pendant' (italics mine).

4

Donatist Strategy and Catholic Response, 403–5

The Catholics referred to specific laws when asking the emperor to promulgate additional legislation, culling words and phrases from extant imperial laws and rescripts. Creation was therefore a matter of application: incremental augmentation rather than legislative innovation. The Donatists preceded the Catholics in this strategy, as they had likewise argued that the Maximianists should be subject to heresy laws. The use and manipulation of law by Catholic and Donatist clergy as described in Chapter 3 was of paramount importance in the struggle for domination, but it constitutes only the rarified, top layer of their relationship. It is sometimes difficult to discern in these episcopal embassies the quotidian friction that shaped Catholic–Donatist interactions, but most towns and many hamlets had two churches, two bishops, competing congregations, intermittent defections from one to the other, and occasional shifts in administrative policy that had to be recognized, at least in some degree, by officials and residents. The continuous renegotiation of social and political position that was an inherent aspect of town dynamics often resulted in violence.

Most violence in the Roman world consisted of low-level, personal indignities: the hitting and beatings that articulated the nuances within and among familial relations and the social orders.[1] But violence was also a functional aspect of large institutions, most prominently the Roman government. The Catholics and Donatists often called upon administrators to force opponents into line, but when they felt it was required, the churches employed their own personnel to apply coercion. We know that Catholics kidnapped people and held them prisoner in order to promote conversion.[2] The violence committed

---

[1] See discussion in Michael Gaddis, *There is No Crime for Those Who Have Christ: Religious Violence in the Christian Roman Empire* (Berkeley: University of California Press, 2005), 131–50, esp. 141.

[2] *ep.* 88.9. Other methods of violent coercion would involve, after February 405, imperial cooperation. In 395, Petilianus, the famous interlocutor of Augustine and one of the Donatist representatives at the conference of 411, was kidnapped and forcibly rebaptized by the Donatists when he was a Catholic catechumen (*sermo ad Caesariensis ecclesiae plebem* 8 [CSEL 53]). We do not how know often such abductions occurred on the Donatist side.

by Donatists has a more ominous reputation. The assumption that Donatist aggression was wanton is bolstered by the survival of Catholic literature, and is as subject to exaggeration as the supposed aversion the Donatists felt for government administrations. Certainly, there were attacks by Donatists against Catholic clergy in 403 and 404. Restitutus, the priest at Hippo, and Possidius were only two of their many victims, and we shall see more of them presently. The point is that the assaults occurring at this time were coordinated and measured, designed to intimidate, but not to kill. One can say very justifiably that the violence was brutal, especially if looked at from a Roman perspective, where some of the victims, respectable bishops, ought to have been immune to physical violation, but it is important to recognize the degree of organization and deliberation behind the attacks.

By following the violence against Catholic clergy, we can adumbrate their strategy for response, which culminated in the solicitation of the laws discussed in Chapter 3. The Catholic episcopate viewed the violence as opportunities to call upon the imperial administration to intervene, but the bishops were not unified in their opinion about what, exactly, should be done. Those senior to Augustine wanted to invoke laws that targeted all Donatists, perhaps those that forbade rebaptism. As we have seen, the bishop of Hippo instead advocated the expansion of law to categorize Donatists as heretics. Theodosius' law of 392 specifically targeted those who had the power of ordination, and Augustine said they could consequently pursue Donatist clergy *alone* when Catholics were subjected to attacks. Augustine defines his way of specifying violence as the trigger to activate the law as more lenient,[3] but it is important to note that, first, the actual requests to the emperor to render this law applicable to the Donatists were accompanied by no mitigating stipulations. Second, the qualification of Donatists as heretics made all its members, not just clergy, subject to, among others, the law of 381 which sharply curtailed property and inheritance rights. In efforts to please the other, more conservative, elements in the Catholic episcopate, Augustine and his allies offered greater latitude to prosecute than he cared to admit publicly.

As of the year 405, the Catholics found themselves in a novel position, armed with laws that provided them opportunities to exhort African administrators to fine and exile Donatist bishops. The entire Donatist community was subject to a number of restrictions; bailiffs and lessees were liable to be punished corporally for allowing Donatist rites to occur on land that did not belong to them. Augustine is our best witness to the sudden rush of success that brought with it a whole series of problems for the Catholic Church. The overriding

---

[3] See discussion in Peter Brown, *Augustine of Hippo: A Biography* (Berkeley: University of California Press, 1967; reprint 2000), 229–31.

concern the Catholics had in possessing, for real this time, 'no shortage of laws' was the prudent extent to which they should use them. They wanted the Donatists to convert. They wanted the attacks against Catholic clergy and laypeople to stop. But what they did not want (if we take Augustine as our guide) was to impoverish congregations. Even less did they want corporal penalties. To complicate matters, the burden of prosecution resided with the Catholics. If the laws they asked for demanded punishments the Catholics had no interest in seeing carried out, should they prosecute perceived infractions? From later correspondence of Augustine's we know that he was particularly concerned when Catholic hesitancy was coupled with reluctance on the part of provincial administrators to implement the laws fully.[4] The laws may have been roused, but if neither plaintiff nor judge wanted to enforce them, that would enable adversaries to flaunt them. The solution demanded a great deal of diplomatic and legal skill. The Catholic bishops put themselves between the emperor and provincial administrators—powerful and genuinely scary groups—and played them off each other. The strategy, which the Catholics developed during Possidius' tangle with Crispinus, was to solicit laws from the consistory, bring them back to Africa, prosecute, and then negotiate with provincial administrators to mitigate the penalties. This method of making the law work for them without unduly endangering their opponents was successful, and became for the subsequent decades the primary legal means of coercion. As late as 428, Augustine wrote to Alypius (*ep.* 10*) that he was showing provincial officials an old law of Honorius' (issued between 401 and 405) that forbade the kidnapping of slaves for resale and stipulated that the merchants responsible be whipped with lead-tipped thongs. The circumstances were slightly different now, Augustine told Alypius, in that those being kidnapped and sold were free persons, but Augustine said he was using the old and not-quite-fitting law anyway in efforts to move the African administration to action: 'We have begun to make use of it as much as is necessary to free people, but not to bring terrible penalties down upon these traders.... For we wish to constrain those whom we can by invoking this law, but we do not wish to punish' (*ep.* 10*.4).

THE VIOLENCE

Few transcripts (or précis) from Donatist conferences survive, save the documents appended to Optatus' work *On the Donatist Schism* and excerpts from

---

[4] See, for example, Augustine's *ep.* 100 to the African proconsul Donatus.

the councils of Cebarsussa and Bagai that Augustine incorporated into his own treatises.[5] The Donatist embassies to Constantine the Great, referred to by the Catholics frequently because he rejected their appeals, as well as Emperor Julian's aid in allowing them to reclaim their property and churches in Africa, also referred to by the Catholics as proof of Donatist collusion with a pagan emperor, offer only glimpses of Donatist facility with Roman law. They also utilized violence as another method of engagement. Many people, Donatists as well as Catholics, found these hard-edged attempts at persuasion unpalatable, but it is important to remember that the violence was political: a rhetoric by other means.

Attacks against Catholics surged in 403. The victims were clergy as well as laymen, but the literature emphasizes attacks against bishops and priests.[6] The targeting of Catholic clergy, as opposed to incursions (or what may be reclamations) on churches and church property, and attacks on landowners, seems to be a new development.[7] The increase was in response to a variety of efforts by Catholics to force a confrontation with the Donatists. The conclusion to the Maximianist controversy in the mid-390s, for example, wherein the

---

[5] Most of the documents related to the Donatists are collected in Jean-Louis Maier, *Le Dossier du Donatism*, 2 vols. (Berlin: Akademie Verlag, 1987–9). For discussion of the documents pertaining to the Donatists in the early 300s, see T. D. Barnes, 'The Beginnings of Donatism', *JTS*, 6 (1975), 13–22; and Serge Lancel, 'Les debuts du Donatisme: La Date du Protocol de Cirta et de l'élection épiscopale de Silvanus', *RÉAug*, 25 (1979), 217–29.

[6] Optatus of Milevis and Augustine (*epp.* 108.6.18 and 185.15) describe much of the pre-400s circumcellion/Donatist threats and attacks as directed toward landowners and people of financial means. See Optatus *de schism. Don.* 3.4: 'No one could be secure in his own possessions; the records of debts had lost their force, no creditor at that time had the freedom to enforce payment, all were terrified by the letters of those who boasted that they had been leaders of the saints; and if there was any delay in obeying their behests, a raging multitude suddenly flew to their aid, and, as terror went before them, besieged the creditors with dangers, so that those who should have had suitors on account of their loans were forced into groveling prayers through fear of death.' Translation from Mark Edwards, *Optatus, Against the Donatists* (Liverpool: Liverpool University Press, 1997), 69.

[7] From Optatus' *de schism. Don.* we know that know that during the reign of Julian, in 362, two Donatist bishops (those of Zabi and Flumen Piscensis) led an armed band to the walled hamlet of Lemellefern (Kherbet Zembia); they attacked the Catholic Church and killed two deacons (2.16–18). For further discussion, see W. H. C. Frend, *The Donatist Church: A Movement of Protest in Roman North Africa* (Oxford: Clarendon Press, 1952; reprint 1971), 189–90. This *appears* to be the only planned attack against Catholic *clerics* about which we have good evidence until about 403, but it is to be associated with the Donatist bid to claim churches and property restored to them by Julian's declaration of tolerance (*CTh.* 6.5.37).There exists evidence to the contrary. In 395, when Gildo, vicar of Africa, and Seranus, proconsul, ruled in Africa, there were attacks on numerous churches and church property: *c. litt. Petil.* 2.83.184 and *ep.* 29. Augustine does not assert that Catholic clergy were wounded or killed at that time. These acts may, too, be attributed to bids to claim property, not a deliberate attempt to target and injure individuals.

Also from Optatus *de schism. Don.* 2.17–18, we know that during the reign of Julian, there were armed attacks against Tipasa and Carpi, both of which involved the expulsion of Catholics from churches and the towns. We do not know if there were specific attacks on Catholic clergy.

supporters of Primian (in the majority) accepted their schismatic colleagues back into communion without rebaptism, constituted, in Augustine's opinion, Donatism's mortal failure. The bishop of Hippo exploited what he perceived to be the source of their vulnerability. Modern readers may lament Augustine's frequent review of events in the Maximianist controversy, but the argument apparently succeeded in persuading some Donatist clerics to switch allegiance.[8] Repetition proved effective, and the clerics who 'turned' were subsequently targeted for attack.

Restitutus, whose treatment at the hands of the Donatists, we saw, prompted Augustine to try to activate Theodosius' law of 392, was a Donatist priest who left to join the Catholics, not inspired by the force of law, but 'moved by the reason of truth' ('veritatis ratione promotus'). He was kidnapped, beaten, and imprisoned for almost two weeks. Other clerics shared similar experiences: Marcus, a priest of Casphaliana (close to Hippo), as well as a subdeacon serving under Marcian, the bishop of Urga (also located near Hippo). Marcus, Augustine says, joined the Catholic Church of his own free will, as had Marcian (Marcian had gone into hiding and the Donatists apprehended his subdeacon, whose name we do not know). Marcus was beaten and would have been killed, claims Augustine, if a group of passersby had not intervened. The subdeacon of Urga was beaten too, as well as hit with rocks. Like Marcus, he was said to have barely survived. Augustine says that the three men had joined the Catholic Church of their own accord, indicating that their conversions predated the promulgation of the Edict of Unity in February 405. As Augustine groups the story of Restitutus and these two other clergy members together, it is likely that these attacks occurred around the same time (403–4).

The Catholics also believed that their previous attempt in August 403 to force the Donatist bishops to meet them in a series of public debates promoted violent responses.[9] The Donatist episcopate declined the invitation, but as the proconsul had issued a letter supporting the gathering, the bishops were individually called out before their respective municipal councils to explain the refusal. The Catholics reported that the initial silence from the

---

[8] *ep.* 185.17 and *Cresc.* 3. 45 (49) indicate that Catholic efforts to advertise the Donatist handling of the Maximianist controversy prompted conversions, in as far as the Donatist clergy felt it necessary to apply violence against Catholics in order to keep them quiet. Possidius (*v. Aug.* 10.4–5) also indicates that persuasion lessened Donatist numbers to the point they felt it necessary to respond with violence.

[9] *Concilia Africae, Registri Ecclesiae Carthaginensis Excerpta* 93: 'Sed quia diffidentia premebantur, nihil paene ausi sunt respondere. Unde, quia impletum est erga eos episcopale officium, et illi qui veritati respondere nequiverunt ad immanes violentias sunt conversi, ita ut multos episcopos multosque clericos, ut de laicis taceamus, insidiis oppresserint, ecclesias etiam aliquas invaserint, aliquas invadere pertentaverint.'

Donatists soon turned to assaults. Besides Possidius, Augustine was the target of an ambush around this time, but he accidentally took the wrong road and therefore escaped injury. The recent discovery of Augustine's sermon *Contra paganos* (Dolbeau s. 26) allows us to place the aborted attack between September and December 403, the same months within which we think Possidius was beaten. In this new sermon, preached, it is believed, on 1 January 404,[10] Augustine clearly indicates he had already made his escape: 'That's why they [the Donatists] hate us, and if they get the chance kill us at the hands of the circumcellions. But because the Lord was at hand to help us, we escaped, giving thanks to the Lord's mercy' (§45).[11]

In 401, Catholic bishops had agreed to assert their presence more by exhorting residents in Donatist territories to embrace Catholicism.[12] These missions would have been resented, but we have little idea of the extent to which they occurred.[13] Possidius was traveling on a preaching mission in Donatist territory when he was ambushed, but most clerics who were beaten in 403 and 404 were at home, in their own towns. This brings us to the third reason for the increased attacks. Some bishops were engaged in legal proceedings at the local level to repossess churches once owned by Catholics but now in Donatist hands. What constituted their legal grounds for laying claim to the churches is unclear. Possession was more fluid than we sometimes suppose. Emperors Constantine, Constans, Julian, and Valentinian had issued contradictory

---

[10] See François Dolbeau, *Vingt-six sermons au peuple d'Afrique* (Paris: Institut d'Études Augustiniennes, 1996), 354–6. The only hesitation Dolbeau feels regarding the dating of this sermon comes from the location of the story in Possidius' *Vita*. Possidius places the story of Augustine's failed attack before his own, thus opening up the possibility that Augustine's brush with the Donatist gang could have come before 403. The placement is a matter not of dating or historical sequence, but of narrative structure. He places himself next to Augustine as a mark of his position as Augustine's heir. Moreover, Possidius is notoriously loose on structuring his narrative with precise chronological markers: see Brigitta Stoll, 'Die *Vita Augustini* des Possidius als hagiographischer Text', ZKG, 102 (1991), 4.

[11] 'Propter hoc oderunt nos et, si facultas detur, occidunt manu circumcellionum. Sed quia dominus adiuvit, evasimus, gratias agentes misericordiae domini.' There is also a brief allusion to the attack in Dolbeau s. 4, which was most likely preached on 29 June 404. For an English translation of the new sermons, see *Sermons: Newly Discovered Sermons*, translated by Edmund Hill in *The Works of Saint Augustine: A Translation for the 21st Century* (Brooklyn: New City Press, Hyde Park, 1997).

[12] *Concilia Africae, Registri Ecclesiae Carthaginensis Excerpta* 69: 'Deinde placuit ut his peractis legati etiam praedicandae pacis atque unitatis, sine qua salus christiana non potest obtineri, e numero nostro ad ipsorum Donatistarum sive quos habent episcopos sive ad plebes mittantur, per quos omnibus in notitiam perferatur, quam nihil habeant quod adversus ecclesiam catholicam iuste possint dicere, maxime ut manifestum fiat omnibus per gesta etiam municipalia, propter documentorum firmitatem.' See also Frend, *Donatist Church*, 252.

[13] The participation of local magistrates was expected at these meetings between Donatists and Catholics. The minutes of the 401 conference state that one of the goals of the Catholic mission was to expose and exploit the split between the Maximianists and Primianists. See A. C. De Veer, 'L'Exploitation du schism maximianiste par saint Augustin dans sa lutte contre le Donatisme', *RecAug*, 3 (1965), 219–37.

legislation assigning ownership. Donatists and Catholics both referred to favorable laws and defined themselves as existing within their confines. The back-and-forth struggle relied on legal documents and physical pressure. Hence, Donatist efforts in the early 360s (under Julian) to reclaim churches, sometimes by violent means, as well as the strategy of Optatus, the Donatist bishop of Timgad, who tried to secure Catholic churches in the 390s.[14] While Optatus tried to evict Catholic congregations from churches once belonging to the Donatists, Catholic bishops pushed back in 403 and 404 with their own claims for ownership in front of local administrators. We may be witnessing Catholic efforts to take what the Donatists had claimed in previous legal battles.[15]

Servus, the bishop of Thubursicu bure (Teboursouk), sought to reclaim a church occupied by the Donatists in his district. He took his case to the proconsul.[16] Procurators listened to the Donatist and Catholic representatives, but before a ruling was announced, Servus found himself facing an angry mob of his fellow townspeople. He was beaten and, according to Augustine, barely left alive.[17] Servus' father, a presbyter of advanced age and weak health, was so upset by the attack on his son and the Church that he died a few days later.[18] Maximianus, the bishop of Bagai,[19] was the victim of the most dramatic assault meted out by the Donatists. Like Servus, Maximianus sought to reclaim a church currently owned by the Donatists. The verdict favored Maximianus. Soon after, when Maximianus was attending to his duties in church, a Donatist group attacked him with weapons, including the wooden legs they had wrenched

See Serge Lancel, *Saint Augustine*, translated by Antonia Nevill (London: SCM Press, 2002), 287: 'This project for an itinerant embassy certainly failed; at least nothing further is known about it. Two years later, it was not resumed but replaced by far more precise and exacting measures devised by the council that met at Carthage on 25 August 403.' Cf. Frend, *Donatist Church*, 257–8.

[14] Optatus, as representative of the true Catholic Church at the time, would be at liberty to ask the African administration to lend aid of *apparitores* or soldiers to help in securing these building complexes.

[15] Pierre-Marie Hombert, *Nouvelles recherches de la chronologie augustinienne* (Paris: Institut d'Études Augustiniennes, 2000), 569–71 and A. C. De Veer commentary in *BA*, 31, 811.

[16] Hombert suggests that these attempts by Catholics to reclaim the churches occupied by Donatists may have their origins in the previous successes of Optatus, who was backed by Gildo, to push Catholics out of these churches. *Nouvelles recherches*, 570, and supra n. 7.

[17] *Cresc.* 3.43 (47): 'Servus...cum invasum a vestris locum repeteret et utriusque partis procuratores proconsulare praestolarentur examen, repente sibi in oppido memorato vestris armatis inruentibus vix vivus aufugit.'

[18] *Cresc.* 3.43 (47): 'A quibus pater eius presbyter aetate ac moribus gravis ea caede, qua vehementer adflictus est, post dies paucos excessit e vita.'

[19] A man with a very colorful past: 'Maximianus 6', *PCBE Afrique*, 723–5. Perhaps a former Donatist, Maximianus resigned his episcopate in 402 (we do not know why save for the risk of potential scandal; Augustine spoke of him highly); Augustine's *ep.* 69 invites a man by the name of Castorius, perhaps Maximianus' brother, to take the job. Either Maximianus' retirement was short lived or he managed to reconcile himself and his Catholic colleagues to the idea of his retaining the bishopric.

from the altar. Augustine says Maximianus bled profusely, having sustained a stab wound to the groin area. The bleeding may have been life-threatening, but his attackers dragged him outside where apparently the amount of dust and dirt entering the wound stemmed the flow. The Donatist gang left and soon after a group of Catholics, singing psalms, held Maximianus to carry him to safety. A superior number of Donatists returned and sent the Catholics running. The Donatists dragged Maximianus away. After sunset, they took him up the steps of a tower and pushed him off. Augustine believes that he would have died, but he landed in a pile of burnt excrement that cushioned his fall.[20] Later that night, a poor man approaching the place in the dark to relieve himself discovered the bishop, recognized him, and, terrified, called his wife to bring the lamp; she had been standing some steps away (*procul*) to afford her husband some privacy. Together, they brought him to the house not knowing whether he was dead or alive. Maximianus recovered slowly, having more scars, Augustine says, than limbs.[21]

The beatings of Servus and Maximianus are of particular interest because both bishops were engaged in suits to reclaim churches. Servus was attacked before a decision was rendered, but Maximianus won his case and attained possession. Nothing is known as to the substance of their arguments, but aside from using older historical precedents from emperors who issued their decisions regarding the possession of churches decades ago, these clergy may have submitted pleas based on Possidius' recent appearance before the proconsul. Both Servus and Maximianus made trips to the imperial court in the second half of 404 as 'living evidence'. They presented their scars to the emperor to demonstrate the extremes to which Donatists would go to intimidate the Catholics. Servus was already at court when Maximianus arrived, and we know that Maximianus' arrival was just prior to, or consonant with, the embassy of Evodius and Theasius, who were sent to Rome in June 404. Servus and Maximinus showed the emperor their *recent* wounds. They must have therefore submitted their cases, and received their punitive beatings, in just the past few months. As such, arguments made for the return of the churches may have been based on Possidius' case as presented to the proconsul, which was heard as early as January 404.[22]

---

[20] *Cresc.* 3.43 (47). Cf. *ep.* 185.27, where Augustine says he was thrown off the tower because his attackers thought he was already dead.

[21] See *Cresc.* 3.43 (47) and *ep.* 185.27.

[22] Augustine was in Carthage from late August to late September 403: see Othmar Perler and J. L. Maier, *Les Voyages de saint Augustin* (Paris: Études Augustiniennes, 1969), 246–9. He returned to the city by December 403 where he delivered a number of sermons, including the 1 January sermon *s.* Dolbeau 26, likely preached on the new year celebrations of 404 because Augustine refers to the foiled attempt by the Donatists to ambush him. Dolbeau (*Vingt-six sermons*) and Hombert (with the latter more convinced) believe that there is a distinct possibility that Augustine was in Carthage from December 403 into the new year. See Hombert, *Nouvelles*

The Donatists and the circumcellions are known for their hotheaded violence,[23] but the events of 403 and 404 indicate that not only were the assaults against bishops and priests carefully timed and planned, but more importantly, their perpetrators held themselves to a limit of damage imposed. Augustine and Possidius speak of numerous unnamed clerics who suffered invasion of their homes, beatings with clubs and swords, and a mixture of lime and acid thrown into their eyes.[24] Possidius says that some of these clerics

recherches, 563–88, esp. 571, for discussion of dating. Hombert strongly argues, taking up the assertion of Dolbeau's, for the dating of a series of sermons on the Psalms—147, 103, 80, 146, 102, 57 and 66—as being delivered in Carthage in December 403 and early January 404. A. M. La Bonnardière had previously dated the series to December 409: 'Les Enarrationes in Psalmos prêchées par saint Augustin à Carthage en décembre 409', *RecAug*, 11 (1976), 52–90.

From the opening lines of *De oboedientia* (Dolbeau *s.* 2) which was preached in Carthage on 23 January 404, Augustine said he had not expected to be in the city at that time. Aurelius' letter of invitation to Carthage had been insistent and forceful, and Augustine finally consented to go, much against his will. It was cold, and he was not feeling up to the long trip. He was also expected in the city of Constantine by 28 January for a council of Numidian bishops, to be hosted by Xanthippus. Augustine excused himself to Xanthippus and arrived in Carthage, 'not so much brought as hauled' ('non adducerent, sed adriperent' [2]). If he had already been in the city for over a month, it is not clear why he told Aurelius' congregation how unexpected and sudden this visit was. Certainly, Augustine's emphasis on his personal discomfiture was an effective method of expressing his annoyance with the congregation's behavior (their rudeness on the preceding day had prompted Augustine to retire to his seat without delivering his sermon), but this day's sermon (23 January) alludes to a quick relay of letters, interrupted plans, and hurried travel. I am wondering if Augustine's presence in Carthage in December and January represents two separate trips: December through early January and then an urgent recall in the middle of the month. Aurelius may have summoned Augustine to Carthage in January because of the Crispinus affair; this may have been the pressing need that required a mid winter trip (Dolbeau, *Vingt-six sermons*, 325). January is only a guess, and it is a conservative one.

[23] See F. Van der Meer, *Augustine the Bishop: The Life and Work of a Father of the Church*, translated by Brian Battershaw and G. R. Lamb (London: Sheed and Ward, 1961), 79–128. Associated with the randomness of circumcellion violence is the belief that the circumcellions were neither under the jurisdiction of Donatist clergy nor subject to ecclesiastical directives. See Robert A. Markus, 'Christianity and Dissent in Roman North Africa: Changing Perspectives in Recent Work', in D. Baker (ed.), *Schism, Heresy and Religious Protest* (Cambridge: Cambridge University Press, 1972), 21–36.

Many times, Augustine speaks of the clergy and the circumcellions acting in concert (*Cresc.* 3.43 [47]) and Frend says that we should take Augustine at his word: *Donatist Church*, xvii. More recently, Leslie Dossey has noticed that despite the opinion of many scholars of the circumcellions as acting outside the church directives altogether, their leaders, when named by Augustine, all turn out to be Donatist clergy. See 'Judicial Violence and Ecclesiastical Courts in Late Antique North Africa', in Ralph W. Mathisen (ed.), *Law, Society, and Authority in Late Antiquity* (Oxford: Oxford University Press, 2001), 110.

[24] See Possidius *v. Aug.* 10.6; Augustine *ep.* 88.8, *Cresc.* 3.42 (46). We know that Catholic priests and bishops were murdered in 407, 408, and 411. In *ep.* 88.8, Augustine uses the verb *concido* (as in: 'non tantum nos fustibus quassant ferroque concidunt'). While Teske translates this as 'to kill', it need not be that extreme. Although these anonymous attacks cannot be dated with certainty, both Possidius and Augustine place them in their narratives as accompanying descriptions of specific attacks that are datable, such as that against Restitutus or Possidius. These attacks against unnamed Catholic clergy were occurring in 403 and 404.

were murdered, but his chronology sometimes is so compacted that the span of decades flows through the length of only one sentence, and thus he may be referring to other, later, occurrences.[25] On the other hand, Augustine asserts that all the (unnamed) clerics attacked were left 'semivivos', which clearly means that they were not killed.[26] The attacks described by our sources were injurious and terrifying: forced disrobing, rolling in mud and blood, and public parading.[27] The confrontations with Catholic personnel, carefully choreographed, were humiliating, but halted before they proved fatal.[28]

Augustine is adamant that these attacks were deadly in intent, but as we progress through their retelling, it is evident that all the clerics who were assaulted—those specifically named and those who remained anonymous—survived their ordeals. The exception is the father of Bishop Servus, but his death is attributable to old age and emotional trauma, not wounds.[29] The weapons used by circumcellions, reputed to be clubs or other bludgeoning instruments, may have played a part in the survival rate, but we know that they did not limit themselves exclusively to non-piercing tools.[30] Cutting weapons were part of the arsenal (as we saw in the case of Maximianus of Bagai), so

---

[25] See *v. Aug.* 10.5–6: 'ipsisque catholicis sacerdotibus et ministris adgressiones diurnas atque nocturnas direptionesque rerum omnium inferebant. Nam et multos Dei servos caedibus debilitaverunt, aliquibus etiam calcem cum aceto in oculos miserunt, *aliosque occiderunt*' (italics mine). Two bishops were murdered in 408, and a certain Restitutus of the Hippo area who may, or may not, be the same Restitutus beaten in 403, was murdered by Donatists after the 411 conference.

[26] *Cresc.* 3.42 (46): 'Namque horrendis armati cuiusque generis telis terribiliter vagando non dico ecclesiasticam, sed ipsam humanam quietem pacemque perturbant, nocturnis adgressionibus clericorum catholicorum invasas domos nudas atque inanes relinquunt, ipsos etiam raptos et fustibus tunsos ferroque concissos *semivivos* abiciunt. Insuper novo et antehac inaudito sceleris genere oculis eorum calcem aceto permixto infundentes et inferciunt, quos evellere conpendio poterant, excruciare amplius eligunt quam citius excaecare.'

[27] Note that in Honorius' imperial letter of 409, which we know as Sirmondian Constitution 14, the emperor complains of bishops' hair being pulled, which is clearly a form of humiliating harassment. By this time, clerics were tonsured (*coronati*). See Chapter 5, n. 61.

[28] See *ep.* 29.11 (*c.*395), referring to a *basilica haereticorum*, and *ep.* 43.1 (397 or 398), where Augustine, in his bid to persuade, flatters the Donatist recipients of this letter that they are not heretics because they do not exhibit 'stubborn animosity'. In *c. litt. Petil.* 1.1 Augustine does name the Donatists as heretics. Hombert, among others, spaces the writing of the *c. litt. Petil.* over several years, with the third book composed as late as 405 (with the acknowledgment that our guess must remain between 403 and 405). The first book, however, maintains its date of composition at 400: Hombert, *Nouvelles Recherches*, 53–6, 189–93.

For discussion, see commentary by A. C. De Veer, *BA* 31, 759–64.

[29] Restitutus, Marcus, a subdeacon under Marcian, Possidius, Augustine, Servus Dei, the father of Servus, and Maximian of Bagai (and a number of unnamed others surrounding the Restitutus narrative and at the court when Maximian arrived).

[30] In the *sermo de passione Donati ep < iscopi > Abiocalensis* 6, a Donatist martyrdom account, we are told that Catholics too used blunt instruments in their attacks in order to avoid the spilling of blood. See J. L. Maier, *Le Dossier du Donatism*, i, 206–7; and Peter Brown's review of Tengström's book *Donatisten und Katholiken*, *JRS*, 55 (1965), 282.

self-imposed restraint by Donatists must explain why all the clerics survived.[31] As to who ordered these attacks, Primian, the Donatist bishop of Carthage, was partial to utilizing physical methods when he thought them appropriate.[32] Violence may have been a matter of general discussion among the Donatist bishops at their council in 403, and they could have decided that threats and encroachments could be met with physical resistance against clergy.[33] Catholics, after all, were specifically targeting Donatist clergy with pursuit of Theodosius' law. As for the assault on Possidius, the one case for which we have evidence regarding the impetus of the attack, the identity of the assailants, and information about the aftermath, the order seems to have been given by Calama's bishop. The Donatists were nothing but brutal to Possidius, but they did not intend to kill the Catholic bishop. Maximianus, the bishop of Bagai, was treated with particular contempt, but did his attackers want to murder him? Augustine thinks so, and he says that surviving a push from a tower was no less than a miracle. Both, the humiliation implied by the pile of manure at the bottom and the soft landing it afforded Maximianus were, I believe, intentional.

THE RESPONSE

The Catholics had responded to Donatist aggression since the mid-390s with consistent application to heresy laws, but pursuit of this kind of conviction was not their only option. In cases dealing with free adult people removed from the context of the *familia* (the extended household), the law stipulated that a leader of an organization, religion, or institution was not responsible for infractions perpetrated by his subordinates.[34] Roman law of *iniuria*, however, under which category violent treatment of Catholic clergy would fall, deemed culpable not just those who performed violent deeds, but those who were complicit in them.[35] There was room to prosecute and convict if the

---

[31] Augustine tells us the Donatists also used slings or catapults, as well as cutting instruments, including swords. *c. litt. Petil.* 2.88.194, 2.96.222; *c. ep. Parm.* 1.11.17 ('qui primum tantummodo fustibus, nunc etiam ferro se armare coeperunt'). Maximian, bishop of Bagai, was cut with a sword ('ferro etiam crudeliter caesus,' *Cresc.* 3.43 [47]).

[32] Frend, *Donatist Church*, 213; Monceaux, *Histoire littéraire de l'Afrique Chrétienne*, vi, 57 ff.

[33] We should not forget that many Donatist bishops and clergy deplored the violence occurring in their sees. Many tried to stop it or rebuked their congregations sharply. See *c. ep. Parm.* 1.11.17; *c. litt. Petil.* 1.24.26; *Cresc.* 3.49 (54); *epp.* 93.11 and 49.

[34] For example, in the *Theodosian Code*, heresy laws predating the Restitutus case clearly indicate that owners of property were not liable to punishment (in this case, fines) if they did not know that their tenants were engaging in illegal activities (see *CTh.* 16.5.21, dated 15 June 392 and *CTh.* 6.5.34, dated 4 March 398).

[35] See Chapter 3, n. 8.

Catholics could allege that Donatist bishops had procured the attacks against Catholic clergy, but they also could be considered liable if they had merely used persuasion (rather than tangible remuneration) to solicit attacks. But prosecution based on the delict itself was not part of the Catholic strategy. They wanted to combat violence with heresy charges as opposed to those of *iniuria* or *vis*.

Augustine provided the explanation why the Catholics pursued this strategy. Activation, he said, would exercise a great deal of control over the Donatists without requiring large-scale penalties against laypeople. Ensuring the 'good behavior' of the Donatist congregations would be the responsibility of the Donatist bishops, who would be the ones fined if any violence was perpetrated against Catholic clergy in their respective dioceses.

> But before these laws by which they are being forced to come into the holy banquet were promulgated in Africa, some brothers, among whom I was included, thought that, though the madness of the Donatists was raging everywhere, we should not ask the emperors to give orders that this heresy be completely eliminated by establishing a punishment for those who chose to remain in it. Rather, we thought that we should ask that they establish laws so that those who preach the Catholic truth by speaking it or who read the scriptures to determine it should not suffer the Donatists' insane acts of violence. We thought that this could be achieved in some measure if they reaffirmed more explicitly against the Donatists, who denied that they were heretics, the law of Theodosius of most pious memory, which he promulgated against all the heretics in general, namely, 'that any bishop or cleric of theirs, wherever he is found, should be fined ten pounds of gold.' We did not want all of them to be fined in that way but only those in whose territories the Catholic Church suffered some acts of violence from their clerics, from the circumcellions, or from their people, so that, following a complaint from the Catholics who had suffered such violence, their bishops or other ministers would be held to the payment of the fine by the care of those in charge. For we thought that, if they were thoroughly frightened and did not dare to do anything of the sort, we could freely teach and hold the Catholic truth so that no one would be forced to it, but that those who wanted to follow it without the risk of having false and hypocritical Catholics. Other brother bishops of mine thought otherwise, who were older than I and who observed the examples of many cities and locales where we saw the solid and true Catholic Church, which was nonetheless established and strengthened there by such benefits from God, when human beings were forced into the Catholic communion by the laws of earlier emperors. (*ep.* 185.25)[36]

---

[36] See *retr.* 2.74. This letter is also known as *De correctione Donatistarum liber unus* (Goldbacher [ed.], CSEL 57). 'Verum tamen antequam istae leges, quibus ad convivium sanctum

Augustine wrote this in a letter to Boniface, the *comes Africae*, in 417, a far distance in time from the events related. The perspective is totally historical. As to the difference of opinion that existed between the Catholic bishops as to the best approach to suppress Donatism, some wanted to target all its followers. Augustine and his allies thought it better to restrict Donatist clergy so as to gain time and opportunity to persuade Donatist laypeople to enter, willingly, the Catholic fold. As for the older bishops, they may have had in mind injunctions against rebaptism that had been issued before 404. One example that we know about was promulgated in 377 (*CTh.* 16.6.2).[37] This declaration denied churches to those who practiced rebaptism and ordered them to be given over to Catholics. These kinds of laws and the Catholic bishops in 404 who told Augustine they wanted them reissued

coguntur intrare, in Africam mitterentur, nonnullis fratribus videbatur, in quibus et ego eram, quamvis Donatistarum rabies usque quaque saeviret, non esse petendum ab imperatoribus, ut ipsam haeresem iuberent omnino non esse poenam constituendo eis, qui in illa esse voluissent, sed hoc potius constituerent, ut eorum furiosas violentias non paterentur, qui veritatem catholicam vel praedicarent loquendo vel legerent constituendo. Quod eo modo fieri aliquatenus posse arbitrabamur, si legem piissimae memoriae Theodosii, quam generaliter in omnes haereticos promulgavit, ut, quisquis eorum episcopus vel clericus ubi libet esset inventus, decem libris auri multaretur, expressius in Donatistas, qui se negabant haereticos, ita confirmarent, ut non omnes ea multa ferirentur, sed in quorum regionibus aliquas violentias a clericis vel Circumcellionibus vel populis eorum ecclesia catholica paterentur, ut scilicet post protestationem catholicorum, qui fuissent ista perpessi, iam cura ordinum ad persolvendam multam episcopi sive ministri ceteri tenrentur. Ita enim existimabamus eis territis et nihil tale facere audentibus posse libere doceri et teneri catholicam veritatem, ut ad eam cogeretur nemo, sed eam, qui vellet, sine formidine sequeretur, ne falsos et simulatores catholicos haberemus. Et quamvis aliis fratribus aliud videretur iam aetate gravioribus vel multarum civitatum et locorum exempla curantibus, ubi firmam et veram catholicam videbamus, quae tamen ibi talibus beneficiis dei constituta esset atque firmata, dum per priorum imperatorum leges ad communionem homines catholicam cogerentur, obtinuimus tamen, ut illud potius, quod dixi, ab imperatoribus peteretur.'

See also *ep.* 88.7, where Augustine offers essentially the same explanation: 'ex consilio autem nostri episcopi legatos ad comitatum miserunt, qui impetrarent, ut non omnes episcopi et clerici partis vestrae ad eandem condemnationem X librarum auri, quae in omnes haereticos constituta est, tenerentur sed hi soli, in quorum locis aliquas a vestris violentias ecclesia catholica pateretur.'

ep. 93.15–16 on being convinced by colleagues that the Donatists should be forced to unity.

[37] See *CTh.* 16.6.1, 16.6.2, and 16.5.5, dated to 373, 377, and 379, respectively. At least one of them was issued to the proconsul of Africa. It is likely that the African Catholics solicited laws against rebaptism, but they seem not to have pursued these laws in the time of Augustine, perhaps in part because the Donatists argued that they never performed 'rebaptism'. Theirs was the first, as the previous had been illegitimate and ineffective. The first letter against rebaptism was issued to the proconsul of Africa, Julianus. The second (16.6.2) is preserved in the *Theodosian Code* as written to Flavianus, the vicar of Africa, but discrepancies in the evidence regarding the date and location of issue led Mommsen to conclude that this letter was written to Florianus, vicar of Asia (as preserved in the text of the *Justinianic Code*).

See *ep.* 105.9 for reference to laws Augustine claims were issued against the Donatists by Gratian (i.e. in the same years these laws on baptism were promulgated).

did not prescribe physical coercion, but it would have been hard to avoid when government forces faced congregations during transference.[38] We do not know the extent to which the Catholics even tried to utilize these laws. Support by local administrators for Donatists along with religious and legal arguments they could employ to great effect made it difficult for the Catholics to get a foothold. Genethlius (died *c*.393), the bishop of Carthage who preceded Aurelius, was praised by the Donatists for not having enforced a decree directed against them (*ep*. 44. 12), but that may be attributable as much to powerlessness as to kindness.

To Augustine's thinking, the heresy charge provided a precise weapon, powerful in that the direct evidence of a bishop's complicity in violent acts against the Catholics was unnecessary to win the case. It was one thing to prove that a bishop was part of a conspiracy to harass Catholic clergy; it was another, and a much more simple matter, to pinpoint the Donatist bishop who presided over the territory wherein the violence took place and present the bishop, a man whom everyone knew, to the judge. He performed the act of ordination and he himself had been ordained.[39] Episcopal defendants were therefore guilty by profession, not by act, and would be liable to heavy fines as well as restrictions on their ability to inherit or bequeath wealth. This strategy provided the Catholics with a great deal of latitude at the episcopal level. At the same time, it provided the Catholics a broad, but indirect, weapon for use against the whole Donatist community. Target the bishops and the Donatist congregations would fall into line, disciplined more by the hand of their own beleaguered (and ever-poorer) bishops than by any potential threat from the Catholic camp. Ten pounds of

---

[38] As we see in the *sermo de passione sancti Donati episcopi Abiocalensis* (in Maier, *Le Dossier de Donatism*, i, 201–11), where parishioners remained in their churches when Emperor Constantine issued laws that they cede to the Catholics. When troops came to escort them out, violent clashes ensued.
Cf. Frend, *Donatist Church*, 262. Frend's evidence that the conservative bishops of 404 wanted physical punishment, to the point of capital sentences, comes from a letter (esp. *ep*. 100.2) written after issue of what we call Sirmondian Constitution 14 (early 409) when Honorius stated that judges must apply capital sentences to those guilty of physically harming Catholic bishops. Augustine's discussion in *ep*. 185.26—his notice that the death penalty was not to be invoked against the Donatists—seems to me to pertain to what grounds the Donatists should be prosecuted, whether on charges related to religious laws or on the basis of the violent crimes committed (the latter could be construed as a capital crime).
See also *ep*. 93.16–17, written in 407 or 408. The 'fear of the imperial laws' mentioned here has been assumed to mean fear of physical coercion. Augustine is referring to judgments against the Donatists from the age of Constantine to the promulgation of the Edict of Unity, where the punishments stipulated were, for the most part, financial. As of 405, *conductores* and *procuratores* who were responsible for allowing Donatist rites to be observed on estates were to be whipped (*CTh*. 16.6.4).

[39] 'vel ordinasse clericos vel suscepisse officium clericorum.'

gold was a large sum, a burdensome fine for even wealthy congregations. As such, the law was harsh, but it had a 'gentle' side in that the cases regarding violence against clerics would be tried in civil court, relieving the Catholic Church from being party to criminal cases where torture was habitually used in questioning, and conviction resulted in physical punishments.

Augustine's solution, however, was in truth much broader in punitive force than he admitted and, in theory, could be used by more aggressive Catholic bishops in ways that Augustine, perhaps, never intended. The legal slippage between the letter and spirit of Theodosius' law of 392, as Augustine and his allies envisioned its application, was enormous. Augustine and those who shared his opinion wanted this law to be used only against the Donatist bishops in whose territories violence had occurred. Such parameters, however, were never part of the legislation itself. Thus, the assertion that the law would be invoked only under specific circumstances depended completely on the will and inclination of the Catholic bishops pursuing suits. Augustine himself said that the local bishops would be the ones responsible for bringing Donatists in front of the judges. The understanding, at least to Augustine, was that this would happen only when violence set in motion the Catholic means of self-defense. But there was nothing in the law proper to keep Catholics restricted in its use. A bishop need not require a violent episode to haul up his Donatist counterpart in front of the local judge or the proconsul. We remember that the law as first promulgated also held accountable landowners, procurators, and lessees (*curatores*). Landowners cognizant of heretical services observed on their estates would forfeit their property. Moreover, in his letter to Boniface (*ep.* 185), Augustine neglects to mention that classifying all Donatists as heretics would render laypersons vulnerable to a variety of established injunctions. The expansion of the law of 381, which Augustine decidedly supported, compromised the property rights of every adherent (although, of course, the wealthy were more visible and had more to lose). Thus, the 'diplomatic' strategy defended and carried by Augustine was in reality very flexible, and far more potentially damaging to the Donatists than he seemed willing to admit.

Augustine also tells us that in 404 Evodius and Theasius carried with them to Rome suggestions as to how the laws should be shaped and directed, namely, that the Theodosian law only be applicable to clerics and bishops in whose territories there were episodes of violence against the Catholic Church (*epp.* 88.7 and 185.25). Again, there is no such stipulation to be found in the council minutes. True, we possess only its synopsis,[40] but there is no indication that

---

[40] F. L. Cross, 'History and Fiction in the African Canons', *JTS*, 12 (1961), 227–47 discusses the creation and the collecting of the manuscripts.

the Catholics planned to ask that the Theodosius' law be changed in order to specify the targeting of clerics in violent sees.[41] The only actual adjustment suggested allows for those whose inheritances were confiscated (under the 381 inheritance law against heretics) to keep them if they converted to Catholicism. This would be an effective control on people 'who cared more for earthy belongings than the judgment of heaven'.[42]

This is the second time we have encountered Augustine's assurance of strict association between the charge of heresy and an act of violence, but the evidence does not support him. It was left to a bishop's discretion to prosecute when he thought it appropriate. A degree of control could be imposed on Catholic bishops if heresy suits were brought to the attention of the imperial consistory only after having received permission from primates, but the evidence does not suggest tight coordination. Authority was apportioned to individual Catholic bishops regarding suits brought before local or provincial authorities.[43] And, we have evidence that bishops could easily circumvent the church's self-imposed restrictions on imperial embassies and ignore the parameters—explicit or not—governing the submission of cases to adjudication.

Here is an extreme example. In 419, Augustine wrote to Possidius about the problem of replacing the recently deceased Deuterius, the Catholic bishop of Caesarea (Cherchel).[44] Emeritus, the Donatist bishop of the same town who

---

[41] The council minutes indicate that the promulgation of Theodosius' law will offer the Catholics a useful means of controlling those who are wicked or do wicked things; the minutes do not specify for the law as it stands now to be changed. Who would be held accountable to this law would be a matter for Catholic discretion: 'ut in eos valeat, contra quos propter eorum insidias catholici provocati contestationem deposuerint, ut hoc saltem terrore a schismatica vel haeretica pravitate desciscant, qui consideratione aeterni supplicii emendari corrigique dissimulant' So that it may have influence with them, against whom, on account of their treachery, the Catholics, having been called forth lodged a suit, so that at least by this dread, they may leave off from their schismatic or heretical wickedness, who avoid being corrected and set right even upon consideration of eternal punishment.

[42] *Concilia Africae, Registri Ecclesiae Carthaginensis Excerpta* 93: 'non metu caelestis iudicii, potius quam terreni commodi aviditate.'

[43] We do not know how much control Augustine and his close colleagues had over the legal activities of the other Catholic bishops. Even someone like Florentius, who appeared with Possidius before the emperor in 410, managed to keep his episcopal Donatist counterpart imprisoned for three years (*Coll. Carth.*, I, 142).

[44] A letter of Augustine (23*A in the Divjak collection) is thought to be addressed to Possidius, although the absence of a salutation makes definitive ascription impossible. Circumstantial evidence marks Possidius as the recipient, but the argument as first put forward by Marie-François Berrouard and augmented by Serge Lancel, is convincing. Berrouard, 'L'Activité littéraire de saint Augustin du 11 septembre au 1ᵉʳ décembre 419 d'après la Lettre 23*A à Possidius de Calama', in *Les Lettres de Saint Augustin découvertes par Johnannes Divjak: Communications presentees au colloque des 20 et 21 Septembre 1982* (Paris: Études Augustiniennes, 1983), 301–27 and Serge

is mentioned in the *Vita Augustini* and is best known for dominating the conference of 411, was one of Deuterius' blood relatives.[45] Augustine was surprised that many people of the city were anxious to appoint in Deuterius' place a man named Honorius, who currently held the episcopal seat at Cartenna. Ecclesiastical law maintained that such a transfer was impossible, but Honorius' supporters were determined to see him installed. Precedent was easy to find. Deuterius may have, in fact, been Honorius' father, and he left his seat at Cartenna years before to become the bishop of Caesarea.[46] Honorius' supporters employed all their rhetorical and political reserves. We know from *ep.* 22* to Alypius that a letter was sent to the primate of the province of Caesarea—Augustine is dubious that it was, as stated, sent in the name of the people of Cherchel—that requested the primate to grant permission for Honorius to go to court. A favorable answer from the imperial administration could smooth the way for him to make the transfer. The primate refused, but Honorius thought that he could still get what he wanted if he went on personal business, which did not necessitate permission from higher ecclesiastical authority. His private agenda included disagreement over compensation to a man who had circulated a tract opposing Honorius' episcopacy, and this could provide an entrée to address the court on ecclesiastical matters.

The concern shared by Augustine, Possidius, and Alypius was that once at court, Honorius would call upon extant heresy laws to suppress the Catholics who resisted his transfer to Caesarea (22*10). Honorius apparently accused those opposed to him of being heretics; he then inserted this denunciation into the formal records (*acta*) of the church. When these men found out about Honorius' declaration, they confronted the bishop, but he denied he had ever said such a thing. They were not, however, allowed access to the documents. They told Augustine that Honorius, who was currently a guest of Augustine's, had the *acta* with him. Honorius in turn denied that there was any mention of the oppositional party in the documents, but clearly Augustine was not granted access to them either. 'Above all', Augustine writes to Alypius, 'I am concerned for the ones who sent us letters from there about him, lest perchance he sail and bring about at the court certain dangers for them' (22*.10). Honorius could submit the records as evidence to persuade administrators to declare his enemies heretics. They would be treated as if they were Donatists (22*.11).

Lancel, 'Saint Augustin et la Maurétanie Cesarienne (2): L'affaire de l'évêque Honorius (automne 419-printemps 420) dans les nouvelles Lettres 22*, 23*, et 23* A.', *RÉAug*, 30 (1984), 251–62.

[45] *Emer.* 10.
[46] Henry Chadwick, 'New Letters of Augustine', *JTS*, 34 (1983), 447.

A DISPLAY OF THE WOUNDED

A number of Catholic clerics went to court in 404.[47] Several bishops, including Maximianus of Bagai and Servus, came to seek safety and support from the emperor.[48] The dramatic stories had their intended effect. According to Augustine, those at court who saw the wounds and heard the accounts felt an *ingens invidia* rising against the Donatists. These visits may have coincided with the lodging of Crispinus' appeal, and the overlap may explain why Honorius' rescript railed against Donatist behavior (certainly Crispinus had not been the one to tell him about it) and came down so hard on the African administrators for not imposing fines in cases involving physical abuse.[49] Augustine says that Honorius' ruling against Crispinus was inspired by his disgust with the 'wicked' behavior of the Donatists.[50]

According to Augustine (*ep.* 185), the emperor's mind seems to have already been made up by the time Evodius and Theasius arrived. The visits of Maximianus and other injured bishops so appalled the court that before the official episcopal delegation was announced, the emperor renewed previously promulgated heresy laws against the Donatists and issued new ones.[51]

> His great mercy brought it about that our delegates were not able to obtain what they had wanted to obtain. For there preceded us some very serious complaints of bishops from other places, who had suffered many evils from the Donatists and been removed from their sees. In particular the horrible and unbelievable attack on Maximian, the Catholic bishop of Bagai, caused our legation not to get what it was after. For the law had already been promulgated that the heresy of the Donatists with all

---

[47] *Cresc.* 3.43 (47): 'Hic cum illic invenisset collegam Thubursicensem, quem paulo ante commemoravi, et alios nonnullos similia vel non multo inferiora perpessos.' It may be this parade of 'walking wounded' that inspired Pope Innocent to ask the African bishops to be more restrained in sending their own to court. See *Concilia Africae, Registri Ecclesiae Carthaginensis Excerpta* 94.

[48] The traditional date of their attacks is some time in 403 or 404, before the Edict of Unity was issued (February 405). *Cresc.* 3.43 (47): 'Omitto ante quanta commiserint, quibus easdem leges adversus errorem vestrum constitui coegerunt, magis christiana mansuetudine temperatas quam in tam magna scelera vi congrui vigoris exertas.'

[49] On the timing of Crispinus' appeal, including whether the Catholics knew of the emperor's response at the June 404 council, see Chapter 3, n. 110.

[50] *ep.* 88.7: 'This was the reply to appeal. Was it not your previous behavior that brought down this penalty?' 'Cuius appellationi quod ita responsum est, nonne vestorum praecedens improbitas...extorsit, ut fieret?'

[51] *Cresc.* 3.43 (47): 'Ingens in vos conflagravit invidia atque inde factum est, ut et praeteritae omnes contra vos leges excitarentur et istae conderentur novae. Quarum tamen universarum severitas, si vestrorum inordinatae ac sine ulla lege grassanti saevitiae comparetur, mira lenitas appellanda est.'

its great savagery—for it seemed more cruel to spare them than they themselves were cruel—not merely be prevented from using violence but not be permitted to go completely unpunished. And yet capital punishment was not to be imposed in order to maintain Christian gentleness even toward those unworthy of it, but fines were to be levied and exile established for their bishops and ministers. (*ep.* 185.26)[52]

This letter does not tally with Augustine's other reminiscences regarding the legation's visit. While the excerpt above indicates that Evodius and Theasius were preempted by the wounded bishops, *ep.* 88.7 says something quite different: 'But when the envoys came to Rome, the fresh and shocking scars of the Catholic bishop of Bagai so affected the emperor that such laws were passed which were passed before.'[53] Not only do the laws, including the Edict of Unity, seem to emerge from the consistory only after the delegation arrived, but the Latin indicates the arrival of the bishops was coterminous with the bishop of Bagai's dramatic appearance. Maximianus may have been a part of the episcopal delegation. The bishops were not only willing to solicit laws with more punch than Augustine admitted, but they also wanted to elicit reactions to the shocking appearance of Maximianus.

THE EDICT OF UNITY

Honorius published the Edict of Unity and the other anti-Donatist directives in February 405 (preserved, in part, in the *Theodosian Code* as 16.5.38, 16.6.3 [the Edict proper], 16.6.4, 16.6.5, and 16.11.2).[54] In light of these pronouncements,

---

[52] 'Sed dei maior misericordia...id egit, ut legati nostri, quod susceperant, obtinere non possent. Iam enim nos praevenerant ex aliis locis quaedam episcoporum querelae gravissimae, qui mala fuerant ab ipsis multa perpessi et a suis sedibus exturbati; praecipue horrenda et incredibilis caedes Maximiani catholici episcopi ecclesiae Bagaiensis effecit, ut nostra legatio iam, quid ageret, non haberet. Iam enim lex fuerat promulgata, ut tantae immanitatis haeresis Donatistarum, cui crudelius parci videbatur, quam ipsa saeviebat, non tantum violenta esse, sed omnino esse non sineretur impune non tamen supplicio capitali propter servandam etiam circa indignos mansuetudinem Christianam sed pecuniariis damnis propositis et in episcopos vel ministros eorum exilio constituto.'

[53] 'Sed sic cum legati Romam venerunt, iam cicatrices episcopi catholici Bagaitani horrendae ac recentissimae imperatorem commoverant, ut leges tales mitterentur, quales et missae sunt.'

The *Contra Cresconium* as well as *ep.* 88 (these works written at the same time, closer to the events themselves than *ep.* 185, and utilizing many of the same phrases and words), provide information contrary to that offered in *ep.* 185 regarding the time of Maximianus' arrival and the promulgation of anti-Donatist laws by Honorius. See Hombert, *Nouvelles recherches*, 195–200.

[54] Notice that the time between the decision to send an embassy (June 404) and the promulgation of the Edict of Unity (February 405) is over six months. This does not account for the time

the assurance Augustine offers us in *ep.* 185 that the episcopal delegation's arrival had little to do with the laws promulgated falls under more suspicion. The desiderata expressed by the Church council of 404 are very much present in the imperial letters as are some distinctly African Catholic notions regarding the placement of Donatists in the category of heretics.

The Edict of Unity is a harsh document containing much more uncompromising language than the other letters issued in February and March 405. This directive alone (as far as we can tell from what survives of the texts) lumped the Donatists together with the Manichaeans and states that those persevering in the practice of heretical worship were subject to laws previously enacted against them, specifically those issued by Honorius. Donatists were now subject to all antiheretical legislations, including those against the Manichaeans, which since the days of Diocletian had been particularly stringent.[55] The Edict also states that if seditious mobs assembled, 'sharp goads of a more severe punishment will be applied'.[56] Seditious mobs could mean Church congregations, and the goads indicate physical punishments, but this is the only time in Honorius' slate of legislation that he threatens to inflict physical harm on large groups of laypeople. We do not have the entire edict, of course, but the vagueness here may be deliberate, a rhetorical tour de force admonishing all by forceful language to abandon their foolishness without delineated particulars.[57] The other legislation issued in February and March 405 was much more direct, targeting Donatist clergy and practitioners with, for the most part, financial penalties.

Donatist clergy took the brunt of the new laws. Those who were convicted of rebaptizing were not fined ten pounds of gold, but were left bereft of their property. For all but the wealthiest members of the clergy, the distinction was negligible (*CTh.* 16.6.4 and 16.6.5). If their children were not Donatists or had abandoned their fathers' religion for Catholicism, they had the right to retain the property.[58] Estates where Donatist services were observed were to be absorbed by the imperial fisc. If the owners were not cognizant of Donatist activity, the estate would remain with the owners, but the lessee or procurator responsible would be flogged with whips tipped with lead and sent into permanent exile.

---

required to return to Africa. We know that Evodius and Theasius visited Paulinus of Nola after their visit to the court.

[55] Peter Brown, 'The Diffusion of Manichaeism in the Roman Empire', *JRS*, 59 (1969), 92–103 and Richard Lim, *Public Disputation, Power, and Social Order in Late Antiquity* (Berkeley: University of California Press, 1995).

[56] 'Et si turbae forte convenerint seditionis, concitatos aculeos acrioris conmotionis non dubitet exserendos.'

[57] Lancel, *Saint Augustine*, 290.

[58] This accords with the request from the council of 404 to alleviate penalties upon conversion. See *supra* n. 42.

Honorius also pressured landowning Donatists by cutting into their slaveholding rights. Slaves forced to embrace the master's religion could seek asylum in the Catholic Church and be protected from the owners by a grant of freedom. We know that Donatist landowners—Crispinus, bishop of Calama, being the prime example—rebaptized their tenants. Landowning, rents, and agricultural sales had suddenly become much more problematic for the Donatist church. The extent of their holdings is unknown, but to judge from Crispinus, the bishop of a respectable but not exceptional city, they must have been sizeable.

Those who rebaptized, participated in the rebaptism, and/or were aware of this activity and did not report it were not allowed to make wills; they could not inherit or make contracts. Those who attended Donatist churches fell under the same restriction, which would be lifted for those who abandoned their practices. Judges, municipal officials, and decurions who condoned Donatism would be fined twenty pounds of gold. We also know from Augustine that Honorius called for the exile of Donatist bishops and clergy who did not comply with the emperor's exhortation to unity.[59] These laws, one may argue, were tougher than the ones envisioned by the Catholics at the council of 404, but the degree of difference is slight. The Catholics had asked for financial coercion: ten pounds of gold for clergy and suspension of inheritance and bequeathal rights for all Donatists. The first part, the Theodosian law against heretics, has changed from ten pounds of gold to the threat of perpetual poverty, and again in keeping with Catholic requests, the children of the convicted who denied Donatism could retain the property. The ruling on estates is similar to Theodosius' law save one significant difference: notice of whipping and exile of the lessee or procurator ('per conductorem procuratoremve' [*CTh.* 16.6.4]) responsible for the observance of Donatist rites on estates. In the law of 392, freeborn lessees were to pay the fine; those of slave status were to be beaten with clubs and exiled. In the updated law of 405, social status was not a factor. All responsible lessees and procurators were to be punished with flogging, and Honorius makes no distinction between private and imperial estates.[60] Whipping with lead-tipped thongs, as Honorius advocates, gouged the flesh, and Augustine remarked that people who were beaten like this often died.[61] This aside, what Honorius legislated is essentially what the Catholic bishops had commissioned Evodius and Theasius to obtain. The Edict of Unity constitutes the acceptance of suggestions offered by the Catholic episcopate.

---

[59] *Cresc.* 3.47 (51); *ep.* 185.26: 'in episcopos vel ministros eorum exsilio constituto.'

[60] The tightening of the law on religious rites performed on estates must have been a central concern to the Catholics, but it is not a regular topic in the record of the church councils.

[61] *ep.* 10*.4: 'The flogging with lead...easily brings about the man's death.' See Peter Brown, *Power and Persuasion in Late Antiquity: Towards a Christian Empire* (Madison: University of Wisconsin Press, 1992), 54.

In sum, Augustine's letter to Boniface (*ep.* 185) distorts the events. Augustine's apparent control over a strategy to stem Donatist violence is tendentious as is his assignment of the promulgation of the Edict of Unity to bishops other than those sent by the Catholic council. Exactitude more than a decade removed from the events is perhaps asking too much, but Augustine was a man who liked to turn to documents to refresh his memory. It is true that Boniface, a general dedicated to a largely Arian military force stationed in Africa, required careful treatment. Augustine's version of Honorius' reception of Catholic bishops places the onus on Donatist violence and Catholic bishops other than himself, but still gets the message across: forced unity was a good idea as well as a success.[62] The most interesting point about this letter is what it tells us about Augustine's influence over the councils. Like Possidius' *Vita*, *ep.* 185 has been accepted as more proof of Augustine's emerging preeminence over the Catholic bishops, but we may have doubts. Augustine says the hope of free and true conversion propelled the council's decision, but it is more likely that other considerations, especially the effectiveness of any previous laws promulgated against Donatism, would have had greater priority. The argument the bishops were having in 404 indicates that they had produced minimal change. It was time to try something new, and this may have played a part in persuading the majority of bishops. In the end, however, acquiescence to Augustine's view actually required little compromise. Although he says differently, the episcopal conference agreed to ask for laws whose range and flexibility allowed bishops, if they so willed and had support from local administrators, to apply a great deal of pressure on their territories. The older bishops were not forced to concede much of anything.

THE PROBLEM WITH SUCCESS

The Donatists' long-standing protection from African administrators began to erode at the end of the fourth and the beginning of the fifth centuries; history,

---

[62] The author of the fictional letters exchanged between Augustine and Boniface (*PL* 33, 1095–8) knew Augustine as the quintessential bishop whose duty it was to forgive, not punish. A Goth who had assaulted a consecrated virgin was threatened with punishment by a *gladius ultor*. Boniface pleads to Augustine that he not be executed or imprisoned, but given a good reprimand; that way he will be given time to repent. 'It is not right,' Boniface says 'that a defendant be executed at the suggestion of a bishop, who is set aside for pardoning if the guilty repents' ('fas enim non est ut reus episcopi suggestionibus occidatur, qui veniae, si poenituerit, reservatur'). Emperor Honorius says something similar, stating that it is the duty of a bishop to forgive (*Sirm.* 14): 'sacerdotii sanctitas ignoscendi solam gloriam derelinquit.'

precedent, and the law were no longer trusted allies. But as the Catholics concomitantly rose in power, they found that the provincial courts still presented obstacles. The Catholics continued to send delegations to the imperial consistory because the provincial courts could not (or would not) help them to the degree they wished. Judges were reluctant to change or widen extant laws beyond what was outlined in the imperial directives. They did constantly interpret, and thus fashion, the law, but it is evident from the surviving correspondence between the provinces and the imperial court that judges and administrators resisted overinterpretation.[63]

The natural conservatism and potential bias of the local judges prompted the Catholics to appeal to the imperial court for 'satisfactory' answers.[64] The legal privileges afforded by proximity to the emperor, however, introduced a different kind of problem. The Catholics, now armed with laws to cower their opponents, were reluctant to collect the penalties they stipulated. We have seen Possidius ask the African proconsul to waive the penalty against Crispinus, but the episode illustrates well the risk of interfering as the bid for clemency rebounded in the form of an imperial rebuke directed at the African administration. The stakes increased as Honorius' reaction to violence against priests and bishops became progressively more severe. The Catholics hoped the laws would serve the purpose of discouraging attacks, but bishops like Augustine did not want them fully enforced. Augustine argued that the episcopate would be hesitant to initiate proceedings if they knew those convicted of violent acts would be beaten, or fare even worse. As for the local and provincial magistrates, they, too, may have been hesitant to take up these kinds of cases. Aside from the real issues of partisanship or even indifference, the awful punishments the laws demanded meant that local officials would feel it best to deal with imperial pronouncements as they saw fit. That sometimes meant ignoring laws altogether. Thus, there are many imperial injunctions threatening administrators with heavy fines for not discharging their duties in protecting Catholic interests. The problem, then, is that if imperial laws discouraged both administrative and Catholic parties to follow through with prosecution, it was quite possible that the relaxation of pressure from both sides would result in the emboldening of transgressors.

---

[63] Jill Harries, *Law and Empire in Late Antiquity* (Cambridge: Cambridge University Press, 1999), 53–5.

[64] A sample: Evodius and Theasius went to court in June 404. In August 405 another delegation was sent to thank the emperor for the promulgation of the Edict of Unity. There was an official embassy in 407, three in 408, and one in 410. These are the ones, at least, of which traces remain in the *Concilia Africae*. The fact that Evodius and Theasius arrived at court to find numerous Catholic bishops there and that when the Donatists went to Italy in 406 they found a North African bishop waiting for an audience (*ep.* 88.10) indicates that these 'official' visitations commissioned by the annual council at Carthage (and for which evidence is extant) were only a portion of the total.

The solution the Catholics hit upon was to continue to apply to the consistory, but to negotiate with provincial administrators so as to lessen or negate the penalties demanded by the emperor. There are numerous letters of Augustine that ask administrators, including Donatus (*proconsul; ep.* 100), Macedonius (*vicar; epp.* 152–3), Apringius (*proconsul; ep.* 134), and Marcellinus (*tribunus et notarius; epp.* 133 and 139), not to apply the full measure of the law against the convicted.[65] Modern scholarship mistakes Augustine's remarks such as these for the pleas of an outsider to an overly active and independent judiciary, but we need to keep in mind that these bids for mercy more often than not resulted from Catholic prosecutions. The bishops brought cases to the attention of the local and provincial administrations, and it was the bishops who sought to pressure the same administrators through the solicitation of imperial support. The requests we see for reduction in punishment, therefore, constitute one of two situations: one, the Catholics, having 'gone over the heads' of the provincial administrators to ask for what they wanted of the consistory, subsequently requested that local governments forgive the very penalties stipulated in the laws they asked for; or, two, the Catholics had asked the provincial administrations to render judgments, and then asked that these sentences be reduced.

In Chapter 5, Possidius provides an illustrative example of how the Catholic bishops negotiated among the local, provincial, and imperial administrations in the face of religious competition and challenge. This time we will turn to Possidius' fellow residents of Calama, who rioted and burned down his basilica when he tried to stop their holiday parade, which he deemed too 'pagan'. In 408, he and three other bishops went to court to complain of continuing attacks against Catholic personnel. They returned to Africa with a law that declared physical harassment of bishops a capital crime as well an order from the emperor to round up innocent residents of Calama so that they would be forced to reveal the identities of those who rioted against the bishop. How Possidius could restore his basilica, his dignity, and the authority of the Catholic Church in Calama while submitting to Augustine's exhortation not to employ corporal punishment was a matter of international consultation (with Paulinus of Nola acting as adviser) and a great deal of anguish for Augustine. He was not sure how they would resolve the matter. He was not even sure at this point, he told Paulinus, how the justice of this world could be of any help in the correction and healing of souls.

---

[65] See 'Donatus 24', *PCBE Afrique*, 309–10; 'Macedonius 2', 659–61; 'Apringius', 84–6, and 'Flavius Marcellinus 2', 671–88.

5

Possidius Goes to Court, 408–9

The summer months of 408 were difficult for the Catholic Church in Africa.[1] The townspeople of Calama rioted in protest of Possidius' attempts to break up a procession that was heading for his basilica. The unrest that began on 1 June lasted for a week, and when it was over, one of Possidius' clergy was dead. The basilica was looted and partially burned. After sporadic and unsuccessful negotiations between the Church and Calama's municipal council, news arrived that many high-ranking men in Stilicho's administration, and Stilicho himself, had been executed. Donatist hopes of a change in imperial policy awakened. There was consequently more unrest, this time around Utica, a coastal town in Africa proconsularis. Two Catholic bishops were killed by mobs; another three, including Evodius and Theasius, whose embassy in 404 helped secure the implementation of the Edict of Unity, were seriously wounded. Possidius and three of his colleagues traveled to the imperial court in the second half of 408 to tell the emperor that violence against Catholic clerics continued even in the face of his repeated legal admonitions.

Using Augustine's letters, Church council minutes and extant laws (the *Theodosian Code* and Sirmondian Constitutions 12 and 14), we can trace the bishops' legal activities in 408 and 409. Citing the contents of what we know as *Sirm.* 12, Possidius exhorted Calama's magistrates to prosecute those guilty of rioting against his church. Possidius was ignored, so he proceeded to Ravenna, where the emperor issued legislation in the Church's favor, which exists as *Sirm.* 14.[2] This imperial law affirmed all legislation enacted against heretics by previous administrations, but also demanded capital punishment for those who 'dared to take advantage of episcopal mildness' with acts of violence against Catholic bishops. The episcopal embassy found favor with Honorius, but his ideas of justice were unacceptable to Augustine, who immediately appealed to the proconsul of Africa, Donatus, not to issue any such sentence as dictated by the law.

We have seen that successive appeals to imperial law were largely responsible for the success the Catholics enjoyed against the Donatists in 404 and 405.

---

[1] A version of this chapter was published under the title 'Catholic Bishops and Appeals to the Imperial Court: A Legal Study of the Calama Riots in 408', *JECS*, 12 (2004), 481–521.

[2] Jill Harries, *Law and Empire in Late Antiquity* (Cambridge: Cambridge University Press, 1999), 88–91.

The events of 408 and 409 show how the Catholics could effectively apply force even when they remained a minority interest. When Calama rioted, no one, it seems, was willing to side with Possidius. Certainly no one intervened when the crowds attacked his basilica. When Possidius went to court, members of Africa's Christian elite, like Nectarius and the proconsul Donatus, were wary of episcopal plans. Yet, Possidius was able exert a great deal of pressure on Calama's municipal council by simply announcing he was sailing for Italy. Whereas the local senate had first ignored him, now they conceded their wrongdoing and offered to pay for damages in hopes Possidius would remain in Africa. The offer was not good enough for Possidius, and he went to Italy in hopes of attaining an even stronger position from which to negotiate. We are not sure what, exactly, he wanted, but restitution alone was not enough. We know that Augustine wanted heavy financial penalties that, in his own words, would render the perpetrators incapable of contemplating such action again. It was up to the local courts to determine the damages, and as they were not sympathetic to Possidius' cause, appealing to the emperor may have been the sole means of satisfying their demands. It is, however, possible that Possidius may have wanted even more.

The *Vita Augustini* insists that all Catholic bishops supported Augustine unconditionally, and while we know this is untrue, the events of 408 allow us to see that the legal wrangling in the aftermath of the riots caused tension among Possidius and Augustine. The strategy of imposing a Catholic agenda by means of legal threats, which some found unpalatable but others thought desirable, could strain relations between colleagues and friends. Bishops were divided regarding the extent to which coercion should be used, in terms of both numbers and extremes. Augustine refused to subject the participants in the Calama riots to physical punishment, but Possidius' sentiments are not as clear. In Augustine's letter to Paulinus of Nola (*ep.* 95), he seems to indicate unease with, even desperation at, the turn of events, and might be engaging in efforts, with Paulinus of Nola acting as a third party, to persuade Possidius to desist from pursuing his ambition to make the people of Calama suffer more than what the standards of episcopal wisdom and mercy dictated.

THE RIOTS AT CALAMA, JUNE 408

On 1 June 408, a group of people parading in celebration proceeded toward the doors of Possidius' basilica.[3] Many of them were dancing. The procession

---

[3] Except where noted, all descriptions of the Calama riots are taken from *ep.* 91 of Augustine.

may have included the display of a silver statue representing a pagan god (*ep.* 104.5). When the clerics barged into the crowd and attempted to break up the parade, the pagans threw stones at the church. One full week later, Possidius, citing legal texts that supported the Catholic cause, demanded protection and recompense from the town officials. Their response was ambiguous, and the townspeople, encouraged by the hesitation shown by the magistrates, returned and stoned the church again. Augustine admitted that the clerical staff had no power to cower opponents, for on the following day, when Possidius was rebuffed once more in his efforts to lodge a formal complaint ('apud acta dicere volentibus publica iura negata sunt'), the crowd stoned the church for a third time. This third confrontation was preceded by a hailstorm. Augustine assumed that hail should have served as a divine warning against further violence, but the storm may well have been interpreted as a sanction to the protest. The gods, too, were angered by the untimely halt of the celebration and were throwing rocks of their own ('ne vel divinitus terrerentur, grando lapidationibus reddita est').[4] Immediately following the third round of rock throwing, the crowd began to hurl firebrands. They first threw fire at the church roof, then at the clerics who, now feeling physically threatened, scattered. The crowd pursued. One cleric was killed on the street. The others fled to safety, hiding where they could. Possidius holed up in a cramped space and listened to the hurried footfall of enraged townspeople as they uttered curses and called for his death. Possidius remained there long into the night. The basilica burned (*ep.* 104.17) and the adjoining church buildings were looted.

Augustine goes on to say that no authority in the town ('quorum esse gravis posset auctoritas') did anything to quell the rioters. No one at all, in fact, seems to have interfered save a stranger ('peregrinum'), whose status is unknown, but Augustine's description of him emphasizes his lack of influence.[5] This stranger

---

Possidius, who is forthcoming about his dealings with Crispinus, mentions none of the events of 408 in his *Vita Augustini*. The Crispinus narrative leads to vague mention of what may be the Edict of Unity of 405 ('de die in die maugebatur et multiplicabatur pacis unitas' [13.1]), and then Possidius immediately proceeds to the conference of 411.

[4] Cf. F. Van der Meer, *Augustine the Bishop: The Life and Work of a Father of the Church*, translated by Brian Battershaw and G.R. Lamb (London: Sheed and Ward, 1961), 40, and Gerald Bonner, *St. Augustine of Hippo: Life and Controversies* (Philadelphia: Westminster, 1963), 125.

[5] Right at this time (in 408, shortly after the death of Arcadius and during the proconsulship of Porphyrius), one of the region's *curatores*, named Valentinus, completed the restoration and repair of the roof on a facility in Calama that housed 'strangers' (*peregrini*). This appears not to be a house for the poor. Since Valentinus' repairs fulfilled duties to his municipal office, the house he maintained might have been affiliated with the imperial transport system or government interest in agrarian export. Our lone stranger who helped the Catholics may have stayed here. See Claude Lepelley, *Les Cités d'Afrique romaine au Bas-Empire* (Paris: Études Augustiniennes, 1979–81), ii, 94. The inscription may be found at *CIL* 8.5341 and *I.L. Alg.* 1.263.

managed to protect several clerics from harm and recover objects stolen in the midst of the confusion. His actions, Augustine says, prove how easy it would have been for others to stop the violence. Augustine assigns the reticence of the Christians to fear of the local authority, and he indicates that he knows who instigated the riots but refuses to name the individuals.[6] The town officials, it seems, had turned away and allowed the protesters free rein because they themselves were among the participants.

Augustine distinctly calls the initial parade a 'pagan' one ('paganorum sacrilega'), but it is unclear to what degree, or with what intentions, Calama's residents were attending to non-Christian ideas or deities. The use by Augustine and the Catholic bishops of a word like 'pagan' often indicates an ill-defined non-Catholicism rather than a specific belief system.[7] The townspeople may have been performing the annual celebrations held on the Kalends of June, but the crowd was unusually provocative.[8] Not even under the reign of Julian the Apostate, Augustine says, had the pagans dared to approach the basilica doors. As far as we know, Possidius' church was located at the far northern extreme of the town. The celebrants may have deliberately walked past it.[9] Despite this directed antagonism, the residents were surprised that the bishop felt at liberty to intrude. Possidius' boldness may have been part of a planned strategy designed to test a new imperial law that gave bishops the authority to stop pagan rites.

Augustine says that the townspeople marched on 1 June contrary to the most recent laws (*recentissimas leges* [*ep.* 91.8]). Laws prohibiting public celebration of pagan rites date back to the reign of Theodosius the Great, and Possidius already had solid legal grounds for objecting to the 1 June procession if he could argue successfully that this was, in fact, an outlawed pagan celebration.[10] An imperial letter which we know as *Sirm.* 12 was posted in the forum

---

[6] See *ep.* 91.9: 'Demus etiam veniam timori eorum, qui potius deum pro episcopo et servis eius deprecandum quam potentes inimicos ecclesiae offendendos esse putaverunt.'

[7] James J. O'Donnell, *Augustine: A New Biography* (New York: Ecco, 2005), 195; Peter Brown, 'Religious Coercion in the Later Roman Empire: The Case of North Africa', *History*, 48 (1963), 285; Paul Monceaux, *Histoire littéraire de l'Afrique chrétienne depuis l'origins jusqu'a l'invasion arabe* (Paris: Editions Ernest Leroux, 1912–23; reprint, Brussels: Culture et Civilization, 1966), iv, 381.

[8] Harries, *Law and Empire in Late Antiquity*, 88. According to Macrobius (*Sat.* 1.12.33), the Kalends of June are referred to as the Kalends of the Beans ('nam et Kalendae Juniae fabariae vulgo vocantur') as newly ripened beans were now added to the offerings for the goddess Carna in celebration of the first fruits of the summer. The text of the Codex Calendar of 354 for 1 June mentions the *ludi Fabarici*. See Michele Renee Salzman, *On Roman Time* (Berkeley: University of California Press, 1990), 92.

[9] H. Leclercq, *Dictionnaire d'archéologie chrétienne et de liturgie* (Paris: Letouzey et Ané, 1907–53), vi, 2; Isabelle Gui with Noël Duval and Jean-Pierre Caillet, *Basiliques chrétiennes d'Afrique du nord* (Paris: Institut d'Études Augustiniennes, 1992), i, 343–5 and ii, section 122.

[10] See, for example, *CTh.* 16.10.12 (issued 392) and 16.10.13 (issued 395). Both laws were addressed to Rufinus, the praetorian prefect, and clearly prohibit sacrifice and the establishment of any pagan shrine, including turf ones which may have been commonly used in rural areas (for

of Carthage on 5 June 408. It placed restrictions on heretics and pagans, and is just the kind of law with which Possidius attempted to back his claims to the officials who so studiously ignored him. Is *Sirm*. 12 *recentissima*? The imperial letter outlined specific practices of heretics and pagans that were not to be tolerated and included a clause applicable to the situation in which Possidius was involved: 'It shall in no wise be permitted to hold convivial banquets in honor of sacrilegious rites in such funereal places or to celebrate any solemn ceremony. *We grant to bishops also of such districts the right to use ecclesiastical power to prohibit such practices*' (italics mine).[11] The letter goes on to say that the local authorities and municipal judges had to fulfill their obligations to this law. For disregarding the regulations, they as well as their staffs and the municipal senates ('officiis ordinibusque') were each liable to fines of twenty pounds of gold. It has been suggested that this imperial directive, posted in Carthage on 5 June, was the one the celebrants were violating when they marched on 1 June, and the one Possidius had in hand when he complained to the local officials.[12] The idea is attractive, but the problem is the seemingly insurmountable space between 1 June, which is the day Possidius first interfered with Calama's celebrations, and 5 June, when this antipagan legislation was 'published' at Carthage.

Augustine, it seems, did have the text of *Sirm*. 12 in front of him when he wrote his first letter to Nectarius, a Christian man of importance at Calama, who tried to intercede on behalf of the rioters. Augustine's term for the pagan

---

turf altars see D. Riggs, 'The Continuity of Paganism Between the Cities and Countryside of Late Roman Africa', in T. Burns and J. Eadie [eds.], *Urban Centers and Rural Contexts in Late Antiquity*, [Lansing: Michigan State Press, 2001], 290). Also forbidden is approaching any shrine, and giving of gifts or honoring images. The contents of the *Theodosian Code* do not encompass all laws in circulation before 438, the year of codification, nor does their presence in the *Code* mean that the African bishops were automatically aware of these imperial directives. The point is that laws outlawing pagan processions and sacrifice were in circulation before June 408.

[11] 'Non liceat omnino in honorem sacrilegi ritus funestioribus locis exercere convivia vel quicquam sollemnitatis agitare. Episcopis quoque locorum haec ipsa prohibendi ecclesiasticae manus tribuimus facultatem.'

We do not know what 'ecclesiasticae manus tribuimus facultatem' means. When dealing with non-Catholics, the options always discussed by Augustine and the Catholics involved the utilization of the imperial courts and the consequent penalties that those bodies were capable of administering. A great degree of latitude, however, should be factored in when dealing with a bishop and his powers over lower-class townsmen, the tenants working Catholic lands, and the people dependent on Church alms for survival. Leslie Dossey in 'Judicial Violence and the Ecclesiastical Courts in Late Antique North Africa', in Ralph W. Mathisen (ed.), *Law, Society, and Authority in Late Antique North Africa* (Oxford: Oxford University Press, 2001), 98–114 (esp. 105–9) has collected evidence of bishops beating heretical preachers, residents of poor houses, and small-time landowners. See also, in the same volume, Noel Lenski, 'Evidence for the *Audientia episcopalis* in the New Letters of Augustine', 83–97.

[12] 'Possidius', *PCBE Afrique*, 891.

festival ('sacrilega sollemnitas agitata est' [*ep*. 91.8]) is identical to Honorius' words in *Sirm*.12: 'non liceat omnino...sacrilegi ritus...quicquam sollemnitatis agitare.'[13] This phrase is unique in Augustine's corpus (although *sollemnitatem agitare* appears three times in distinctly Christian contexts)[14] and is not a standard expression among the bishops to designate pagan celebrations; these words, together or used separately (especially *sollemnitas*), are most often found in legal texts.[15] For Augustine to have consulted this specific law does not solve this particular chronological question, however; Augustine wrote this letter in August 408, well after the posting of the law, so he may in this instance be applying current law to past events. But the verbal association indicates that Augustine and the African bishops used this particular piece of legislation to pursue their case.

The gap between 1 and 5 June can, in fact, be resolved in two different ways. The first scenario involves the amount of time it took for the Calama affair to flare up and subside: the riots consisted of three days of violence stretched out over a nine-day period. The posting of this law (*Sirm*. 12), the initial riots in the town, and Possidius' grounds for legal protest may, initially, have had absolutely nothing to do with one other. In *ep*. 91 Augustine may be chronologically collapsing a week or so when he says that the pagans were acting contrary to the most recent laws. All the players—Possidius, the rioters, and the local authorities—may have been completely unaware of the latest imperial directive. After the disturbances of 1 June, nearly eight days passed before Possidius attempted to bring the matters before the authorities: 'deinde post dies ferme octo, cum leges notissimas episcopus ordini replicasset et dum ea, quae iussa sunt, velut implere disponunt, iterum ecclesia lapidata est.' He may have waited that long because it was not until a week later that he received notification of the new law of Honorius and Theodosius II. Augustine calls the laws 'notissimas' when he describes the events eight days after the initial stoning when Possidius addressed Calama's magistrates, imperial letter in hand. That is perhaps because it was not until that time that this law was, in fact, known. The problem with this reconstruction is the compression of time. The edict was posted on 5 June. Possidius' approach to the authorities, if nearly eight days after 1 June, gives us a date

---

[13] Goldbacher (*CSEL* 58 Index 3, p. 27) used the verbal association to date this letter of Augustine's (*ep*. 91) as well as the one he wrote to Paulinus of Nola (*ep*. 95). See Pierre Courcelle, 'Les Lacunes de la Correspondence entre Saint Augustin et Paulin de Nole', *RÉA*, 53 (1951), 275, n. 3.

[14] *s*. 183 (on the Pentecost), *s*. 383, and *s*. VI *De pluribus Martyribus* (*s. X ex Cod. Cassien*).

[15] See Iacobus Gothefredus (ed.), *Codex Theodosianus* 1665: 'Glossario nomico V. agitare', as noticed by the anonymous commentator of Rufinus, *PL* 20,0289B.

of 7 or 8 June, and thus the document requires a very rapid relay into the African hinterland.[16]

The second scenario permitting Possidius to complain to the Calama authorities by means of *Sirm*. 12 allows for this law to be the impetus for efforts to halt the procession. The proconsul of Africa, Porphyrius, posted the text of what we know as *Sirm*. 12 on 5 June. The law had been issued by the praetorian prefect (PPO) of Italy, Curtius, on 15 November 407 (the traditional date is 25 November). Six months between creation and promulgation means that other copies could have arrived in Africa through faster channels. While ship travel in the winter months was dangerous and unpredictable, the seas opened up by March and grain ships from Rome began to arrive on the shores of Africa in the early spring with travelers (many of them clerical), news, and correspondence.[17] A copy of Honorius' letter may have arrived in Africa and been in the possession of Church officials before 1 June, courtesy of bishops Fortunatianus (probably the bishop of Sicca) and Vincentius. These men had been sent to Italy to petition the court in June 407 and there are several pieces of legislation published late in that year whose promulgation may have been directly inspired by their visit.[18] The annual Church council had sent them in 407 to secure, among other things, laws against pagans and Donatists. This embassy may have solicited a law addressed to Africa's proconsul, Porphyrius, preserved in the *Theodosian Code* as 16.2.38 (15 November 407) and 16.5.41 (also 15 November 407). The first extract decreed that imperial laws regarding Church matters would

---

[16] See Othmer Perler and J. L. Maier, *Les Voyages de Saint Augustin* (Paris: Études Augustiniennes, 1969), 25–56, on overland travel in Africa. Carthage was the major port, of course, but Hippo also serviced the Mediterranean traffic north and south. See Augustine *ep*. 10*.7, where the traffickers of freeborn Africans (captured and sold as slaves in northern provinces) sailed north from the port of Hippo. See also Augustine's *ep*. 149: Rufinus sails to see Paulinus of Nola in 414 from Hippo. Marius, Mercator *Commonitorium de coelestio* 3.3 (*PL* 48, 98): Pelagius landed at Hippo, not Carthage, when he arrived from Italy in 410.

[17] In *CTh*. 13.9.3 (380), Emperor Theodosius informed the African shipmasters that the season of transportation for government goods was from the beginning of April to the beginning of October. Vegetius *De re militari* 4.39 states that the optimal sailing dates were from late May until the middle of September; days still considered acceptable fell after 10 March and before 10 November. See Boudewijn Sirks, 'Sailing in the Off-Season with Reduced Financial Risk', in Jean-Jacques Aubert and Boudewijn Sirks (eds.), *Speculum Iuris: Roman Law as a Reflection of Social and Economic Life in Antiquity* (Ann Arbor: University of Michigan Press, 2002), 147.

[18] C. Munier (ed.), *Concilia Africae, Registri Ecclesiae Carthaginensis Excerpta* 97. See also 'Fortunatianus 4 (Bishop of Sicca Veneria) and 5 (Bishop of Neapolis)', *PCBE Afrique*, 482–7 as well as 'Vincentius 3', 1210–12.

It is my belief that as most of the seven members of the Catholic delegation at the 411 conference had been to the imperial court, the Fortunatianus who went to Italy on the embassies of 407 and 408 (we know that it is the same man who went on both embassies, as the *Excerpta* state that the 408 departure is his second) was the bishop of Sicca.

be defended and represented to judges by trained advocates, not by clerics. This seems an indirect response to the African Church, which charged the embassy to seek permission for the Church to have *defensores scholastici* represent them in legal matters.[19] The second *Code* entry (16.5.41) reiterated that laws regarding heretics (Donatists and Manichaeans are expressly named) remained in effect, but open, sincere, and public rejection of heresy in favor of the Catholic faith would absolve the guilty from punishment. The connection of this extract to Fortunatianus and Vincentius is not based on the substance of the law, but rather because its addressee and date are identical to the above-mentioned 16.2.38. The two excerpts may have once been part of the same letter.

Additional connections can be made between other imperial laws and this episcopal visit to the imperial court. The association of 16.2.38 with the bishops is strong, since the legislation speaks of an issue that the African episcopate commissioned its embassy to raise with the emperor. If we connect 16.2.38 to 16.5.41 because of identical addressee and dates of issue (15 November 407), we should also consider *Sirm.* 12 as a part of this entire legislative series, because this letter quite possibly shares the same date as the previously mentioned entries.[20] *Sirm.* 12 is dated in the manuscripts, probably erroneously, to 25 November 407. That is a ten-day difference, but a link to 15 November is detectable in the two excerpts from what we call *Sirm.* 12 that wound up in the *Code* proper: 16.5.43 and 16.10.19. Both these laws, without doubt, are taken from the text that constitutes *Sirm.* 12 because their language and content mirror that imperial epistle very closely. Both these entries are dated 15 November 408 ('Dat. XVII Kal. Dec. Rom(ae) Basso et Philippo Conss.'). The year cannot be right and should

---

[19] See 'Fortunatianus 5', *PCBE Afrique*, 486–7. *Concilia Africae, Registri Ecclesiae Carthaginensis Excerpta* 97: 'Placuit etiam ut petant ex nomine provinciarum omnium legati perrecturi, Vincentius et Fortunatianus, a gloriosissimis imperatoribus, ut dent facultatem defensores constituendi scholasticos, qui in actu sunt vel in munere defensionis causarum, ut more sacerdotum provinciae, idem ipsi qui defensionem ecclesiarum susceperint, habeant facultatem pro negotiis ecclesiarum, quoties necessitas flagitaverit, vel ad obsistendum obrepentibus, vel ad necessaria suggerenda, ingredi iudicum secretaria.'

See *CTh.* 16.2.38: 'Adque hoc ipsis praecipuum ac singulare deferimus, ut, quaecumque de nobis ad ecclesiam tantum pertinentia specialiter fuerint impetrata, non per coronatos, sed ab advocatis eorum arbitratu et iudicibus innotescant et sortiantur effectum.'

See H. Lecrivan, 'Explicaiton d'une loi du code Théodosien (XVI.2.38)', *Mélanges d'archéologie et d'histoire de l'Ecole française de Rome*, 10 (1890), 253–6, and for more recent discussion, Caroline Humfress, *Forensic Practice in the Development of Roman and Ecclesiastical Law in Late Antiquity with Special Reference to the Prosecution of Heresy* (Ph.D. diss., Cambridge University, 1998),164–7.

[20] For discussion of dating, see John F. Matthews, *Laying Down the Law: A Study of the Theodosian Code* (New Haven: Yale University Press, 2000), 151–5 and Otto Seeck, *Regesten der Kaiser und Päpiste für die Jahre 311 bis 476 n. Chr.* (Stuttgart: J. B. Metzlersche Verlagsbuchhandlung, 1919; reprint, Frankfurt: Minerra, 1964), 312.

be changed to 407.[21] That then leaves the question as to whether these laws (*Sirm.* 12, 16.5.43, and 16.10.19) were issued on 15 or 25 November. The date 15 November is more likely the correct one, and thus it is possible that all the laws discussed above (16.2.38, 16.5.41, *Sirm.* 12, and, by extension, 16.10.19 and 16.5.43) were imperial responses to one episcopal delegation to the emperor at Rome.[22] Thus, the suggestion that Fortunatianus and Vincentius were the bishops who conveyed what we know as *Sirm.* 12 to the African Church before it was posted in the forum at Carthage becomes more plausible, as they may have been the very bishops whose embassy successfully solicited this letter from the emperor. If this embassy returned to Africa with a copy now in Possidius' possession, and that it had not passed through usual channels as part of the process of promulgation, including receipt by the emperor's representative in Africa and his official posting of the letter in a public place, may explain why Calama's elite would essentially ignore an imperial letter. For them, it was not—at least, not yet—a legitimate and active piece of legislation.[23]

LOCAL RULE AND IMPERIAL LAW

Despite pushing legal claims by twice citing legislation and demanding that charges be brought against the perpetrators, the municipal council ignored Possidius. Many of Calama's elites were partial to traditional forms of polytheistic worship and civic observance.[24] They were protecting their own. Possidius may also have been disliked in Calama. The town would already have been at loggerheads with Possidius, and with his Donatist counterpart, Crispinus, as well,[25] if these bishops had previously pressured its people, via imperial laws

---

[21] Bassus and Philippus were the consuls in 408. That tallies, but both laws were issued in Rome and Emperor Honorius was not in Rome in November 408. He had left the city before he received confirmation of the death of his brother, Arcadius, in late May. He was in Rome in November 407. In addition, both *Code* entries were addressed to the praetorian prefect, Curtius. Curtius was prefect in November 407, but not in 408. By November 408, Curtius had been replaced first by Longinianus (Zos 5.32.6): all citations from Zosimus are found in F. Paschoud (ed.) (Paris: Paris, Bekes Lettres, 1971–1989; reprint, 2003). See also Matthews, *Laying Down the Law*, 147–55.

[22] Roger S. Bagnall, Alan Cameron, Seth R. Schwartz, and Klaas A. Worp, *Consuls of the Later Roman Empire* (Atlanta: Scholars Press, 1987), 77. The date 15 November is more likely since in rendering the days VII Kal. Dec. (25 November) versus XVII Kal. Dec. (15 November), the 'X' could be easily dropped in the copying process, but it is unlikely that it would have been added.

[23] See Matthews, *Laying Down the Law*, 180–1. The language used to describe announcement and display of law was standardized (*accepta* and *proposita*, abbreviated as *acc.* and *pp.*) and integral to the process of promulgation.

[24] Lepelley, *Les Cités*, ii, 97–101.

[25] For evidence of Donatist efforts against paganism, see Augustine *ep.* 93.3 and *c. ep. Parm.* 1.10.16. See also Bonner, *St. Augustine of Hippo*, 298.

or personal influence, to abandon their practices.[26] Possidius may have tried, perhaps unwisely, to apply pressure to the municipal council with the contents of *Sirm*.12, which threatened penalties of twenty pounds of gold from local senates and their staffs who neglected to enforce the antipagan measures. Bishops were able to maintain control over some local residents, especially those of lower-class status who received financial support from the Church, but success along a broader social spectrum was largely dependent on the will of the local administrations to enforce the laws. Municipal senates were often beyond the reach of bishops' control, and Calama's leaders may have long been irritated with Possidius' enthusiastic initiatives. We also need to remember that since early 405, Possidius had been cajoling the Donatists in and around Calama to Catholic unity. The legal options as outlined in Honorius' legislation of 405 were numerous, and as much as we know Possidius, he would have eagerly invoked them. He certainly would have been within his rights to attempt to force the exile of Calama's long-standing Donatist bishop or squeeze the Donatist congregations with threats of financial ruin. The bishop of Calama may have made many enemies in the years previous to 408. Interference with the June parade and the strong resistance he encountered may represent a culmination of years of frustration from all sides, not a momentary collapse of normally peaceful relations.[27]

Augustine visited Calama shortly after the disturbances to support Possidius, and his reception by the town elite was decidedly cool.[28] An audience was granted him, but terms favorable to the Church were not forthcoming (*ep.* 91.10). Augustine and Possidius failed to reach a satisfactory arrangement with the authorities and they possessed insufficient leverage to impose their wishes. The solution was to appeal to higher authority, and Possidius

---

[26] Lepelley, *Les Cités*, ii, 97–101.

[27] We have almost no information about Crispinus after his appeal to Honorius in 404. All we know is that he died shortly before the convening of the 411 conference. See *Coll. Carth.*, I, 139: 'Petilianus episcopus dixit "Crispinus proximo tempore exivit de corpore."'

s. Dolbeau 27, preached, perhaps, in the last months of 406, may have been delivered in Calama. Its subject was the forcing of the town's Donatists into the Catholic fold. See F. Dolbeau, *Vingt-six sermons au peuple d'Afrique* (Paris: Institut d'Études Augustiniennes, 1996), 300–1.

[28] Perler, *Les Voyages de Saint Augustin*, 269, is confident that Augustine's visit to Calama precludes the possibility that Augustine attended the Church conference in Carthage, held on 16 June. The time is too tight; if Augustine learned about the final day of the Calama riots on 9 or 10 June, that means he arrived in Calama on 11 June at the earliest. He had only a day or two to negotiate with all the parties before he had to proceed to Carthage; it took three full days to get there from Calama. The assumption is that Augustine hurried to Calama as soon as he heard news of Possidius, but Augustine's visit to Calama may have occurred after his return from the Church council. To some degree, historians may push for an immediate visit by Augustine since it is often assumed, even if unintentionally, that Augustine, not Possidius, was the one capable of reestablishing order.

eventually informed Calama's magistrates that he was taking his case to the imperial court. The benefits accrued from seeking an imperial audience may outweigh the anger he provoked among the elites back home, but even if Possidius could persuade the imperial consistory to issue legislation that called for the local government to act against the rioters (many of them, it seems, of municipal status), could imperial law be translated effectively from Ravenna to Calama? The local administration was ignoring Possidius now; additional directives could be ineffectual in the face of studied neglect.[29]

It could be even more difficult for all involved if Possidius found consistent support among all levels of the imperial administration. An emperor's violent judgments required cooler heads and more temperate implementation at the local level. If the proconsul, vicar, and local judges were willing to execute the emperor's orders against rioters who murdered a cleric on the street, Possidius and his colleagues would have to interfere to save property and lives. After the episode with Crispinus in 404, when the emperor demanded the proconsul pay a fine for not upholding the law and its penalties, administrators would likely be cautious about undermining the emperor's sentence in order to please a litigious Numidian bishop.

The residents of Calama did not want Possidius to go to Ravenna. Relations between the local council and the Catholic bishop had deteriorated too far to sustain fruitful negotiations, so one of the town's citizens, Nectarius, turned to Augustine for help.[30] Nectarius was a gentleman whose relationship with Augustine had gone back several years.[31] They had an awkward encounter in

---

[29] Peter Brown, *Power and Persuasion in Late Antiquity: Towards a Christian Empire* (Madison: University of Wisconsin Press, 1992), 3–34.

[30] Possidius' *Indiculum* (X⁵ *Epistulae* 50) reads 'Nectario quattor'. There exist two letters from Augustine to Nectarius, not four. It is likely, however, that the two written by Nectarius to Augustine are mistakenly accounted for in this way. See A. Wilmart, 'Operum S. Augustini Elenchus a Possidio eiusdem discipulo Calamensi episcopo digestus: Post Maurinorum labores novis curis editus critico apparatus numeris tabellis instructus', in *Miscellanea agostiniana* ii (Rome: Tipografia Poliglotta Vaticane, 1931), 185.

[31] Finding a successor for Megalius was a difficult and prolonged task which Augustine and his colleagues assigned themselves. Megalius did not like Augustine and had tried to block his ordination as co-bishop of Hippo. The Catholic aristocrats in Calama may have shared Megalius' opinion. Augustine's efforts to replace Megalius involved the cooperation of bishops who were former inmates at Augustine's own monastery: Profuturus, bishop of Constantine; Severus, bishop of Milevis; and Possidius, soon to be the bishop of Calama. The difficulties and frustrations adumbrated by Augustine in *ep.* 38 may have stemmed from Calama's ground-level resistance to the search for, and appointment of, a bishop whom the people of Calama may have viewed, not as a man of their choice, but as a 'crony' of Augustine. See 'Megalius', *PCBE Afrique*, 742. The reasons for Megalius' opposition ranged from general anger (*Cresc.* 3.80 [92]) to the accusations that Augustine was a crypto-Manichaean (*Cresc.* 4.64 [79]) to the rumors that he had tried to seduce a woman using love potions (*c. litt. Petil.* 3.16 [19]).

the mid- to late 390s when Calama's bishop, Megalius, died and the African episcopate was trying to appoint his replacement. Nectarius told Augustine that he did not want to be consulted about the matter (*ep.* 38.3). Augustine's expectation of Nectarius' participation is important and means that Nectarius was probably a Catholic.[32] His religious affiliation is not secure, however, because while Augustine called Nectarius' father a Christian (*ep.* 91), he chided the son, saying, 'One must not give up hope that you [Nectarius] can attain that fatherland or even now plan with greatest wisdom to attain it' (91.2). That may mean Nectarius was not a Christian or a baptized Catholic, but it is more likely that Augustine was engaging in emotional blackmail by questioning Nectarius' loyalty.[33] Nectarius saluted Augustine 'in the Lord' ('Fratri Augustino Nectarius in Domino Salutem' [*ep.* 103]), and he offered a reminder (in *ep.* 90) of what constituted a bishop's duties regarding the succoring and saving of men, a liberty more fitting for a Catholic, rather than a non-Catholic, magistrate.

A wealthy gentleman of Calama who was most likely a Catholic Christian interceding for the rioters never mentions Possidius' name or indicates that Calama had a bishop. He reminded Augustine of episcopal responsibilities in a letter requesting clemency, indicating that Calama's bishop had not been responsive to similar pleading. Nectarius had turned to Augustine in attempts to persuade Possidius' hopefully more congenial colleague. If Nectarius, inspired by Possidius' announcement of his departure to court, began his quest for clemency with Possidius, it seems that judging from Nectarius' letter to Augustine, this initial approach had failed. Possidius was in no mood for clemency, or, from a more practical standpoint; he felt it necessary to display unsympathetic resolve in order to buttress his negotiating position and his dignity, both of which must have been severely compromised by the humiliating treatment he had received.

We know that Megalius was dead by August 397 (*Concilia Africae, Registri Ecclesiae Carthaginensis Excerpta* 33), but Possidius seems to be junior to Florentius, who was ordained bishop in September 401 (*Concilia Africae, Registri Ecclesiae Carthaginensis Excerpta* 107). This indicates that the see of Calama remained vacant or a there was a successor to Megalius before Possidius was installed. Crescentinus, whose see remains unknown, first appears in the historical record in August 397 as the primate of Numidia. He was dead by November 401 (*ep.* 59). Could he have occupied Calama's see during those years? See 'Crescentianus 3', *PCBE Afrique*, 226.

[32] O'Donnell, *Augustine: A New Biography*, 185–8.

[33] The contradictions in the evidence have introduced speculation that it was the elder Nectarius, a Christian, who begged off participation in finding a replacement for Megalius and it was his still-pagan son who was Augustine's correspondent in 408 and 409. Only eleven years separate the death of Megalius and the riots at Calama, and Nectarius himself had a son named Paradoxus, who was old enough to be described as *adulescens* in 409 (*ep.* 104.15). *Adulescens* was usually reserved for youths who are fifteen years of age and older. The Nectarius of 408 is most likely the same man who removed himself from discussion regarding the appointment of Calama's new bishop. See 'Nectarius', *PCBE Afrique*, 776–9, esp. 779.

Augustine's meeting with town authorities had likewise been frustrating. Calama's elite had demanded too much. 'They themselves asked much from us', Augustine wrote to Nectarius, 'But heaven forbid that we should be the sort of servants who are pleased to be asked for things by those who do not ask them of our Lord' (*ep.* 91.10). Augustine believed that the residents of Calama were not taking the riots seriously. What, then, had the officials offered as recompense before Augustine, and then Possidius, left Calama? Nectarius wrote in his first letter to Augustine that he and the town recognized that they violated the law; an assessment of damages could be tabulated by the courts and the payment to the Church made in full. All he asked for was that the guilty be excused from corporal punishment ('haec [colonia]...non levi populi sui errato prolapsa est....De damnis facilis potest haberi taxatio; tantum supplicia deprecamur' [*ep.* 90]).[34] These may be the original terms presented to Augustine when he was at Calama, but more likely the offer improved when Possidius set out for Hippo to confer with Augustine before he sailed to Italy. Now that Calama was faced with potential clarification and execution of the law through imperial channels, the town became more tractable.[35] Possidius was initially at a disadvantage while treating with the elite of Calama, but Nectarius' first letter indicates that they did not want him to appeal to the consistory and tried to forestall his trip. Possidius now had leverage, but thinking he could do better if he circumvented the local courts which might be biased in the determination of damages, he departed for Italy in September or, more likely, October 408.[36]

THE FALL OF STILICHO AND VIOLENCE IN AFRICA

Possidius' trip must have been extraordinarily difficult. Italy during these months was very unstable because the western administration had just been purged. On 13 August 408, the murder of many of the empire's highest

---

[34] *Taxatio* in a legal context (which this is) was an estimate of costs for restitution that the plaintiff would submit to a judge, who used that figure as the upper limit not to be exceeded when he made his ruling. On other occasions, the judge could set the limit himself. See Peter Garnsey, '*Taxatio* and *Pollicitatio* in Roman Africa', *JRS*, 61 (1971), 116–29, esp. 118–19.

[35] Nectarius says that if they were to be judged by the strict measure of the law, their punishment would be too severe: 'quod quidem si iuris publici rigore metiamur, debet plecti severiore censura.'

[36] The dating assumes that Augustine and Possidius knew of the appointment of Theodorus as praetorian prefect of Italy before Possidius left for Ravenna. The news would have reached Africa in September. See Erika T. Hermanowicz, 'Book Six of Augustine's *De musica* and the Episcopal Embassies of 408', *AugStud*, 35 (2004), 165–98.

administrators (including the praetorian prefects of Gaul and Italy) was carried out by order of Olympius. The execution of Stilicho soon followed on 23 August. The remainder of his supporters continued to be arrested, tortured, and killed. His widow, Serena, and their son, Eucherius, were also apprehended and executed.[37] Stilicho's brother-in-law, Bathanarius, is thought to have been serving as *comes Africae* at the time of Stilicho's murder. He was on friendly terms with the Catholic bishops, and Severus, the bishop of Milevis, once told Augustine of a dinner he enjoyed at Bathanarius' house where he witnessed a demonstration of the properties of magnets.[38] News of Stilicho's death, which probably reached Africa by mid to late September, may have been accompanied by orders to recall or execute the *comes*.

Stilicho's regime had continually pressed the senatorial class for cash in order to neutralize military threats from abroad (Constantine in Gaul and Alaric and his brother, Athaulf, in Upper Pannonia and northern Italy). Olympius' replacements of the high-ranking administrators whom he had murdered in August included men who had deeply resented the financial demands placed upon them by Stilicho's regime. The new administration granted major tax concessions to Italian landowners[39] and refused Alaric's request to settle his people permanently in Noricum and Pannonia (Zos. 5.36.1–3). Rebuffed in his demands for payment and land, Alaric, with Athaulf, began a coordinated march south through Italy.

About the time Possidius arrived in Italy with plans to travel north from Rome to Ravenna, Alaric and Athaulf had marched south along the Po,

---

[37] Eucherius had previously been accused by Olympius of plotting, at the behest of his father, to replace the young Augustus, Theodosius II, with himself. Olympius sent two of his agents to Rome to execute Eucherius and his remaining supporters. Before those orders could be carried out, Eucherius tried to garner support from the senate and people of Rome by issuing directives that allowed greater freedom to pagan worship. See Orosius 7.38 (CSEL 5): 'Occisus Eucherius, qui ad conciliandum sibi favorem paganorum restitutione templorum et eversione ecclesiarum inbuturum se regni primordia minabatur, paucique cum isdem satellites tantarum molitionum puniti sunt.'

This may be one reason why Augustine urged Olympius (*ep.* 97) to reiterate that the religious laws promulgated under Stilicho were, in fact, still in force. To assert that the decisions of now-disgraced imperial officials were no longer in force was a known tactic. In August 414, the emperors wrote to Julianus, the proconsul of Africa, stating that the decisions reached in the 411 conference at Carthage were to be upheld even if the imperial judge in that council, Marcellinus, had been accused of treason and executed by imperial order (*CTh.* 16.5.55).

[38] *Civ. Dei* 21.4. See *PLRE* ii, 221 and 'Bathanarius', *PCBE Afrique*, 136–7.

[39] *CTh.* 11.28.4, dated 13 September 408. See John F. Matthews, *Western Aristocracies and Imperial Court*, A.D. 364–425 (Oxford: Clarendon Press, 1975), 286–7. African estates would have picked up much of the monetary burden (some of these estates were owned by the same people who held lands in Italy), but Africa would see that tax pressure lessened by Honorius' relief measures promulgated in 410. See *CTh.* 11.28.6 (25 June 410).

circumvented Ravenna, and then proceeded across Apennines and south to the outskirts of Rome. Alaric cut the city off from Ostia and proceeded to squeeze the city into submission. Rome was hungry, and Zosimus tells us that starvation and disease rendered the streets overflowing with corpses (5.39.3).[40] When the city finally paid him the required ransom and Honorius had delivered the demanded hostages, Alaric lifted the blockade and withdrew his troops north into Etruria. He made concerted efforts to keep the roads safe for travelers, but there were attacks. It is at this point, with Alaric in Etruria, that Zosimus reports that the year 408 came to an end (5.42.3).

Possidius was only one of at least five African clerics trying to get to Ravenna during the second half of 408. Two Church councils had been convened at Carthage after the Calama riots.[41] The first, the annual conference on 16 June, commissioned the bishop Fortunatianus to go again to the imperial court to present the Catholic case to the emperor against heretics and pagans.[42] No particulars have come down to us about the details of this embassy ('legationem iterum suscepit episcopus Fortunatianus contra Paganos et haereticos') except that during this conference, convened no more than ten days after the proconsul Porphyrius posted what we call *Sirm.* 12 in the forum of Carthage (close to where the bishops were meeting in the Basilica Restitutus), the bishops decided it was necessary to send Fortunatianus to Ravenna.[43] Here was yet another embassy asking for reaffirmation of the kind of legislation that had just been promulgated. Clearly, the Church felt the need to complement this broadly encompassing legislation with more assurance from the emperor. Honorius had just confirmed all previous heresy laws against Manichaeans, pagans, Donatists, Priscillianists, and the Caelicolae. All their property was subject to confiscation. Legal authorities were responsible for overseeing the law put into effect under pain of severe financial penalties. After Calama, however, the Church believed that the imperial court needed to know of the reluctance with which the emperor's laws were being enforced.

---

[40] Cf. *ep.* 99.

[41] See Monceaux, *Histoire littéraire de l'Afrique Chrétienne*, i, 381–2 for a review of the documents and councils under discussion.

[42] *Concilia Africae, Registri Ecclesiae Carthaginensis Excerpta*, 106. Fortunatianus went on the embassy of June 407. He was one of seven bishops to present the Catholic arguments at the conference of 411.

[43] Possidius' decision to go to court could have been discussed and approved at this 16 June conference or the one in October 408. The Church council of 407 decreed that bishops seeking an audience with the imperial court must have in their possession formal papers issued by the primate (or a council) and ratified by the Church in Rome in order to approach the emperor. Possidius' mission would have been cleared during one of these sessions. It makes more sense to assume that permission was granted in October, for, as far as we know, during the month of June the residents of Calama and the African bishops were still in negotiation as to how the parties could resolve the crisis.

The second council, held on 13 October, sent two bishops to court this time, Restitutus and Florentius. Since mid-June, the Church's opponents had become bolder, the situation in Africa more fractious. The remaining records of the second council at Carthage of this season report that two bishops, Severus and Macarius, had recently been murdered.[44] Three others—Evodius, Theasius,[45] (these men constituting the embassy to court in June 404), as well as Victor, the bishop of Utica[46]—were attacked ('caesi sunt').[47] The bishops Restitutus and Florentius, like Fortunatianus before them, were sent to the emperor with a request for laws *contra paganos et haereticos*.

The evidence from the Church councils and Augustine clearly indicates that the escalation in violence was due to news of Stilicho's fall and the belief, circulated by the Donatists, that his death meant also the suspension of the laws he had promulgated.[48] Augustine wrote at least twice to Olympius (the man promoted to *magister officiorum* after Stilicho's murder), and he reported in his second letter (*ep.* 97), written in November or December 408, that the situation in Africa had sharply deteriorated. Augustine asked Olympius to state publicly that the antiheresy laws enacted under the supervision of Stilicho were not defunct.

> I also want to advise you to speed up your good work with much diligence and concern in order that the enemies of the Church may know that those laws which were sent to Africa concerning the destruction of idols and the correction of heretics, when Stilicho was still alive, had been established by the will of the most pious and faithful emperor. They deceitfully boast or rather choose to think that these laws were

---

[44] We know nothing about the careers of Severus and Macarius, but the injured had their sees in what is today the northwest of Tunisia, in and around Utica.

[45] Theasius, bishop of the modern Sidi Ahmed bou Farès, had traveled before with Evodius to the imperial court by order of the Council of Carthage, convened on 16 June 404. In light of the aggressions by the Donatists, their mission in 404 was to ask the emperor to confirm the authority of the laws against heretics as applicable to the Donatists (see Chapter 4). At the 411 conference, the Donatist bishop Petilianus singled out these two men, Theasius and Evodius, as being bishops whose pursuit and prosecution of Donatists were more violent and virulent than most (*Coll. Carth.*, I, 141]). See 'Theasius', *PCBE Afrique*, 1105–6.

[46] 'Victor 23', *PCBE Afrique*, 1161. He attended the conference of 411.

[47] The council of October records that Evodius, Theasius, and Victor were wounded 'on account of the cause' of the murdered bishops. Perhaps Evodius, Theasius, and Victor were wounded in attempts to defend Severus and Macarius; all the five men may have been assaulted in one coordinated attack. Another possibility: the wounded bishops may have been set upon when they arrived in town subsequent to the murders in order to investigate the crime. Most Donatist violence, historically, occurred in Numidia, unquestionably the geographic and religious center of African Donatism. All these five Catholic bishops seem to have been set upon in Utica, a northern urban center, not a place where such Donatist sorties usually occurred.

[48] See Augustine *ep.* 105.6, addressed to the Donatists: 'Et tamen quid est melius, proferre veras imperatorum iussiones pro unitate an falsas indulgentias pro perversitate, quod vos fecistis et mendacio vestro subito totam Africam implestis?'

established without his knowledge or against his will, and for this reason they cause the minds of the ignorant to be very upset and dangerous and deeply hostile to us. (97.2)[49]

That makes four African bishops seeking audiences with the emperor between June and October: Fortunatianus, Possidius, Restitutus, and Florentius.[50] A priest from Milevis followed in the winter carrying *ep*. 97, which reported on the situation in Africa.[51] It is in this letter that Augustine warned Olympius that several bishops were on their way to Ravenna:

> And many [*multi*] brothers, holy colleagues of mine, went off, when the Church was severely disturbed, almost in flight to the most glorious imperial court. Either you have already seen them, or you have received their letters from the city of Rome when they found some opportunity.[52]

Augustine enclosed further instructions for them that Olympius was asked to deliver to the bishops when they presented themselves.

Possidius visited Bishop Memorius[53] as well as Possidius of Nola before going to Ravenna,[54] but he and his episcopal colleagues were also obliged to

---

[49] 'Quo noverint inimici ecclesiae leges illas, quae de idolis confringendis et haereticis corrigendis vivo Stilichone in Africam missae sunt, voluntate imperatoris piissimi et fidelissimi constitutas; quo nesciente vel nolente factum sive dolose iactant sive libenter putant atque hinc animos inperitorum turbulentissimos reddunt nobisque periculose ac vehementer infestos.' Augustine clearly includes laws against the pagans as needing reaffirmation. This letter takes in more than the Donatist question.

[50] This may be argued based on the evidence of other embassies. For example, Fortunatianus and Vincentius had gone to the emperor, then residing in Rome, in June 407, but their request to be heard was not answered, we think, until November of the same year. If we are dealing with roughly the same time schedule, Fortunatianus was probably still at court (this time, Ravenna) by at least early November 408.

[51] For the dangers of winter travel, see Sirks, 'Sailing in the Off-Season'. We hear from Paulinus of Nola (*ep*. 49) of orders from the emperor that the grain ships sail for Rome earlier than usual, resulting in a number wrecking off the coast of Sardinia. One in particular, whose entire crew, save one older man, abandoned the ship, drifted twenty-three days before being pulled to shore by Sicilian fishermen. The fact that the emperor urged an early departure has inspired some readers to speculate that this episode dates to the crises of 409–411. Emin Tengström, *Bread for the People: Studies of the Corn-Supply of Rome during the Late Empire* (Stockholm: Acta Instituti Romani Regni Succiae [Paul Åström Förlag], 1974), 41, argues for the winter of 409 when our African priest is making his crossing. Cf. Dennis Trout, *Paulinus of Nola: Life, Letters and Poems* (Berkeley: University of California Press, 1999), 188, n.163.

[52] *ep*. 97.2: 'Et fratres quidem multi sancti collegae mei graviter ecclesia perturbata profecti sunt paene fugientes ad gloriosissimum comitatum, quos sive iam videris sive litteras eorum ab urbe Roma opportunitate cuiusquam occasionis acceperis.'

[53] Known by tradition as the bishop of Capua, but J. Lössel argues that Memorius was the bishop of Eclanum, the town where Julian, Memorius' son, eventually became bishop, and also Julian's birthplace. See *Julian von Aeclanum: Studien zu seinem Leben, seinem Werk, seiner Lehre und ihrer Überlieferung* (Leiden: Brill, 2001), 19–43.

[54] For African clerics conducting business with the imperial court, delivering epistles to Paulinus was part of the standard itinerary. Bishops Theasius and Evodius, returning from court after

spend time in Rome. The visit was necessary for all bishops before proceeding to the court, as the Church council at Carthage in June 407 had agreed that those submitting petitions to the emperor needed to attain permission to do so from their respective primates in Africa and the Roman pontiff in the form of written documentation. Clerics attempting to circumnavigate this stricture would be excommunicated.[55] Augustine knew the bishops were experiencing some difficulty getting to and around that city, but an extended stay would allow them to cultivate a number of valuable contacts. One of the consuls of 408, Anicius Auchenius Bassus, had known Augustine from their days together at Milan and honored Monica by composing her funerary epitaph.[56] Italica, probably the daughter-in-law of Petronius Probus, must have seen the bishops at least intermittently, as Augustine became concerned that she offered no news of them in one of her letters.[57] Thus, at the time of the composition of *ep.* 97 ('media hieme'), Augustine had received no confirmation that any of the bishops had reached Ravenna, but was aware that they had been inconvenienced by Alaric's push against Rome. That means the bishops could not have reached Ravenna until the late fall or early winter season.

---

their embassy of 404, delivered a letter of Augustine to Paulinus. A few months later, Fortunatianus, identified as a priest from Thagaste, but perhaps later named as bishop (and the Fortunatianus who traveled to court in 407 and 408), delivered another letter to Paulinus while on his way to Rome (*ep.* 80). See Sigrid Mratschek, *Der Briefwechsel des Paulinus von Nola: Kommunikation und soziale Kontakte zwischen christlichen Intellektuellen* (Göttingen: Vandenhoeck & Roprecht, 2002), 553–61, and the same author's prosopographical study of visitors, including African clerics, to Nola in 'Multis enim notissima est sanctitas loci: Paulinus and the Gradual Rise of Nola as a Canter of Christian Hospitality', *JECS*, 9 (2001) 511–53, esp. 531–9. See also Trout, *Paulinus of Nola*, 202–6.

[55] *Conciliae Africae, Registri Ecclesiae Carthaginensis Excerpta* 106. In cases of emergency, African bishops in Rome who were not carrying such documentation could attain permission from the pope alone. See J. E. Merdinger, *Rome and the African Church in the Time of Augustine* (New Haven: Yale University Press, 1997), 98–9.
  Brown, 'Religious Coercion in the Late Roman Empire', 303, n. 194, urges caution regarding this kind of legislation; these formal declarations may not have been rigorously observed by the bishops themselves. That this kind of injunction was submitted several times in various African councils speaks of the bishops' lack of observance (*Concilia Africae, Breviarium Hipponense* 27; *Concilia Africae, Registri Ecclesiae Carthaginensis Excerpta* 94; *Concilia Africae, Canones in Causa Apiarii* 23). On the other hand, our bishops planned to go to Rome. That they did this in such difficult times may offer evidence that the 407 and 408 delegations took these stipulations seriously.

[56] 'Anicius Auchenius Bassus 7', *PLRE* and F. Buecheler and A. Riese (eds.) *Anthologia Latina* (Leipzig: Teubner 1894; reprint, Amsterdam: Hakkert 1964), 1.670.

[57] For familial identification, see 'Italica 1', *PCBE Italie*, 1.1162–3. Augustine responds to her in *ep.* 99: 'Some letters of the brethren which reached us earlier described a dangerous and difficult situation, but less serious than we feared. I am more surprised than I can say that our brothers, the holy bishops, did not take advantage of the journey of your messengers to write to us, and that your letter gave us no news of your great trials, which are also ours because of the kinship of our charity.'

SIRMONDIAN CONSTITUTION 14

The law we know as *Sirm*. 14 was addressed from the emperor to the praetorian prefect of Italy, Theodorus, and issued on 15 January 409.[58] It is the response to an embassy of African bishops. The letter is neither an unsolicited edict, nor is it a rescript sent in response to Theodorus asking for clarification on behalf of the African bishops. The violence against a bishop described by Honorius is the first the emperor has heard of it, and he castigates the African judges for not prosecuting these cases on their own. They certainly did not refer the matter to him.[59] It was the bishops who alerted him to the situation.[60]

The law consists of two parts. The first addresses a particular event. A bishop was set upon by a mob, and the local authorities did nothing to punish the guilty. This is another instance, the emperor says, of bishops being mistreated outside their houses and basilicas. In the recent past, he continues, several clerics have been beaten and humiliated in full view of their towns' citizens and these clerics have suffered physical harm. Specific details are not offered, save the kind of degrading treatment we saw in 403 and 404: hair pulling (clerics by this time were tonsured, *coronati*,), beating, and parading in public.[61] The constitution orders that local authorities prosecute such crimes and punish those responsible. As to this one particular circumstance of violence that inspired the imperial letter, wherein it is clear that numerous people participated, the law demands that as many as possible of those involved be found. The guilty are to be sentenced to deportation or the mines, and all their property will cede to the imperial fisc. For the future, Honorius orders Theodorus to notify those under his jurisdiction that subsequent violence against bishops will be punished with a capital sentence. Accusations and prosecutions against perpetrators are invited, and the local governors must take action on such cases. All responsible parties must do their utmost to protect the bishops: 'Thus for this reason at least the audacity of evil men shall fear because of the accusation

---

[58] Cf. the theory, recently revisited, that the Sirmondian Constitutions are Merovingian forgeries: Élisabeth Magnou-Nortier, 'Sur l'Origine des Constitutions sirmondiennes', *Revue de droit canonique*, 51 (2001), 279–303, esp. 292–3.

[59] 'Tanti sceleris nefas et immane flagitium numquam ante conpertum Africanorum iudiciorum auctoritas nec creditae sibi potestatis iure persequitur nec debita cura referendi in nostram fecit notitiam pervenire.'

[60] 'Expectandum fuit institutis accusationibus contra professionis propriae sanctitatem, ut episcopi suas persequerentur iniurias et reorum nece deposcerent ultionem, quos invitos decet vindicari?'

[61] See Innocent I, *ep*. 3 (*PL* 20,491) and *CTh*. 16.2.38. Both mention tonsured clerics. The first dates from the Council of Toledo, 400, and the second, 15 November 407.

of others the action which they are confident cannot be brought against them through a bishop.'[62]

The second part of the letter shifts in subject. Here is a reminder that the previous laws against Donatists, Jews, and pagans retain their force. For no reason should people assume that promulgated legislation has diminished in power or scope. Provincial administrators are subject to heavy financial penalties and loss of station if for any reason they do not prosecute. Failure on the part of municipal councils to report violators to the proper authorities will result in deportation and loss of all property. This second part of the Constitution is clearly a response to African bishops' concerns that Stilicho's death rendered previous religious legislation void and can be linked to Augustine's letters to Olympius and the mission statement of the 13 October embassy.

What about the first section of the imperial letter? Can it be connected to the riots at Calama? I think so, and for three reasons. First, Augustine noted in his correspondence that the local authorities did nothing to ensure compensation for injuries to clerics and damage done to church property. The same neglect provides impetus for Honorius' anger in *Sirm.* 14. Second, the situation at Calama and that as described by Honorius involve riots with many people involved. True, we do not have much information about the attacks on the bishops discussed at the Church council of October, but here, too, local authorities did not handle the situation to the satisfaction of the Catholic Church, and it is likely that this assault against numerous bishops involved the participation of many people.

Third, and this point is more convincing, Honorius directs officials as to the means by which they may uncover the perpetrators: the first when dealing with the specific (unnamed) events that prompted the letter and, second, when anticipating more mob violence against the Catholic Church. As to the first directive, African judges are ordered to investigate the matter and bring as many defendants as possible to court. They are to do this 'without injury to innocent people' ('sine innocentium laesione'), which means that when information about the identities of perpetrators is not readily available, many people, directly involved or not, will have to be questioned. The methods by which judges are to narrow their search, are adumbrated in the second directive: 'Moreover, if the offense is said to have been perpetrated by a multitude, some, if not all, can nevertheless be recognized, and by a confession of these, the names of their accomplices may be disclosed.'[63] 'Possunt...cognosci': as a

---

[62] 'ut hac saltem ratione, quod agi adversum se per episcopum non posse confidit, at aliorum accusationibus malorum audacia pertimescat.'

[63] 'Et si per multitudinem commissum dicitur, si non omnes, possunt tamen aliquanti cognosci, quorum confessione sociorum nomina publicentur.'

matter of judicial procedure, the questioning will require torture. The emperor gives the judges the right to call on the armed troops (*apparitores*) employed by the *comes Africae* to aid in the rounding up of numerous people ('multitudo violentia').[64]

In March 409 Augustine received another letter from Nectarius (*ep*. 103), almost eight months after the initial discussion between the two men.[65] Its arrival at Hippo so many months after he sent his first letter suggests that this was not one in a series of polite exchanges. Nectarius was writing for a reason. His epistle lacks cohesion and speaks of beatings, scars, and humiliation. Even Augustine was confused, and he told Nectarius to explain himself more clearly. Augustine repeats (in *ep*. 104) that the kind of physical abuse mentioned in Nectarius' latest letter is of no interest to the Church. If his pleas were inspired by news that Possidius won his case (of which Augustine says he has heard nothing, indicating that by late March 409 Possidius had not returned to Africa), then he should just speak plainly and tell him everything so that he, Augustine, might prevent such events and prevent others from carrying them out.[66]

Nectarius' letter has three parts, with the third and last being of most import to Augustine and to us. The first two are elaborate, flowery responses to Augustine's previous letter and are couched in the rhetoric and literary imagery used in polite correspondence. Nectarius returns to the subject of his first letter (*ep*. 90), Cicero's *De republica*, wherein he states again that it is through service to the state that great men attain the heaven Augustine admonishes him to contemplate.[67] Then he acknowledges that Augustine (and the Church) will not ask for physical punishment, but this comment is not prompted by the case itself; Nectarius is using Augustine's sentiments as way of introducing a philosophical reason why the Catholics should retract all requests for punishment. Nectarius sets out to prove that, first, poverty can be considered worse than death (oblivion) and, second, that the Stoics argued wrongdoing or sin (*peccatum*) should not be distinguished by degree. Sin is sin; wrongdoing is

---

[64] 'Et si multitudo violentia civilis apparitionis exsecutione et adminiculo ordinum possessorumve non potuerit praesentari, quod se armis aut locorum difficultate tueantur, iudices Africani armatae apparitionis praesidium, datis ad virum spectabilem comitem Africae litteris praelato legis istius tenore deposcent ut rei talium criminum non evadant.'

[65] *ep*. 104.1: The dating is secure for Augustine's receipt of the letter because he was so annoyed with Nectarius' delay that he pointedly remarks that he received this on 27 March, 'post menses ferme octo, quam scripseram'.

[66] *ep*. 104.1: 'Absit, ut, ista cuiquam inimicorum nostrorum vel per nos vel per quemquem quod ingerantur, instemus; sed, ut dixi, si aliquid tale ad te fama pertulit, apertius edissere, ut noverimus, vel quid agere, ne ista fiant, vel quid haec credentibus respondere debeamus.'

[67] For discussion, see Margaret Atkins, 'Old Philosophy and New Power: Cicero in Fifth-Century North Africa', in Gillian Clark and Tessa Rajak (eds.), *Philosophy and Power in the Graeco-Roman World* (Oxford: Oxford University Press, 2002), 251–69.

wrongdoing. It follows, then, that repentance of sin—whatever that sin may be, since all have the same value—demands a pardon that is as well without grade. Forgiveness should be complete and universal.[68]

It is only in the third part of the letter that Nectarius introduces the matters that prompted the revived correspondence. 'Nunc quoniam, non quantum debui, sed quantum potui, maius, ut dicitur, minusve respondi, oro atque obsecro': 'Now, since I have responded more or less, as it is said, not as much as I ought to have but as much as I could, I beg and pray' (103.4). Nectarius asks that Augustine excuse the people of Calama from physical punishment. Men would return to their homes, with a source of grief and humiliation to themselves and their families because of visible wounds and scars ('vulnerum et cicatricum' [103.4]). The men to whom Nectarius refers to here are the town elite: they have reputations to lose, and their friendship and gratitude should be welcomed by Augustine.[69]

Nectarius is not actually saying that those found guilty of rioting are going to be beaten. The scenario Nectarius describes (the beating, the humiliation, the scars) is all in the subjunctive, and thus presented as hypothetical.[70] The worst that these men could experience was forestalled because Augustine (in the perfect tense) pardoned them, as established in their previous correspondence. 'And let these things hold for those who are bound by the true guilt of what they confessed. By the consideration of the law of your religion, you have already pardoned them, something I do not cease from praising.'[71] What Nectarius has just written is both a reminder of Augustine's promise and a rhetorical prelude to the next matter of concern. Nectarius asks Augustine to contemplate what could have happened to these guilty persons if the Church had not pardoned them, and then introduces a different set of potential victims who are just now entering the proceedings. After Nectarius finishes with the

---

[68] Augustine voices his impatience with what he considered the untenable sophistry of this Stoic exercise in paradox with a play upon the name of Nectarius' son, which was Paradoxus, *ep.* 104.15: 'tu vero, vir merito laudabilis, ne, quaeso, ista paradoxa Stoicorum sectanda doceas Paradoxum tuum, quem tibi optamus vera pietate ac felicitate grandescere.'

[69] *Sirm.* 14 acknowledges that upper class people may be among the guilty: 'Of whatsoever dignity and honor the offenders are proved to be, such judges shall either deliver them to the mines or shall compel them to undergo the penalty of deportation.'

[70] *ep.* 103.4: 'Etiam atque etiam cogites, intendas, quae sit illius species civitatis, ex qua ad supplicium ducendi extrahuntur, quae sit matrum, quae coniugum, quae liberorum, quae parentum lamentatio, quo pudore ad patriam venire possint liberati sed torti, quos renovet dolores aut gemitus consideratio vulnerum et cicatricum. Et his omnibus pertractatis deum primo consideres hominumque cogites famam, bonitatem amicam potius familiaremque coniunctionem et ignoscendo potius laudem quam vindicando conquiras.'

[71] *ep.* 103. 4: 'Atque haec de his dicta sint, quos verus confessionis suae reatus astringit, quibus quidem legis contemplatione, quod laudare non desino, veniam tribuisti.'

convicted who have been pardoned at the behest of the bishop, he begins the next sentence with *iam*, indicating a shift in subject and focus:

> Now this can scarcely be expressed, what cruelty it would be to seek out innocent people and to bring them under judicial examination of a capital crime, who, it is clear, have nothing to do with the crime. If it comes to pass that these very people are cleared, just think, I beg you, they will be freed with enormous damage to the reputations of the accusers, since the accusers, having lost their case, will have dismissed the defendants by their own accord and forsaken the innocent.[72]

Nectarius assumes that the Roman authorities are interested in involving clearly innocent people in the case and not because their innocence is in question and the ensuing questions will clarify matters. Nectarius indicates that these people (the *innocentes*) are recognized, at the outset, as having no direct involvement. The motivation for questioning these people then seems to point to their ability to disclose just who the guilty perpetrators are (*devocare* is not so much a term of indictment as it is demand of action, like the discharge of duty or presence at a location).[73] The following *quos* links these *innocentes* to the circumstance of being ultimately released ('quos si purgari contigerit'). When these *innocentes* are later dismissed, much *invidia*, Nectarius says, will come to those who pressed the charges in the first place. The *accusatores* (i.e. the bishops and clerics bringing cases to the attention of the provincial administrators), having lost their cases (*victi*), will have to let the defendants go (the defendants meaning the *rei*). The bishops, having started this messy process, which in this kind of capital investigation necessitated that the innocent questioned be routinely tortured, will come away with nothing. In the end, the bishops will have no case against those accused, and the innocent having been dragged into this 'witch hunt' will be let go. The outcome, Nectarius warns, is that the Catholics will look very poorly indeed. This particular translation requires a separation of identity between the *rei* and the *innocentes*. If these people are one and the same, it is not clear why Nectarius repeats the *innocentes* at the end of

---

[72] *ep*. 103.4: 'Iam illud explicari vix potest, quantae crudelitatis sit innocentes appetere et eos, quos a crimine constat esse discretos, in iudicium capitis devocare. Quos si purgari contigerit, cogites, quaeso, quanta accusatorum liberabuntur invidia, cum reos sponte dimiserint victi, reliquerint innocentes.'

This translation, which has benefited greatly from the suggestions of Peter Brown, differs from H. Huisman (*Augustinus' Briefwisseling met Nectarius* [Amsterdam: Babeliowsky, 1956], 55), who renders the meaning that the accused will be freed from being hated by the accusers, if the accusers admit defeat and drop legal proceedings. That interpretation does not satisfactorily explain why Nectarius would think this scenario so cruel. See also E. M. Atkins and R. J. Dodaro (eds.), *Augustine: Political Writings* (Cambridge: Cambridge University Press, 2001), 10 and 254–5.

[73] For *devoco*, see *CTh*. 8.4.1 and 15.3.1: both instances use the verb in terms of service or payment required. See also *TLL* 5.1.868–9. Ms. V reads *devorare*.

the sentence; by doing so, he links them with the *innocentes* mentioned at the beginning of the previous sentence. They are the same people, distinguished from the third party, the *rei*.[74] It is important to remember that in the Calama riots (as in most disturbances in small towns), the innocent and the guilty, the accusers and the accused, all knew each other. Some of those involved were the town's elite; if we speak of small-town social distinctions, the innocent, who may not have exercised as much power in Calama as the defendants, could be vulnerable to later retribution. He has clearly stated before that the elite were among those responsible, and that well might be a reason why Nectarius is convinced the *innocentes* would not make denunciations.

Nowhere in previous correspondence did Nectarius or Augustine mention that the judicial investigations surrounding the Calama riots would entail a capital trial. The residents of Calama, Nectarius says, would be happy to pay their fines; all that they ask is to be let off corporal punishment. Matters of fines and (the rejection of) beatings continued to constitute the subject matter of the correspondence. Here, and only here, Nectarius speaks of people brought into court for a capital case ('in iudicium capitis devocare'). And I think he did this because he was reacting and responding to Honorius' letter, *Sirm.* 14. Directly subsequent to Honorius' order to cast a wide net of questioning to find the guilty, he says that, from now on, people convicted of participating in violence against the Church would, as well, suffer capital punishment: *iudicium capitis* usually meaning death, the mines, or exile.[75] The severity of the sentence is extreme, as Honorius himself admits, because it aims to thwart those who assume that bishops, because of the nature and the moral parameters of their office, would never bring these cases to the attention of the authorities. It is the duty of the empire to protect bishops; the duty of bishops is to forgive.

Nectarius is our best witness to the episcopal embassy that inspired the promulgation of *Sirm.* 14. While we readily detect the presence of Restitutus and Florentius, whose efforts entailed the reaffirmation of antiheresy laws after Stilicho's death, Nectarius' panicked letter to Augustine, which points to the emergency generated by the stipulation of broad questioning and imposition of capital punishment for violence against the Catholic Church, connects the imperial letter with the events at Calama.

---

[74] Note that Honorius makes the same distinction later in the letter when he allows armed *apparatores* assigned to the *comes Africae* to round up large crowds for questioning: the *multitudo violentia* will be brought to court so that the *rei* (defendants) in such a crime cannot evade the law.
[75] 'Adque ita provinciae moderator, sacerdotum et catholicae ecclesiae ministrorum, loci quoque ipsius et divini cultus iniuriam capitali in convictos vel confessos reos sententia noverit vindicandam.'

POSSIDIUS AND AUGUSTINE IN DISAGREEMENT?

Augustine's attitude toward coercion, as well as his willingness to court imperial power, has been well explored in modern scholarship.[76] Throughout 408, Augustine's views seem to have been consistent with those held by other Catholic bishops, especially Possidius. Augustine, too, was dissatisfied with initial negotiations at Calama. He appealed to Olympius to uphold the rigor of the imperial law against heretics and pagans, and, in anticipation of Possidius' meeting with the imperial consistory, may have sought the support of the praetorian prefect of Italy, Theodorus, who may be Mallius Theodorus, well known to Augustine from their days in Milan together, a friend of Monica's, and the dedicatee of one of Augustine's treatises written at Cassiciacum, the *De beata vita*. It is well known (from Augustine's *ep.* 101) that Possidius traveled to Italy in 408 with Book 6 of Augustine's *De musica* as a gift for Bishop Memorius (the father of Julian of Eclanum). Possidius may have brought another copy to give to the praetorian prefect.[77] Augustine continued to seek recognition from a legal apparatus whose methods of judgment were extreme, but he was just as eager as ever to dull the laws' force when applied at the local level.

An abiding unease toward imperial law and, perhaps, Possidius' embassy emerges from a letter of Augustine's addressed to Paulinus of Nola that Possidius carried with him to Italy (*ep.* 95). We should note that Paulinus was very likely reading the letter aloud to visitors with Possidius in company; the matter under discussion is Possidius' travails at Calama, not the Donatists.[78] Augustine offers a thoughtful discussion of the psychological effects of punishment,

---

[76] See Chapter 3, n. 3.

[77] See supra n. 36.

[78] Those visitors may have been some of the 'stars' of the aristocratic Christian world. Melania the Younger, in the company of Pinianus (her husband) and Albina (the elder Melania's daughter-in-law), had departed Rome as Alaric's troops approached, probably in the fall of 408, and headed south to Nola, perhaps with Rufinus of Aquileia also in attendance. This party continued on to their estates in Sicily, but the arrival date might be as late as August 410. If Possidius' departure for Italy occurred in the fall of 408, when Alaric had already started to press for Rome, there is a chance that he arrived at Nola to find this company already assembled; they would have been the first audience for this letter of Augustine's. See Trout, *Paulinus of Nola*, 119–20; C. P. Hammond, 'The Last Ten Years of Rufinus' Life and the Date of his Move South from Aquileia', *JTS*, 28 (1977), 372–428, esp. 372; and F. X. Murphy, 'Rufinus of Aquileia and Paulinus of Nola', *RÉAug*, 2 (1956), 79–91. Cf. Mratscheck, 'Multis enim notissima est sanctitas loci', 547, n. 211.

For Possidius' contacts with Volusian, the uncle of Melania the Younger, see A. Chastagnol, 'Le Sénateur Volusien et la conversion d'une famille de l'aristocratie romaine au Bas-Empire', *RÉA*, 58 (1956), 240–53 and Peter Brown, 'Aspects of Christianization in the Roman Aristocracy', *JRS*, 51 (1961), 1–11.

and articulates the tension, as Augustine saw it, between the Catholics and the imperial court, as well as the African political administrators and the prosecuted. The strain under which the Catholic bishops operated in pursuing these imperial injunctions is evident in that Augustine cites disagreements among his colleagues and friends. Not all bishops were sensitive or astute regarding the government's punishment of transgressors at the behest of the Church. The brutal strictures of Roman law were, in the end, poor substitutes for heavenly rule, and to Augustine, the two were so distant that he doubted the appropriateness of an emperor's *oracula*.[79]

Letter 95 begins with the news that Possidius was forced to join Paulinus' company because of a regretful duty, the particulars of which the bishop of Calama will relate in his own words. Augustine intimates that he cannot travel for social calls, as duty requires him to remain in Hippo. For him, no imminent danger now presses, but the burden is difficult nonetheless.[80] Augustine's letter is dramatic, made more so by his delayed and what seems halfhearted response to Paulinus' questions posed in *ep.* 94; Paulinus had asked about the nature of heavenly speech, more to the point, if angels had tongues. That is an interesting question and one which Augustine would have enjoyed answering. He does not until the end of the letter, and the response is brief, restricted to the plausibility of angels' corporality.

Augustine instead focuses on Paulinus' earlier exhortation to anticipate the pleasures of heaven by withdrawing from the world. This elicits a weary response from Augustine: it is impossible. The responsibility of holy men entails intimate involvement in quotidian affairs, including proximity with those who are concerned with only earthly matters.[81] Augustine then swoops down to the specifics of remove versus involvement: 'What should I say about punishing or not punishing?' ('Quid dicam de vindicando vel non vindicando?' [95.3].) Here is the issue and the central thrust of the letter. Punishment is not an unambiguous matter whose implementation inevitably improves the one punished or, at large, the society that supposedly derives benefit from chastising its erring members. The complexity resides in the necessity of listening to the ticking of human minds in order to ascertain what is most effective for the redemption of souls. Careful attention to the potential effects of

---

[79] *Oraculum* is the term used to describe law issued by the emperor. See Chapter 6, n. 10.
[80] *ep.* 95.1: 'Utrum exerceamur his an potius plectamur, nescio.'
[81] *ep.* 95.2: 'Thus' says Augustine, 'we are dragged down by these dusty and earthy desires, and we have a hard time lifting our sluggish hearts to God, so as to live the life of the Gospel by dying the death of the Gospel.' ('Ita pulvereis quibusdam vel etiam luteis affectibus nostras animas praegravantes, laboriosius et pigrius levamus ad deum, ut vivamus evangelicam vitam moriendo evangelicam mortem.')

punishment, while always keeping in mind to what end chastisement leads (correction, redemption, salvation), elicits necessary questions and demands finely wrought answers.[82] What punishment is enough for what crime? Each person responds differently to corrective treatment, so how does one gauge the appropriate measure for each? How does one punish with love and in hope of redemption and at the same time avoid inflicting excess pain and humiliation? The decision to chastise or suspend punishment may harm or benefit anyone who finds himself, at some point, affected by the activities of the transgressor. Augustine admits that he makes wrong decisions about such complicated matters everyday, especially since scripture seems to enumerate many seemingly contradictory precepts about justice and judgment. Augustine's method of sifting through these directives is both pragmatic and charitable. Appropriate answers which help to solve fundamental problems are found in the quiet nuances of scripture when applied at that time, at that moment, to the situation at hand.

> Does it not mean that the divine words of the Lord are merely touched upon by us rather than thoroughly studied by us as long as in many more passages we are seeking what we should hold rather than hold something settled and definite? And though this caution is filled with worry, it is much better than rashness in making assertions. (95.4)[83]

Augustine then turns to problems that arise when dealing with others who are not finely attuned to these matters. To argue with these men or to give in to them constitutes a distasteful and dangerous choice. Unpleasantness, even jeopardy to the soul, is an unavoidable consequence:

> If someone does not think in accord with the flesh, something that the apostle says is death, will he not be a scandal for another who still thinks in accord with the flesh in a case where it is most dangerous to say what

---

[82] On the philosophical aspects of the correspondence between Nectarius and Augustine, see Robert Dodaro, *Christ and the Just Society in the Thought of Augustine* (Cambridge: Cambridge University Press, 2004) as well as his 'Augustine's Secular City' in Robert Dodaro and George Lawless (eds.), *Augustine and His Critics: Essays in Honor of Gerald Bonner* (New York: Routledge, 2000), 231–59.

[83] 'Quid? ipsa divina eloquia domini nonne palpantur potius quam tractantur a nobis, dum in multo pluribus quaerimus potius, quid sentiendum sit, quam definitum aliquid fixumque sentimus? Et ea cautio cum sollicitudinis plena sit, multo melior est tamen quam temeritas adfirmandi.'

Augustine's letter to Vincentius, the Donatist bishop of Cartenna (*ep.* 93), which may well have been written before Possidius' troubles at Calama, raises many of the same questions regarding punishment and its uses that are found in the letter to Paulinus. Chastisement, Augustine tells Vincentius, motivated by love and desire to correct, helps all concerned, transgressors and victims alike. This approach also mirrors God's methods: punishment for the purification and redemption of those whom he loves, the most famous example being Paul, who was blinded and struck by God to achieve his spiritual recovery.

you hold and most troublesome not to say this, but most deadly to say something other than what you hold?[84]

The letter advances from discussion of punishment and the need for subtlety in its use to the acknowledgment of the existence of those who did not have the perspicacious sensitivity required to live the scripture's exhortations. What then follows can only be construed as criticism of men within the Church—'qui intus sunt'—who make it difficult to speak one's mind.[85] When Churchmen disagree with one another, an assumed prerogative essential to the liberty of *fraterna charitas*, as Augustine calls it, some construe this as a personal attack motivated by ill will and unkindness, and these misunderstandings rupture friendships: 'Certe hinc existunt inimicitiae plerumque etiam inter carissimas familiarissimasque personas' (95.4).

The reference to 'qui intus sunt' does not involve Donatists or any other non-Catholic Christian group. That the phrase refers to the Donatists cannot be sustained because of Augustine's complaint that arguments with 'those within' damaged relations between dearest friends, a circumstance applicable almost exclusively to Augustine's intimate associations with his Catholic colleagues.[86] Moreover, Augustine confirms that this whole discussion is not hypothetical. The events and the frustrations they caused were real. They were happening to him.

> For, whether the dangers in which anyone is involved seem more serious than those not previously experienced or whether they are truly such, any fearfulness and storm of the desert seems to me less bothersome than that which we either suffer or fear amid tumults.[87]

Again, it is important to remember that the composition as well as the reading of this letter involved Possidius' physical presence. Did Augustine think Possidius mistaken for having embarked on an embassy to the court? More pointedly, did Possidius depart Africa in hopes of securing a stronger sentence against the rioters than what Augustine had previously demanded from

---

[84] *ep.* 95.4: 'Nonne in multis, si non secundum carnem homo sapiat, quam mortem esse dicit apostolus, magno scandalo erit ei, qui adhuc secundum carnem sapit, ubi et dicere, quid sentias, periculosissimum et non dicere laboriosissimum et aliud, quam sentis, dicere perniciosissimum est?'

[85] Goldbacher indicates a lacuna in this sentence, but it does not seem to interfere with the meaning or interpretation of 'qui intus sunt'.

[86] A sentiment that would have not been lost on Paulinus, and certainly not on Rufinus and Melania, if they too were present at Nola. Rupture among Christian friends over belief and practice and personality described the company's history of relations with Jerome. See Trout, *Paulinus of Nola*, 218–26, and Pierre Courcelle, 'Paulin de Nole et saint Jérôme', *RÉL*, 25 (1947), 250–80.

[87] *ep.* 95.4: 'Sive enim quia pericula, in quibus quisque versatur, graviora sunt quam inexperta sive quia re vera ita est, quaelibet pusillanimitas tempestasque deserti minus mihi videtur molesta quam ea, quae vel patimur vel timemus in turbis' (Teske translation reads 'crowds' for 'turbis').

Nectarius? Augustine had spoken of heavy financial penalties that would prohibit such behavior from happening again, but he had categorically excluded corporal punishment. As we have seen, the emperor and praetorian prefect, the latter of whom perhaps an old friend of Augustine's, ruled otherwise. One assumes that the capital sentence decreed was merely the manifestation of imperial law's typical harshness and not the wish of Possidius and his fellow bishops, but they could have anticipated a stringent sentence. Perhaps they were, in fact, surprised, but Augustine's intimations to Paulinus of Nola indicate a difference of opinion between himself and his colleagues.

Augustine reiterates to Paulinus his fear about making mistakes regarding the nuances of judgment,[88] and he explains that one of the reasons his job and the decisions demanded from it are so bewildering is that his power, in whatever form, is exercised not in a clear way as it is demarcated in Roman law, but with a view to heavenly rule.[89] The second does not offer the crisp definitions and tabulated penalties as prescribed by Roman law. The distinction between earthly and heavenly rule is not a rare subject in Augustine's corpus, but it is noteworthy that such a sentiment occupies much of the substance of the correspondence between Nectarius and Augustine (especially the beginning of ep. 91).[90] The statement also serves as a reminder that the duties of Christian

---

[88] *ep.* 95.5: 'maximeque in his, quae breviter, ut potui, commemoravi, periculosissime laborare me sentiam.'

[89] *ep.* 95.5: sed quia omnis haec ignorantia et difficultas hinc mihi videtur existere, quod in magna varietate morum et animorum et inter occultissimas voluntates atque infirmitates hominum rem populi gerimus non terreni atque Romani sed Hierosolymitani caelestis.

[90] The reference to the kind of government one rules also draws us back to *ep.* 259 (CSEL 57) addressed to Cornelius (identified as Romanianus by Aimé Gabillon 'Romanianus, alias Cornelius: Du nouveau sur le bienfaiteur et l'ami de saint Augustin', *RÉAug*, 24 [1978], 58–70). Cornelius asked Augustine for a *consolatio* on the recent passing of his wife, the kind that Paulinus of Nola wrote for one Macarius (see Trout, *Paulinus of Nola*, 188, n. 162, for identification). Augustine refused Cornelius' request on the grounds that his behavior, notably his commerce with concubines, required reform before Augustine would comply with his wishes. Augustine aligned his refusal with Cicero's hard stance against Catiline (*In Cat.* 1.2): 'Tully inveighed against an enemy, and his preoccupation with the government of an earthly state [*terrenam rem publicam*] was far different from mine, yet he said: "I wish, conscript fathers, to be kind [*me esse clemeniam*], but in the midst of these great perils to the state I do not wish to seem remiss [*non dissolutum videri*]." I have been appointed to the service of the eternal city, as minister of the divine word and sacrament [*in aeternae civitatis servitio constitutus minister verbi sacramentique divini*], and how much more justly can I say—especially as you know what a friendly feeling I have for you—"I wish, brother Cornelius, to be kind, but in the midst of such great perils to you and me I do not wish to seem remiss."'

Dom de Bruyne dated this epistle by its consistent pairing in medieval manuscripts with securely datable letters. He asserted that it was written in 408, just about the time Augustine wrote his two letters to Olympius, the new *magister officiorum*. See 'Les anciennes Collections et la chronologie des lettres de saint Augustin', *RBén*, 43 (1931), 284–95. Dom de Bruyne's assertion is strengthened by the letter's internal evidence.

clergy necessitate rejection of the unambiguous rule to which the Roman government adheres. Complex hearts—each one made distinct by respective weaknesses, distinct psychologies, and unique processes and intentions—populate the heavenly Jerusalem. The clear and decisive judgments pronounced by the emperor and his staff are not appropriate in their bluntness and brutality.

Perhaps Augustine is articulating a conclusion that all three bishops—Augustine, Paulinus, and Possidius—have reached: life on earth with its attendant responsibilities over souls necessitates decisions that strain bishops' adherence to the apostolic life. The bishops would prefer not to gird themselves with pronouncements from the consistory,[91] but it was a fact of living and leading others in this world. The lament, however, over disagreements with 'those within' which refers to Augustine's present concerns, gives pause. The problem is immediate and has to do with Possidius' embassy to Ravenna. Augustine concludes this section of the letter by asking Paulinus to ponder his words and discuss the problem with 'some kind doctor of the heart' ('cum aliquo mansueto cordis medico' [95.6]) at Nola and Rome. I take this to mean that Paulinus should discuss the Calama riots and the embassy with Possidius in order to ensure that his address to Honorius remained directed toward the appropriate, not the vengeful.

After promulgation of Honorius' law against those who attack Catholic clerics, it was Augustine who appealed to local authorities not to impose the stipulated sentence. Donatus, the proconsul of Africa, who we know deliberately snubbed Augustine by not granting him an audience, also may not have answered his letters.[92] In the first letter that Augustine sent (*ep.* 100), he asks that the capital conviction not be pronounced on those who commit acts of violence ('nefariis iniuriis' [100.2]) against the Church.[93] The letter has been traditionally dated to late 408 or early 409 and is taken by modern readers as

---

[91] *ep.* 100.1 to Donatus: 'Nollem quidem in his afflictionibus esse Africanam ecclesiam constitutam, ut terrenae ullius potestatis indigeret auxilio.'

[92] See *Codex Theodosianus*, Mommsen edition, Vol. 1, *Prolegomena*, cxciii. 'Donatus 24', *PCBE Afrique*, 309–10. His family owned lands near Hippo; his father was Catholic (*ep.* 112.3). Augustine wrote to Donatus in late 409 or early 410, after the latter had left office (*ep.* 112). There is no evidence indicating whether Donatus answered Augustine's first letter, but he did not grant Augustine an audience during his proconsular tenure, and not, it seems, because of busy schedules or infelicitous near misses; Augustine's first sentence of *ep.* 112 speaks of Donatus' inaccessibility, even when the proconsul was geographically near: 'Quod te administrantem multum desiderans, etiam cum Tibilim venisses, videre non potui' (*ep.* 112.1).

Thibilis (modern Announa) was a small town whose closest neighbor of size and distinction was Calama (twenty-three kilometers to the northeast of Thibilis). Augustine may have requested an audience with Donatus from Possidius' see. See Lepelley, *Les Cités*, ii, 477–85.

[93] *ep.* 100.2: 'Quaesumus igitur, ut, cum ecclesiae causas audis, quamlibet nefariis iniuriis appetitam vel afflictam esse cognoveris, potestatem occidendi te habere obliviscaris, petitionem nostrum non obliviscaris.'

an indication that the proconsul, without the consent of the Catholic Church, was in the process of violently repressing assumptions on the part of non-Catholics that Stilicho's legislation was no longer valid.[94] Instead, I think that Augustine is asking Donatus to resist carrying out the capital sentences as prescribed by Honorius in the text of *Sirm.* 14.[95]

Augustine's letter follows the progress of *Sirm.* 14. The first part discusses capital sentences imposed on those who have attacked the Church and refers to anyone who would commit crimes against Catholic clerics. If Donatus acquiesces to Augustine's request, the perpetrators will have the opportunity to repent of their sins.[96] Augustine told Donatus that imposing radical sentences actually worked against the efforts of the bishops. Implementation of stringent penalties was not a prudent tactic. Because injured Catholic parties would shoulder the burden of reporting incidences of violence against themselves, recourse to the law would be impossible when the bishops knew that the people they accused might actually be executed or exiled. Bishops, he said, would rather be killed than be responsible for the deaths of others, and this would offer more incentive for perpetrators to step up attacks.[97] In the text of

[94] Frend intimates that Donatus' decision to impose death on perpetrators was his own and not generated by any imperial edict. The proconsul's dedication to the Catholic cause rendered his judicial decisions harshly conservative: Frend, *The Donatist Church*, 271–2 and Bonner, *St. Augustine of Hippo*, 267. Neil McLynn, 'Augustine's Roman Empire', *AugStud*, 30 (1999), 29–44, redates the letter to shortly after the news of Stilicho's death reached Africa, late August or September 408. His interpretation of the letter suggests that Augustine's request for rejection of the death penalty was based on a hypothetical argument. The second part of the letter asks Donatus to affirm that the legislation enacted under Stilicho is still valid; McLynn believes that once Donatus did this, that is, underscored the legitimacy of previously promulgated legislation, then in his observance of these very laws Donatus was planning to inflict capital punishment on those convicted. Thus, as Augustine was gauging the mood of the proconsul's office to see whether Donatus intended to consider all promulgated laws still valid, means that this letter should be dated to the turbulent months of late summer, when everyone was still trying to understand the shifts in imperial personnel and the new direction of the court. Both these scenarios, their dates, and the position of Donatus require the proconsul to be largely acting on his own (whether by fact or potential) in assigning capital punishment to the Donatists. This seems to be a stretch; it makes more sense if the sentence was coming from the imperial administration.

[95] The letter should be dated after 15 January 409 and receipt by Augustine probably after March 409, as Possidius had not returned to Africa before that month. These dates are close, but do tally. Augustine would have seen a copy of the imperial decree after 27 March when Augustine told Nectarius that he still was not aware of the outcome of the African embassy to court. Gaudentius, the next proconsul, did not replace Donatus until (late?) April of the same year. Mommsen, *Prolegomena*: 289. The first letter to Gaudentius in the *Codex* is dated 29 April.

[96] *ep.* 100.1: 'corrigi eos cupimus, non necari; nec disciplinam circa eos neglegi volumus nec supplicia, quae digna sunt, exerceri. Sic ergo eorum peccata compesce, ut sint, quos paeniteat peccavisse.'

[97] *ep.* 100.2: 'Illud quoque prudentia tua cogitet, quod causas ecclesiasticas insinuare vobis nemo praeter ecclesiasticos curat. Proinde si occidendos in his homines putaveritis, deterrebitis nos, ne per operam nostram ad vestrum iudicium aliquid tale perveniat, quo comperto illi in nostram perniciem licentiore audacia grassabuntur necessitate nobis impacta, ut etiam occidi ab eis eligamus, quam eos occidendos vestris iudiciis ingeramus.'

Sirm. 14, Honorius declared that it was not the place of bishops to demand vengeance when instead it was their duty to forgive. The emperor's injunctions for local administrators to initiate cases on behalf of the beleaguered bishops, with the punch behind that directive in the form of stiff penalties for non-compliance, demonstrates amply Augustine's quandary. If penalty stipulations were increased, this left both Church and local officials even more reluctant to prosecute cases; added leverage was only granted to those who would attack Church interests.

Exhortations to reject this first part of *Sirm.* 14, however, do not necessitate the rejection of the entire imperial law. The second part of Augustine's letter is much more specific and addresses the validity of previous heresy laws promulgated against the Donatists. Augustine makes the transition to a new request ('cito iterim'), wherein he asks proconsul Donatus to reiterate the legitimacy and permanency of laws against the Donatists. Augustine says that the Donatists still assume that the laws previously enacted against them by Stilicho have lost their force. They may have been pressing this point into the spring of 409. Augustine has clearly shifted focus here. Nothing about death sentences or severe punishments is in question. Augustine wants Donatus to fulfill his obligations to the law, working from legislation previously promulgated that stipulates confiscation of property and monetary fines. In other words, this second section of the letter addresses the Donatist question only in terms of their status as heretics; he is not discussing them in terms of the first section, wherein all those who perform violent acts against the Church are liable to much more stringent penalties. The former kind of cases (heresy) Augustine was very willing to bring to the attention of the authorities, and he assumes that, as usual, the Donatists will appeal to the proconsul for more favorable rulings.[98]

Augustine's request to Donatus to ignore an imperial injunction placed him, once again, in the potentially awkward position of asking an imperial official to ignore the very laws which had been solicited by Catholic bishops. When Possidius and Augustine acted in concert in the Crispinus affair in 404, the proconsul's attentions to the Church were strongly rebuffed by the emperor, resulting in fines and a letter of rebuke from Honorius. Donatus never answered this letter of Augustine.[99] There are many reasons why a Christian proconsul would ignore a bishop's request, but in this case, Donatus may have been wary of putting himself in the position of being fined and demoted because the bishops wanted to have it both ways.

---

[98] *ep.* 100.2: 'sed eos, cum hoc abs te petitur, rerum certarum manifestissimis documentis apud acta vel praestantiae tuae vel minorum iudicum convinci atque instrui patiaris.'

[99] That Donatus did not respond to *ep.* 100 is made clear by Augustine's remarks at the beginning of *ep.* 112.

6

The Conference of 411

If there is a lighter side to the sack of Rome in 410, it may be found in the *Histories* of Procopius, which report that when an imperial bird-keeper told Honorius that Rome had fallen, the emperor at first appeared stricken, but was then visibly relieved to discover the slave was referring to the city, not his favorite gamecock of the same name.[1] The true story of what Honorius was doing when the awful news reached Ravenna is similarly fantastic. The gates of Rome opened to Alaric's plundering army on 24 August. The following day, the emperor ruled to favor requests submitted by an embassy composed of four North African bishops. One of the legates was Possidius.[2]

It had been a fast trip for the bishops. The embassy, composed of Florentius, Possidius, Praesidius, and Benenatus, received orders to sail during the Council at Carthage on 14 June 410, just two months before the emperor's pronouncement. The speed at which they gained both an audience and affirmation may be attributable in part to the presence of Pope Innocent at court.[3] The African bishops were commissioned to complain about the Donatists and protest a recently promulgated law that stated 'each one could take up the worship of Christianity according to his own free will'.[4] This 'edict of toleration' as it has been called, does not survive, but in a letter to Heraclianus, *comes Africae*, the emperor declared that his previous law (*oraculum*), which provided an excuse for

---

[1] *Historia bellorum* 3.2.

[2] *CTh.* 16.5.51.

[3] See Orosius *hist.* vii, 39: 'apud Ravennam tunc positus.' For brief discussion, see É. Demougeot 'A propos des interventions du pape Innocent Ier dans le politique séculière', *Revue Historique*, 212 (1954), 23–38 at 32. I thank Michele Salzman for calling to my attention Pope Innocent's presence at Ravenna.

The African bishops are listed in order of seniority (*Concilia Africae, Registri Ecclesiae Carthaginensis Excerpta* 107). See *PCBE Afrique* 'Florentius 4', 471–3. He acted as one of the seven *consiliarii* at the 411 conference. See also *PCBE Afrique* 'Praesidius 1', 899–900, and 'Benenatus 3', 139–40, the latter of whom was a correspondent of Augustine's (*epp.* 253 and 254).

[4] *Concilia Africae, Registri Ecclesiae Carthaginensis Excerpta* 107: 'legationem susceperunt contra Donatistas…eo tempore quo lex data est, ut libera voluntate quis cultum christianitatis exciperet.'

heretics to 'creep back' to their former practices, was now void.[5] He used the same kind of language in a letter to Flavius Marcellinus (written on 14 October 410) wherein he expressed his concern that an incorrect interpretation of a ruling was being used to the profit of the Donatists. He ordered this law be abolished lest more occasion be given for their 'misguided' beliefs.[6]

> Now we also decree that this legal manipulation must be hindered by a similar command; we justly say this, that we willingly rescind that which had been promulgated, so that no one may presume he is able to transgress against divine worship by means of our decrees.[7]

Honorius' sudden display of tolerance is surprising, and the decision to recall his own pronouncement just a few months later makes the initial issue even more suspect. The emperor may indeed have decided that Africa's diligent continuation of grain shipments to Rome in the emergency of 410 merited reward, with cancellation of taxes accompanying a relaxation of heresy laws.[8] Such a supposition, however, requires Honorius to dismantle all his previous injunctions against the Donatists, a group with whom he was personally and politically at odds. It has been suggested that perhaps the ruling was instead of local derivation, promulgated by the proconsul of Africa, Macrobius, but if it did come from the emperor, he himself spoke of it (twice in two different places) as an *oraculum*, which may mean that this was a verbal, not written, statement.[9] His incautious words escaped the palace walls, were infelicitously taken up by eager provincial administrators, and had to be stopped by subsequent imperial directives.

The above-mentioned scenarios are unlikely. The law originated from court and was both tangible and intentional, as *oraculum* is a word used to describe written documents emerging from the consistory through

---

[5] *CTh.* 16.5.51 (dated 25 August 410): 'Oraculo penitus remoto, quo ad ritus suos haereticae superstitionis obrepserant, sciant omnes sanctae legis inimici plectendos se poena et proscriptionis et sanguinis, si ultra convenire per publicum execranda sceleris sui temeritate temptaverint.'

[6] *Coll. Carth.*, I,4: 'Nec sane latet conscientiam nostram sermo caelestis oraculi, quem errori suo posse proficere scaeva donatistarum interpretatio profitetur; qui quamvis depravatos animos ad correctionem mitius invitaret, aboleri eum tamen etiam ante iussimus, ne qua superstitionibus praestaretur occasio.'

[7] *Coll. Carth.*, I,4: 'Nunc quoque excludendam subreptionem simili auctoritate censemus; illudque merito profitemur, libenter nos ea quae statuta fuerant submovere, ne in divinum cultum nobis se quisquam auctoribus aestimet posse peccare.'

[8] Tax remission at *CTh.* 11.28.6, issued to the proconsul of Africa, Macrobius, on 25 June 410.

[9] Louis Leschi, 'Le dernier Proconsul païen de la province d'Afrique (410 ap. J-C.)', *Congrès national des Sciences historiques*, 2 (1932), 253–60.

accustomed channels.[10] The 'edict of toleration', whose rapid adoption by Donatists surprised and angered the emperor, probably had its origin in his immediate needs. A story in the Historia nova of Zosimus refers to Honorius' relationship with General Generidus, whose services were in high demand in 410 (5.46.4).[11] Generidus was not a Catholic, and he announced that his convictions and the laws against them prevented him from attending the emperor at the palace. When Honorius said that the laws were not applicable to him, Generidus replied that he could not receive such an honor when imperial injunctions were still causing injury to others. Honorius, Zosimus says, then ordered their cancellation so that qualified men could rule in a civil or military capacity while staying loyal to their own beliefs. We need not remain wedded to the story itself to understand the circumstances under which this particular law probably found its way to Africa. Honorius obviously intended his tolerance to be limited in scope, but he must have not properly articulated the parameters of his generosity. Donatist bishops, like their Catholic counterparts, listened carefully for laws emerging from the consistory. For all we know, they may have had a representative at court when this particular law was issued.[12] When news of Honorius' ruling reached Africa, the Donatist bishops approached their local senates and members of the provincial administration to begin dismantling the current strictures against them. It is the same process we have seen before: the seeking of favor through employment of precedents whose affiliation with the issue at hand, however tangential, is emphasized when presenting arguments before administrative bodies. We do not know the extent of Donatist success, save for the emperor's remarks regarding their exploitation of a law not intended for them. Augustine says that after dissemination ('illa perditionis libertate concessa'), many former Donatists, having come to the Catholic side after promulgation of the Edict of Unity, chose not to return to their previous allegiance.[13] It is true, however, that the new Donatist bishop of Hippo, Macrobius, openly processed into

---

[10] Marcellinus refers to Honorius' rescript of 410, clearly a written document, as an *oraculum* (*Coll. Carth.*, I, 140). When Symmachus asks for legal clarification by ruling from Theodosius I, he asks for the promulgation of *oracula*. See R. H. Barrow (trans.), *Prefect and Emperor: The Relationes of Symmachus A.D. 384* (Oxford: Clarendon Press, 1973) as well as Jill Harries, 'The Roman Imperial Quaestor from Constantine to Theodosius II', *JRS*, 78 (1988), 148–72.

[11] Albert C. de Veer, 'Une Mesure de Tolérance de l'Empereur Honorius', *Revue des études byzantines*, 24 (1966), 189–95.

[12] The events between 404 and 411 show that the Donatists of Africa went to court with some regularity. The Donatist bishop of Rome as well acted as a conduit of information between Italy and Africa. He was in Carthage for the conference in 411.

[13] *Contra Gaudentium* 1.24 (27): 'quorum quidam in regionibus vestris etiam quibusdam nostris maiores apparuerunt, quando vobis illa perditionis libertate concessa ad vos redire noluerunt.'

that city and reoccupied a church that, until recently, had been under Catholic control (*ep.* 108.14). The situation was unsettling enough to prompt the sending of Catholic bishops to Italy in very unstable times, but at least two of the men were used to difficult travel. As we saw in Chapter 5, Possidius was still at court in early 409. His senior in the 410 delegation, Florentius, had also been sent to Ravenna in June 408.

Aside from the request for Honorius to clarify his law, Possidius and the embassy asked the emperor to arrange for the Donatists and Catholics to meet in a council mediated by an imperial representative. This is the genesis of the conference of 411. The Donatist and Catholic bishops met in Carthage at one of the city's baths, the Thermae Gargilianae, on 1, 3, and 8 June.[14] They debated in front of Flavius Marcellinus, *tribunus et notarius*, a devoted Catholic, a man of talent, and the brother of the proconsul of Africa, Apringius.[15] He executed his duty as judge impeccably, but that meant making sure that the Catholics emerged as the winners. To say that he was an impartial mediator is decidedly exaggerated, but he always remained courteous.

---

[14] For overview, see Jeremy Williams, 'Collatio of 411', in Allan D. Fitzgerald (ed.), *Augustine Through the Ages: An Encyclopedia* (Grand Rapids: William B. Eerdmans Publishers, 1999), 218–19.

The bishops met in the *scriptorium* of the baths. The structure was apparently cool, filled with light, and spacious enough to accommodate all the bishops (close to 600 near the end of the first day when the Catholic bishops were called in) without, apparently, too much discomfort. See *C. Don.* 35.58: 'tam spatioso et lucido et refrigeranti loco'.

Possidius' description of the 411 conference in the *Vita Augustini* is typical: little detail, but with all the credit going to Augustine (*v. Aug.* 13.1–3): 'And more and more by the aid of Christ, the unity of peace, that is, the fraternity of the Church of God, grew and multiplied from day to day. This was especially advanced after the conference which was held a little later at Carthage by all the Catholic bishops with these same bishops of the Donatists at the command of the most glorious and devout Emperor Honorius, who, in order to bring this about, had sent the tribune and notary Marcellinus from his own court to Africa as judge. In this conference they were completely silenced, and being convicted of error by the Catholics, were reprimanded by sentence of the judge.' ('ac magis magisque, iuvante Christo, de die in die maugebatur et multiplicabatur pacis unitas et ecclesiae Dei fraternitas. Et id maxime factum est post conlationem quae ab universis episcopis catholicis apud Carthaginem cum iisdem Donatistarum episcopis postmodum facta est, id iubente gloriosissimo et religiosissimo imperatore Honorio, propter quod perficiendum etiam a suo latere tribunum et notarium Marcellinum ad Africam iudicem miserat. In qua controversia illi omnimodis confutati, atque de errore a catholicis convicti sententia cognitoris notati sunt.')

[15] Marcellinus was a good friend of Augustine to whom Augustine dedicated the first three books of *De civitate Dei*. For a discussion of their correspondence see Madeline Moreau, *Le Dossier Marcellinus dans la correspondance de saint Augustin* (Paris: Études Augustiniennes, 1973).

See also *PCBE Afrique* 'Favius Marcellinus 2', 671–88. Marcellinus was executed on 13 September 413. Augustine's account of his last visit with Marcellinus while the latter was incarcerated may be found in *ep.* 151 to Caecilianus. For the profound effect Marcellinus' murder had on Augustine's view of the alliance between Catholic Church and empire, see Peter Brown, *Augustine of Hippo: A Biography* (Berkeley: University of California Press, 1967; reprint 2000), 337–8.

Possidius was the only Catholic delegate who seemed to tax Marcellinus' patience.[16] The bishop of Calama was one of seven appointed to present arguments for the Catholic side, and he made little effort to temper his speech or suppress his exhilaration when suggesting an examination of the Donatist correspondence with Constantine the Great, evidence which proved the Donatists, not the Catholics, first sought the intervention of imperial authorities.[17] Marcellinus twice cut him off mid-sentence (II, 29; III, 11). When the Donatists asked to submit their response to the Catholic mandate on 8 June, an *exceptor* named Romulus who was employed by the city government of Carthage began to read it aloud. Bishop Emeritus interrupted with the complaint that Romulus was slurring the phrases together to the detriment of comprehension, to which Augustine suggested that a member of the Donatist staff perform the recitation. The Catholic bishops had previously demanded that noisy outbursts on the Donatist side be noted in the transcripts, and Possidius was following their lead when he demanded: 'Let it be noted that they asked that the *gesta* which they have submitted be read by their own *notarii*!' To which Marcellinus tartly responded, 'It does not matter who reads it.'[18] On the whole, however, we do not hear as much from Possidius as we would expect from a man so eager for confrontation. He may have been advised to hold back on the morning of the 8 June, as the discussion revolved around his embassy of 410. The Donatists wanted the Catholics to provide the names of the legates in order to question them as to the contents of the written requests (first the *preces* and then the *mandatum*) they brought with them on their visit to the emperor. With the aid of Marcellinus, the Catholics were spared scrutiny of these documents, but I believe Possidius' sparse comments underscore a tactical decision that he remain quiet lest he reveal too much.[19]

THE CONFERENCE OF 411: PRELIMINARIES

Stenographers recorded all the sessions. To ensure the satisfaction and confidence of bishops who had accumulated a century of mutual mistrust, Marcellinus established an elaborate procedure of recording and transcribing to guarantee

---

[16] The *Gesta cum Emerito* (4) tells us that the transcripts from the 411 conference were read aloud every year during Lent in the sees of Carthage, Thagaste, Cirta, Hippo, and all other diligent churches ('apud omnes diligentes ecclesias'). Since Possidius was there with Augustine in his 'debate' with Emeritus, one would think that he would have specifically named Calama if the transcripts were read aloud at Possidius' basilica.

[17] *Coll. Carth.*, III, 148; 152; 168; 178.

[18] Ibid. III, 256: '"Scriptum sit ipsos petisse ut a suis notariis gesta quae proferunt recitentur." Marcellinus, vir clarissimus, tribunus et notarius, dixit: "Nihil interest a quo relegantur."'

[19] Cf. Serge Lancel, *Actes de la Conférence de Carthage en 411* (Paris: Les Éditions du Cerf, 1972), Vol. 1, 242–3.

acceptance of the record (I.10). A select group of eight bishops (four Donatist and four Catholic) monitored the stenographers. The speakers themselves were required to read over the fair copies and acknowledge the accuracy of the transcripts by affixing their signatures after each of their respective entries.[20] One manuscript of this transcript survives, but it breaks off in the middle of the third day of discussion. Augustine's partisan *Breviculus collationis cum Donatistis* and an extant list of chapter headings from the manuscript help fill in the lacuna that obfuscates what transpired on the final day.[21]

It is agreed that the transcript of the 411 conference is a remarkable document. The most distinguished bishops in Africa of the late fourth and early fifth centuries speak directly to us here. Despite its privileged position as evidence, however, the transcript remains underutilized. Readers find it disappointing as they may, with some justification, come away thinking that the conference never really got started. This was to be a discussion about religious differences so as to identify and define the true Church. Statements and declarations from the first day attest to promises of developing arguments using scriptural evidence, as opposed to the kind of technical approaches based on documentation one finds in civil cases.[22] It seems the Donatists, however, offered little save procedural objections, with theology and its attendant metaphors only entering the proceedings just before the transcript breaks off. Many of those familiar with the conference, even those who approach it with only a historical eye, believe the Donatists were simply filling time, larding the discussion with superfluous arguments. This sentiment repeats the accusation made by the Catholics themselves.[23] In public debates it was common for the

---

[20] Emin Tengström, *Die Protokollierung der Collatio Carthaginensis: Beiträge zur Kenntnis der römischen Kurzschrift nebst einem Exkurs über das Wort sceda (schedula)* (Göteborg: Elanders Boktryckeri Aktiebolag, 1962); and H. C. Teitler, *Notarii and Exceptores*: An Inquiry into the Role and Significance of Shorthand Writers in the Imperial and Ecclesiastical Bureaucracy of the Roman Empire (Amsterdam: J. C. Gieben Publisher, 1985), 6–13.

[21] James S. Alexander, 'Methodology in the *Capitula gestorum conlationis Carthaginiensis*', *Studia Patristica*, 17 (1982), 3–8.

[22] *Coll. Carth.*, I, 40–54.

[23] See, for example, Paul Monceaux, *Histoire littéraire de l'Afrique Chrétienne depuis les Origins jusqu'a l'Invasion arabe*. (Paris: Éditions Ernest Leroux-reprint Culture et Civilizaton, 1912–23; reprint Brussels, 1966), iv, 413, 'Là-dessus s'engage une controverse interminable et très confuse, coupée par d'autres chicanes.' See also Geoffrey Grimshaw Willis, *Saint Augustine and the Donatist Controversy* (London: (Willis) S.P.C.K, 1950), 72; É. Lamirande, 'Augustine and the Discussion of the Sinners in the Church at the Conference of Carthage', *AugStud*, 3 (1972), 97–112. More recently, Robert A. Markus, 'Africa and the Orbis Terrarum: The Theological Problem', in Pierre-Yves Fux, Jean-Michel Roessli, and Otto Wermelinger (eds.), *Augustinus Afer: saint Augustin, africanité et universalité: actes du colloque international, Alger-Annaba, 1–7 Avril 2001* (Fribourg: Éditions Universitaires Fribourg Suisse, 2003), 325; and Serge Lancel, *Saint Augustine*, translated by Antonia Nevill (London: SCM Press, 2002), 296–300. The exception is Maureen A. Tilley, 'Dilatory Donatists or Procrastinating Catholics: The Trial at the Conference of Carthage', *Church History*, 60 (1991), 7–19, esp. 14, who rightly argues that Donatist strategy focused on procedural issues.

actors to accuse each other of unwarranted 'digressions' as a way of criticizing their presentations.[24] The Donatists said the same of the Catholics with almost equal frequency.[25] Others instead call Donatist actions 'strategic', but this merely serves as a kindly explanation for behavior some have interpreted as desperate and ill prepared.[26] Augustine was the first to suggest (repeated to this day) that the Donatists intentionally bloated the transcript to make it too confusing to understand.[27] The Catholics were confident of the outcome, but the Donatists deflated their heightened anticipation by making an indecipherable mess out of what should have been an unambiguous victory.[28]

The seeming lack of direction and sense exhibited by the transcript is a function of a correlative lack of context. The emperor and Marcellinus called this meeting a *disputatio* and *collatio*, respectively, but contrary to these names, the conference of 411 was a legal hearing, whose parameters were established by the issue of an imperial rescript.[29] Marcellinus, acting as a representative of the emperor through receipt of *mandata*, issued additional directives, and these had to adhere to the strictures set by the initial rescript. The Catholics and Donatists were restricted by the limitations imposed by these documents. All their actions, therefore, especially the seemingly obtuse ones introduced by the Donatists, were informed by the conference's legal boundaries. When analyzed in terms of civil procedure and the degree to which it can be manipulated, the conference of 411 begins to make more sense.

---

[24] Augustine accused Pelagius and Julian of wordiness and indulging in irrelevancies. See *De gratia Christi et de peccato originali*. 1.32.35 and *Contra Iulianum opus imperfectum* 3.20. For other examples, see Mathijs J. G. P. Lamberigts, 'The Italian Julian of Aeclanum about the African Augustine of Hippo', in Pierre-Yves Fux, Jean-Michel Roessli, and Otto Wermelinger (eds.), *Augustinus Afer: Saint Augustin, africanité et universalité: Actes du colloque international, Alger-Annaba, 1–7 Avril 2001* (Fribourg: Éditions Universitaires Fribourg Suisse, 2003), 89, nn. 67 and 68.

[25] For example, *Coll. Carth.*, III, 68, 75, 88, 89. Notice that Marcellinus' injunction against trifles that waste time 'nebulis (I.10)' are repeated in the Donatist accusations against the Catholics (see e.g. III, 89 and III, 153 ['nebulas']).

[26] Gerald Bonner, 'Carelessness', *St. Augustine of Hippo: Life and Controversies* (Philadelphia: Westminster Press, 1963), 269; Frend, 'the Donatists prepared their case indifferently', *The Donatist Church: A Movement of Protest in Roman North Africa* (Oxford: Clarendon Press, 1952; reprint, 1971), 279.

[27] See preface to *brev.*: 'sed quia hoc obtinere minime potuerunt, id efficerunt multiplicitate gestorum, ut quod actum est non facile legeretur.'

[28] Brent Shaw, 'African Christianity: Disputes, Definitions and "Donatists"' in Malcolm R. Greenshields and Thomas A Robinson (eds.), *Orthodoxy and Heresy in Religious Movements: Discipline and Dissent* (Lewiston: Lampeter, 1992), 32: 'From their point of view, the more the "debates" were reduced to a chaos and a shambles, the better.'

[29] Notice that the meeting is nowhere called a *concilium*, which is defined in Du Cange's *Glossarium* as 'Episcoporum consessus de rebus Ecclesiasticis deliberantium'. A *collatio* as defined in the *TLL* is more a gathering, Christian or not, where the parties engage in discussion and disputation. Possidius (*v. Aug.* 16.4) describes Augustine's meetings with the Manichaean Felix as a *collatio*.

In a typical civil case (i.e. a *cognitio* of the later empire), a person interested in initiating a case approached a magistrate with a request (*preces*) for a hearing. Generally, if a presiding magistrate believed the allegations had merit, he would issue an official subpoena (usually called a *litis denuntiatio*), which, within four months of its issue, had to be accompanied by a written statement from the person who submitted the complaint (*libellus conventionis*) and a written response from the defendant. The case itself as heard in a court employed this dossier of documents to define the parameters of the trial. The accuser spoke first, and only after hearing the charge would the defense respond. Summons to trials worked on a strict timetable. While extensions could be granted, if the defendant exceeded the time span allotted and did not fulfill his obligations (including showing up in court), he was ruled contumacious and automatically lost the case. If it was the plaintiff who did not appear at the appointed time, the case would usually be dismissed.[30]

The process just described looks a lot like the situation that precipitated the 411 conference. Possidius' legation of 410 presented a request (*preces*) to the emperor, and the latter responded with a rescript appointing a judge to preside over the trial. The Catholics had asked for the conference, and so they were not officially summoned to appear, unlike the Donatists, who, like civil defendants, were given a deadline of four months and threatened with a judgment of contumacy if they did not meet their legal obligations. As in a court case, there was to be a winner and a loser, with consequences in store for the 'guilty' who did not comply with the ruling.

The 411 conference, therefore, is a legal proceeding, but it is highly unusual one for several reasons, not least of which is the emperor's proleptic condemnation of the Donatists in the very rescript that ordered the convening of this meeting. He called them adherents of wrong belief and liars (I, 5), wording his pronouncement in such a way that definitions could not shift when subjected to interpretive scrutiny. The terms 'Catholic' and 'Donatist' were fixed, so despite objections to the assignment of 'Catholicism' to one party before the convening of a conference whose purpose was to determine who deserved that appellation, Marcellinus continued to use it, justifiably, he said, as he was following the dictates of Honorius' rescript.[31]

---

[30] Lancel's discussion of the legal aspects of the conference of 411 is indispensable: *Actes de la Conférence*, 1, 66–88. See also Artur Steinwater, 'Eine kirchliche Quelle des nachklassischen Zivilprozesses', *Acta congressus iuridici internationalis VII saeculo*, 2 (1935), 125–44; W. W. Buckland, *A Text-Book of Roman Law from Augustus to Justinian* (Cambridge: Cambridge University Press, 1963), 662–7, and André Chastagnol, *La Préfecture urbaine à Rome sous le Bas-Empire* (Paris: Presses Universitaires de Trance, 1960), 375–8.

[31] *Coll. Carth.*, III, 92. Augustine himself was careful not to use the word 'Catholic' in referring to his Church (see Markus, 'Africa and the Orbis Terrarum,' 326). The Donatist objections were mostly directed at Marcellinus, who kept using the term 'Catholic' as determined by Honorius'

One cannot but agree with modern judgments that Honorius' letter, and thus the whole council, were irretrievably biased.[32] Marcellinus may have been a gentleman, but he was obligated by law to subscribe to Honorius' directives. He was to repress Donatism in favor of Catholicism and all that 'antiquity and religious authority had established' (I, 4). The conference was to confirm the Catholic faith. Honorius had said as much.[33] And while Marcellinus' comments may have been more temperate, his language underscored the emperor's assumptions.[34] The parameters of the case as established by the imperial rescript made it impossible for the Donatists to escape condemnation. Their response to this legal 'trap' was to try to undermine the validity of the law that summoned them to Carthage. If they could discredit that imperial rescript, they just might escape its anticipated verdict.

THE LEGAL DETAILS: RESCRIPTS AND MANDATES

Before discussing what transpired at the conference, we need to look more closely at the documents that framed it. Honorius' rescript commissioning Marcellinus to convene the conference was read aloud on its first and third days (I,4 and III, 29).[35] The emperor declared that the Donatists had sullied Africa with 'vain error and unnecessary dissension' ('vano errore et dissensione superflua'). So that future generations would not find fault with the emperor's attention to duty, he was called now, as previous emperors had been, to protect Catholicism. It did not escape Honorius that the Donatists deliberately misinterpreted the substance and intent of a recent imperial law to their

---

rescript, and *repeated* by the directives issued prior to the conference by Marcellinus. One of the many times the Donatists objected to the use of nomenclature, Marcellinus responded: 'If Your Holiness claims that they [the Catholic side] are called by a false name, let it finally be accounted the proper time to discuss the business at hand, and in as much we are talking about this name being presumed, if it can be proved, the opposing side will be refuted in all these matters (III, 96).'

[32] Lancel, *Actes de la Conférence de Carthage en 411*, Vol. 1, 29: 'Tant de partialité nous confound.'
[33] 'Ut quid ad confirmandam catholicam fidem praeceptio nostra profecerit celerius possimus agnoscere.'
[34] *Coll. Carth.*, I, 5 (the words of Marcellinus): 'Quid clementissimus princeps dominus noster Honorius pro catholicae fidei confirmatione decreverit....Cunctos etenim tam catholicae quam donatianae partis episcopos in unum voluit congregari, ut, lectis ab utraque parte peritioribus viris, certae fidei veritate discussa, superstitionem ratio manifesta convincat.'
[35] The second reading was in response to the Donatist query as to who called this conference. The rescript clarifies that it was the Catholics who asked for this particular meeting, but Marcellinus' first edict makes it clear that the Catholic action did not automatically qualify them as the plaintiffs.

advantage. It was to be annulled so as to provide no opportunity for indulging in *superstitio*. 'We judge that this manipulation needs to be repressed with a repeated injunction.'[36] The emperor wrote that he had received an embassy of Catholic bishops and agreed to commission a select gathering of Catholic and Donatist bishops at Carthage.[37] Honorius expected that 'clear reason would defeat superstition', with Catholicism constituting *ratio*.

The emperor's letter delineated further specifics. The meeting would occur after a lapse of four months.[38] Three separate announcements, spaced twenty days apart, would forestall the opportunity of pleading ignorance to the summons. As the ones called forward, the Donatists would be declared contumacious if they did not appear by the stipulated date. Noncompliance would result in automatic rule against them, which included ceding of Donatist basilicas and congregations to the Catholics.[39] Honorius then named Marcellinus as the emperor's representative, ordering him to execute his duty while keeping within the parameters established by the imperial rescript.[40]

The emperor's letter was in the form of a pragmatic rescript (*pragmaticum rescriptum*). While this became a popular means to issue legislation in late antiquity, this is the first time this kind of document appears in the extant evidence.[41] From what is known about them, such rescripts had the force of law but pertained to corporations, not individuals. Thus, in the conference of 411, the bishops themselves were not subject to individual ruling

---

[36] 'Nunc quoque excludendam subreptionem simili auctoritate censemus.'

[37] (I, 4): 'Studio < tamen > pacis et gratiae venerabilium virorum episcoporum legationem libenter admisimus, quae congregari donatistas episcopos ad coetum celeberrimae desiderat civitatis, ut, electis sacerdotibus, *quos pars utraque delegerit*, habitis disputationibus, superstitionem ratio manifesta confutet' (italics mine).

[38] Honorius' rescript is dated October 410. The four-month time allotment began with the issue of Marcellinus' first edict (February 411), which meant a deadline of 19 May 411. The Donatists marched through the city on 18 May to make their point.

[39] 'trini edicti < evocationem volumes custodiri, ita ut vicensis diebus in e > vocatione contumacium tempora concludantur. Quibus emensis atque transactis, si provocati adesse contempserint, cedat cum ecclesiis populus.'

Possidius protests subsequent Donatist complaints that they lodged, accusing Marcellinus of being irreparably partial. If they held him suspect, Possidius says, they could have refused the meeting. The statement is, to say the least, disingenuous. See *v. Aug* 14.2: 'poterant utique suspectum eum habentes, recusare congressum.'

[40] I, 4: 'ut et ea quae ante mandata sunt, et quae nunc statuta cognoscis, probata possis implere sollertia.'

[41] For discussion, see Theodor Mommsen, 'Sanctio Pragmatica', in *Gesammelte Schriften* 2.2 (Berlin: Mommsen-publishers Weidmann, 1905), 426–8; Jean Gaudemet, *La Formation du droit séculier et du droit de l'église aux IVe et Ve Siècles* (Toulouse: Siney, 1957), 35–8; Peter Kussmaul, *Pragmaticum und Lex: Formen spätrömischer* (Göttingen: Vandenhoeck & Ruprecht, 1981), esp. 87–9; Ralph Mathisen, '*Adnotitio* and *Petitio*: The Emperor's Favor and Special Exceptions in the Early Byzantine Empire', in Dennis Feissel and Jean Gascou (eds.), *La pétition à Byzance* (Paris: Association des Amis du Centre d'Histoire et Civilization de Byzonce, 2004), 23–32, and Lancel, *Actes de la Conférence*, Vol. 1, 67–8.

(such as being labeled plaintiffs or defendants). Instead, the two Churches, as institutions, were the bodies attending the conference. It seems that this approach was preferred by the Catholics. Possidius and his embassy asked for a discussion among only a few bishops, rather than as many as could come, which was the accustomed tradition for Church councils.[42] The issue of a pragmatic rescript authorized some bishops to act as representatives for all.[43] This is why on the morning of the first day, when the entire Donatist episcopate insisted that Marcellinus identify which party was the plaintiff and defendant, he responded that in public and corporate law, chosen delegates and not a crowd (*multitudo*) were assigned a legal identity (*persona*).[44] The Catholics often spoke of the appointment of representatives as an excellent way to avoid the unpleasantness of scenes that hundreds of bishops might make with their unruly noise and anger. It is more important, however, that such an arrangement protected the delegates from being subjected to personal accusation. For example, if a Catholic delegate had in his 'lineage' a clergy member thought in Donatist opinion to be, or have been ordained by, a *traditor*, the bishop at the conference could not be personally impugned, as he was acting on behalf of his church, not in *propria persona*. Hence, when the Donatists asked Augustine who ordained him, Alypius and Possidius protested that, as bishops sent to debate according to the instructions of a mandate, this was not a legitimate question (*Coll. Carth.*, III, 244–5). Marcellinus agreed, and reminded the Donatist side that matters concerning individuals did not affect this case.[45]

---

[42] Presentation by representatives was also the plan for the 403 conference, but we have seen that this meeting never took place. *Concilia Africae Registri Ecclesiae Carthagenensis Excerpta* 92: 'deligatis ex vobis, quibus causam assertionis vestrae committatis'.

[43] Supra n. 37 and Marcellinus' remark that it was the emperor who ordered representatives to present arguments at *Coll. Carth.*, III, 74.
See also III, 38 and 248.

[44] I, 34: 'Numquam habere potuit certam multitudo personam, cum hoc etiam in publicis actionibus atque corporibus soleat custodiri, ut per ordinatas atque firmatas omnia peragantur.'
If this were really a *collatio*, such a restriction would not have been imposed on the Donatists. Emeritus responded (*Coll. Carth.*, I, 35): 'I have your word, Exalted Sir, that nothing is demanded of me according to civil law when the matter is conducted according to faith [ecclesiastical law]: 'Teneo fidem tuam, vir sublimis, nihil mihi de iuris lege praescribi, ubi agitur < de > fide.' Marcellinus explained that the demand for both sides to employ representatives was designed to hinder unnecessary talking. Petilian answered with the exclamation (*Coll. Carth.*, I, 37): 'optimus moderator!' There is more sarcasm and disappointment here than praise.

[45] *Coll Carth.*, III, 248: 'licet haec quae de personis aguntur cognitionem differre non debeant.' See also the Catholic mandate (I, 55 [lines 361–6]) where they remind the Donatists that accusations against the delegates have nothing to do with accusations lodged against the Church: 'Quaecumque autem crimina quibuslibet collegis nostris, non iam more conferentium vel disputantium, sed maledicentium et litigantium obicienda putaverint, respondendum est eis nec eorum causas ad ecclesiae causam, quam nunc defendendam iniungimus, pertinere.'

Aside from Honorius' rescript, there were two edicts (*edicta*) issued by Marcellinus. They also had the force of law, as they were legally associated with the imperial rescript by means of *mandata* the emperor had given to Marcellinus (I, 4). The word 'mandate' makes frequent appearances, and it is best to clarify the term now since several kinds are mentioned during the course of the conference. First, the mandates Honorius sent to Marcellinus: they allowed Marcellinus to act on the emperor's behalf, including issuing further directions to the bishops as the conference drew near. The Catholics and Donatists also served their churches through the use of mandates. Whenever episcopal embassies traveled to the imperial court, they took these with them, which authorized them to act for all the bishops. Thus, when Possidius and his colleagues went to the emperor, they submitted *preces* requesting a meeting with the Donatists, but they also carried with them a document issued by the Catholic bishops at the June 410 council. This mandate detailed exactly what they had to do, and by whose authority they were to act. Bishops had to remain faithful to their instructions. Improvisation was discouraged.

So far, this is reasonably clear, but pragmatic rescripts complicate the picture somewhat. In most civil trials, the *preces*—the complaints lodged by a plaintiff to request action by a judge—were accessible to the defendants, as they made their counterarguments based on their contents. But in a trial activated by a pragmatic rescript, the actors were corporations, not individuals, and so the *preces* were not included in the proceedings. In terms of the 411 conference, those who made up the embassy, including Possidius, were not conducting personal business, but acting on behalf of a larger body. To include the *preces* in the proceedings of the conference assumed that the bishops who delivered the request were the same who composed it, and this was not necessarily correct. The bishops who made the trip to Ravenna were themselves not lodging a suit, so instead of including the *preces* to which the defense would ordinarily respond, Marcellinus required of both parties to submit letters, signed by all the bishops, that ratified the words and actions of the bishops chosen to represent them.[46] These statements were referred to as mandates, too, because they delineated the parameters of the arguments to be employed by the representatives

---

[46] The words of Marcellinus (*Coll. Carth.*, I, 10): 'Igitur episcopi memorati soli in praedictum locum tempusque conveniant, ita tamen ut reliqui omnes utriusque partis episcopi, ante diem qui praedestinatus examini est, ratum se habituros quicquid a septenis utrimque coepiscopis suis fuerit actitatum epistulis ad mean dicationem currentibus utrimque designent; quibus epistulis tamen etiam testimonium omnes apud me propriae suscriptionis adiungant.'

The Donatist bishops announced, rightly, that the submission of mandates was a function of secular, not ecclesiastical law (*Coll. Carth.*, I, 53): 'Quia haec causatio forensis est, non legalis. Nam uti mandato, his formulis praesumere non est ecclesiasticae consuetudinis sed forensis ludi atque certaminis, et illius exercitii quod magis argumentis quam fide aliqua saepe substitit.'

chosen by their respective collectives. In addition, Marcellinus also asked both parties to write him letters affirming that they understood and would obey Marcellinus' directives, including the election of delegates (I, 14–18). Both of these documents (the mandates and the letters of confirmation) constituted legal promises, violations of which were actionable.[47]

NEITHER COUNCIL NOR COURT CASE

As far as the Donatists were concerned, everything about the establishment of this conference was to their disadvantage. They were justified in their suspicions, but to a modern audience, their consequent maneuverings often appear to be little more than histrionics. Take these two famous examples. First, the whole of the second day was taken up by their objections to the continuation of the debate when the transcripts from the first session were not ready in fair, readable copies. Their protests are often ascribed to dilatoriness, but they were simply arguing for the proper observance of Marcellinus' second edict, which declared that each day of discussion would be followed by a day wholly dedicated to transcribing the record, which would then be examined and signed by the participants.[48] The stenographers had not finished transcribing the events of 1 June by the morning of 3 June. The Donatists insisted: no fair copy, no discussion. They were well within their legal rights to refuse. The date assigned for reconvening followed, and was subsidiary to, the availability of the transcript. Readers should be cautious of believing the Catholics when they attribute their acquiescence to benevolent indulgence in the face of Donatist stalling.

And then there was the awkwardness about who, if anybody, was going to sit down during these proceedings. Upon being invited to do so, the Donatists thanked Marcellinus but declined, declaring that they would stand before their prosecutors as Christ stood before Pilate (*Coll. Carth.*, I, 144–5 and III, 3–7). And so everyone, Donatists, Catholics, and Marcellinus, stood for all of the first, second, and, probably, the third day.[49] To assume the mantle of Christ and

---

[47] The legal term is *cautio ratam rem habere*. See the final sentence of *Coll. Carth.*, I, 10.

[48] *Coll. Carth.*, I, 10: 'Post primum autem collationis diem descriptioni subscriptionique gestorum locum diei subsequentis efficiet procrastinata cognitio; ita ut, si quid forte praecedenti collationi supererit, in diem tertium recurrat examen. Omne igitur spatium conferendi vicissim diei unius intercapedo distinguet, quo possint in medio gesta subinde subscribenda describi, memoratorum praestante custodia, qui hoc fine suum metiantur officium, non ut aliquid dicant, sed ut dicta custodiant.'

[49] Since the first half of the third day was dedicated to Donatist arguments as to their position as defendants, it is very unlikely that they were seated when arguing their points. Marcellinus did not bother to ask them to sit, and thus no exchange was included in the transcript.

the martyrs added a certain amount of drama, but we should remember that like those they emulated, the Donatists assumed that they were defendants in a court case. Sitting indicated equality among the parties and acquiescence to the proceedings. The Catholics submitted *preces* to the emperor asking for a hearing. According to the law, this should place them in the position of plaintiff. Honorius' subsequent rescript, with its judicial summons and precipitous opinion as to the required conclusion, only affirmed for the Donatists that they must be the defendants.

The problem was that the meeting in 411 does not adhere to the usual procedure for court cases (*cognitiones*), councils (*concilia*), or, as far as we know about them, conferences (*collationes*). We have already noted Honorius' anticipatory verdict, but this is a strikingly 'hybrid' affair. A church council would never assign its attendees the roles of defendant or plaintiff, nor does this kind of identification occur in *collationes*, which were not affiliated with the judicial system, but it happened in 411, and much of the first and third days of the conference were occupied with discussion as to which party was the accuser. On the other hand, Marcellinus never allowed for a traditional assignment of persons (*personae*), that is, defendant and plaintiff. The Catholics lodged the complaint with the emperor, but in his first edict of February 411, Marcellinus declared that *both* the Catholics and the Donatists had asked for this conference.[50] This alleged Donatist 'request' referred to an embassy that met with the praetorian prefect in 406 to ask for relief from pressures placed upon them by enforcement of the Edict of Unity. A Catholic bishop named Valentine also happened to be at court on unrelated business.[51] The Donatists said that they wanted to be heard along with him, but the prefect declined on behalf of Valentine: 'that bishop had not come for that purpose, nor had he received some such mandate from his bishops' (*ep.* 88.10).

This alone appears to constitute their request for a conference with the Catholics. On the morning of 8 June, the Donatists vehemently denied that this was their intention:

> That is what we were wishing to hear declared before the tribunal, if they (the Catholic embassy) insinuated to the emperor that we presented

---

[50] *Coll. Carth.*, I, 5: 'Consona siquidem utriusque partis petitio ad hanc principem sententiam provocavit. Nam sicut a catholicis nuper conlatio postulata est, sic ante brevissimum tempus donatistarum episcopos in iudicio inlustrium potestatum *conlationem postulasse non dubium est*. Et quoniam libenter assensum tribuit clementia principalis et concilium fieri intra Africam universale decrevit, utriusque partis iuxta poscentibus < episcopis > huic me disputationi principis loco iudicem voluit residere.'

[51] *PCBE Afrique*, 'Valentinus 2', 1130–2. He was the bishop of Vaienen (location unknown) and became the primate of Numidia after 411.

ourselves voluntarily before the praetorian prefect or indeed that we asked for a debate. If this is in fact what you said, I am able to refute you before the tribunal on the basis of the text of the *gesta*. (III, 129)[52]

Unfortunately, we never see the *gesta* from 406. Despite its apparent ability to absolve them, the Donatist bishops Petilian and Emeritus adamantly protested its being put forward for review. This may rouse suspicions as to what the *gesta* actually contained, but the Donatists were not bluffing here. In civil cases there was a strict order about the submission of documents as evidence. One of the first rules, reasonably enough, is that one submitted evidence after, not before, identification of the plaintiff and defendant. Marcellinus, as we shall see presently, had different ideas about settling on *personae*, and as it turns out, the transcript from the 406 embassy was the first one put before the conference to serve as a *means* of identifying the plaintiff. It was simply intolerable to the Donatists that in light of standard procedure, as well as the fact that it was the Catholics who submitted the *preces* initiating the 411 hearing—which had not yet, and would never be, examined—their 406 visit should be submitted to scrutiny first.[53]

The repercussions of the 406 embassy and the consequential designation of *personae* were several: first, Marcellinus declared that the identification of the plaintiff and defendant would be based, not on who asked for this particular meeting, but on historical accusations: when and what church accused the other of doing.[54] This means that the two sides had to enter the discussion (and submit documentation) prior to classification. Concomitantly, Marcellinus told the bishops that the emperor appointed him to judge without prejudice on the

---

[52] 'Hoc est quod volebamus in iudicio prodi, utrum imperialibus auribus intimarint nos in iudicio praefecturae vel voluntarios adstitisse vel quaesisse conflictum. Si enim ista dixisses, possem te de gestorum fide in iudicio confutare.'

[53] I think it is telling that when a reading of the 406 *gesta* actually commenced, it was the Catholics who emphatically stopped its recitation. They said there existed earlier *gesta* (from 403) that revealed the Catholics requested the African proconsul to call a meeting before 406. Why were Possidius and Alypius anxious to circumvent the 406 transcript in order to present evidence that pointed to them as the plaintiffs? See *Coll. Carth.*, III, 168–74.

[54] See *Coll. Carth.*, III, 114 (Emeritus speaking): 'Your Excellency understands that without appealing to the law the *persona* of the one defending is irrelevant, nor is it possible for someone to be called a defendant unless first there will have existed someone to call him forth. Therefore, if he stands in the position of the one seeking—this is what is said of a plaintiff—let him initiate an action to which I am able to respond, Indeed, they frequently say that we engage in superfluous delays, so that we won't come to the business at hand. Accordingly, since this is the very heart of the case, that he who calls another to court ought to begin the action in a court of law and to call forth a reply, let your Excellency heed that they need to proceed as to whether, or what, kind of action they are undertaking against us, so that we may respond.

points the parties chose to discuss. Of course, he and all present were constrained by the dictates of the law (i.e. Honorius' rescript), and he would intervene if he found it necessary to maintain the legal bounds, but he would not rule on what they were to discuss.[55] The subject of the conference was to be the *causa erroris*, its object was to choose *ratio* over *superstitio*, but *how* the bishops wanted to address the emperor's demands was up to them. That means, again contrary to the rules of civil procedure, that the plaintiff's arguments would not be followed by the defendant's response. There was no set order of speaking. Third, in his February edict, Marcellinus told the Donatists that they could choose another judge (*cognitor*) sympathetic to the Donatist cause, who would, like Marcellinus, be limited to ruling on matters of procedure. This appointment would obviously compromise their position as defendants, so they immediately declined:

> Marcellinus: If it pleases, let the other *cognitor*, chosen by your side, preside with me. If he is present, let him enter.
>
> Petilian: It is not fitting for us, who did not ask for the first judge, to choose another.
>
> Marcellinus: It is most evidently declared by the tenor of the divine constitution that a conference, not a judge, was asked for [by the Catholics].[56]

In sum, the Donatists had been summoned and restrained as if they were defendants, but were not given the opportunity to be defendants when the conference began.

THE LEGAL STRATEGY

Presenting themselves as the persecuted party was consonant with Donatist notions of what constituted the Church. True Christians suffered at the hands

---

Marcellinus answers (*Coll. Carth.*, III, 120): 'If it is established that the conference was requested by both parties, it also stands that the plaintiff is the one who has put forth an accusation.' ('Si conlationem ab utrisque partibus constat esse postulatam, constat eum esse petitorem qui crimen intendit.')

[55] Ibid. I, 5: 'Nihil aliud me nisi quod allegationes partium examinatae potuerint demonstrare, et quod veri invenerit fides, per admirabile mysterium trinitatis, per incarnationis dominicae sacramentum, et per salutem supramemoratorum principum iudicaturum me esse promitto.'

[56] Ibid. I, 6–8: Marcellinus: '…si placeret, electus a vestra parte mecum alius cognitor resideret; qui si praesto est, introire dignetur. Petilian: Non decet nos cognitorem eligere alterum, qui non petivimus primum. Marcellinus: Evidentissime praeceptionis augustae tenore declaratum est collationem, non cognitorem, fuisse postulatum.'

of the false.[57] But Donatist strategy at Carthage, it needs to be emphasized, did not have the *identity* of the Church at its center. In this setting of part conference and part court case, the Donatists pushed for the proceedings to look more like the second.[58] The Catholics pulled in the opposite direction. It was their hope that they could base the discussion on the texts of the mandates, and thus keep separate two contested areas of debate: the Church (*causa ecclesiae*) and the individuals who constituted, and according to the Donatists, compromised it (*causa Caeciliani*).[59] For the first, the Catholics said, the groups should argue from scripture. For the second, the parties were free to introduce legal and ecclesiastical documentation. The Donatists were warned, however, that an investigation of these would reveal that the imperial administration absolved both Caecilian and his *ordinator*, Felix of Abthungni (I, 55).

The Donatists believed that human actions affected the purity of the Church, so a Catholic separation of the two presented its own set of problems. More importantly, the Donatists wanted to settle immediately on the identity of parties through recourse to imperial law; it was the likes of such documents, after all, that brought them to Carthage under duress. Only after that pronouncement would they speak according to scripture. Imperial law, therefore, had procedural meaning for the Donatists in this conference, but to the Catholics (and Marcellinus), it was a matter of historical consequence. The introduction of past *gesta* constituted an entry into the discussion of the *causa Caeciliani*, at the end of which was the answer of who first accused the other of wrongdoing.[60] Thus, from the outset, the parties were poised to speak at cross-purposes. The Catholics planned their approach impeccably. They effectively checked Donatist strategy, for as much as the Donatists wanted a ruling on the parties, the Catholics would respond in equal measure with a damaging recall of the *gesta* stretching back to Caecilian's case. That said, the Catholics were certainly ready for a strictly legal contest if it became necessary. The seven bishops the Catholics chose to represent them—Aurelius, Alypius, Augustine, Vincentius, Fortunatus, Fortunatianus, and Possidius—were well experienced in the fields of forensics and law. Alypius was trained as a

---

[57] Ibid. I, 53. Petilian says: 'If one forsakes divine law, he shows that he is not a bishop. If he truly adheres to divine law, then I am obliged to answer him as one who desires to be Christian' ('si a lege discesserit, episcopum se non esse demonstret; si vero legem tenuerit, tunc ei ut illi qui christianus esse desiderat debeam respondere').

[58] Tilley, 'Dilatory Donatists or Procrastinating Catholics', 14.

[59] Lancel, *Actes de la Conférence*, Vol. 1, 46–50; Monceaux, *Histoire littéraire d'Afrique*, iv, 414; Émilien Lamirande, 'Augustine and the Discussion of Sinners'.

[60] Determination of the 'initial' accuser was alien to the law, as a number of imperial and provincial pronouncements after the age of Constantine determined the Donatists to be correct in their beliefs. Most recent law was always invested with greater authority.

lawyer and went to court many times in the latter half of his career. Vincentius and Fortunatianus had been to court in 407; Fortunatianus went again in June 408.[61] Possidius had been to see the emperor in 408 and 410. The Catholics may have said they anticipated arguing from scripture and debating over history, but all of them were fully prepared to engage the law.[62]

On the morning of 1 June, the 18 Catholic representatives watched as more than 250 Donatist bishops processed into the scriptorium. They had indeed already chosen their delegates as directed by Marcellinus' edict, but they asked him a few days before if they could all appear. It was important, they said, to demonstrate their number, as the Catholics regularly, and falsely, insisted on its paucity.[63] Number and Catholic lies about it will later emerge as a prominent aspect of this conference, but we return to the beginning of the first day when Marcellinus ordered a series of documents to be read and entered into the *gesta* (the rescript, his two edicts, the letters of commitment from the Catholics and the Donatists, and then one more from the Catholics, which voiced concern over the Donatist request for all the bishops to attend the proceedings). Between the reading of the first and second of Marcellinus' edicts, the Donatists asked for the correct observance of civil procedure (I, 9). Before any of these documents were introduced, they said, it was appropriate to identify the plaintiff and defendant. Marcellinus remonstrated, declaring that their concerns would be addressed in accordance to the law, but he had decreed that the documents would be read first. Emeritus, the Donatist bishop of Caesarea responded:

> It seems to me that the trial has already begun and to this point the identity [*persona*] of those entering it has not been determined. Nothing else is incumbent upon you, most true judge, other than to uphold the truth. If we heed the procedure of all these affairs, first the issue of [whether

---

[61] See Chapter 5, n. 19.

[62] The Catholics knew they were going to win. To make forced unity more palatable, the Catholics offered an accommodation to their rivals just a few days before the conference. If the Catholics were favored by Marcellinus, they promised that the now united bishops—the Catholic and formerly Donatist—would each keep their congregations and basilicas. A single episcopal chair would be occupied only upon the death of one of these; or, if the townspeople rejected the idea of two bishops, both would step down in favor of a third acceptable to all. This offer, made in the name of all the bishops, may be found in the collection of Augustine's letters, assigned number 128 in the Maurist catalogue. See also Émilien Lamirande, 'L'Offre conciliatrice des Catholiques aux Donatistes relativement à l'épiscopat (*Gesta collationis Carthaginiensis* I. 16)', *Église et Theologie*, 2 (1971), 285–308.

[63] *Coll. Carth.*, I, 14: 'Qua de re sinceritatem tuam plurimum exhortamur ut prioris edicti fide servata, cunctos nos ad te venire praecipias, ut quamprimum de numero nostro constet, quos adversarii paucos esse saepe mentiti sunt.'

the Catholic party arrived on] time, the mandate, the nature of *persona*, and the suit must be addressed, and then finally the merits of the case.[64]

Much of the subsequent Donatist conversation with Marcellinus consists of the push for establishing these preliminaries before speaking about the central issue (*negotium*). The Donatists wanted one of two outcomes. The first was that external stipulations be dropped, including the imperial rescript and Marcellinus' participation, and then the two parties could argue from scripture alone. They were well aware, and subsequently reminded by the judge, that this was an impossibility (III, 49). Since legal constraints tilted the proceedings in Catholic favor and restrained the Donatists as if they were called to a civil trial, they would assume it *was* a trial.[65] Therefore, the second, more Strategic choice, and the one they pursued, consisted of a debate based on scripture only after insisting that legal preliminaries be settled. If the Donatists could use procedure to their advantage, they might shut down the conference before having to enter the theological debate Honorius required that they lose. Hence their first point: *de tempore*. The Catholics announced their arrival in the city on 25 May. The four-month deadline as outlined in Honorius' rescript and, more specifically, Marcellinus' first edict was the 19 May. The Donatists argued that the Catholics were late, and according to the rules of procedure, the case should be dismissed (I, 29; III, 203–7). Marcellinus rejected the point on factual, not procedural, grounds, although he did note that the objection was more relevant to secular (*forensis*) than ecclesiastical procedure (I, 30). He told the Donatists that he ordered the parties to convene on 1 June (I, 23).[66] Even if that were not enough time for all to gather, the emperor had given him liberty to extend the deadline for two more months (I, 30).[67] This first attempt at forcing a collapse failed, but the Donatists had made their point. Neither the Catholics nor Marcellinus cared to respond to the Donatist complaint that if they, the Donatists, had arrived after 19 May, the Catholics would have seen to it that their opponents were immediately pronounced the losers.[68]

---

[64] I, 20: 'Acta est, ut arbitror, causa et adhuc conflictantium non est statuta persona. Tibi enim, iudicum verissime, nihil aliud incumbit quam tenere veritatem. Si enim omnium negotiorum advertamus instantiam, primo de tempore, de mandato, de persona, de causa, tum demum ad merita negotii veniendum est.'

[65] Cf. Frend, *The Donatist Church*, 279.

[66] Notice the Donatist challenge to Marcellinus (I, 24). They asked if the day of convening was determined by Marcellinus' edict or by the imperial decree. Marcellinus responded: 'The day was established from my edict according to the form of the imperial judgment...We need not dwell over this any longer.'

[67] See Lancel, *Actes de la Conférence*, Vol. 1, 74–8.

[68] *Coll. Carth.*, I. 29: 'Qui si non adessemus, iam pars adversa sine dubio flagitaret in contumaces dicendam esse sententiam, tempusque iam fuisse definitum quo nec post venientibus agere quicquam aut respondere licuisset.'

The next, and most sustained, debate over procedure dealt with Possidius' embassy to Honorius in 410: *de mandato*. On 1 June, the Catholics read aloud their mandate, a representative statement signed by all the Catholic bishops, which the Donatists insisted on verifying through a review of all the signatories. Thus, we see all the Catholic bishops identify themselves and receive recognition from their episcopal rivals (I, 112–43). This mandate established the position from which the Catholic delegation would commence their 'defense'. The Donatists in response read out a very short declaration announcing that the seven Donatist episcopal representatives had the authority to be the 'defenders against the *traditores* and our persecutors who wish to discomfit us with a law promulgated at their request in the court of the *clarissimus spectabilis tribunus* and *notarius*, Marcellinus' (*Coll Carth.*, I, 148). They refused to make any statements until Marcellinus determined *personae*. When summoned, each Donatist bishop stepped forward for verification by their Catholic counterparts. So ended the first day of the conference.

Augustine writes in the *Breviculus* that the morning of the third day witnessed the Donatists abandoning their promise, made, he says, on the first, to base their arguments from scripture once the business about the mandates was settled. Instead, they reverted to more 'time-wasting' arguments about secular law and procedure.[69] Augustine is referring to the attention the Donatists now focused on the *preces* that Possidius and his colleagues submitted to the emperor. As far as they were concerned, Marcellinus should rule the Catholics as the plaintiffs based on the submission of this document alone. Marcellinus reminded them that these were not admitted into proceedings governed by a pragmatic rescript (*Coll. Carth.*, III, 38). Emeritus' response was to ask for clarification: Well, who were the legates, then? When they left for the court, were they acting on the orders of an official mandate from all the Catholic bishops? What were the implications if they were charged to speak on behalf of all the bishops? If the *preces* remained unavailable, certainly it was possible to establish *personae* by an examination of the legates and the *mandatum* they brought with them.[70] This suggestion upset the Catholics, but the Donatists replied that it seemed to them

---

[69] Cf. Marcellinus' comments at III, 3.
[70] *Coll. Carth.*, III, 39. Emeritus: 'Si pragmatico rescripto preces inseri non solere praestantiae tuae interloquutione signatum est, eos quos legatos esse dixerunt, utrum ex omnium voluntate, utrum ex communi mandato perrexerint doceant, ut, si non in precibus, certe vel in legatis possit stare persona.'

The Donatists transit so smoothly from *preces* to the *mandatum* that it takes time to notice that they are referring to two different kinds of documents. Augustine makes the distinction clear in the *Breviculus* 3.2.2: 'Then the Donatists began to demand the *preces* by which this *collatio* was sought by the Catholics. Here, when the Cognitor himself [Marcellinus] made an answer to

that there were two actions before the court, the first one having emanated from the rescript, which had its source in the *preces*, the other constituting the arguments found in the Catholic mandate that had been read on 1 June. If what they presented to the emperor was the same as this mandate, they should offer proof of the similarity. If these documents differed, one should be discarded (*Coll. Carth.*, III, 43).[71]

Marcellinus was in no position to accept this proposition. He stepped in and reminded the Donatists that the whole point of this meeting was to discover the *causa erroris* through a discussion of scripture. The emperor, he said, outlined no clear form or procedure for the conference; he only ordered that it should take place. The Donatists replied that it was apposite to the discussion to know the names of the legates, as well as the contents of the first mandate. Without that information, nothing regarding the convocation of the council could be established. What were the accusations lodged against them at court, accusations which the Donatists could surely confute using evidence from Scripture? What kind of information was Honorius working with when he wrote his letter? Surely, it was legally justified that they, the Donatists, should understand the basis on which they had been called forth before they engaged the court? If nothing could be proved regarding the genesis of the conference, the case should be thrown out.[72]

Marcellinus stated flatly that the conference would continue (III, 58), so the Donatists then argued that in order for them to make a fitting response in front of the tribunal, they needed to know what had been said against them (III, 62). The information would be especially pertinent if the Catholics alleged untrue things.

> Augustine: Why do [you] ask when I sought [the conference] when you can see at what time I have come? Why do you ask whether I sought [the

---

them that in a *pragmaticum rescriptum*, *preces* were not accustomed to be included, to this they then turned themselves: that they give over and transcribe into the records the *mandatum* of the Catholics, in which they ordered that the *collatio* be sought from the emperor, and the [names of the] legates whom they sent to ask for it.' ('Tunc Donatistae etiam preces, quibus ab eis illa collatio petita est, postulare coeperunt. Hic cum eis ipse cognitor responderet in pragmatico rescripto preces inseri non solere, ad id se converterunt, ut mandatum catholicorum, quo mandaverant peti ab imperatore collationem, eosdemque legatos, quos ad hoc impetrandum miserant, sibi ederent atque proderent.')

[71] Ibid. III, 49: 'Igitur, quia nihil ab re est quod in iudicio postulamus, petimus ut primitus aut rescripti iacturam aut mandati sui faciant cessionem, ut ad causam venire valeamus.'

[72] Ibid. III, 56: 'He said that his own legates went neither whose names, nor rank nor mandate he wished to be introduced into the proceedings. Therefore, let him lose this action, because he is not able to prove [anything], let the case be dismissed.' ('Dixit enim suos isse legatos quorum neque nomina, neque ordinem, neque mandatum vult iudicio publicare. Igitur, aut huius rei iacturam faciat, quia non potest adprobare.')

meeting] when all the Catholics here in this city gave the council a copy of its mandate? A mandate which they signed and then affirmed the signatures in person, at your insistence?

Montantus: Let it be noted that the opposing party is engaging in dilatory maneuvers because they won't give over that which is demanded by our party. Therefore if they wish the delay in the proceedings to be over, let them produce what we ask for. Let them produce the mandate, let them hand over the names of the legates. Only then will we arrive at the heart of the matter.

Marcellinus: The most clement emperor did not want this to be investigated. He ordered that the reason for the disagreement and the cause of the error be looked into.

Montantus: But the most clement emperor made it known in his own rescript that these very men sent a legation. And then, because of his clemency he wished to give to us the possibility to inquire of this at the tribunal, it is fitting that they hand over the mandate and the names of the legates, so that we may know how they most likely lied in that document, so that we may be cognizant in all these matters under discussion the merit of the people we debate, and so that we may follow procedure in responding to these honorable men.

Marcellinus: The text of the mandate of the general council and list of signatures shows clearly that they gave their consent to the delegation. And when the names of all the signatories were read out for purposes of confirmation, your holiness said you would not be satisfied with that unless they all were physically present, so that they could personally indicate whether it was these very men who, respectively, had signed and given the mandate by their own declarations....

Montanus:...but I ask for the identity of those who gave the mandate to our most clement emperor, not those who have come today before this tribunal. Your honor, it is right for these men to reveal the action, which they refuse to do, in the court of your Nobility. Let them now give over the mandate, let them name the legates so that, when we have reviewed these documents [*his recensitis*] and what it is they commissioned these men to do, then we will be able to respond to their allegations.[73]

Marcellinus: Those whom you say went on this embassy, if you know that they are present or that they signed the mandate in person, please indicate that clearly. But if they are absent, they need to be here so that the whole matter can be addressed. (III, 66)

Montanus: Yes, your honor, those need to be present who crossed the sea to visit our clement emperor. Let their presence here confirm what they were ordered to do at the behest of these men [*istis*] so that I may

---

[73] See also *Coll. Carth.*, III, 129.

understand from this mandate what they wished to introduce into this case, and what lies, perhaps, they said about us in that legation. It is always the ambition of the Catholics to whisper rumors about their adversaries. How will I be able to know whether the episcopal—as they claim themselves to be—delegation [*personam*] under the pretext of telling the truth was able to suggest something untoward to the emperor unless I am able to read through the names of the legates or the mandate entrusted to them and to evaluate them for myself? (III, 62–7)

In the above intervention (III, 66), Marcellinus reveals an inclination to assent to the Donatists' request, but they were not able to capitalize by answering to his satisfaction why they were so interested in the names of the legates (III, 70, 77, 81). The emperor, Marcellinus said, had not ordered him to investigate the embassy, and it was not for him to go beyond the dictates of the imperial rescript, which protected their identities. The representatives, before them, had been confirmed and validated by the personal confirmation of all the signatories from 1 June. To what ends a review of the embassy to the emperor? What were they insinuating: that the emperor had done something contrary to the law (III, 77)? The Donatists argued that even in the face of the pragmatic rescript, the emperor admitted to receiving an embassy of Catholic bishops, so questions about them were legitimate (III, 73):

> Now I have announced and ruled that I am not able to deport from the guidelines of the imperial *oraculum*, Indeed, it is certain that in my investigation the *personae* of the legates ought not to be examined. So let the *gesta* be read [of the Donatist embassy to the praetonian prefect in 406] So that it may be more clearly demonstrated who is in the position of plaintiff.[74]
>
> Adeodatus: The emperor did not order that the *gesta* of the illustrious authorities [meaning the praetorian prefect of Italy and the *gesta* of 406] be presented before the tribunal, but the liberty is given to the opposing side to bring that forward. They bring forward anything they want but it is not permitted for us to get what we ask for. (III, 140)[75]

Augustine himself made exertions to keep the Donatists away from the 410 embassy. He announced that the contents of the *mandatum* could not be handed over as they also dealt with matters alien to this particular conference.

---

[74] See also *Coll. Carth.*, III, 84 and 86.

[75] Marcellinus: 'Iam pronuntiavi atque iudicavi formam me excedere non posse imperialis oraculi. Nec enim in iudicio meo legatorum certum est discuti debere personas. Unde gesta relegantur, ut quis petitoris loco adsistat clarius demonstretur. Adeodatus: Hoc imperator non praecepit ut gesta inlustrium potestatum in iudicio prodantur, et tamen datur adversae parti licentia prodendi. Produnt ipsi quae volunt, nobis non sinitur accipere quod poscimus.'
See also *Coll. Carth.*, III, 73.

Revealing secrets of personal import would be inappropriate and make them look like traitors (*proditores*) to the people who had entrusted them with sensitive information (III, 162). The Donatist bishop Adeodatus sharply challenged him: it was not normal procedure, he said, for documents of this kind to cover a diverse set of topics. The explanation could not be true: 'I have caught you out in your lie, I grasp your falseness' (III, 163).[76]

The Donatists asked Marcellinus repeatedly if he would offer a definitive pronouncement regarding preliminaries, namely, the identification of the *personae* (III, 118). Marcellinus was slow to do this, to the point that the Donatists asked him if the question they were asking was appropriate (III, 112). Indeed it was, Marcellinus said, but it was his understanding that since the conference was requested by both parties, the plaintiff was to be identified as the one who first put forth accusations (III, 120). Were not the Donatists, he asked, the ones who had first alleged that the Catholic Church had been stained with crime? Did the Donatists have anything to say about this (III, 113)? All that the Donatists believed the Catholics had done, including misdeeds performed by individuals, they regarded as matters of discussion for the conference proper, that is, for the debate conducted according to scriptural law. They did not want to enter this kind of conversation until the Catholics had been ruled plaintiffs as part of the preliminary rulings.[77] But they now found themselves not only bound to appear in court like defendants but then also wedged into the infuriating position of being accounted the plaintiff. Their efforts to extricate themselves from Marcellinus' 'trap' proved costly: they asked the court to demonstrate that the conference had actually been requested by both parties. The Catholics were waiting for this question. Aside from the Donatist appearance before the praetorian prefect in 406, the Catholics had proof of their initial contact with Emperor Constantine. The documentation began to roll out, despite continual pleas by the Donatists to stop in favor of pronouncing on preliminary matters before addressing the main issues (III, 129, 131, 133, 135, 137, 140). Thus, Petilian's exasperated remark: 'Sensim in causam inducimur'(III, 151). As the documents relating to the Donatists' embassy to Constantine came closer to being presented before the tribunal, Petilian objected that the discussion had degenerated into one of secular law. If the main business of the trial was to abandon ecclesiastical law in favor of the earthly ('si forensis est actio' [III, 183]), they, the Donatists, could bring up 'secular' objections as well, such as revisiting the tardiness of the Catholics ('de tempore').

---

[76] *Coll. Carth.*, III, 163: 'Non possunt in uno mandato diversa mandari negotia…teneo tuum mendacium, teneo falsitatem.'

[77] When Emeritus saw the trial running away into an examination of historical documents, he said in frustration: 'So it goes like this, this is the procedure followed by the tribunal. Thus is the truth examined so that there is no mention of *persona*', ('Sic agitur causa, haec iudicii forma est, sic veritas inquiritur ut de persona taceatur' [III, 114]).

Marcellinus thought it profitable to review the historical documents.[78] For him, locating the one who first lodged accusations would determine the identity of the plaintiff. The Catholics simultaneously assured the Donatists they would back away from recounting the Donatist embassy to Constantine and concentrate on ecclesiastical law if the Donatists refrained from 'attacking' the characters of individual men. Marcellinus, however, insisted that the transcripts continue to be read even while the Catholic bishops promised they would not (III, 194, 201–2, 214–15, 223).

> Petilian [addressing Marcellinus]: Your honor, as you know, I received from the elders of my Church orders [*mandatum*] to respond to accusations, not to accuse. I am not here as a plaintiff, but as one who is obliged to respond...I would respond to the charge if only they would have recourse to divine law and would seek responses and judgments from this kind of law. But they mix both issues, that is clear. What I want to know is the kind of action [they plan to lodge], that no one will reproach me in public, no one will judge me a poor defense for a good case...(III, 193)
>
> Marcellinus: There are two items which your holiness insists must be dealt with. One, that the mandate in which the legates were chosen be read aloud; the other, that they state clearly whether they will depart from the divine law.
>
> Petilian: Let them briefly answer both.
>
> Marcellinus: One of these points I will respond to myself because it concerns me. I am not able to call the legates into question regarding whose embassy the emperor made his pronouncement lest it seem, to his detriment, that the entire matter is being reopened [*ne in eius iniuriam refricari aliquid videretur*]. As for the other, it is plainly established through their own declarations [*prosecutionibus*] with whereby it is shown that they wish to steer away from secular law on the condition that you do not make personal accusations. So as this is all dependant on who is identified as the plaintiff, and since the *gesta* presented by your party have been read out, allow those that were submitted by the opposing party be read by the official [the *gesta* of 403, which is the request by the Catholics to the proconsul of Africa to summon the Donatists to a council]. (III, 194)

DONATIST NUMBERS AND CATHOLIC LIES

The Donatists never saw the Catholic *preces* or their first *mandatum*. While the Donatists thought the introduction of these documents would help make the trial proceed to their advantage, their relentless insistence, even in the face of

---

[78] Brown, *Augustine of Hippo*, 332–4.

legal injunctions against the exposure of these documents and the men who carried them, may seem more obdurate than strategic. Access, however, offered advantages even beyond the crucial identification of the parties. One has to do with public perception. What the Catholics wrote to Honorius was inevitably more strident than the contents of the *mandatum* they delivered on the first day of the conference. If we take history and the declarations of the imperial rescript as guides, the 410 embassy undoubtedly asked Honorius to affirm extant legislation against the Donatists. In as much as both sides courted the crowds attending to the events, this episode of a visit to the emperor only affirmed the impression held by many people that the Catholics were the aggressors who used imperial law to suppress the opposition.[79]

There is also the issue of honesty. The Donatist bishops assured Marcellinus that they pushed on the mandate only so that no one could later accuse them of remaining silent in the face of lies (III, 138). Even if the Catholics had done nothing untoward and the deceit alleged was rumor only, it looked very bad when the Donatist bishops accused them of lying to the emperor. Certainly, the Catholics were under no obligation to release the *preces* or *mandatum*, but their refusal, as well as Augustine's flimsy explanation for it, made the insinuations look plausible. The Donatists positioned themselves as the ones who maintained the truth. This spoke to their understanding of what it meant to be the Catholic Church of North Africa. Augustine and his colleagues at this conference referred to the true Church as the one spread across the globe, a totality joined in communion as promised in the scriptures (e.g. III, 100–1). The Donatists replied that the Church was not proven through a tabulation of geographical areas, but a totality generated by purity. Wholeness was a matter of morality: pure, holy, and without stain. This was not a question of physical space (III, 102). The mandate, therefore, was an excellent illustration of what differentiated the two groups. The former may have had the support of some in faraway lands, but whatever they garnered through alliances came by illicit means (Petilian is speaking):

> That the Catholic Church is in my possession, both our pure pure form of worship as well as your sins and your outrages makes true. The whole Church of God will be under obligation to be pure, holy, without stain or wrinkle. That is why, therefore, so that we may agree to a discussion of this matter and utilize at the appropriate time divine testimony, the first matter of business is—that I ask from you, if you have enough

---

[79] During the conference, the Catholics insisted that they were only defending themselves against the Donatist charge of having betrayed the Church (III, 110). This the Donatists found laughable (III, 165), not only because the assignment of terms in their opinion was being made in contradiction to correct judicial procedure (III, 114), but they were the ones who, accused of heresy and schism (III, 193) had long suffered from imperial laws solicited by the Catholics.

confidence, especially since Our most just judge is conducting this part of the case—that whatever must be done be disseminated among the people. It is clear enough that you lied to Our most clement emperor, Since you hesitate to reveal what you said, what you did, what you ordered, what that legate assumed, what mandate he accepted, what he accomplished. Let the consciousness of the people know these things, let all the provinces know, let the *acta* and this controversy fully preserve it, let them know that you most evidently have no faith in your lie and that you tie deylays on to the proceedings so that, by your deception and obstructing frifles, it may never arrive at the truth. (III, 75)[80]

The moral consequence of mendacity is here, however, secondary to its legal uses. There are at least seven occasions during the conference when the Donatists accuse the Catholics of lying.[81] The first reference to what they thought was deliberate dishonesty appears in their official letter to Marcellinus submitted before the conference began. They announced that the presence of all the bishops was crucial to assure the court that their numbers were significant, something they said the Catholics often lied about.[82] The Catholics responded to the accusation in measured tones. They made no denials, but assured Marcellinus that in comparison to all the empire, Donatist numbers were, in fact, small.[83] Most of the accusations of lying centered on the contents of the Catholic mandate. The Catholics, they said, refused to reveal its contents because the court would then know that they had lied to the emperor.

Injunctions against manipulating the law, especially the solicitation of favorable rescripts by lying to government administrators, is a common refrain in the *Theodosian Code*.[84] Rescripts written in response to *preces* that contained

---

[80] 'Ecclesiam catholicam penes me esse, et pura observatio nostra facit et vitia vestra atque flagitia vestra. Omnis ecclesia Dei pura, sancta, sine macula et ruga esse debebit. Quare igitur, ut ad huius disputationem rei possimus descendere et congruo tempore testimoniis dominicis uti, prius est—quod de te flagito, si non diffidis, maxime cum id agat causae iustissimus cognitor—ut quicquid agendum sit populo publicetur. Mentitum te igitur clementissimo imperatori sat constat, cum dubitas proferre quid dixeris, quid egeris, quid mandaveris, quid susceperit ille legatus, quod mandatum acceperit, quid peregerit. Noverit haec conscientia populi, sciat universa provincia, hoc acta istaque controversia plene contineant, sciant vos apertissime de mendacio vestro diffidere morasque innectere actioni ne ad veritatem aliquando vestris praestigiis nebulisque obstantibus veniatur.'

[81] I, 14; III, 65; III, 67; III, 75; III, 89; III, 138; III, 163.

[82] 'I, 14: 'Qua de re sinceritatem tuam plurimum exhortamur ut prioris edicti fide servata, cunctos nos ad te venire praecipias, ut quamprimum de numero nostro constet, quos adversarii paucos esse saepe mentiti sunt.'

[83] I,16 = *ep*. 129.6: 'If our people have said this at times, they could have said it with perfect truth of these places where the number of our fellow bishops, clerics, and laypeople is far greater, especially in Africa Proconsularis. And yet, apart from Numidia Consularis, our numbers easily surpass them even in the other African provinces. Or at least we are absolutely correct to say that they are very few in comparison with all the nations through which the Catholic communion is spread.'

[84] Jill Harries, *Law and Empire in Late Antiquity* (Cambridge: Cambridge University Press, 1999), 30–1.

false information were subject to immediate cancellation.[85] The technical term for the illegal solicitation of law was *subreptio*, and in his rescript, Honorius declares it was the Donatists who were guilty of this infraction, having deliberately misunderstood his previous *oraculum* to their undeserving benefit.[86] When the Donatists accuse the Catholics of misleading the emperor, they use nouns like *mendacium* and the verb *mentior*, but their intentions are clear. If Catholic documentation prompting Honorius to call this conference contained untruths, the Donatists would have grounds to demand a dismissal.[87] A judge cannot proceed in cases where the plaintiff has falsified his complaints. Again, Petilian is speaking:

> They speak although they are silent about the fact that they are ashamed to reveal this, that they lied to our most clement emperor. If they are, therefore, trusting of the virtues of their claim in purpose and order, why are they hesitant to air it? And since your Honor deigns to have remembered that it was debated at the first day that either they would conduct the meeting according to secular law or they would agree to argue by the authority of divine law, and this they promised to me by their own consensus; however, your Nobility stated this expressly, that it was not appropriate for him that he be removed from the laws, If is your role, your Nobility; to maintain that which is the law; however, the necessity was promised by than that they ought to make proofs with the divine law. If, therefore, in your presence it is conduced according to civil law, since you have acknowledged to preside over them, enforce what the laws contain If, however, an ecclesiastical disputation is placed front and center, I ask you, I who desires to dislose this way, what you sought, what you did, what you said against me. If I have found that this man has said true things, I consider it necessary to engage in a dispute of this [ecclesiastical] law; if, however, I have found that you began with treachery and lies, it is necessary that I flee for and utterly from your person. What benefit is it to me to offer instruction to a liar? What benefit is if to render account to someone opposing me and one bent on continuing to do so?(III, 89)[88]

---

[85] *CTh.* 1.2.6: 'Even if it is not a trial, but an execution, that is ordered, inquiry must be made in regard to the veracity of supplications to the emperor, so that if fraud should have intervened, there shall be an investigation of the entire case.' See Jean Gaudemet, *La Formation du droit séculier*, 34–5.

[86] Supra n. 36.

[87] Cf. *ep.* 141.3 and 7: Augustine states that the Donatists tried to prevent the conference from taking place after the parties had gathered in front of Marcellinus. This could be a reference to the Donatist protest that the Catholics were late, but Augustine's vagueness allows for other possibilities.

[88] 'Loquuntur enim cum tacent se vereri id proferre quod clementissimo imperatori mentiti sunt. Si igitur freti sunt bona petitionis voluntate atque ordine, quid eam dubitant ventilare? Et quoniam potestas tua meminisse dignatur id priore controversia agitatum ut aut iure publico agerent aut legis dominicae auctoritate descenderent disputare idque suo mihi promisere consensu, nobilitas autem tua id sibi exceperit a legibus tolli se minime oportere, tuarum partium est, vir nobilis, id tenere quod legum est, illorum autem est promissa necessitas ut lege divina debeant experiri. Si igitur apud te legibus publicis agitur, quoniam tu hisdem praesidere professus es, exige quod leges habent. Si autem disputatio legalis in medium mittitur, interrogo te,

The Donatists, who, like the Catholics, regularly recorded their own church councils, planned to utilize Marcellinus' elaborate transcribing protocol to their advantage. Pragmatic rescripts, as their names imply, were designed to deal with specific legal issues and, like the kind of rescripts called *adnotationes*, were not allowed to function as precedents in future cases.[89] That said, the transcript of the 411 conference was considered a legal document and could certainly function as evidence in appeals. On 1 June, just after the Catholics read out their mandate, it was announced that all 266 of the Catholic bishops had signed said document. Petilian asked, 'Where are they who signed it?' (I, 58–9) So begins the Donatist action to catalogue the bishops: number and location.[90] Thus, the transcript itself contains a ratified count, which constituted evidence required to contradict Catholic assurances of a tiny Donatist presence.[91] If Marcellinus had allowed the Catholic mandate to be inserted in the *gesta* and found, in fact, the Catholics had informed the emperor that the Donatists constituted a minority interest in Africa and offered this as a reason why now was the right time to silence them, the question becomes whether Marcellinus would dissolve the conference.[92]

That seems impossible, but we can think of two ways in which a 'withdrawal' of Honorius' rescript might have worked. The first is a theoretical 'invalidation', involving a severing of the conference from imperial law by virtue of superior moral stance. The Catholics always justified themselves to the Roman government by pointing to alliances across geographical boundaries. For them, the bishops and administrators in Roman territories were joined in alliance with Catholic Africans through the promise related through Scripture that the true Church was spread throughout the world. To the contrary, the Donatists believed their disagreement with the Catholics was not a matter of concern for external parties (III, 102). It was an internal dispute regarding, among other things, the basis on which religious and ecclesiastical legitimacy was founded. The focus was on the moral integrity of believers, not in directives and support from outside parties. A kind of moral extraction of Honorius' rescript from the conference would constitute a reorientation of the conference away

---

hic qui desideras disputare, quid petieris, quid egeris, quid contra me dixeris; quem si invenero vera dixisse, necesse habeo eius legis disputationem committere; si autem cognovero a perfidia atque mendacio te coepisse, necesse est ut tuam personam longe prorsus evitem. Quid enim mihi prodest docere mendacem? Quid mihi prodest refragatori ac refragaturo reddere rationem?'

[89] Mathisen, 'Adnotatio and Petitio', 23–32.

[90] The Donatists protested that the number of Catholic bishops was artificially inflated by assigning bishops to places little larger than hamlets.

[91] The Donatists also wanted to demonstrate that the Catholics 'packed' small hamlets and villages with bishops so as to appear to have the majority (*Coll. Carth.*, I, 61 and 65).

[92] Another candidate for the basis of accusation of mendacity would be the Catholic interpretation of the Donatist embassy of 406.

from outsiders and toward a domestic context. Marcellinus was there at the behest of Ravenna, but a decrease (or collapse) of authority previously exerted by Honorius' letter offered a chance for the proceedings turning on questions of *African* Christianity.

The Donatists, however, were not naive and understood that Marcellinus remained unmoved by their arguments.[93] They also preferred the practical to the abstract, conceiving the conference of 411 as an event not necessarily determinative of their future. Certainly, the *gesta* served as evidence for both sides in the courting of loyalties among fellow Africans, and we know that both Catholics and Donatists wanted the transcripts to be read out in public in the years following 411. More important, to cast doubt on the validity of Honorius' letter, even if they lost the case, increased their chances of lodging a successful appeal at a later date. Thus, from the beginning of day three (III, 8), the Donatists began to verify their comments in the transcript 'without prejudicing their right to appeal'.

After Marcellinus issued his ruling in favor of the Catholics, a Donatist embassy departed for Italy. They must have brought a transcript of the conference with them and shown it to Honorius in hopes he would overturn Marcellinus' decision (*v. Aug.* 13.3 and *c. Don.* 12.16). Even the legitimate objection that one of the seven representatives on the Donatist side had to withdraw before the conclusion of the conference left the emperor unmoved.[94] He did, however, rescind the rescript that convened the 411 conference, but not for the reasons the Donatists hoped. While working from the emperor's mandate, Marcellinus had directed African provincial authorities in February 411 to return to the Donatists the basilicas they occupied previous to the promulgation of the Edict of Unity (*Coll. Carth.*, I, 10). Marcellinus warned local governments not to overlook these orders, which would remain in force until he rendered a decision.[95] Despite the fact that pragmatic rescripts could not act as precedent and despite the short-term nature of Marcellinus' injunction, Honorius felt compelled to remind his praetorian prefect, Seleucus, that the stipulations he had made prior to the conference were to be annulled.[96] It is a

---

[93] At III, 234 Petilian says, 'By God, you sure defend them enough!' ('Satis illos defendis per Deum.')

[94] *Capit.* III, 540–2. It was Marcellinus who told the Donatists that they now had legitimate cause to appeal: 'Interloquutio, cum septeni adstent, de unius defectu querelam esse posse.'

[95] Pretensions to a suspension of judgment were superficial, as Marcellinus also made it clear that *ratio* was to best *superstitio*. Since Honorius ruled that *ratio* equaled Catholicism, the niceties extended to the Donatists were strictly meant to be temporary.

[96] *CTh.* 16.5.53: 'Those provisions which were able to be impetrated by a pragmatic sanction or by an annotation of Our hand shall be annulled. Those limitations which were formerly defined on this subject shall remain in force, and the sanction of the former Emperors shall remain in force.' Clearly, these 'provisions' are those Marcellinus articulated in *Coll. Carth.*, I, 10, as they are referred to as emanating from a *pragmaticum sanctio*, which is the same as Honorius' *pragmaticum rescriptum*.

comment on the legal adeptness of the Donatists that Honorius took precautions to declare his rescript now invalid. They would undoubtedly have used it to make their arguments before African administrators.

ENDING TO BEGIN AGAIN

We rely largely on Augustine to fill in the details of the conference after its transcript breaks off. Calling into question of the authenticity of *gesta*, the clarification of names and the way that documents should, or should not, be dated: all these he interprets as desperate maneuvers to waste time and obfuscate the proceedings. We may greet these sentiments with justified skepticism. The Donatists continued to call upon their legal knowledge to dissect Catholic evidence, but it is true that the Donatists were not able to make much forward motion, and even lost ground when they believed they could impugn the authenticity of imperial correspondence recording the absolution of Caecilian with a passage from Optatus, who, as it turned out, did not support their argument (*brev.* 19.37–20.38 = *Capit.* III, 530–7; *ep.* 141.8]).[97] Petilian, who along with Emeritus spoke the most forcefully on the Donatist side, retired at that point, saying he could continue no longer (*Capit.* III, 540).

There are critical exchanges during the conference that shift its direction and momentum: the places where Marcellinus inclined toward, then fell away from, questioning Possidius and the legates of the 410 embassy; or where Marcellinus decided to pursue the identification of parties through investigation of documents that led back to Caecilian; even where Petilian dramatically withdrew before the third day was over. In terms of legal strategy, the defining moment was the Donatist abandonment of their attempt to have Marcellinus rule on identity as a function of civil procedure. As the insertion of documents into the *gesta* traveled back in time, closer to Constantine's hearing of the case of Caecilian, the Donatists vehemently protested that the Catholics were having it both ways: they were able to argue about secular matters, that is, recall and enter evidence appropriate to a civil court, without having had pronouncement on identities or any other preliminary matter (III, 203). The Catholics promised, the Donatists said, to base their arguments on divine law (III, 213). 'Yes', Augustine responded, 'but as regards the Church [*causa ecclesiae*] and not about Caecilian and his colleagues [*causa Caeciliani*], against whom you lodge allegations' (III, 214). The sides again spoke past each other: the

---

[97] See also *ep.* 141.8.

Donatist interest in having a plaintiff named (who asked for *this* conference) was rendered synonymous, and yet in reality was wholly incompatible, with the Catholic defense against Donatist accusations against specific members of the clergy. 'All these things have been often repeated', says Marcellinus, 'since it appears that first the identity of the plaintiff should be determined, let the *gesta* be read' (III, 215).

At this moment the Donatists chose to pursue another tactic. After a few minutes' attempt to argue for a reconciliation between the *causa ecclesiae* with the *causa Caeciliani* by illustrating the connection between the actions of men and the well-being of the Church (III, 221–49),[98] the Donatists announced that they wanted to read a response to the Catholic mandate (the one they heard on 1 June). After the preamble, which declared episcopal support for the delegates presenting the statement, Marcellinus stopped them: 'I see that you have again submitted another mandate' (III, 252). He had no quarrel with the document itself, but after the submission of their first declaration (i.e. the short statement of defense they called their mandate), the hearing had started ('constat transisse negotium'), and any response to the Catholics, Marcellinus said, should have been made in the representatives' names, not the entire Donatist episcopate (III, 253). The meaning is clear: well on into the third day and just a few pages from where the transcript breaks off, the conference as Marcellinus and the Catholics envisioned it finally begins. The Donatists had repeatedly argued that they would speak with the Catholics on matters of divine law upon the establishment of legal preliminaries, but Marcellinus accepted the Catholic method of determining who the accuser was (based not on law but on history). The Donatists consequently abandoned their strategy and resigned themselves to a case where the documentary evidence could come forward in an unaccustomed, and detrimental, sequence.[99] At least they would submit their mandate, which articulated their views based on Scripture and could anoint themselves the defendants in the historical sense, as ones who suffered persecution, confiscation, and proscription (III, 258).

Certainly, the Donatists could have pursued any number of approaches to this conference. That a debate according to theology alone never occurred

---

[98] See, for example, Emeritus' comment (III, 249): 'Divine law is filled with many examples in which the pure life of clergy may be proven by divine testimony.' (Multis etiam documentis lex divina diffunditur, quibus inmaculata vita pastoris debeat caelestibus testimoniis adprobari.')

[99] One can, I believe, detect some mockery in Marcellinus' words when the Donatists asked to introduce this new mandate (III, 250): 'I had wanted first to establish whether it could be demonstrated from a reading of the *gesta* who was the plaintiff. But if you want me to leave off from this phase of the inquiry, go ahead and show that these things which you put forward ought to be read out.' ('Constare quidem primitus volueram ut quis loco petitoris adstaret ex recitatione gestorum evidentissime monstraretur. Sed si vultis ab hac me parte discedere, evidenter ostendite ut ea quae offertis debeant recitari.')

seems a matter of regret to modern readers. If one looks back to the middle of May 411, when the Donatist bishops were gathered in the city and about to receive their second and final edict from Marcellinus, it is easier to understand why the Donatists responded the way they did. They had read the rescript. They also had words from Marcellinus declaring that the impending meeting was to be a *collatio*, but he provided no further details until the first day of the conference. Only then did the Donatists learn that their assumptions about legal procedure, by all standards reasonable ones, were incorrect.

Basing their response on the questioning of the legitimacy of an imperial rescript required ambition and confidence. This is why the conference of 411 records an important historical moment. It is not about confusion, nor attempted sabotage, but instead the knowledge and use of law by Catholic and Donatist bishops. A man less keen than Marcellinus could have provided access to the documentation the Donatists asked to be entered into the court proceedings. The event would have then turned out very differently. As it is, the Donatists took the transcript to the public, promoting its reading and declaring its contents proof that Marcellinus' judgment was biased.[100] Rumors of malfeasance also played their part. The transcript repeatedly alleged Catholic mendacity, and thus legal infraction, while verifying the Donatist numbers. There would come a day when they could present this information when appealing to more sympathetic ears. Emperors lived for only so long.

---

[100] *v. Aug.* 14.1. See also *retr.* 2.46 (*Ad Emeritum episcopum Donatistarum post conlationem liber unus*, which is not extant) and the *Gesta cum Emerito*, both of which refer to the unfairness of the trial.

Conclusion

After the 411 conference, the provincial administration supported Catholic efforts to absorb Donatist congregations. A Donatist bishop could keep his church if he adhered to Marcellinus' ruling, and so continue in his post by alternating basilicas with his Catholic counterpart. Former competitors-now-turned-colleagues were expected to show each other 'mutual deference' (*ep.* 126.3). We do not know how many chose to follow Marcellinus' exhortations to abandon their 'errors' and embrace the 'unity' of the Catholic Church.[1] As for Possidius, his job was made more challenging by the fact that Crispinus was recently deceased, and his replacement had not been chosen as of the conclusion to the conference (*Coll. Carth.*, III, 139). As unilaterally stipulated by the Catholic side, when one of the two bishops died, his joint colleague should succeed him, and so upon returning to Calama, Possidius was suddenly bishop to roughly double the number of congregants as when he left for Carthage.[2]

Augustine's letters indicate that the process of consolidating land, buildings, congregants, and other assets required time and repeated exhortations to steadfastness. The scale of transfer was not one that encompassed large territorial or provincial areas, but instead progressed town by town and hamlet by hamlet. The Catholic episcopate, however, was in a hurry to supply clergy where there were too few, one indication that Marcellinus' offer may have been frequently refused. Precipitous decisions resulted in mistakes, the appointment of Anthony of Fussala to a former Donatist stronghold being one of the most dramatic.[3] We have no idea if Possidius encountered resistance from

---

[1] Serge Lancel, 'Le sort des évêques et des communautés donatistes après la Conférence de Carthage en 411', in Cornelius Mayer and Karl Heinz Chelius (eds.), *Internationales Symposion über den Stand der Augustinius-Forschung* (Würzburg: Augustinus-Verlag, 1989), 149–67. The division of territories and congregants was still a matter of lengthy discussion at the Church Council of Carthage in 418: *Concilia Africae, Registri Ecclesiae Carthaginensis Exerpta* 117 and 118.

[2] *ep.* 126.3 stipulates that in case of refusal by the congregation to accept two bishops, either because of incompatibility of personalities or because of the solution's irregularity, both should resign and another should be appointed. Possidius remained the bishop of Calama until his exile in 437.

[3] *epp.* 209 and 20* as well as *s. Guelferbytanus* 32 on the religious demography of the area before 411. *ep.* 209.2 tells us that Catholic clergy who tried to establish themselves in the environs of Fussala before the arrival of Anthony were attacked and beaten.

the Donatists at Calama, but surely he would have called upon the governmental apparatus to enforce the law. A tranquility of sorts, likely aided by the unifying presence of the shrine to St Stephen, did allow Possidius the freedom to travel widely throughout Africa in the following years: Hippo, Carthage, and Caesarea Mauretania.[4] We do not think he went again to Italy while Augustine was alive. After 411, Alypius became the primary liaison between the African Church and the imperial court. As we can see from his correspondence with Augustine, Alypius' missions remained committed to Catholic interests by the presentation of appeals, requests for clarification, and the solicitation of legal declarations from the consistory.

Many issues occupied the bishops at home.[5] Preliminary treatises against Pelagius and Caelestius were followed by the assembling of detailed historical dossiers for submission to papal and imperial authorities. Matters regarding clerical discipline received the same kind of evidentiary scrutiny. Augustine and Possidius were both involved in the affair of Apiarius, a case famous not so much for the infractions committed by this priest, but for the tension between the pope and the African episcopacy that arose over which party had the greater authority in matters of discipline and overseas (papal) appeals. The African episcopate met with papal legates and argued their points, but structured their case around two separate dossiers that contained transcripts of councils, comparative historical documents, and canons from the Council of Nicaea.[6]

Possidius and the Catholic episcopate continued to engage the law and defend the Church's positions—legal, clerical, and even theological—by use of documentation based on historical precedent and extant law. I have presented about sixteen years' worth of detailed evidence pertaining to the legal aspects of Possidius' career. The materials gathered for the second part of this book themselves serve as a representative dossier to demonstrate how the Catholics and Donatists sought political gains by application to those who issued law. For Possidius, the exercise was more than just a convenient means to power in this world. Law could be cajoled, pushed, and manipulated, but once promulgated, it carried great authority. As it was possible for the law to define orthodoxy, it rose above its earthly provenance and spoke on behalf of the divine. In the *Vita Augustini*, the end of Donatism and Pelagianism comes with an imperial pronouncement. The

---

[4] James J. O'Donnell, *Augustine: A New Biography* (New York: Ecco, 2005), 175–9, on the effects of the shrines and St Stephen.

[5] *ep.* 23*A serves as a good reminder of how many issues the bishops dealt with: intercession on behalf of criminals, appeals to the court, episcopal succession, and clerical discipline.

[6] See *Concilia Africae, Canones in Causa Apiarii* as well as the article by Charles Munier, 'La Tradition littéraire des Dossiers africains', *Revue de droit canonique*, 29 (1979), 41–52. There is further discussion in J. E. Merdinger's *Rome and the African Church in the Time of Augustine* (New Haven: Yale University Press, 1997).

administration's laws against Arianism expose those who represent its beliefs as crafty abusers of rhetoric. Rhetoric, and not the authoritative texts of legislation and transcripts, is alone what remains to those outside the protection of the law. Manichaeism stands apart in that Ambrose's and Augustine's sermons, extemporaneous and unexpected, constitute the impetus for the heresy's rejection. And yet Possidius marks the beginnings of the sect's defeat in Africa as the moment when secretaries opened their notebooks ('*apertis notarii tabulis*' [*v. Aug.* 6.6]) and recorded the debate between Augustine and Fortunatus, which was the first encounter Augustine faced after his ordination to the priesthood. The final mention of Manichaeism in the *Vita* comes in the form of two separate hearings conducted by Augustine, separated historically by seventeen years, but placed side by side in the biography. Augustine questioned members of the elect in cooperation with a procurator of the imperial household, and then met in debate with Felix of the *Contra Felicem Manichaeum* fame.[7] The transcripts, which were considered legal documents and, as Possidius tells us, available for review to all those who were interested, proved the truth and precipitated the conversion of many (*v. Aug.* 17.6 and 8).

Defeat of his opponents, conversion of heretics to right belief, ratification by governmental authority, and the historical permanence of the collection demonstrated that Augustine produced authoritative texts. In his assertion, Possidius set himself at odds with Augustine, who believed that all writings save scripture were subject to error. Augustine trusted council decisions and cited these, as well as law, to argue his points. Later in life, Augustine also began to refer to specific authors to lend weight to his opinion, but as Éric Rebillard has argued, he did so for the purposes of polemic, not as a demonstration of doctrinal truth.[8] The fluid nature that Augustine understood to be an aspect of one's own writings applied to all literary creations. Possidius challenged Augustine's assertion by elevating Augustine's texts to a uniform, unassailable correctness. The *Vita*'s *Indiculum* lists Augustine's works by subject, a kind of categorization Augustine employed only in draft form in order to write what would be for him a more accurate and meaningful catalogue. The biography itself prioritizes Augustine's texts, the emphasis being placed on those that probably would not have been ranked first in Augustine's mind. The greatest theological challenge

---

[7] In about 421, Ursus, the *procurator domus regiae*, brought these elect to the bishops for a hearing. Augustine discusses the case in *On Heresies* (*haer.* 46.9). See also *PCBE Afrique* 'Ursus 3', 1236. The debate with Felix took place in early December 404. See *PCBE Afrique* 'Felix 20', 417–18. Placing the two incidents side by side is more evidence that Possidius is not concerned with chronology as much as he is with subject.

[8] Rebillard's articles are crucial: see 'A New Style of Argument in Christian Polemic: Augustine and the Use of Patristic Citations', *JECS*, 8 (2000), 559–78, and 'Augustine et ses autorités: l'Élaboration de l'argument patristique au cours de la controverse pélagienne', *Studia Patristica*, 38 (2001), 245–63.

Augustine faced in his last two decades of life was the trans-Mediterranean debate over grace and free will. Possidius was quite aware of the volume of material that crossed the sea regarding the subject, and he obliquely addressed the exchange by staunchly defending Augustine's value as a theologian, but writings on Pelagian and Massilian concerns do not appear in the *Vita*. The importance of the dispute as well as its resolution lay in the dossier of collected documents that were ruled on by the emperor. The *Vita* gives pride of place to transcripts from debates because, in tandem with their use by authorities to form law, they defined orthodox Christianity. Other books may enjoy a prominent place within the *Vita*, but Possidius denies them their intended function. The *Confessions* and *Retractationes* are employed as evidence of Augustine's literary and doctrinal stability when in fact their purpose was to chart the points of evolution in Augustine as a man and thinker. Possidius thus mutes the shifts in Augustine's life and oeuvre by means of a paradox: he promotes Augustine's texts to the level of unchangeability through their blatant manipulation, with the result that Augustine's own books and words stand forever at variance with themselves. Possidius learned to do this from his years of engagement with legal texts. A pronouncement of the emperor, signed in a distinctive, and by law exclusive, script was greeted by provincial administrators with awe and careful choreography.[9] The finality of receipt, however, was the end result of frenetic action by competing groups who in their use of evidence and argument often set truth at defiance.

Peter Brown once said that the *Vita* portrayed Augustine's life as deceptively tranquil and uncomplicated.[10] As far as the bishop's intellectual experiences are concerned, we now know this is a matter of Possidius' deliberate construction. Concomitantly, the ease with which legal victories come to Augustine in the *Vita* belie the tremendous exertions made by the entire African episcopate, from which Possidius emerged as one of its most active members.[11] There was constant movement of people and texts between Africa and Italy, but the historical reality is subsumed under Possidius' image of a solitary Augustine who single-handedly makes gains through his rational speech and writing. A gigantic figure too large for the landscape and its other occupants, Augustine overshadows historical traces of corporate movement and collective effort.

---

[9] See *CTh.* 9.19.3 for the script used only by the emperor. In this letter of Valentinian and Valens, the proconsul of Africa is chided for imitating this handwriting. Later in the fifth century, the emperors signed letters in purple ink (*CJ* 1.23.6). See discussion in John F. Matthews, *Laying Down the Law: A Study of the Theodosian Code* (New Haven: Yale University Press, 2000), 168–99.

[10] *Augustine of Hippo: A Biography* (Berkeley: University of Califonia Press, 1967; reprint 2000), 136.

[11] The correspondence with Macedonius as represented in the *Vita* (*v. Aug.* 20) being a perfect example. Possidius muted the extent to which Augustine and his colleagues actively solicited the law. The cooperation by the imperial authorities is presented as a function of the correctness of the Catholic stance rather than the result of repeated visits and constant appeals.

In the end, the Augustine of the *Vita* even supersedes his mortal self. Possidius turns away from the bishop's fallible body. Personal salvation is pushed aside to make room for the immortality of his texts. The commemorative epitaph that Possidius borrows refers to Augustine's literary corpus, not the man. So, too, with the *Vita*: the books will always be there. They will always be the truth.

Augustine resisted the notion that nonscriptural texts by individual authors could constitute authoritative statements, and that they could be cited in a fashion similar to the Bible. But he lost this particular historical argument. The years immediately following Augustine's death witnessed the nascence of patristic literature, which we may define as a body of texts, written by a select group of authors, whose contents were thought to offer correct pronouncements on scriptural interpretation and doctrinal issues. There has been important discussion of late regarding the origins of patristics, but little is said as to the institutional forces that informed their development.[12] True, it has been noted that the Roman Christian and Roman legal cultures share many structural similarities. In the first step toward 'disservering' rhetorical, legal–imperial, and religious discourse in order to understand how, exactly, these three literary entities functioned in relation to each other, Mark Vessey comments on what others have also noticed: that Roman law seems to have had a direct effect on procedures adopted by Christians in their Church councils.[13] In Africa, the legalistic trappings that informed the protocol of these meetings emerged as early as the episcopate of Cyprian.[14] Substantive, as opposed to procedural, consequences included the creation of creeds, those authoritative statements that marked out correct doctrine, as well as regulations that established guidelines for clerical action and discipline. Augustine, who, as we have seen, rejected the doctrinal authority of a body of nonscriptural texts, regarded the decisions made by (approved) Church councils as unquestionably worthy of obedience.[15]

---

[12] The discussion I am thinking of is among James J. O'Donnell, 'The Authority of Augustine', *AugStud*, 22 (1991), 7–35; Mark Vessey, 'Opus Imperfectum: Augustine and His Readers. A.D. 426–35', *V Chr*, 52 (1998), 264–85, and 'The Forging of Orthodoxy in Latin Christian Literature: A Case Study', *JECS*, 4 (1996), 495–513, and Éric Rebillard (supra n. 8).

[13] 'Sacred Letters of the Law: The Emperor's Hand in Late Roman (Literary) History', *An Tard*, 11 (2003), 353–4, citing Jill Harries, *Law and Empire in Late Antiquity* (Cambridge: Cambridge University Press, 1999), vii and Tony Honoré, *Law in the Crisis of Empire, 379–455 A.D.: The Theodosian Dynasty and Its Quaestors* (Oxford: Clarendon Press, 1988), 8.

[14] See Introduction, n. 34.

[15] An attitude Possidius wanted to emphasize, as Augustine was accused of not following the decision of the Council of Nicaea when he was ordained as bishop when Valerius still alive. See *v. Aug.* 21.1: 'Sanctorum concilia sacerdotum per diversas provincias celebrata cum potuit frequentavit, non in eis quae sua sunt, sed quae Iesu Christi quaerens, ut vel fides sanctae ecclesiae catholicae inviolata maneret.' Of course, there were church councils that for Augustine did not carry the weight of authority, the Donatist Councils of Cebarsussa and Bagai being prime examples. See Robert Eno, 'Doctrinal Authority in Saint Augustine', *AugStud*, 12 (1981), 158–65.

It is likely that the emergence of a canon of Christian 'fathers' is, in some way, connected to the establishment of Christian 'law' by Church councils. A study of the careers of Possidius and Augustine, however, shows us that this offers only a partial explanation. Clearly, the bishop of Hippo invested different meaning in these two kinds of texts—council decisions and the writings of individuals—and he was not alone in so far as the authority of councils had been recognized a full century before the emergence of what we call patristics. How did the focus of authority migrate to another set of texts, whose origins and impetus, it can be argued, are quite different? In what specific way are they related? To answer these questions, the study of Roman law and the study of conciliar tradition, usually conducted along separate lines, need to be integrated. The two spheres of action interacted constantly, with the level of engagement reaching new heights after the early 390s when Theodosius I legislated orthodox homogeneity. Such an imperial demand, not necessarily enforced from the top down, elicited responses, bottom up, from numerous Christian interests with the assurances that they adhered to his expectations, however loosely defined.[16] The point is that the striving for recognition, with simultaneous vilification for one's opponents, had entered a new, more intense, legal phase. There was much at stake, not least of which were the enormous financial benefits in store for the favored.[17] While we may attribute the inauguration of annual African Church councils in 393 to the personal resolve of Aurelius and Augustine, the opportunities and challenges presented by increased legal pressure (and promise) should not be discounted.[18] As we have seen, these meetings became exercises in preparation for approaching the imperial consistory. Adopting legalistic protocols were not designed solely for internal use, but employed to discuss, adopt, and craft Roman law. In the end, the push to gain access to the consistory may explain heightened conciliar

---

[16] As discussed in Neil McLynn's '"Genere Hispanus": Theodosius, Spain, and Nicene Orthodoxy', in Kim Bowes and Michael Kulikowski (eds.), *Hispania in Late Antiquity* (Boston: Brill, 2005), 77–120. Caroline Humfress's article, 'Roman Law, Forensic Argument and the Formation of Christian Orthodoxy III–VI Centuries)', in S. Elm, É. Rebillard, and A. Romano (eds.), *Orthodoxie, Christianisme, Histoire* (Paris, 2000), 125–47, is fundamental École Française de Rome.

[17] The rewards went both ways. See Christopher Kelly, *Ruling the Later Roman Empire* (Cambridge: Harvard University Press, 2004), 171–6, for discussion of the amount of money churches and their representatives presented to authorities for the opportunity to be given a favorable hearing.

[18] In the Council of 407, the Catholic bishops decided that annual councils at Carthage were no longer imperative. The African primates were invited to call meetings when they deemed them necessary, thereby relieving the bishops from having to travel great distances every year. By 407, the Edict of Unity had been promulgated, and the episcopate had refined their methods for appealing to the consistory. Like the commencement of the Carthage council, its termination is squarely attributable to historical circumstances. See *Concilia Africae, Registri Ecclesiae Carthagenensis Excerpta* 95.

activity among African Catholics, meaning that these meetings resulted from, and were not the origins of, the episcopate's command over the law.

Looking closely at how groups seeking to capitalize from imperial law engaged in its imitation may help us understand the origins of patristic literature. The distances in Augustine's mind between, first, scripture and the authority of council decisions, and, second, between council decisions and the written works of individuals, could precipitously narrow for someone like Possidius when all these texts constituted legal documents. Once items like letters, treatises, and transcripts had become part of an evidentiary dossier, and more important, a dossier that had helped persuade a judge to issue a favorable ruling, their status, or textual function, changed. The extent to which they were invested with authority, of course, was overstated for the purposes of persuasion. Possidius had to lean hard on Augustine's books, as the African episcopate leaned on the law, in order to lend to the bishop's works a permanence he was afraid they did not yet possess. Authority was a goal in the sights of men like Possidius, not the starting point. One can make a similar remark about Augustine's library at Hippo: in the midst of conquest and disruption, Possidius insisted on the collection's permanence and ease of circulation.

Roman law and the legal process offered an effective and familiar paradigm through which texts could rise above the transient noise of indistinct voices. Granted there may be other, additional contributors to the phenomenon. Authority over texts was also the purview of grammarians and rhetors, but what we are looking for is the origin of authority within the texts themselves, not as it was wielded by their interpreters.[19] The kind of 'globalization' the empire experienced in late antiquity when the autonomy of regional, or urban, law-making bodies ceded to centralized pronouncements—the culminations being the issue of Gregorian and Hermogenian Codes in the reign of Diocletian, and then the distribution of the *Theodosian Code* in 438—had its counterpart, one may argue, in the international dialogue that went on among

---

[19] Robert Dodaro has written a compelling series of articles on correctness in scriptural interpretation and doctrine as a function of literary decorum (see his 'Quid deceat videre [Cicero, *Orator* 70]: Literary Propriety and Doctrinal Orthodoxy on Augustine of Hippo', in S. Elm, É. Rebillard, and A. Romano (eds.), *Orthodoxie, Christianisme, Histoire* (Paris: École Françise de Rome, 2000), 57–81, and 'The Theologian as Grammarian', *Studia Patristica*, 38 [2001], 70–83). But the starting point for both of them is an excerpt from Latham's *Handlist of Rhetorical Terms* (Berkeley: University of California Press, 1968; reprint 1991), which locates literary authority in a reader, not a text. In other words, the text is an inert object: its authority is a function of the reader who possesses the expertise to make appropriate pronouncements about it. And while literary conventions exist, and consensus is possible through knowledge of precedent, reason, and use (*auctoritas, ratio,* and *usus*), in the end, evaluation remains subjective. This is not the same view expressed by the *Vita*, which portrays Augustine's corpus as superseding the man. Authority emanates from the oeuvre. What distinguishes it further from other texts, I have argued, is its validation of yet another kind, that being the law.

learned Christians, a dialogue that traversed time and locale. For example, the known correspondence between Augustine and Paulinus of Nola, as well as what must have been a significant amount of private communication, constitutes their interaction. They never met. When texts become the dominant medium of communication for far-flung communities, they may take on additional significance by embodying the people, churches, and cities whence they came, while simultaneously unifying disparate populations and places through the dialogues they engender. Augustine's community of like-minded thinkers that he called upon to respond to Julian of Eclanum pointedly included a range of texts from a wide geographic and chronological span, most pointedly those written by Greek bishops (*Contra Iulianum* 1.5.15). Jerome, too, created his own disparate community of scholars, included himself as a member, and wrote of their lives as constituting the books they wrote.[20] But a Christianity consisting of communities defined in relation to each other by distance and written communication had been a reality since the days of Paul.[21] The difference now, at the time Possidius wrote the *Vita*, was that the empire's homogeneous administrative apparatus provided a touchstone by which Christian texts could be tested for what, in the end, were identical measures: orthodoxy and legality. We need to think of these texts as moving, not just among Christian communities such as churches and councils, but also through offices of provincial judges and the imperial consistory. In the case of Roman Africa, and more specifically, for Possidius, Augustine's texts had a right to permanence because they were the law.

[20] See Mark Vessey, 'The Forging of Orthodoxy in Latin Christian Literature: A Case Study', *JECS*, 4 (1996), 495–513. He makes the point (508–9) that this kind of catalogue was not new. We recall that Galen, for example, wrote two separate autobiographies, both of which plotted his life through the books and treatises he wrote.

[21] Keith Hopkins, 'Christian Number and Its Implications', *JECS*, 6 (1998), 185–226, for discussion on the correspondence among Churches that has been lost.

Bibliography

Primary Sources

I use the abbreviations in *Augustine Through the Ages* for the titles of Augustine's works.

1. Works of Augustine

brev.	*Breviculus conlationis cum Donatistis*, ed. M. Petschenig CSEL 53 (1910).
civ. Dei	*De civitate Dei*, ed. Dombart and Kalb, CCL 47 and 48 (1955).
conf.	*Confessiones*, ed. James J. O'Donnell (Oxford: Oxford University Press, 1992); Available at http://www.stoa.org/hippo.
Cresc.	*Ad Cresconium grammaticum et Donatistam*, ed. M. Petschenig, CSEL 52 (1909).
c. Don.	*Contra Donatistas post conlationem*, ed. M. Petschenig, CSEL 53 (1910).
Emer.	*Gesta cum Emerito*, ed. M. Petschenig, CSEL 53 (1910).
en. Ps.	*Ennarationes in Psalmos*, CCL 38–40.
ep.	*Epistulae*, ed. Goldbacher, CSEL 34.1 and 2, 44, 57 (1895–1923); new letters, ed. J. Divjak, CSEL 88 (1981).
c. ep. Parm.	*Contra epistulam Parmeniani*, ed. M. Petschenig, CSEL 51 (1908).
c. Faust.	*Contra Faustum Manicheum*, ed. I. Zycha, CSEL 25.1 (1891).
f. et symb.	*De fide et symbolo*, ed. I. Zycha, CSEL 41 (1900).
c. Gaud.	*Contra Gaudentium*, ed. M. Petschenig, CSEL 53 (1910).
gest. Pel.	*De gestis Pelagii*, ed. C. Urba and I. Zycha, CSEL 42 (1902).
haer.	*De haeresibus ad Quodvultdeum liber unus*, ed. Plaetse and Beukers, CCL 46 (1969).
c. litt. Petil.	*Contra litteras Petiliani*, ed. M. Petschenig, CSEL 52 (1909).
mor.	*De moribus ecclesiae catholicae et de moribus Manichaeorum*, CSEL 90.
persev.	*De dono perseverantiae*, PL 45.
praed. sanct.	*De praedestinatione sanctorum*, PL 44.
retr.	*Retractationes*, ed. Mutzenbecher, CCL 57 (1984).
s.	*Sermones*, PL 38, 39, PL Supplementum 2, *Vingt-six sermons au peuple d'Afrique* (new sermons), ed. F. Dolbeau (Paris: Institut d'Études Augustiniennes, 1996).

2. Other Ancient Sources

Coll. Avell.	*Epistulae imperatorum pontificum aliorum...Avellana quae dicitur Collectio*, ed. O. Günther, CSEL 35.1 (1895).

GENNADIUS

de script. eccl.	*Liber de scriptoribus ecclesiasticus*, PL 58, 1059–1120.

OPTATUS OF MILEVIS

de schism. Don.	*De schismate Donatistarum*, CSEL 26.

OROSIUS
hist.   *Historiae adversum paganos*, ed. C. Zangemeister, CSEL 5 (1882).
lib. Apol.   *Liber apologeticus de arbitri libertate*, ed. C. Zangemeister, CSEL 5 (1882).

PAULINUS OF MILAN
v. Amb.   *Vita di S. Ambrogio*, ed. M. Pellegrino (Rome: Editrice Studium, 1961).

POSSIDIUS
v. Aug.   *Vita Augustini*, ed. A. A. R. Bastiensen in *Vite dei Santi*, iii: *Vita di Cipriano, Vita di Ambrogio, Vita di Agostino* (Fondazione Lorenzo Vallc, 1975).
Indiculum   *Operum S. Augustini Elenchus a Possidio eiusdem discipulo Calamensi episcopo digestus: Post Maurinorum labores novis curis editus critico apparatus numeris tabellis instructus*, ed. A. Wilmart in *Miscellanea Agostiniana* (Rome: Tipographic Poliglotta Vaticana, 1930–1), ii, 149–233.

PROSPER OF AQUITAINE
Chron.   *Prosperi Tironis epitoma de chronicon*, in *Chronica Minora* I (*MGH* IX), ed. T. Mommsen (Berlin: Weidmann, 1892).
Contra collat.   *De gratia et libero arbitrio liber contra collatorem*, CCL 68A (1900).
Resp. Gall.   *Pro Augustino responsiones ad capitua obiectionum Gallorum calumniantium*, CCL 68A (1900).
Resp. Gen.   *Pro Augustino responsiones ad excerpta Genuensium*, CCL 68A (1900).

VICTOR OF VITA
Victor Vit.   *Historia persecutionis Africanae provinciae*, ed. M. Petschenig, CSEL 7 (1881).

ZOSIMUS
Zos.   *Histoire nouvelle*, ed. and tr. F. Paschoud (Paris: Belles lettres, 1971–89; reprint, 2003).

Secondary Sources

Adesi, G. Barone, 'Eresie "sociali" e inquisizione Theodosiano', in *Atti dell'Accademia romanistica costantiniana: VI Convegno internazionale* (Perusii: Studium generale civitatis, 1986), 119–66.
Alexander, James S., 'A Note on the Interpretation of the Parable of the Threshing Floor at the Conference of Carthage of A.D. 411', *Journal of Theological Studies*, 24 (1973), 512–19.
——, 'Count Taurinus and the Persecutors of Donatism', *Zeitschrift für antikes Christentum*, 2 (1998), 247–67.
——, 'Methodology in the *Capitula gestorum conlationis Carthaginiensis*', *Studia Patristica*, 17 (1982), 3–8.
Alexander, Loveday, 'The Living Voice: Scepticism towards the Written Word in Early Christian and in Graeco-Roman Texts', in D. J. A. Clines, S. E. Fowl, and S. E. Porter (eds.), *The Bible in Three Dimensions: Essays in Celebration of Forty Years of Biblical Studies in the University of Sheffield* (Worcester Billing & sons Ltd., 1990), 221–47.
Altaner, Berthold, *Kleine Patristische Schriften* (Berlin: Akademic Verlag, 1967).

Ando, Clifford, 'Augustine on Language', *Revue des Études Augustiniennes*, 40 (1994), 45–78.

Andt, Édouard, *La Procédure par rescrit* (Paris: Recueil Sirey, 1920).

Atkins, Margaret, 'Old Philosophy and New Power: Cicero in Fifth-Century North Africa', in Gillian Clark and Tessa Rajak (eds.), *Philosophy and Power in the Graeco-Roman World* (Oxford: Oxford University Press, 2002), 251–69.

Atkinson, J. E., 'Out of Order: The Circumcellions and *Codex Theodosianus* 16,5,52', *Historia*, 41 (1992), 488–99.

Bagnall, Roger S., Alan Cameron, Seth R. Schwartz, and Klaas A. Worp, *Consuls of the Later Roman Empire* (Atlanta: Scholars Press, 1987).

Barnard, Laurette, 'The Criminalization of Heresy in the Later Roman Empire: A Sociopolitical Device?', *Journal of Legal History*, 16 (1995), 121–46.

Barnes, T. D., 'The Beginnings of Donatism', *Journal of Theological Studies*, n.s., 26 (1975), 13–22.

Barrow, R. H., *Prefect and Emperor: The Relationes of Symmachus, A.D. 384* (Oxford: Clarendon Press, 1973).

——, 'The Inaccuracies in the *Vita Augustini* of Possidius', *Studia Patristica*, 16 (1985), 480–6.

Batiffol, Pierre, 'Le Règlement des premiers conciles africains et le règlement du sénat romain', *Bulletin d'Ancienne Littérature et d'Archéologie Chrétiennes*, 3 (1913), 3–19.

——, 'L'Église et les survivances du culte impérial', in Louis Bréhier (ed.), *Les Survivances du culte impérial romain, à propos des rites shintoïstes* (Paris: Auquste Picord, 1920), 5–33.

Berrouard, Marie-François, 'L'Activité littéraire de saint Augustin du 11 septembre au 1er décembre 419 d'après la lettre 23*A à Possidius de Calama', in *Les Lettres de saint Augustin découvertes par Johnannes Divjak: Communications presentées au colloque des 20 et 21 septembre 1982* (Paris: Études Augustiniennes, 1983), 301–27.

——, 'Un Tournant dans la vie de l'Église d'Afrique: Les deux Missions d'Alypius en Italie à la lumière des *lettres* 10*, 15*, 16*, 22* et 23*A de saint Augustin', *Revue des Études Augustiniennes*, 31 (1985), 46–70.

Bethe, Erich, *Buch und Bild im Alterum* (Amsterdam: A. M. Hakkert, 1964).

Beyenka, Sister M. Melchior, 'St. Augustine and the Hymns of St. Ambrose', *American Benedictine Review*, 8 (1957), 121–32.

Bonner, Gerald, *St. Augustine of Hippo: Life and Controversies* (Philadelphia: Westminster Press, 1963).

——, 'Augustine's Visit to Caesarea in 418', in C. W. Dugmore and Charles Duggan (eds.), *Studies in Church History* (London: Nelson, 1964), 104–13.

——, 'Pelagianism and Augustine' Part 1, *Augustinian Studies*, 23 (1992), 33–51.

——, 'Pelagianism and Augustine' Part 2, *Augustinian Studies*, 24 (1993), 27–47.

——, '*Dic Christi veritas ubi nunc habitas*: Ideas of Schism and Heresy in the Post-Nicene Age', in William E. Klingshirn and Mark Vessey (eds.), *The Limits of Ancient Christianity: Essays on Late Antique Thought and Culture in Honor of R. A. Markus* (Ann Arbor: University of Michigan Press, 1999), 63–79.

Bouhot, Jean-Paul, 'La Transmission d'Hippone à Rome des oeuvres de saint Augustin', in Donatella Nebbiai-Dalla Guarda and Jean-François Genest (eds.), *Du copiste au collectionneur: Mélanges d'histoire des textes et des bibliothèques en l'honneur d'André Vernet* (Turnhout: Brepols, 1998), 23–33.

Brisson, Jean-Paul, *Autonomisme et christianisme dans l'Afrique romaine* (Paris: Éditions de Boccord, 1958).

Brown, Peter, 'Aspects of the Christianization of the Roman Aristocracy', *Journal of Roman Studies*, 51 (1961), 1–11.

——, 'Religious Coercion in the Later Roman Empire: The Case of North Africa', *History*, 48 (1963), 283–305.

——, 'St. Augustine's Attitude to Religious Coercion', *Journal of Roman Studies*, 54 (1964), 107–16.

——, 'Christianity and Local Culture in Late Roman Africa', *Journal of Roman Studies*, 58 (1968), 85–95.

——, 'Pelagius and His Supporters: Aims and Environment', *Journal of Theological Studies*, 19 (1968), 93–114.

——, 'The Diffusion of Manichaeism in the Roman Empire', *Journal of Roman Studies*, 59 (1969), 92–103.

——, *The Cult of the Saints: Its Rise and Function in Latin Christianity* (Chicago: University of Chicago Press, 1981).

——, *Power and Persuasion in Late Antiquity: Towards a Christian Empire* (Madison: University of Wisconsin Press, 1992).

——, *Authority of the Sacred* (Cambridge: Cambridge University Press, 1995).

——, 'Augustine and a Practice if the *imperiti*', in Goulven Madec (ed.), *Augustin prédicateur (395–411): Actes du Colloque International de Chantilly (5–7 septembre 1996)* (Paris: Institut d' Études Augustiniennes, 1998), 367–75.

——, *Augustine of Hippo: A Biography* (Berkeley: University of California Press, 1967; reprint, 2000).

——, 'Augustine and a Crisis of Wealth in Late Antiquity', *Augustinian Studies*, 36 (2005), 5–30.

Burnett, Carole C., 'Dysfunction at Diospolis: A Comparative Study of Augustine's *De gestis Pelagii* and Jerome's *Dialogus aversus Pelagianos*', *Augustinian Studies*, 34 (2003), 153–73.

Burns, J. Patout, 'Augustine's Role in the Imperial Action against Pelagius', *Journal of Theological Studies*, n.s., 29 (1978), 67–83.

——, 'The Interpretation of Romans in the Pelagian Controversy', *Augustinian Studies*, 10 (1979), 43–79.

——, 'On Rebaptism: Social Organization in the Third-Century Church', *Journal of Early Christian Studies*, 1 (1993), 367–403.

——, 'The Atmosphere of Election: Augustinianism as Common Sense', *Journal of Early Christian Studies*, 2 (1994), 325–39.

——, *Cyprian the Bishop* (New York: Routledge, 2002).

Burns, Paul C., 'Augustine's Use of Varro's Antiquitates Rerum Divinarum in his *De civitate Dei*', *Augustinian Studies*, 32 (2001), 37–64.

Büttner, Theodora and Rodney Wener, *Circumcellionen und Adamiten: Zwei Formen mittelalterlicher Haeresie* (Berlin: Akademic Verlag, 1959).

Cavadini, John C., 'Ambrose and Augustine *De bono mortis*', in William E. Klingshirn and Mark Vessey (eds.), *The Limits of Ancient Christianity: Essays on Late Antique Thought and Culture in Honor of R. A. Markus* (Ann Arbor: University of Michigan Press, 1999), 232–49.

Chadwick, Henry, 'New Letters of St. Augustine', *Journal of Theological Studies*, n.s., 34 (1983), 425–52.

——, 'History and Symbolism in the Garden at Milan', in F. X. Martin and J. A. Richmond (eds.), *From Augustine to Eriugena: Essays on Neoplatonism and Christianity in Honor of John O'Meara* (Washington: Catholic University of America Press, 1991), 42–55.

——, 'Donatism and the *Confessions* of Augustine', in Glenn W. Most, Hubert Petersmann, and Adolf Martin Ritter (eds.), *Philanthropia kai Eusebeia: Festschrift für Albrect Dihle zum 70. Geburtstag* (Göttingen: Vandenhoeck & Ruprecht, 1993), 23–35.

——, 'On Re-reading the *Confessions*', in Fannie Lemoine and Christopher Kleinhenz (eds.), *Saint Augustine the Bishop: A Book of Essays* (New York: Garland Publishers, 1994), 139–60.

——, 'New Sermons of St. Augustine', *Journal of Theological Studies*, n.s., 47 (1996), 69–91.

Chastagnol, André, 'Le Sénateur Volusien et la conversion d'une famille de l'aristocratie romaine au Bas-Empire', *Revue des Études Anciennes*, 58 (1956), 241–53.

——, *La Préfecture urbaine à Rome sous le Bas-Empire* (Paris: Presses Universitaires de France, 1960).

——, *Les Fastes de la préfecture de Rome au Bas-Empire* (Paris: Nouvelles Éditions Latines, 1962).

Cimma, M. Rosa, *L'episcopalis audientia nelle costituzioni imperiali da Costantino a Giustiniano* (Turin: G. Giappichelli, 1989).

Clark, Elizabeth A., *The Origenist Controversy: The Cultural Construction of an Early Christian Debate* (Princeton: Princeton University Press, 1992).

Clover, Frank M., 'Carthage in the Age of Augustine', in J. H. Humphrey (ed.), *Excavations at Carthage 1976 Conducted by the University of Michigan* (Ann Arbor: The Kelsey Museum at the University of Michigan, 1978), 1–14.

Cooper, K., 'Insinuations of Womanly Influence: An Aspect of the Christianization of the Roman Aristocracy', *Journal of Roman Studies*, 82 (1992), 150–64.

Courcelle, Pierre, 'Sur les dernières paroles de saint Augustin', *Revue des Études Anciennes*, 46 (1944), 205–7.

——, *Recherches sur les Confessions de saint Augustin* (Paris: Éditions de Boccard, 1950).

——, 'Les Lacunes de la correspondance entre saint Augustin et Paulin de Nole', *Revue des Études Anciennes*, 53 (1951), 253–300.

——, *Les Confessions de saint Augustin dans la tradition littéraire: Antecedents et Postérité* (with special attention to Appendix iv: *Emprunts et compléments de Possidius aux Confessions*) (Paris: Études Augustiniennes, 1963).

——, *Late Latin Writers and Their Greek Sources*, tr. Harry E. Wedeck (Cambridge, MA: Harvard University Press, 1969).

Courtois, Christian, *Les Vandales et l'Afrique* (Paris: Arts et Métiers Graphiques, 1955).

Cox Miller, Patricia, *Biography in Late Antiquity: A Quest for the Holy Man* (Berkeley: University of California Press, 1983).

Coyle, J. Kevin, 'Saint Augustine's Manichaean Legacy', *Augustinian Studies*, 34 (2003), 1–22.

——, 'The Self-Identity of North African Christians in Augustine's Time', in Pierre-Yves Fux, Jean-Michel Roessli, and Otto Wermelinger (eds.), *Augustinus Afer: Saint Augustin, africanité, et universalité: actes du colloque international, Alger-Annaba, 1–7 avril 2001* (Fribourg: Éditions Universitaires Fribourg Suisse, 2003), 61–73.

Cranz, F. Edward, 'The Development of Augustine's Ideas on Society before the Donatist Controversy', *Harvard Theological Review*, 1 (1954), 255–316.

Crespin, Rémi, *Ministère et sainteté: Pastorale du clergé et solution de la crise donatiste dans la vie et la doctrine de saint Augustin* (Paris: Études Augustiniennes, 1965).

Cross, F. L., 'History and Fiction in the African Canons', *Journal of Theological Studies*, 12 (1961), 227–47.

Dagemark, Siver, 'Possidius' Idealized Description of St. Augustine's Death', in *Vescovi e pastori in epoca teodosiana: In occasione del XVI centenario della consacrazione epsicopale di S. Agostino, 396–1996*, Studia Ephemeridis Augustinianum 58 (Rome: Institution Patristicum Augustinianum, 1997), 719–41.

De Bruyne, D., 'Le Texte et les citations bibliques de la *Vita S. Augustini* de Possidius', *Revue Bénédictine*, 42 (1930), 297–300.

——, 'La Chronologie de quelque sermons de Saint Augustin', *Revue Bénédictine*, 43 (1931), 185–93.

——, 'Les anciennes Collections et la chronologie des lettres de saint Augustin', *Revue Bénédictine*, 43 (1931), 284–95.

Decret, François, 'Saint Augustin, témoin du manichéisme dans l'Afrique romaine', in Cornelius Mayer and Karl Heinz Chelius (eds.), *Internationales Symposion über den Stand der Augustinus-Forschung* (Würzburg: Augustinus–Verlag, 1989), 87–97.

——, 'Le Traité d'Evodius *Contre les Manichéens*: Un Compendium à l'usage du parfait controversiste', *Augustinianum*, 2 (1991), 387–409.

Deferrari, Roy J., 'Verbatim Reports of Augustine's Unwritten Sermons', *Transactions of the American Philological Association*, 46 (1915), 35–45.

De Giovanni, Lucio, *Chiesa e stato nel codice Theodosiano: Saggio sul libro XVI* (Naples: Tempi Moderni Edizioni, 1980).

De Guibert, J., 'La Notion d'hérésie chez saint Augustin', *Bulletin de Littérature Ecclésiastique*, 21 (1920), 369–82.

Dell' Oro, Aldo, 'Sul concetto di "Pragmatica sanction"', *Studia et Documenta Historiae et Iuris*, 11 (1945), 314–18.

Delmaire, Roland, 'Étude sur les souscriptions de quelques lois du Code théodosien: Les Lois reçues a Regium', in Michel Christol et al. (eds.), *Institutions, société, et vie politique dans l'Empire romain au IVe siècle ap. J.-C.* (Rome: École Française de Rome, 1992), 315–28.

——, *Les Institutions du Bas-Empire romain, de Constantin à Justinien: Les Institutions civiles palatines* (Paris: Les Éditions du Cerf, 1995).

Demougeot, E., 'Sur les lois du 15 Novembre 407', *Revue Historique de Droit Français et Étranger*, 28 (1950), 403–12.

——, *De l'unité a la division de l'empire romain, 395–410: Essai sur le gouvernement imperial* (Paris: Librarie d'Amérique et d'Orient, 1951).

——, 'A propos des interventions du pape Innocent 1ᵉʳ dans la politique séculiere', *Revue Historique*, 212 (1954), 23–38.

de Plinval, Georges, 'Prosper d'Aquitaine interprète de saint Augustin', *Recherches Augustiniennes*, 1 (1958), 339–55.

De Veer, Albert C., 'Le dernier Proconsul païen de la province d'Afrique (410 ap. J.-C.)', in *Congrès national des sciences historique, 14–16 Avril 1930* (Alger: Société Historigue Algérienne, 1932), 253–60.

——, 'L'Exploitation du schisme maximianiste par saint Augustin dans la lutte contre le Donatisme', *Recherches Augustiniennes*, 3 (1965), 219–37.

——, 'Une Mesure de tolérance de l'Empereur Honorius', *Revue des études byzantines*, 24 (1966), 189–95.

Diesner, H. J., 'Die Circumcellion von Hippo Regius', *Theologische Literaturzeitung*, 85 (1960), 497–508.

——, 'Possidius und Augustinus', *Studia Patristica*, 6 (1962), 350–65.

Dihle, Albrecht, *The Theory of Will in Classical Antiquity* (Berkeley: University of California Press, 1982).

Dodaro, Robert, 'Augustine's Secular City', in Robert Dodaro and George Lawless (eds.), *Augustine and His Critics: Essays in Honour of Gerald Bonner* (New York: Routledge, 2000), 231–59.

——, '*Quid deceat videre* (Cicero, *Orator* 70): Literary Propriety and Doctrinal Orthodoxy in Augustine of Hippo', in S. Elm, É. Rebillard, and A. Romano (eds.), *Orthodoxie, christianisme, histoire* (Rome: École Française de Rome, 2000), 57–81.

——, 'The Theologian as Grammarian: Literary Decorum in Augustine's Defense of Orthodox Discourse', *Studia Patristica*, 38 (2001), 70–83.

——, *Christ and the Just Society in the Thought of Augustine* (Cambridge: Cambridge University Press, 2004).

Dolbeau, 'La Survie des oeuvres d'Augustin: Remarques sur l'*Indiculum* attribué à Possidius et sur la bibliothèque d'Anségise', in Donatella Nebbiai-Dalla Guarda and Jean-François Genest (eds.), *Du copiste au collectionneur: Mélanges d'histoire des textes et des bibliothèques en l'honneur d'André Vernet* (Turnhout: Brepols, 1998), 3–22.

Dossey, Leslie, 'Judicial Violence and the Ecclesiastical Courts in Late Antique North Africa', in Ralph W. Mathisen (ed.), *Law, Society, and Authority in Late Antiquity* (Oxford: Oxford University Press. 2001), 98–114.

Dunn, Geoffrey D., 'Heresy and Schism According to Cyprian of Carthage', *Journal of Theological Studies*, n.s., 55 (2004), 551–74.

Du Roy, O., *L'Intelligence de la foi en la Trinité selon saint Augustin: Genèse de sa théologie trinitaire jusqu'en 391* (Paris: Études Augustiniennes, 1966).

Duval, N., 'Notes d'epigraphie chrétienne III: Epsicopus unitatis', *Karthago*, 9 (1958), 137–49.

Duval, Yves-Marie, 'Julien d'Éclane et Rufin d'Aquilée Du Concile de Rimini a la répression pélagienne: L'Intervention impériale en matière religieuse', *Revue des Études Augustiniennes*, 24 (1978), 243–71.

——, 'La Date du "De natura" de Pélage: Les Premières Étapes de la controverse sur la nature de la grâce', *Revue des Études Augustiniennes*, 36 (1990), 257–83.

——, 'Pélage en son temps: Données chronologiques nouvelles pour une présentation nouvelle', *Studia Patristica*, 38 (2001), 95–118.

Duval, Yves-Marie, 'Note sur la letter d'Evodius à l'abbé Valentin d'Hadrumète', *Revue des Études Augustiniennes*, 49 (2003), 123–30.

Dvornik, Francis, 'Emperors, Popes and General Councils', *Dumbarton Oaks Papers*, 6 (1951), 3–23.

Elm, Eva, 'Die *Vita Augustini* des Possidius: The Work of a Plain Man and an Untrained Writer? Wandlungen in der Beurteilung eines hagiographischen Textes', *Augustinianum*, 37 (1997), 229–40.

——, *Die Macht der Weisheit: Das Bild des Bischofs in der Vita Augustini des Possidius und anderen spätantiken und frümittelalterlichen Bischofsviten* (Leiden: Brill, 2003).

Eno, Robert, 'Some Nuances in the Ecclesiology of the Donatists', *Revue des Études Augustiniennes*, 18 (1972), 46–50.

——, 'The Work of Optatus as a Turning Point in African Ecclesiology', *The Thomist*, 37 (1973), 668–85.

——, 'Doctrinal Authority in Saint Augustine', *Augustinian Studies*, 12 (1981), 133–72.

Feissel, Denis, 'L'Adnotatio de Constantin sur le droit de cité d'Orcistus en Phrygia', *Antiquité Tardive*, 7 (1999), 255–67.

Fitzgerald, Allan D., 'Tracing the Passage from a Doctrinal to an Historical Approach to the Study of Augustine', *Revue d'Études Augustiniennes et Patristiques*, 50 (2004), 295–310.

Fredriksen, Paula, 'Paul and Augustine: Conversion Narratives, Orthodox Traditions, and the Retrospective Self', *Journal of Theological Studies*, n.s., 37 (1986), 3–34.

——, 'Beyond the Body/Soul Dichotomy: Augustine on Paul against the Manichees and the Pelagians', *Recherches Augustiniennes*, 23 (1988), 86–114.

Frend, W. H. C., *The Donatist Church: A Movement of Protest in Roman North Africa* (Oxford: Clarendon Press, 1952; reprint 1971).

——, 'The Gnostic-Manichaean Tradition in Roman North Africa', *Journal of Ecclesiastical History*, 4 (1953), 13–26.

——, 'The Early Christian Church in Carthage', in J. H. Humphrey (ed.), *Excavations at Carthage 1976 Conducted by the University of Michigan*, iii (Ann Arbor: University of Michigan Press, 1977), 21–40.

——, 'Donatist and Catholic: The Organisation of Christian Communities in the North African Countryside', in *Cristianizzazione ed organizzazione ecclesiastica delle campagne nell'alto Medioeve: Espansione e resistenze* (Spoleto: Scttimane di Studio del Centro Italiano di Studi Sull'alto Medioevo, 1982), 601–37.

——, *Archaeology and History in the Study of Early Christianity* (London: Variorum Reprints, 1988).

——, 'Augustine and Orosius on the End of the World', *Augustinian Studies*, 20 (1989), 1–38.

——, 'Donatus paene totam Africam decepit. How?', *Journal of Ecclesiastical History*, 48 (1997), 611–27.

Gabillon, Aimé, 'Romanianus, alias Cornelius: Du nouveau sur le bienfaiteur et l'ami de saint Augustin', *Revue des Études Augustineinnes*, 24 (1978), 58–70.

Gaddis, Michael, *There Is No Crime for Those Who Have Christ: Religious Violence in the Christian Roman Empire* (Berkeley: University of California Press, 2005).

Garnsey, Peter, '*Taxatio* and *Pollicitatio* in Roman Africa', *Journal of Roman Studies*, 61 (1971), 116–29.

——, 'Lactantius and Augustine', in A. K. Bowman et al. (eds.), *Representations of Empire: Rome and the Mediterranean World* (Oxford: Proceedings of the British Academy, 2002), 153–79.

Gaudemet, Jean, *La Formation du droit séculier et du droit de l'église aux IVe et Ve siècles* (Toulouse: Sirey, 1957).

——, 'Quelques aspects de la politique legislative au Ve siècle', in *Studi in onore di Edoardo Volterra* (Milan: A. Guiffré, 1971), 225–34.

——, 'Politique ecclésiastique et législation religieuse après l'édit de Théodose I de 380', in *Droit et société aux derniers siècles de l'Empire romain*, Antiqua 66 (Naples: Jovene, 1992), 175–96.

Gaudemet, Jean, P. Siniscalco, and G. L. Falchi, *Legislazione imperiale e religione nel IV secolo* (Rome: Institute Partristico Augustinianum, 2000).

Gebbia, C., 'Sant' Agostino e l'episcopalis audienti', *L'Africa Romana*, 8 (1989), 683–95.

Geerlings, Wilhelm, 'Haeresis und Schisma in den Canones der nordafrikanischen Konzilien von 345 bis 525', in André Gabriels and Heinrich J. F. Reinhardt (eds.), *Ministerium Iustitiae: Festschrift für Heribert Heinemann zur Vollendung des 60. Lebensjahres* (Essen: Ludgerus Verlag Hubert Wingen, 1985), 161–7.

Gilliard, Frank D., 'Senatorial Bishops in the Fourth Century', *Harvard Theological Review*, 77 (1984), 153–75.

Glorie, F., 'Das "zweite Aenigma" in Augustins Opusculorum Indiculus cap X^4, 1–4 "Tractatus Psalmorum"', in *Corona gratiarum: Miscellanea patristica, historica, et liturgica Eligio Dekkers O.S.B. XII lustra complenti oblata* (Brussels: Sint Pictersabdij, 1975), 289–309.

Gorman, Michael M., 'Eugippius and the Origins of the Manuscript Tradition of Saint Augustine's "De Genesi ad Litteram"', *Revue Bénédictine*, 93 (1983), 7–30.

Grafton, Anthony and Megan Williams, *Christianity and the Transformation of the Book* (Cambridge, MA: The Belknap Press of Harvard University Press, 2006).

Grasmück, Ernst Ludwig, *Coercitio: Staat und Kirche im Donatistenstreit* (Bonn: L. Röhrscheid, 1964).

Greenslade, S. L., *Schism in the Early Church* (SCM Press, Ltd.,1953).

Grégoire, Reginald, 'Riflessioni sulla tipologia agiografica della *Vita Augustini* de Possidio', *Augustinianum*, 25 (1985), 21–6.

Gui, Isabelle, with Noël Duval and Jean-Pierre Caillet, *Basiliques chrétiennes d'Afrique du nord* (Paris: Institute d'Études Augustiniennes, 1992).

Hamilton, Louis I., 'Possidius' Augustine and Post-Augustinian Africa', *Journal of Early Christian Studies*, 12 (2004), 85–105.

Hammond, C. P., 'The Last Ten Years of Rufinus' Life and the Date of His Move South from Aquileia', *Journal of Theological Studies*, n.s., 28 (1977), 372–429.

Harnack, Adolf, *Possidius Augustins Leben* (Berlin: Verlag der Akademic der Wissenschaften, 1930).

Harries, Jill, 'The Roman Imperial Quaestor from Constantine to Theodosius II', *Journal of Roman Studies*, 78 (1988), 148–72.

——, 'Constructing the Judge: Judicial Accountability and the Culture of Criticism in Late Antiquity', in Richard Miles (ed.), *Constructing Identities in Late Antiquity* (New York: Routledge, 1999), 214–33.

——, *Law and Empire in Late Antiquity* (Cambridge: Cambridge University Press, 1999).

Harries, Jill and Wood, Ian (eds.), *The Theodosian Code* (Ithaca: Cornell University press, 1993).

Härtel, Gottfried, 'Zur Problematik der pragmatischen Sanktionen spez. zur Sanctio pragmatica pro petitione Vigilii', *Iura*, 27 (1976), 33–49.

Hermanowicz, Erika T., 'Book Six of Augustine's *De musica* and the Episcopal Embassies of 408', *Augustinian Studies*, 35 (2004), 165–98.

——, 'Catholic Bishops and Appeals to the Imperial Court: A Legal Study of the Calama Riots in 408', *Journal of Early Christian Studies*, 12 (2004), 481–521.

Holmberg, Erik J., *Zur Geschichte des Cursus Publicus* (Uppsala: A.-B. Lundequistska Bokhandeln, 1933).

Hombert. Pierre-Marie, *Nouvelles recherches de chronologie augustinienne* (Paris: Institut d'Études Augustiniennes, 2000).

Honoré, Tony, 'The Making of the Theodosian Code', *Zeitschrift der Savigny-Stiftung für Rechtsgeschichte: Romanistische Abteilung*, 103 (1986), 133–221.

——, *Law in the Crisis of Empire, 379–455 AD: The Theodosian Dynasty and Its Quaestors* (Oxford: Clarendon Press, 1988).

Hopkins, Keith, 'Christian Number and Its Implications', *Journal of Early Christian Studies*, 6 (1998), 185–226.

Humfress, Caroline, *Forensic Practice in the Development of Roman and Ecclesiastical Law in Late Antiquity, with Special Reference to the Prosecution of Heresy*, Ph.D. dissertation, Cambridge University, 1998.

——, 'Roman Law, Forensic Argument, and the Formation of Christian Orthodoxy (III–VI Centuries)', in S. Elm, É. Rebillard, and A. Romano (eds.), *Orthodoxie, christianisme, histoire* (Paris: École Française de Rome, 2000), 125–47.

——, 'A New Legal Cosmos: Late Roman Lawyers and the Early Medieval Church', in Peter Linehan and Janet L. Nelson (eds.), *The Medieval World* (New York: Routledge, 2001), 557–75.

Jacques, François, 'Le Défenseur de cité d'après la lettre 22* de saint Augustin', *Revue des Études Augustiniennes*, 32 (1986), 56–73.

——, 'Propriétés impériales et cités en Numidie Méridionale', *Cahiers du Centre G. Glotz*, 3 (1992), 123–39.

Jacobsson, Martin, *Aurelius Augustinus, De musica liber VI: A Critical Edition with a Translation and an Introduction* (Stockholm: Almquist and Wiksell International, 2002).

Jansen, Tore, *Prose Prefaces: Studies in Literary Conventions* (Stockholm: Almquist, 1964).

Jones, A. H. M., 'Were Ancient Heresies National or Social Movements in Disguise?', *Journal of Theological Studies*, n.s., 10 (1959), 280–98.

——, *The Later Roman Empire, 284–602: A Social, Economic, and Administrative Survey* (Norman: University of Oklahoma Press, 1964).

Jones, B. V. E., 'The Manuscript Tradition of Augustine's *De civitate Dei*', *Journal of Theological Studies*, n.s., 16 (1965), 142–5.

Kaden, Erich-Hans, 'Die Edikte gegen die Manichäer von Diokletian bis Justinian', in *Festschrift Hans Lewald* (Basel: Helbing & Lichtenhahn, 1953), 55–68.

Kalinka, E., 'Die älteste erhaltene Abschrift des Verzeichnisses der Werke Augustins', *Sitzungsberichte Akademie der Wissenschaften in Wien Philosophisch-historiche Klasse*, 203 (1925), 1–34.

Kany, Roland, 'Der vermeintliche Makel von Augustins Bischofsweihe', *Zeitschrift für antikes Christentum*, 1 (1997), 115–25.

Kardong, Terrence G., 'Monastic Issues in Possidius' *Life of Augustine*', *American Benedictine Review*, 38 (1987), 159–77.

Kaster, Robert, 'Macrobius and Servius: Verecundia and the Grammarian's Function', *Harvard Studies in Classical Philology*, 84 (1980), 219–62.

Kaufman, Peter Iver, 'Augustine, Macedonius, and the Courts', *Augustinian Studies*, 34/1 (2003), 67–82.

——, 'Patience and/or Politics: Augustine and the Crisis at Calama, 408–409', *Vigiliae Christianae*, 57 (2003), 22–35.

Kelly, Christopher, *Ruling the Later Roman Empire* (Cambridge: Harvard University Press, 2004).

Kemper, Francis, *De vitarum Cypriani, Martini Turonensis, Ambrosii, Augustini rationibus: Commentatio philologica quam consensu et auctoritate amplissimi philosophorum ordinis in alma litterarum universitate regia monasteriensi ad summos in philosophia honores rite consequendos scripsit* (Münster: Monasterius Guestfalus, 1904).

Klingshirn, William, 'Charity and Power: Caesarius of Arles and the Ransoming of Captives in Sub-Roman Haul', *Journal of Roman Studies*, 75 (1985), 183–203.

Kussmaul, Peter, *Pragmaticum und Lex: Formen spätrömischer Gesetzgebung 408–457* (Göttingen: Vandenhoeck & Ruprecht, 1981).

La Bonnardière, Anne-Marie, *Recherches de chronologie augustinienne* (Paris: Études Augustiniennes, 1965).

Lamberigts, Mathijs J. G. P., 'The Italain Julian of Aeclanum about the African Augustin of Hippo', in Pierre-Yves Fux, Jean-Michel Roessli, and Otto Wermelinger (eds.), *Augustinus Afer: Saint Augustin, africanité et universalité: Actes du colloque international, Alger-Annaba, 1–7 avril 2001* (Fribourg: Éditions Universitaires Fribourg Suisse, 2003), 83–93.

Lambot, C., 'Lettre inédite de S. Augustin relative au "*De civitate Dei*"', *Revue Bénédictine*, 51 (1939), 109–21.

Lamirande, Émilien, 'L'Offre conciliatrice des Catholiques aux Donatistes relativement à l'épiscopat (*Gesta collationis carthaginiensis* I.16)', *Église et Théologie*, 2 (1971), 285–308.

——, 'Augustine and the Discussion on the Sinners in the Church at the Conference of Carthage (411)', *Augustinian Studies*, 3 (1972), 97–112.

——, *La Situation ecclésiologique des donatistes d'après saint Augustine: Contribution à l'historie doctrinale de l'oecuménisme* (Ottawa: Éditions de l'Université d'Ottawa, 1972).

——, 'La Datation de la *Vita Ambrosii* de Paulin de Milan', *Revue des Études Augustiniennes*, 27 (1981), 44–55.

——, *Paulin de Milan et la Vita Ambrosii: Aspects de la religion sous le Bas-Empire* (Montreal: Les Éditions Bellarmin).

Lamoreaux, John C., 'Episcopal Courts in Late Antiquity', *Journal of Early Christian Studies*, 3 (1995), 142–67.

Lancel, Serge, *Actes de la Conférence de Carthage en 411* (Paris: Les Éditions du Cerf, 1972–91).

——, 'Les Débuts du Donatisme: La Date du Protocole de Cirta et de l'élection épiscopale de Silvanus', *Revue des Études Augustiniennes*, 25 (1979), 217–29.

Lancel, Serge, 'A propos des nouvelles letters de S. Augustin et de la Conférence de Carthage en 411', *Revue d'Histoire Ecclésiastique*, 77 (1982), 446–55.

——, 'Saint Augustin et la Maurétanie Césarienne: Les Années 418–419 à la lumière des nouvelles lettres récemment publiées', *Revue des Études Augustiniennes*, 30 (1984), 48–59.

——, 'Saint Augustin et la Maurétanie Césarienne (2): L'Affaire de l'évêque Honorius (automne 419–printemps 420) dans les nouvelles lettres 22*, 23*, et 23* A.', *Revue des Études Augustiniennes*, 30 (1984), 251–62.

——, 'Le Sort des évêques et des communautés donatistes après la Conférence de Carthage en 411', in Cornelius Mayer and Karl Heinz Chelius (eds.), *Internationales Symposion über den Stand der Augustinus-Forschung* (Würzburg: Augustinus–Verlag, 1989), 149–67.

——, ' Évêchés et cités dans les provinces africaines (IIIe–Ve Siècles)', in *L'Afrique dans L'Occident romain* (Rome: École Française de Rome, 1990), 273–90.

——, 'Le Recrutement de l'Église d'Afrique au début du Ve siècle: Aspects qualitifs et quantitifs', in *De Tertullian aux Mozarabes: Mélanges offerts a Jacques Fontaine* (Paris: Études Augustiniennes, 1992), 325–38.

——, *Saint Augustine*, tr. Antonia Nevill (London: SCM Press, 2002).

——, 'Saint Augustin et les Donatistes dans les nouveaux Sermons Dolbeau', in Marcello Marin and Claudio Moreschini (eds.), *Africa cristiana: Storia, religione, letteratura* (Brescia: Editrice Morcelliana, 2002), 201–19.

Lardone, F. G., 'Roman Law in the Works of St. Augustine', *Georgetown Law Journal*, 21 (1932–3), 435–56.

Lawless, George, 'Augustine's First Monastery: Thagaste or Hippo?', *Augustinianum* 25 (1985), 65–78.

——, 'Augustine of Hippo and His Critics', in Joseph T. Linehard, E. C. Miller, and R. J. Tesker (eds.), *Collectanea augustiniana: Augustine presbyter factus sum* (New York: Peter Lang, 1993), 3–27.

Lecrivain, H., 'Explicaiton d'une loi du code Théodosien (XVI.2.38)', *Mélanges d'Archéologie et d'Histoire de l'École Française de Rome*, 10 (1890), 253–6.

Lendon, J. E., *Empire of Honor* (Oxford: Clarendon Press, 1997).

Lenski, Noel, 'Evidence for the *Audientia Episcopalis* in the New Letters of Augustine', in Ralph W. Mathisen (ed.), *Law, Society, and Authority in Late Antiquity* (Oxford: Oxford University Press, 2001), 83–97.

Lepelley, Claude, *Les Cités de l'Afrique romaine au Bas-Empire*, 2 vols (Paris: Études Augustiniennes, 1979–81).

——, 'Un Aspect de la conversion d'Augustin: La Rupture avec ses ambitions sociales et politiques', *Bulletin de Littérature Ecclesiastique*, 88 (1987), 229–46.

——, 'Trois documents méconnus sur l'histoire sociale et religieuse de l'Afrique romaine tardive, retrouvés parmi les *Spuria* de Sulpice Sévère', *Antiquités Africaines*, 25 (1989), 235–62.

——, 'Les Sénateurs Donatistes', *Bulletin de la Société Nationale des Antiquaires de France*, 119 (1990), 45–56.

——, *Aspects de l'Afrique Romaine: Les Cités, la vie rurale, le christianisme* (Bari: Edipuglia, 2001).

——, 'Quelques aspects de l'administration des provinces romaines d'Afrique avant la conquête vandale', *Antiquité Tardive*, 10 (2002), 61–72.

Leyser, Conrad, *Authority and Asceticism from Augustine to Gregory the Great* (Oxford: Clarendon Press, 2000).

Liebs, Detlef, 'Römische Jurisprudenz in Africa', *Zeitschrift der Savigny-Stiftung für Rechtsgeschichte: Romanistische Abteilung*, 106 (1989), 210–47.

Lim, Richard, *Public Disputation, Power, and Social Order in Late Antiquity*. (Berkeley: University of California Press, 1995).

Lizzi, Rita, 'Ambrose's Contemporaries and the Christianization of Northern Italy', *Journal of Roman Studies*, 80 (1990), 156–73.

Lorenz, Rudolf, 'Der Augustinismus Prospers von Aquitanien', *Zeitschrift für Kirchengeschichte*, 73 (1962), 217–52.

——, 'Die Anfänge des abendländischen Mönchtums im 4. Jahrhundert', *Zeitschrift für Kirchengeschichte*, 77 (1966), 1–61.

Lössl, Joseph, '"Te Apulia genuit" (*c. Iul. imp.* 6.18): Some Notes on the Birthplace of Julian of Eclanum', *Revue des Études Augustiniennes*, 44 (1998), 223–39.

——, 'Augustine in Byzantium', *Journal of Ecclesiastical History*, 51 (2000), 267–95.

——, *Julian von Aeclanum: Studien zu seinem Leben, seinem Werk, seiner Lehre und ihrer Überlieferung.* (Leiden: Brill 2001).

Lucas, Christian, 'Notes on the *Curatores Rei Publicae* of Roman North Africa', *Journal of Roman Studies*, 30 (1940), 56–74.

Luck, Georg, 'Die Form der suetonischen Biographie und die frühen Heiligenviten', *Mullus, Jahrbuch für Antike und Christentum*, 1 (1964), 230–41. Also published as 'The Literary Form of Suetonius' Biographies and the Early Lives of Saints', in *Ancient Pathways and Hidden Pursuits: Religion, Morals, and Magic in the Ancient World* (Ann Arbor: University of Michigan Press, 2000), 166–80.

MacCormack, Sabine, 'Sin, Citizenship, and the Salvation of Souls: The Impact of Christian Priorities on Late-Roman and Post-Roman Society', *Comparative Studies in Society and History*, 39 (1997), 644–73.

——, *The Shadows of Poetry: Vergil in the Mind of Augustine* (Berkeley: University of California Press, 1998).

McLynn, Neil B., *Ambrose of Milan: Church and Court in a Christian Capital* (Berkeley: University of California Press, 1994).

——, 'From Palladius to Maximinus: Passing the Arian Torch', *Journal of Early Christian Studies*, 4 (1996), 477–93.

——, 'Augustine's Roman Empire', *Augustinian Studies*, 30 (1999), 29–44.

——, '"Genere Hispanus": Theodosius, Spain, and Nicene Orthodoxy', in Kim Bowes and Michael Kulilowski (eds.), *Hispania in Late Antiquity* (Boston: Brill, 2005), 77–120.

MacMullen, Ramsay, 'The Preacher's Audience (AD 350–400)', *Journal of Theological Studies*, n.s., 40 (1989), 503–11.

Madec, Goulven, 'Possidius de Calama et les listes des oeuvres d'Augustin', in Jean-Claude Fredouille et al., (eds.), *Titres et articulations du texte dans les oeuvres antiques: Actes du colloque international de Chantilly, 13–15 decembre, 1994.* (Institut d'Études Augustiniennes, 1994), 427–45.

——, *Introductions aux 'Révisions' et à la lecture des oeuvres de saint Augustin* (Institut d'Études Augustiniennes, 1996).

Madec, Goulven, *Saint Augustin: La Vie communautaire: Traduction annotée des sermons 355–356* (Institut d'Études Augustiniennes, 1996).

——, 'Augustin évêque', in Goulven Madec (ed.), *Augustin prédicateur (395–411): Actes du Colloque International de Chantilly (5–7 septembre 1996)* (Institut d'Études Augustiniennes, 1998), 11–32.

Magnou-Nortier, Élisabeth, 'Sur l'origine des Constitutions Sirmondiennes', *Revue de Droit Canonique*, 51/2 (2001), 279–303.

Maier, Jean-Louis, *Le Dossier du Donatisme*, 2 vols (Akademic Verlag 1987–9).

Mandouze, André, 'Encore le Donatisme: Problèmes de méthode posés par la thèse de J. P. Brisson', *L'Antiquite Classique*, 29 (1960), 61–107.

——, *Saint Augustin: L'Aventure de la raison et de la grâce* (Paris: Études Augustiniennes, 1968).

——, *Prosopographie chrétienne du Bas-Empire: Prosopographie de l'Afrique chrétienne (303–533)* (Paris: Éditions de Centre National de la Recherche Scientifique, 1982).

Mansfeld, Jaap, *Prolegomena: Questions to Be Settled before the Study of an Author, or a Text* (Leiden: Brill, 1994).

Markus, Robert A., *Saeculum: History and Society in the Theology of St. Augustine* (Cambridge: Cambridge University Press, 1970).

——, 'Christianity and Dissent in Roman North Africa: Changing Perspectives in Recent Work', in Derek Baker (ed.), *Schism, Heresy, and Religious Protest* (Cambridge: Cambridge University Press, 1972), 21–36.

——, 'Country Bishops in Byzantine Africa', in Derek Baker (ed.), *The Church in Town and Countryside* (Oxford: B. Blackwell, 1979), 1–15.

——, *Sacred and Secular: Studies on Augustine and Christianity* (Norfolk: Variorum, 1984).

——, 'Chronicle and Theology: Prosper of Aquitaine', in Christopher Holdsworth and T. P. Wiseman (eds.), *The Inheritance of Historiography, 350–900* (Exeter: University of Exeter, 1986), 31–43.

——, 'Augustine's *Confessions* and the Controversy with Julian of Eclanum: Manicheism Revisited', in B. Bruning, M. Lamberigts, and J. van Houtem (eds.), *Collectanea augustiniana: Mélanges T. J. van Bavel* (Leuven: University Press, 1990), 913–25.

——, *The End of Ancient Christianity* (Cambridge: Cambridge University Press, 1992).

——, 'L'Authorité épiscopale et la définition de la Chrétienté', in *Vescovi e pastori in epoca teodosiana*, Studia Ephemeridis Augustinianum 58 (Rome: Institutum Patristium Augustinianum, 1997), 37–43.

——, 'Africa and the Orbis Terrarum: The Theological Problem', in Pierre-Yves Fux, Jean-Michel Roessli, and Otto Wermelinger (eds.), *Augustinus Afer: Saint Augustin, africanité, et universalité: Actes du colloque international, Alger-Annaba, 1–7 avril 2001* (Fribourg: Éditions Universitaires Fribourg Suisse, 2003), 321–7.

Marrou, Henri-Irénée, 'La Technique de l'édition à l'époque patristique', *Vigiliae Christianae*, 3 (1949), 208–24.

——, 'La Division en chapitres des livres de la "Cite de Dieu"', in *Mélanges Joseph de Ghellinck* (Gembloux: J. Duculot, 1951), 235–49.

——, *Saint Augustin et la fin de la culture antique* (Paris: Éditions E. de Boccard, 1958).

Martroye, M. François, 'La Repression du Donatisme et la politique religieuse de Constantin et de ses successeurs en Afrique', *Mémoires de la Société Nationale des Antiquaires de France*, 13 (1914), 23–140.

Maschio, Giovanni, 'L'Argomentazione patristica di s. Agostino nella prima fase della controversia pelagiana', *Augustinianum*, 26 (1986), 459–79.

Mathisen, Ralph W., Ecclesiastical Factionalism and Religious Controversy in Fifth-Century Gaul (Washington: Catholic University of America Press, 1989).

——, 'For Specialists Only: The Reception of Augustine and His Teachings in Fifth-Century Gaul', in J. T. Lienhard, E. C. Miller, and R. J. Tesker (eds.), *Collectanea augustiniana: Augustine presbyter factus sum* (New York: Peter Lang, 1993), 29–41.

——, 'Sigisvult the Patrician, Maximinus the Arian, and Political Stratagems in the Western Roman Empire, c.425–40', *Early Medieval Europe*, 8 (1999), 173–96.

——, '*Adnotatio* and *Petitio*: The Emperor's Favor and Special Exceptions in the Early Byzantine Empire', in Dennis Feissel and Jean Gascou (eds.), *La Pétition à Byzance* (Paris: Association des Amis du Centre d'Histoire et Civilization de Byzance, 2004), 23–32.

Matthews, John F., *Western Aristocracies and Imperial Court, AD 364–425* (Oxford: Clarendon Press, 1975).

——, *Political Life and Culture in Late Roman Society* (London: Variorum Reprint, 1985).

——, 'The Making of the Text', in Jill Harries and Ian Wood (eds.), *The Theodosian Code* (Ithaca: Cornell University Press, 1993), 19–44.

——, *Laying Down the Law: A Study of the Theodosian Code* (New Haven: Yale University Press, 2000).

Merdinger. J. E., *Rome and the African Church in the Time of Augustine* (New Haven: Yale University, 1997).

Merrills, A. H., *History and Geography in Late Antiquity* (Cambridge: Cambridge University Press, 2005).

Moatti, Claudia. 'Translation, Migration, and Communication in the Roman Empire: Three Aspects of Movement in History', *Classical Antiquity*, 25 (2006), 109–40.

Modéran, Yves, 'Gildon, les Maures, et l'Afrique', *Melanges de l'École Française de Rome, Antiquité*, 101 (1989), 821–72.

——, 'L'Établissement territorial des Vandales en Afrique', *Antiquité Tardive*, 10 (2002), 87–122.

——, 'Une Guerre de religion: Les Deux Églises d'Afrique à l'époque vandale', *Antiquité Tardive*, 11 (2003), 21–44.

Mohrmann, Christine, *Die altchristliche Sondersprache in den Sermones des hl. Augustin* (Nijmegen: N. V. Dekker & Van de Vegt en J. W. van Leeuwen, 1932).

——, 'Zwei Frühchristliche Beschofsviten: *Vita Ambrosii, Vita Augustini*', *Österreichische Akademie der Wissenschaften Philosophisch-Historische Klasse Anzeiger*, 112 (1975), 307–31.

Mommsen, Theodor, 'Sanctio Pragmatica', in *Gesammelte Schriften* 2/2 (Berlin: Weidmann, 1905), 426–8.

Mommsen, Theodor E., 'Orosius and Augustine', in Eugene F. Rice, Jr. (ed.), *Medieval and Renaissance Studies* (Ithaca: Cornell University Press, 1959), 325–48.

Monceaux, Paul, *Histoire littéraire de l'Afrique chrétienne depuis les origins jusqu'a l'invasion arabe*, 7 vols (Paris: Éditions Ernest Leroux, 1912–23; reprint Brussels, Culture et Civilization, 1966).

Moreau, Madeline, *Le Dossier Marcellinus dans le correspondence de saint Augustin* (Paris: Études Augustiniennes, 1973).

——, 'Le Magistrat et l'évêque: Pour une lecture de la correspondence Macedonius-Augustine', *Recherches et Travaux*, 54 (1998), 105–17.

Morgenstern, Frank, 'Die Kaisergesetze gegen die Donatisten in Nordafrika (Mitte 4 Jh. Bis 429)', *Zeitschrift der Savigny-Stiftung für Rechtsgeschichte. Romanistische Abteilung*, 110 (1993), 103–23.

Morin, G., 'Lettres inédites de S. Augustin et du prêtre Januarien dans l'affaire des moines d'Adrumète', *Revue Benédictine*, 18 (1901), 241–56.

Mratschek, Sigrid, 'Multis enim notissima est sanctitas loci: Paulinus and the Gradual Rise of Nola as a Center of Christian Hospitality', *Journal of Early Christian Studies*, 9 (2001), 511–53.

Mratschek, Sigrid, '*Te velimus...consilii participem*: Augustine of Hippo and Olympius, A Case Study of Religious–Political Cooperation in the Fifth Century', *Studia Patristica*, 38 (2001), 224–32.

——, *Der Briefwechsel des Paulinus von Nola: Kommunikation und soziale Kontakte zwischen christlichen Intellektuellen* (Göttingen: Vandenhoeck & Ruprecht, 2002).

Munier, Charles, 'Vers une édition nouvelle des Conciles Africains (345–525)', *Revue des Études Augustiniennes*, 18 (1972), 249–59. Reprinted in *Vie conciliaire et collections canoniques en Occident, IVe–XIIe siècles* (London: Variorum Reprint, 1987).

Munier, Charles, *Concilia Africae (a. 345–a. 525)*, Corpus Christianorum Series Latina 149 (Turnholt: Brepols, 1974).

——, 'La Tradition littéraire des dossiers africains', *Revue de Droit Canonique*, 29 (1979), 41–52. Reprinted in *Vie conciliaire et collections canoniques en Occident, IVe–XIIe siècles* (London: Variorum Reprints, 1987).

——, 'La Tradition littéraire des canons africains (345–525)', *Recherches Augustiniennes*, 10 (1975), 3–22. Reprinted in *Vie conciliaire et collections canoniques en Occident, IVe–XIIe siècles* (London: Variorum Reprints, 1987).

——, 'La Question des appels à Rome d'après la lettre 20* d'Augustin', in *Les Lettres de saint Augustin découvertes par Johnannes Divjak: Communications presentées au colloque des 20 et 21 Septembre 1982* (Paris: Études Augustiniennes, 1983), 287–99. Reprinted in *Vie conciliaire et collections canoniques en Occident, IVe–XIIe siècles* (London: Variorum Reprints, 1987).

——, 'L'Influence de saint Augustin sur la législation ecclésiastique de son temps', in Pierre-Yves Fux, Jean-Michel Roessli, and Otto Wermelinger (eds.), *Augustinus Afer: Saint Augustin, africanité, et universalité: Actes du colloque international, Alger-Annaba, 1–7 avril 2001* (Fribourg: Éditions Universitaries Fribourg Suisse, 2003), 109–23.

Murphy, Francis X., 'Rufinus of Aquileia and Paulinus of Nola', *Revue des Études Augustiniennes*, 2 (1956), 81–91.

Mutzenbecher, Almut, 'Bemerkungen zum Indiculum des Possidius: Eine Rezension', *Revue des Études Augustiniennes*, 33 (1987), 128–31.

Ocker, Christopher, 'Augustine, Episcopal Interests, and the Papacy in Late Roman Africa', *Journal of Ecclesiastical History*, 42 (1991), 179–201.
O'Donnell, James J., 'Augustine's Classical Readings', *Recherches Augustiniennes*, 15 (1980), 144–75.
——, 'The Authority of Augustine', *Augustinian Studies*, 22 (1991), 7–35.
——, *Augustine Confessions* (Oxford: Oxford University Press, 1992).
——, 'The Next Life of Augustine', in William E. Klingshirn and Mark Vessey (eds.), *The Limits of Ancient Christianity: Essays on Late Antique Thought and Culture in Honor of R. A. Markus* (Ann Arbor: University of Michigan Press, 1999), 215–31.
——, *Augustine: A New Biography* (New York: Ecco, 2005).
O'Meara, J. J., *The Young Augustine: An Introduction to the 'Confessions' of St. Augustine* (London: Longman, 1980).
Pellegrino, Michele, 'Reminiscenze letterarie agostiniane nella *Vita Augustini* di Possidio', *Aevum*, 28 (1954), 21–44.
——, *Vita di S. Augustino* (Alba: Edizioni Paoline, 1955).
——, 'S. Agostino visto dal suo primo biografo Possidio', In *Augustiniana: Napoli a S. Agostino nel XVI centenario della nascita* (Naples: Istituto Editoriale del Mezzogiorno, 1955), 45–61.
——, 'Intorno al testo della vita di S. Agostino scritta da Possidio', in *Mémorial Gustave Bardy* (Paris: Études Augustiniennes, 1956), 195–229.
Perler, Othmar, 'Le "De unitiate" (Chap. IV–V) de saint Cyprien interprété par saint Augustin', in *Augustinus magister* (Paris: Études Augustiniennes, 1955), 835–58.
Perler, Othmar, and J. L. Maier, *Les Voyages de saint Augustin* (Paris: Études Augustiniennes, 1969).
Pétré, H., '*Haeresis*, *Schisma* et leurs synonyms latins', *Revue des Études Latines*, 15 (1937), 316–25.
Picard, Gilbert-Charles, *La Civilisation de l'Afrique romaine* (Paris: Études Augustiniennes, 1990).
Pintard, Jacques, 'Sur la succession apostolique selon saint Augustin', in *Forma futuri: Studi in onore del cardinale Michele Pellegrino* (Turin: Bottege d'Erasmo, 1975), 884–95.
Plagnieux, J., 'Le Grief de complicité entre erreurs nestorienne et pélagienne: D'Augustin à Cassien par Prosper d'Aquitaine?', in *Memorial Gustave Bardy* (Paris: Études Augustiniennes, 1956), 391–402.
Raikas, K. K., 'St. Augustine on Juridical Duties: Some Aspects of the Episcopal Courts in Late Antiquity', in Joseph C. Schnaubelt and Frederick Van Fleteren (eds.), *Collectanea Augustiniana: Augustine—Second Founder of the Faith* (New York: Peter Lang, 1990), 467–83.
——, '*Audientia Episcopalis*: Problematik zwischen Staat und Kirche bei Augustin', *Augustinianum*, 37 (1997), 459–81.
——, 'The State Juridical Dimension of the Office of a Bishop in Letter 153 of Augustine to Vicarius Africae Macedonius', *Vescovi Pastori in Epoca Teodosiana, Studia Ephemeridia Augustinianum*, 58 (Rome: Institutum Patristicum Augustinianum, 1997), 683–94.
Rapp, Claudia, 'Storytelling as Spiritual Communication in Early Greek Hagiography: The Use of Diegesis', *Journal of Early Christian Studies*, 6/3 (1998), 431–48.

Rebillard, Éric, *In hora mortis: Évolution de la pastorale chrétienne de la mort aux IVe et Ve siècles dans l'occident latin* (Rome: École Française de Rome, 1994).

——, 'Augustin et le rituel épistolaire de l'élite sociale et culturelle de son temps', in É. Rebillard and C. Sotinel (eds.), *L'Évêque dans la cité du IVe au Ve siècle: Image et authorité* (Rome: École Française de Rome, 1998), 127–52.

——, 'A New Style of Argument in Christian Polemic: Augustine and the Use of Patristic Citations', *Journal of Early Christian Studies*, 8 (2000), 559–78.

——, 'Sociologie de la Déviance et Orthodoxie', in S. Elm, É. Rebillard, and A. Romano (eds.), *Orthodoxie, christianisme, histoire* (Rome: École Française de Rome, 2000), 221–40.

——, 'Augustine et ses autorités: L'Élaboration de l'argument patristique au cours de la controverse pélagienne', *Studia Patristica*, 38 (2001), 245–63.

Reiner, Englebert, 'Sanctio pragmatica', *Revue Historique de Droit Français et Étranger*, 22 (1943), 209–16.

Riggs, D., 'The Continuity of Paganism between the Cities and Countryside of Late Roman Africa', in T. Burns and J. Eadie (eds.), *Urban Centers and Rural Contexts in Late Antiquity* (Lansing: Michigan State Press, 2001), 285–300.

Rist, John M., *Augustine: Ancient Thought Baptized* (Cambridge: Cambridge University Press, 1994).

Roda, Sergio, *Commento storico al libro IX dell'Epistolario di Q. Aurelio Summaco* (Pisa: Giardini Editori e Stampatori, 1981).

Roueché, Charlotte, 'Acclamations in the Later Roman Empire: New Evidence from Aphrodisias', *Journal of Roman Studies*, 74 (1984), 181–99.

——, 'The Functions of the Governor in Late Antiquity: Some Observations', *Antiquité Tardive*, 6 (1998), 31–6.

Rousseau, Philip, 'The Spiritual Authority of the "Monk-Bishop": Eastern Elements in Some Western Hagiography of the Fourth and Fifth Centuries', *Journal of Theological Studies*, n.s., 23/2 (1971), 380–419.

——, 'Augustine and Ambrose: The Loyalty and Singlemindedness of a Disciple', *Augustiniana*, 27 (1977), 151–65.

Rousseau, Philip, *Ascetics, Authority, and the Church in the Age of Jerome and Cassian* (Oxford: Oxford University Press, 1987).

Russell, Frederick H., 'Persuading the Donatists: Augustine's Coercion by Words', in William Klingshirn and Mark Vessey (eds.), *The Limits of Ancient Christianity: Essays on Late Antique Thought and Culture in Honor of R. A. Markus* (Ann Arbor: University of Michigan Press, 1999), 115–50.

Salzman, Michele Renee, 'The Evidence for the Conversion of the Roman Empire to Christianity in Book 16 of the *Theodosian Code*', *Historia*, 42 (1993), 362–78.

——, *The Making of a Christian Aristocracy: Social and Religious Change in the Western Roman Empire* (Cambridge: Harvard University Press, 2002).

Saxer, Victor, *Morts martyrs reliques en Afrique chrétienne aux premiers siècles* (Paris: Éditions Beauchesne, 1980).

Scheele, Jürgen, 'Buch und Bibliothek bei Augustinus', *Bibliothek und Wissenschaft*, 12 (1978), 14–114.

Schindler, Alfred, 'Die Unterscheidung von Schisma und Haresie in Gesetzgebung und Polemik gegen den Donatismus (mit einer Bemerkung zur Datierung von Augustins Schrift: *Contra Epistulam Parmeniani)*', in Ernst Dassmann and K. Suso Frank (eds.), *Pietas: Festschrift für Bernhard Kötting* (Münster: Aschendorffsche Verlagsbushhandlong, 1980), 228–36.

——, 'Die Theologie der Donatisten und Augustins Reaktion', in Cornelius Mayer and Karl Heinz Chelius (eds.), *Internationales Symposion über den Stand der Augustinus-Forschung* (Würzburg: Augustinus–Verlag, 1989), 131–47.

Seeck, Otto, *Regesten der Kaiser und Päpste für die Jahre 311 bis 476n. Chr.* (Stuttgart: J. B. Metzlersche Verlagsbuchhandlung; reprint Frankfurt: Minerra, 1964).

Shanzer, Danuta, '"Arcanum Varronis iter": Licentius' Verse Epistle to Augustine', *Revue des Études Augustiniennes*, 37 (1991), 110–43.

Shaw, Brent D., 'African Christianity: Disputes, Definitions, and "Donatists"', in Malcolm R. Greenshields and Thomas A. Robinson (eds.), *Orthodoxy and Heresy in Religious Movements: Discipline and Dissent* (Lewiston: Lampeter, 1992), 5–34.

——, *Rulers, Nomads, and Christians in Roman North Africa* (Aldershot: Variorum, 1995).

——, 'Judicial Nightmares and Christian Memory', *Journal of Early Christian Studies*, 11 (2003), 533–63.

——, 'Who Were the Circumcellions?', in A. H. Merrills (ed.), *Vandals, Romans, and Berbers: New Perspectives on Late Antique North Africa.* (Burlington: Ashgate, 2004), 227–58.

Sieben, Hermann Josef, *Die Konzilsidee der Alten Kirche* (Paderborn: Ferdinand Schöningh, 1979).

Sirks, Boudewijn, 'From the Theodosian to the Justinian Code', in *Atti dell'Accademia romanistica costantiniana: VI Convegno internazionale* (Persuii: Studium Generale Civitato, 1986), 265–302.

——, 'The Sources of the Code', in Jill Harries and Ian Wood (eds.), *The Theodosian Code* (Ithaca: Cornell University Press, 1993), 45–67.

——, 'Sailing in the Off-Season with Reduced Financial Risk', in Jean-Jacques Aubert and Boudewijn Sirks (eds.), *Speculum iuris: Roman Law as a Reflection of Social and Economic Life in Antiquity* (Ann Arbor: University Michigan Press, 2002), 134–50.

Sotinel, Claire, 'Personnel épiscopal: Enquête sur la puissance de l'éveque dans la cité', in É. Rebillard and C. Sotinel (eds.), *L'Évêque dans la cité du IVe au Ve siècle: Image et authorité* (Rome: École Française de Rome, 1998), 105–26.

Stein, Ernest, *Histoire du Bas-Empire*, tr. Jean-Remy Palanque (Amsterdam: Adolf M. Hakkert, 1959; reprint 1968).

Steinwenter, Artur, 'Eine kirchliche Quelle des nachklassischen Zivilprozesses', *Acta Congressus Iuridici Internationalis VII Saeculo*, 2 (1935), 123–44.

Stock, Brian, *Augustine the Reader: Meditation, Self-Knowledge, and the Ethics of Interpretation* (Cambridge MA: Belknap Press of Harvard University, 1996).

——, 'La Connaissance de soi au Moyen Âge', in *Collège de France, Leçon Inauguarale faite le vendredi 9 janvier 1998* (Paris: Collège de France, 1998), 5–29.

Stoll, Brigitta, 'Einige Beobachtungen zur *Vita Augustini* des Possidius', *Studia Patristica*, 22 (1989), 344–50.

——, 'Die *Vita Augustini* des Possidius als hagiographischer Text', *Zeitschrift für Kirchengeschichte*, 102 (1991), 1–13.

Straw, C., 'Augustine as Pastoral Theologian: The Exegesis of the Parables of the Field and Threshing Floor', *Augustinian Studies*, 14 (1983), 129–51.

Sundwall. J., *Weströmische Studien* (Berlin: Mayer & Müller, 1915).

Teitler, H. C., *Notarii and Exceptores: An Inquiry into Role and Significance of Shorthand Writers in the Imperial and Eccclesiastical Bureaucracy of the Roman Empire* (Amsterdam: J. C. Gieben, Publisher, 1985).

Tengström, Emin, *Die Protokollierung der collatio Carthaginiensis: Beiträge zur Kenntnis der römischen Kurzschrift nebst einem Exkurs über das Wort scheda (schedula)* (Göteburg: Elanders Boktryckeri Aktiebolag, 1962).

——, *Donatisten und Katholiken: Soziale, wirtschaftliche und politische Aspekte einer nordafrikanischen Kirchenspaltung* (Göteburg: Elanders Boktryckeri Aktiebolag, 1964).

——, *Bread for the People: Studies of the Corn-Supply of Rome during the Late Empire* (Stockholm: Acta Instituti Romani Regni Succine[Paul Åström Förlag], 1974).

TeSelle, Eugene, 'Porphyry and Augustine', *Augustinian Studies*, 5 (1974), 113–47.

Tilley, Maureen A., 'Dilatory Donatists or Procrastinating Catholics: The Trial at the Conference of Carthage', *Church History*, 60 (1991), 7–19.

——, *The Bible in Christian North Africa* (Minneapolis: Fortress Press, 1997).

——, 'Sustaining Donatist Self-Identity: From the Church of the Martyrs to the *Collecta* of the Desert', *Journal of Early Christian Studies*, 5 (1997), 21–35.

Trout, Dennis, 'The Dates of the Ordination of Paulinus of Bordeaux and His Departure for Nola', *Revue des Études Augustiniennes*, 37 (1991), 237–60.

Trout, Dennis, *Paulinus of Nola: Life, Letters, and Poems* (Berkeley: University of California Press 1999).

Turpin, William, '*Adnotatio* and Imperial Rescript in Roman Legal Procedure', *Revue Internationale des Droits de L'Antiquité*, 35 (1988), 285–307.

——, 'Imperial Inscriptions and the Administration of Justice', *Journal of Roman Studies*, 81 (1991), 101–18.

Uhalde, Kevin, 'Proof and Reproof: The Judicial Component of Episcopal Confrontation', *Early Medieval Europe*, 8 (1999), 1–11.

Van der Meer, F., *Augustine the Bishop: The Life and Work of a Father of the Church*, tr. Brian Battershaw and G. R. Lamb (London: Sheed and Ward, 1961).

Vega, P. Angelus C., *Opuscula sancti Possidii episcopi Calamensis: Vita sancti Augustini et Indiculum librorum eius* (Escoreal: Typis Augustinians, 1934).

Verheijen, L. M. J., 'La Vie de saint Augustin par Possidius et la Regula Sancti Augustini', in *Mélanges Offerts à Christine Mohrmann* (Utrecht: Spectrum Editeurs, 1963), 270–9.

Verheijen, L. M. J., 'La Règle de saint Augustin: L'État actuel des questions (début 1975)', *Augustiniana*, 35 (1985), 193–263.

Vernay, Eugène, 'Note sur le changement de style dans les constitutions impériales de Dioclétian à Constantin', *Études d'Histoire Juridique Offertes à Paul Frédéric Girard* (Paris: Librairie Paul Geuthner, 1912–13), 263–74.

Vessey, Mark, *Ideas of Christian Writing in Late Roman Gaul*, Ph.D. dissertation, Oxford University, 1988.

——, 'Literacy and *Litteratura*, A.D. 200–800', *Studies in Medieval and Renaissance History*, n.s., 13 (1992), 139–60.

——, 'Jerome's Origen: The Making of a Christian Literary *Persona*', *Studia Patristica*, 28 (1993), 135–45.

——, 'The Origins of the *Collectio Sirmondiana*: A New Look at the Evidence', in Jill Harries and Ian Wood (eds.), *The Theodosian Code* (Ithaca: Cornell University Press, 1993), 178–99.

——, 'Peregrinus against the Heretics: Classicism, Provinciality, and the Place of the Alien Writer in Late Roman Gaul', in *Cristianesimo e specificità regionali nel Mediterraneo latino (sec. IV–VI)* (Rome: Institutum Patristicum Augustinianum, 1994), 529–65.

——, 'The Forging of Orthodoxy in Latin Christian Literature: A Case Study', *Journal of Early Christian Studies*, 4 (1996), 495–513.

——, 'The Demise of the Christian Writer and the Remaking of "Late Antiquity": From H.-I. Marrou's Saint Augustine (1938) to Peter Brown's Holy Man (1983)', *Journal of Early Christian Studies*, 6 (1998), 377–411.

——, 'Opus Imperfectum: Augustine and His Readers, A.D. 426–35', *Vigiliae Christianiae*, 52 (1998), 264–85.

——, 'The Great Conference: Augustine and His Fellow Readers', in Pamela Bright (ed.), *Augustine and the Bible* (Notre Dam: The University of Notre Dame Press, 1999), 52–73.

——, 'Possidius', in Allan D. Fitzgerald (ed.), *Augustine Through the Ages: An Encyclopedia* (Grand Rapids: William B. Eerdmans Publishers, 1999), 668.

——, 'The *Epistula Rustici ad Eucherium*: From the Library of Imperial Classics to the Library of the Fathers', in Ralph W. Mathisen and Danuta Shanzer (eds.), *Society and Culture in Late Antique Gaul: Revisiting the Sources* (Aldershot: Ashgate Publishing Ltd., 2001), 278–97.

——, 'From *Cursus* to *Ductus*: Figures of Writing in Western Late Antiquity (Augustine, Jerome, Cassiodorus, Bede)', in Patrick Cheney and Frederick A. de Armas (eds.), *European Literary Careers: The Author from Antiquity to the Renaissance* (Toronto: University of Toronto Press, 2002), 47–103.

——, 'Sacred Letters of the Law: The Emperor's Hand in Late Roman (Literary) History', *Antiquité Tardive*, 11 (2003), 345–58.

——, 'Introduction', in James W. Halporn (trans.), *Cassiodorus: Institutions of Divine and Secular Learning on the Soul* (Liverpool: Liverpool University Press, 2004), 3–101.

Vidén, Gunhild, *The Roman Chancery Tradition: Studies in the Language of Codex Theodosianus and Cassiodorus' Variae* (Göteborg: Acta Universitatis Gothoburgensis, 1984).

Voltera, Edoardo, 'Appunti intorno all'intervento del vescovo nei processi contro gli eretici', *Bullettino dell'Istituto di Diritto Romano*, 42 (1934), 453–68.

Vössing, Konrad, *Schule und Bildung im Nordafrika der römischen Kaiserseit* (Brussels: Latomus, 1997).

Weaver, Rebecca Harden, *Divine Grace and Human Agency* (Macon: Mercer University Press, 1996).

Weidmann, Clemens, *Augustinus und das Maximianistenkonzil von Cebarsussi: zur historischen und Textgeschichtlichen Bedeutung von Enarrtio in Psalmum 36, 2, 18–23* (Vienna Verlag der Österreichischer Akademic der Wiisenschaffen, 1998).

Weiskotten, H. T., *Sancti Augustini scripta a Possidio episcopo: Edited with Revised Text, Introduction, Notes, and an English Translation* (Princeton: Princeton University Press, 1919).

Wermelinger, Otto, *Rom und Pelagius: Die theologische Position der römischen Bischöfe im pelagianischen Streit in den Jahren 411–432* (Stuttgart: A. Hiersemann, 1975).

Williams, Jeremy, 'Collatio of 411', in Allan D. Fitzgerald (ed.), *Augustine Through the Ages: An Encyclopedia* (Grand Rapids: William B. Eerdmans Publishers, 1999), 218–19.

Willis, Geoffrey Grimshaw, *Saint Augustine and the Donatist Controversy* (London: S.P.C.K., 1950).

Wyrick, Jed, *The Ascension of Authorship: Attribution and Canon Formation in Jewish, Hellenistic, and Christian Traditions* (Cambridge, MA: Harvard University Press, MA, 2004).

Zocca, Elena, 'La figura del Santo Vescovo in Africa da Ponzio a Possidio', in *Vescovi e pastori in epoca theodosiana: Studia ephemeridis augustinianum* 58 (Rome: Institutum Patristicum Augustinianum, 1997), 469–92.

Index

Alaric, king of the Visigoths 169, 170, 173
Alypius, Catholic bishop of Thagaste 11, 18 n. 5, 38, 45, 53, 109 n. 40, 148
 at 411 conference 204
 at court 134, 222
Ambrose of Milan 41 n. 98, 47 n. 123, 75, 223
 in the *Vita Augustini* 26–9, 30, 65, 71, 77
Ammianus Marcellinus 123 n. 86
Anthony, Catholic Bishop of Fussala 221
Apiarius, Catholic priest of Sicca Veneria 222
Apringius, proconsul of Africa 85, 155, 191
audientia episcopalis (bishops' courts) 13, 43, 87, 99, 100
Augustine:
 ambushed 69, 137
 books 14, 45, 65
 conversion 26–28
 death 55, 60–61
 invective against 4, 20, 36–6
 library at Hippo 2, 4, 59, 63, 64, 87, 227
 and Manichaeans 26, 27, 37
 and monastery at Hippo 1, 2, 4, 5, 11, 40–2, 87, 62–63
 and predestination 20, 39
 and Roman law 3, 43–4, 97–9, 133, 145–8, 154
 WORKS:
 Breviculus conlationis 46, 193, 207
 De civitate Dei 7, 43, 78, 79
 Confessiones 1, 5, 11, 17, 18, 25–30, 32, 34, 37, 38, 42, 45, 52, 72, 75, 224
 Contra Cresconium 101
 Ad Donatistas post conlatione 46
 De dono perseverantiae 52
 Contra epistulam Parmeniani 101, 104
 Contra Felicem 46, 223
 De fide et symbolo 35
 Contra Fortunatum 46
 Gesta cum Emerito 46
 De gestis Pelagii 50
 De gratia et libero arbitrio 39, 54
 De haeresibus 46
 indiculum 57–59
 Retractationes 5, 9, 14, 17, 26, 39, 45, 57, 58, 60, 61, 78, 224
 Ad Simplicianum 39, 52
 Speculum 45, 61
 see also *Vita Augustini*
Augustus, emperor 23 n. 23
Aurelius, Catholic bishop of Carthage 53, 145, 204, 226

Bassus, Anicius Auchenius, consul 88, 173
Bathanarius, *comes Africae* 169
Benenatus, Catholic bishop of Chemtou 188
Bernays, Jacob 24 n. 27
Boniface, *comes Africae* 144, 146, 153

Caecilian, bishop of Carthage 88, 89, 126, 204, 218
Caecilianus, vicar of Africa and praetorian prefect 118 n. 71
Caelestius 52, 53, 95, 222
Cassiodorus 9, 13
Catholic councils:
 council of Nicaea 222, 225 n. 15
 council of Carthage in 393 226
 council of Carthage in 403 109, 212
 council of Carthage in 404 123–5, 151, 152
 council of Carthage in 407 162, 170 n. 43, 226 n. 18
 council of Carthage in June 408 170
 council of Carthage in October 408 171, 175
 council of Carthage in 410 188, 199, 207, 210, 213
 council of Milevis in 416 52, 54
 council of Carthage in 418 54
 see also law
circumcellions 85, 67, 86, 121, 122, 137, 140, 141, 143
Claudian 126
Conference of 411 9, 36, 46, 49, 70, 86, 87, 89, 90, 221
 mandates 192, 194, 199, 205, 207, 208, 212, 213
 preces 192, 195, 199, 201, 207, 208, 212, 213
 rescript of Honorius 194, 196–8, 199, 203, 205, 206, 208
 see also Marcellinus
Constans, emperor 137
Constantine (the Great), emperor 13, 89, 126, 135, 137, 145 n. 38

referenced at 411 conference 192, 211, 212, 218
Cresconius, Donatist grammarian 101, 130
Crispinus, Donatist bishop of Calama 69–70, 71, 87, 110, 111, 118, 131 n. 10, 134, 152, 164, 221
  appeal to emperor 117, 149
  attack on Possidius in 403/404 113–14, 154, 166
  as landowner 105–6, 153
  proconsul rules on 97, 115–17, 126
  status 69, 87
Cyprian, bishop of Carthage 13, 21, 22, 31, 54, 55, 57, 71, 72, 128, 225

Deuterius, Catholic bishop of Caesarea 147, 148
Diocletian, emperor 151, 227
Diotimus, proconsul of Africa 118, 119
Donatists 2, 7, 12, 22, 31, 37, 87, 88, 101–2, 106, 120, 121, 122, 123, 124, 132, 188
  Donatist councils: council of Bagai 127, 135; council of 403 110–11, 142; Donatist embassies 49, 116, 119, 201, 202, 210, 211, 217; and the law 89–94, 100, 105; and North Africa 84–6, 98; as represented in the *Vita Augustini* 45, 48–50, 66–71; *see also* law
Donatus, Proconsul of Africa 155, 156, 157, 185, 187

The Edict of Unity (405) 93, 101, 106 n. 34, 118, 119, 136, 156, 165, 190, 201, 217
  description of 150–3
Emeritus, Donatist bishop of Caesarea 71, 147
  at 411 conference 192, 202, 205, 207, 218
  meeting with Augustine in 418 49, 50, 75, 94
Eucherius, son of Stilicho 169
Eugippius 9
Eusebius of Caesarea 56
Evodius, Catholic bishop of Uzalis 8, 11, 18 n. 5, 37, 45, 53
  attacked in 408 156, 171
  embassies to court 125, 139, 146, 149, 150, 152,
  library 42

Faustus, Manichean bishop 130
Felix of Abthungi 88, 89, 204
Firmus, Moorish prince 84
Florentius, Catholic bishop of Hippo

Diarrhytus 1 n. 1, 147 n. 43
  embassies to court 171, 172, 179, 188, 191
Fortunatianus, Catholic bishop of Sicca Veneria 1 n. 3, 11, 45, 164, 204
  embassies to court 162, 170, 172
Fortunatus, Catholic bishop of Constantine 204
Fortunatus, Manichaean priest 46, 223

Genethlius, Catholic Bishop of Carthage 145
Gennadius 9
Gildo, *comes Africae* 84, 85, 86, 104, 126, 135 n. 7

Heraclian, *comes Africae* 85, 188
heresy 92–3, 128–31, 145, 146, 147, 148
Hierus, vicar of Africa 128
Honoratus, Catholic bishop of Thiabe 60, 63
Honorius, Catholic bishop of Cartenna 148
Honorius, emperor 90, 93, 104, 116, 124, 125, 156, 161, 170, 174, 175, 179
  and 411 conference 50, 94, 187–91, 195–7, 199, 206–8, 213, 215–17
  Donatist appeals to 49, 116, 217
  and Edict of Unity 92, 101, 151, 152
  and Pelagianism 53
  receives wounded bishops in 404, 149–150

Indiculum 9, 10, 14, 19, 46, 50, 56–60, 64
Innocent, pope 52, 53, 86, 88, 188
Italica 173

Jerome 9 n. 19, 56, 57, 95, 130, 183 n. 86, 338
John, Catholic bishop of Jerusalem 95
Julian, emperor 97, 126, 135 n. 7, 137, 138, 159
Julian of Eclanum 20, 29, 51, 180, 228

Kemper, Franz 24 n. 26

Lactantius, rhetor at Constantine's court 12, 13 n.32, 79
law 11, 13, 20
  Catholic use of 19, 88, 90–8, 100–8, 120–5, 145
  Donatist use of 85, 86, 89, 119, 126–9, 133–4, 171, 206–8, 214–16, 217
  see also Theodosian Code; Sirmondian Constitutions; Edict of Unity
Leo, Friedrich 24

Macarius, Catholic bishop murdered in 408 171

Index

Macedonius, vicar of Africa 43–4, 155
Macrobius, Donatist bishop of Hippo 107 n. 35, 190
Macrobius, proconsul of Africa 189
Manichaeans 42, 46, 91, 122–3, 151, 163, 223
Marcellinus, *tribunus et notarius* 2, 49, 85, 94, 99 n. 6, 155, 189
   presiding over the 411 Conference 49, 94, 189, 191, 192, 194–201, 204–7, 210–14, 216–21
Marcian, Catholic bishop of Urga 136
Marcus, Catholic priest of Casphaliana 136
Martin, Catholic bishop of Tours 22
Massilians or semi-Pelagians 20, 21, 224
Maximian, Donatist / Maximianist bishop of Carthage 126, 127
Maximianists 91, 105, 132, 135–6
   council of Cebarsussa 126–8, 135
Maximianus, Catholic bishop of Bagai 107 n. 35
   attacked by Donatists 138–9, 141, 142
   at court 149, 150
Maximinus, Arian bishop 47, 71
Megalius, Catholic bishop of Calama 20, 35, 36, 167
Memorius, bishop of Eclanum 5, 18 n. 5, 87, 172, 180
Monica, mother of Augustine 26, 32, 34, 173, 180

Nectarius, gentleman of Calama 157, 160, 166–8, 176, 177, 179, 184
notarii 19, 47 n. 121, 127, 192–3

Olympius, *magister officiorum* 169, 171, 172, 175, 180
Optatus of Milevis 129, 135 n. 6, 134, 218
Optatus, Donatist bishop of Timgad 84, 85, 104, 105, 126, 129, 138
Orosius 6, 7, 95, 96

Pascentius, *comes domus regiae* 46, 47
patristic literature 225–8
Paulinus of Milan 6 n. 12, 22, 52, 53, 75, 76
Paulinus of Nola 3, 56 n. 161
   correspondence with Augustine 155, 157, 180, 181, 184, 228
   Possidius visits 88, 172
Pelagianism 7, 8, 28, 29, 42, 45, 50–4, 87, 222, 224
Pelagius 51–3, 95, 222
Petilian, Donatist bishop of Constantine 21 n. 6, 25 n. 30, 35 n. 69, 49
   at 411 conference 202, 211, 213, 216, 218
   kidnapped by Catholics 132 n. 2
Porphyrius, proconsul of Africa 162, 170
Possidius, Catholic bishop of Calama:
   attitude toward episcopate 21–2, 29, 39, 71
   and Augustine's monastery 1
   education 5, 18
   exile 2
   legal activity 11–13, 20, 88, 93–4, 112–17, 156–73
   personality 3, 87, 137, 164–5, 170, 192
   relationship with Augustine 17, 157
   self presentation in the *Vita* 37, 65, 66
   and the written word 7, 74–6
   see also *Vita Augustini*
Praesidius, Catholic bishop 188
Primian, Donatist bishop of Carthage 110, 111, 126, 127, 129, 136, 142
Proculeianus, Donatist bishop of Hippo 107–8, 110, 111
Profuturus, Catholic bishop of Constantine 36 n. 76, 166 n. 31
Prosper of Aquitaine 4, 9, 20, 39, 40, 48, 54

Restitutus, Catholic bishop 171, 172, 179
Restitutus, Catholic priest of Victoriana villa 106–8, 133, 136
Rufinus 56, 180 n. 78, 183 n. 86

St Stephen, relics and shrines 7–8, 14, 222
schism 129–31
Septiminus, proconsul of Africa 109, 110, 118
Serena, wife of Stilicho 169
Serenus, vicar and proconsul of Africa 88, 89, 104, 105, 112, 129, 135 n. 7
Servus, Catholic bishop of Thubursicu 138, 139, 141, 149
Severus, Catholic clergyman murdered in 408 171
Severus, Catholic bishop of Milevis 18 n. 5, 36 n. 76, 166 n. 31, 169
Sirmondian Constitution 12 156, 159, 160–5, 170
Sirmondian Constitution 14 156, 174–9, 186, 187
Stilicho 76, 93, 156, 169, 171, 175, 186, 187
Suetonius 23, 24, 26, 40, 59

Theasius, Catholic bishop of Memlonitanus 45
   attacked in 408 156, 171
   embassies to court 125, 139, 146, 149, 150, 152

Theodorus, Mallius consul and praetorian
    prefect 85, 88, 118 n. 71, 168 n. 36,
    174, 180
Theodorus, proconsul of Africa and son of
    above 85
Theodosian Code 98, 214, 227
    16.2.27 121
    16.2.29 128
    16.2.34 104 n. 22
    16.2.38 162, 163
    16.5.7 122–4, 125, 133, 146–7
    16.5.21 92, 102–15, 123, 125, 129, 133, 136,
        142, 143, 146, 147, 152
    16.5.39 118
    16.5.41 162, 163
    16.5.43 163, 164
    16.10.19 163, 164
    16.5.38, 16.6.3, 16.6.4, 16.6.5, 16.11.2
        150–3
    see also Edict of Unity
Theodosius I, emperor 84, 90, 122,
    159, 116
Tyconius 130, 107 n. 34

Ulpian, Domitius 12

Valentinian, emperor 137
Valerius, Catholic bishop of Hippo 33, 35,
    36, 40 n. 95, 76, 107 n. 35
Vandals 2, 3, 4, 55, 60, 61–3
Varro, Marcus Terentius 79
Victor, Catholic bishop of Utica 171
Vincentius, Catholic bishop of Culusitana
    162, 164, 204
Vita Augustini:
    Augustine's books 18, 55–7, 59, 73–5,
        77–80
    differs from Augustine's texts 3, 6, 7,
        17–18, 21, 25–32, 77
    documents 45, 46–50
    friendship among bishops 3, 4, 6, 17
    heretics represented in 8, 30, 38, 45
    modern assessments 17, 18, 77, 83
    Roman law in 8, 84
    structure 23, 59
    textual allusion 7, 65, 74, 227
    textual proof 14, 19, 56, 65
    see also *Indiculum*
Volusian, proconsul of Africa 88

Zosimus, pope 53, 54